Y0-BVO-551

COMPUTER-BASED MESSAGE SERVICES

IFIP WG 6.5 Working Conference on
Computer-Based Message Services
Nottingham, England, 1-4 May, 1984

Programme Committee:
G. Antoni, A. Danthine, P. Kirstein, J. Garcia-Luna, R. Miller, N. Naffah, G. Neufeld, J. Palme, S. Ramani, P. Schicker, K. Smaaland, L. Tarouco, J. White, and K. Wimmer

Organizing Committe:
H. T. Smith, W. Dzida, and R. Uhlig

NORTH-HOLLAND
AMSTERDAM • NEW YORK • OXFORD

COMPUTER-BASED MESSAGE SERVICES

Proceedings of the IFIP WG 6.5 Working Conference on
Computer-Based Message Services
Nottingham, England, 1-4 May, 1984

edited by

Hugh T. SMITH

Nottingham University
Nottingham
England

1984

NORTH-HOLLAND
AMSTERDAM • NEW YORK • OXFORD

ISBN: 0 444 87621 9

Published by:

ELSEVIER SCIENCE PUBLISHERS B.V.
P. O. Box 1991
1000 BZ Amsterdam
The Netherlands

Sole distributors for the U.S.A. and Canada:

ELSEVIER SCIENCE PUBLISHING COMPANY, INC.
52 Vanderbilt Avenue
New York, N.Y. 10017
U.S.A.

Library of Congress Cataloging in Publication Data

IFIP WG 6.5 Working Conference on Computer-Based Message Services (1984 : Nottingham, Nottinghamshire)
Computer-based message services ; proceedings of the IFIP WG 6.5 Working Conference on Computer-Based Message Services, Nottingham, England, 1-4 May, 1984.

Bibliography: p.
1. Electronic mail systems--Congresses. I. Smith, H. T. (Hugh T.) II. IFIP WG 6.5. III. Title.
HE6239.E54I35 1984 384.1'4 84-18670
ISBN 0-444-87621-9 (U.S.)

PRINTED IN THE NETHERLANDS

PREFACE

Since its inception in 1979, the objectives of IFIP Working Group 6.5 have been to promote the interchange of information and the discussion of the requirements of computer-based message systems. This conference was the fourth in an annual series of international meetings organised by the Working Group. The three previous meetings were held in Ottawa in 1981, Paris in 1982, and Palo Alto in 1983. In between these annual events, there have been many smaller working meetings of the North American and European Sub-groups. All this activity has resulted in proposals and ideas that have influenced, and continue to influence, emerging international standards.

Until recently, much of this discussion has taken place within the relatively quiet confines of the research community. However, the publication in late 1983 of the CCITT X400 series draft standards for international electronic message interchange has ensured a much wider interest in this work. This conference therefore marks the emergence of the subject into the full glare of commercial light.

At the present time many of the discussions about CBMS centre around system interconnection. As electronic mail facilities move from being the prerogative of the few to the province of the many, so the concern will turn towards what other "value added services" can be offered to the public. Of the issues that will appear important then, many have been addressed in the papers presented at this conference and subsequently developed within the working group's discussions.

The conference brought together twenty seven speakers from eight countries to present papers on computer-based message services. It was attended by 150 people from a total of eighteen countries – one of the largest meetings devoted to such a specialist subject. The papers range across a wide spread of topics, from directory services, multimedia systems, user interface issues, to regulatory and security concerns. In addition to the papers presented at the conference, one and a half days were devoted to working group discussions. The output from these groups is not represented in this book. Readers interested in finding out further details about these groups should contact the Chairman of IFIP WG 6.5 or one of its members.

A great deal of work is involved in planning an international conference. The quality of the papers and the size of the attendance was a testament to the efforts of the members of the Programme and Organizing Committees. Of these, special mention should be made of Wolfgang Dzida, Knut Smaaland and Jose Garcia-Luna who, by force of circumstance, were prevented from attending the conference at the eleventh hour.

As Chairman of the Organizing Committee I would like to acknowledge the invaluable local support of Nottingham University and the Plessey Company. In particular, special thanks go to John Pollard and his staff at Plessey, and Penny Radcliffe and Marion Windsor at the University; without their collective help the conference would have been impossible to stage.

Hugh T. Smith
Computer Science Group
Nottingham University

CONTENTS

PART 3: USER INTERFACE ARCHITECTURE

PART 4: SERVICES AND COST/BENEFIT ISSUES

PART 5: REGULATORY AND SECURITY CONSIDERATIONS

PART 1:

NAMING, ADDRESSING AND DIRECTORY SERVICES

Computer-Based Message Services
H.T. Smith (Editor)
Elsevier Science Publishers B.V. (North-Holland)

IMPLEMENTING DISTRIBUTION LISTS IN COMPUTER-BASED MESSAGE SYSTEMS

Debra P. Deutsch
Bolt Beranek and Newman Inc.
10 Moulton Street
Cambridge, Massachusetts 02238
U.S.A.

This paper models how distribution lists fit into a CBMS and explores some problems that occur in their design and implementation. Operations on distribution lists and access to their definitions are discussed. Options for storing distribution lists are examined. Several issues that arise in the processing of distribution lists are noted. Solutions and approaches are recommended for some of these problems; others are identified for further study.

1. Introduction

A computer-based message system (CBMS) allows communication between "entities" (usually people) using computers. A message, or unit of communication, is sent by its originator to one or more recipients. A distribution list is a stored list of potential message recipients including, perhaps, other distribution lists. The purpose of a distribution list is to allow an originator to send a message to a group of recipients without having to enumerate each member of the group.

Distribution lists are useful when a number of messages are to be sent to the same group of recipients. Since a distribution list is defined just once and then referred to by name, sending a message to a distribution list is more convenient than explicitly naming each of its recipients. Using a distribution list also eliminates the chance that one of its members will be unintentionally omitted as a message recipient. Because access to and maintenance of distribution lists can be shared, a CBMS user can send a message to a distribution list without having to know its exact membership.

After many years of ad hoc implementation in research environments, distribution lists are beginning to receive serious attention. A growing number of working systems, such as Xerox's Grapevine [9] and the CSNET Name Server [10], implement distribution lists. As ISO and CCITT standards committees discuss issues relating to naming and addressing in CBMSs, they will be dealing with distribution lists.

Before implementing a system or designing standards for one, it is best to analyze the problems at hand. This paper characterizes distribution lists by modeling how they fit into a CBMS and exploring some problems that occur in their design and implementation. Section 2 discusses the terminology and model of a CBMS used in this paper. In Section 3, distribution lists are discussed in terms of the operations that can be performed upon them, storage and access to their definitions, and how these factors relate to CBMS architecture. Section 4 identifies and examines some design and implementation problems. The final section makes recommendations for the design of CBMSs that use distribution lists.

2. Model and Definitions

To provide greater clarity, the following paragraphs discuss the CBMS model and terminology used in this paper.

IFIP Working Group 6.5 has developed a functional model for describing CBMSs [7, 8] that has been adopted by several standards bodies [5, 2, 4]. This model divides the components of a CBMS into two classes, User Agents (UAs) and the Message Transfer System (MTS). UAs provide message preparation, display, and management tools to CBMS users. The MTS is used to transfer messages between different UAs. The MTS also makes available a variety of services that are incidental to message transfer. For example, a directory assistance service may be accessed via a request made to the MTS. The MTS is made of one or more Message Transfer Agents (MTAs) that cooperate to provide the MTS services.

The transfer of a message from its originator's UA to the MTS is called <u>submission</u>; the transfer of a message from the MTS to its recipient's UA is called <u>delivery</u>.

Messages consist of two components. The <u>message content</u> is the information that the message originator wishes to communicate to the message recipient. The <u>message envelope</u> is the control information used by the MTS during message transfer. The MTS does not read or alter the message content. Some or all of the message envelope may be available to the recipient's UA upon delivery of the message. It is important to note that there can be redundancy between the message content and envelope. For example, the destination of a message must appear on its envelope; it also is found in the message content itself.

3. Processing Distribution Lists

The purpose of this section is to characterize more fully what distribution lists are, from the standpoint of a CBMS implementor. It begins by describing the operations that can be performed upon distribution lists. Because these operations require varying amounts of access to a distribution list and its definition, the different kinds of access to distribution lists are discussed next. After that the options for storing distribution list definitions are examined, with special attention to how these choices can affect access. A discussion of how limiting access to a distribution list can constrain the way it can be processed is also included.

3.1 Operations on Distribution Lists

Three operations can be performed on distribution lists: modification, citation, and expansion. In the following paragraphs each operation is described in terms of what it does, the contexts in which it is performed, and conditions that must be met for successful completion.

3.1.1 Modification

Modification is used to create and delete distribution lists or to alter their contents. There are two contexts in which modification may take place.

- A user or a UA invokes the operation to create or delete a distribution list or alter its contents.
- An entry is deleted from the contents of a distribution list as part of directory maintenance. Deletion of entries is more fully discussed in Section 4.4.

There are several conditions that must be met before modification can succeed.

1. The entity that requested modification must have permission to make the change in question.
2. If a name is being added to a distribution list, the name must be valid.
3. If a new distribution list is created, its name must be unambiguous within its domain of use. (This rule applies to all new names, not just names of distribution lists.)

When a distribution list name is added to the contents of a distribution list, there may be a check to guard against forming a distribution list loop. A distribution list loop exists when a distribution list contains itself, either directly or indirectly. See Figure 1 for some examples of distribution list loops, which are discussed more fully in Section 4.1.

3.1.2 Citation

Citation is the use of a distribution list name as a destination for a message. There are two contexts in which citation can take place.

- A message originator uses a distribution list name as a destination for a message.
- A distribution list is included in the contents of a distribution list that has been cited.

For citation to succeed, the distribution list name must be valid and the entity that requested citation must have permission to cite the distribution list in question.

3.1.3 Expansion

Expansion is the act of replacing the name of a distribution list with its contents. Since a distribution list can contain another distribution list, expansion may have to be applied more than once in order to obtain the final list of individual message recipients.

There are two contexts in which expansion can occur.

- A distribution list has been cited as the destination for a message.

- o A user or a UA examines the contents of a distribution list.

For expansion to take place, the distribution list must be correctly named, and there must be proper access to its contents.

If expansion is applied more than once, there may be a check for distribution list loops made between expansion operations. If a distribution list loop goes undetected, expansion can become an infinitely long operation. This problem is discussed in more detail in section 4.1.

3.2 Access to Distribution Lists

The ability to modify, cite, or expand a distribution list is contingent on proper access to its definition. There are three different kinds of access to distribution lists: reference, read, and write.

- o Reference access to a distribution list permits an entity to obtain or meaningfully use its name. Reference access is necessary to perform any operation on a distribution list.

- o Read access permits an entity to determine the contents of a distribution list. It is required to perform expansion. It may also be necessary when modifying an existing distribution list.

- o Write access permits an entity to create and delete a distribution list; it also allows an entity to alter its contents. Write access is required to perform modification.

3.3 Storing Distribution Lists

A distribution list can be stored in a directory in the MTS [6, 1] or in a UA. Access to a distribution list can be affected by where the distribution list is stored.

A directory is included in the functional model for a CBMS [3]. It is modeled as a single functional entity containing naming and addressing information about CBMS users. Of course, a directory can be implemented in a distributed manner; it can also be redundant. A directory can be modeled as a database that is queried and updated. Finally, a directory can include access control mechanisms to regulate which of its users may reference, read, or write a given entry.

The directory that stores distribution lists must be able to distinguish between the names of distribution lists and the names of individual users. This ability allows users of a directory to discover if a name refers to a distribution list or not. Access to a distribution list stored in a directory can be very free or restricted, depending upon administrative policy and the desires of the users.

Storing a distribution list in a UA restricts access to it. The UA that stores the distribution list is the only entity with read and write access to it. Therefore, that UA is the only entity that can expand or modify the distribution list.

Normally, if a distribution list is stored in a UA, only that UA has reference access to it. Thus, if a UA wishes to send a message to a distribution list that it stores, it must expand all citations to the distribution list before it finishes submitting the message.

There is an exception to this rule. It is possible to build a UA that, when it receives a message, turns around and sends a copy of the message to each member of a distribution list that it stores. The only way to send messages to the distribution list is by sending them to the UA that stores it. This treatment of distribution lists is more fully discussed in section 4.3.

3.4 The Effects of Limiting Access to Distribution lists

In some situations it is desirable to restrict access to a distribution list. Access restrictions are most often imposed for reasons of data security, privacy, or integrity, but they can also be used to provide differing levels of service to CBMS users. As noted above, the choice of where a distribution list is stored can also restrict access to it.

Regulating the different types of access separately can achieve a number of effects. Restricting reference access to a distribution list limits who can perform any operation on the distribution list or even be told that it exists. Restricting write access to a distribution list limits who can change its contents. Restricting read access to a distribution list limits who can be told its contents.

The choice of which entities have read access to a distribution list is very important because it controls which entities can expand the list. This control can have several repercussions.

Without read access, an originating UA cannot determine the membership or size of a distribution list. This means that the user cannot find out who will get a message sent to the distribution list. If a message originator is charged according to how many copies of a message are sent, it is impossible to know in advance how much sending the message will cost.

If an MTA cannot expand a distribution list, it cannot determine the final destinations of a message being sent to the distribution list. The MTA must route the message to another MTA that has read access to the distribution list. Of course, if no MTA can read a given distribution list, it must be expanded outside of the MTS.

3.5 Choosing Where to Expand Distribution Lists

Expansion of a distribution list to which a message is addressed may take place before or after it is submitted. If expansion takes place in the MTS, the first MTA can request expansion, or the first MTA can route the message toward another MTA, where expansion will take place. The choice between expanding the distribution list in the originating systems (the originator's UA or the first MTA), or in some other MTA depends on two factors - access and delay. The entity that requests expansion must have proper access to the distribution list's definition. Also, if the definition of the distribution lists is stored far away from the originating UA or the first MTA, it may be quicker to route the message toward the place where the definition is stored than to request the information, to receive a response, and then to route the message.

4. Issues

This section examines some design and implementation problems.

4.1 Distribution List Loops

A distribution list can contain other distribution lists. A distribution list loop exists when a distribution list includes itself, either directly or indirectly. Figure 1 illustrates such loops.

<u>Distribution</u> <u>list</u> <u>A</u>:
Joe Jones
Mary Morris
Distribution list B

<u>Distribution</u> <u>list</u> <u>B</u>:
Susan Simmons
Howard Haskins

Distribution list B is contained in distribution list A, but there is no loop formed.

<u>Distribution</u> <u>list</u> <u>C</u>:
Carol Cummings
Distribution list C

This is an example of the smallest possible distribution list loop. It is a loop because distribution list C contains itself.

<u>Distribution</u> <u>list</u> <u>D</u>:
George Greene
Distribution list E

<u>Distribution</u> <u>list</u> <u>E</u>:
Robin Robertson
Distribution list D

This is a loop because the two distribution lists contain each other.

<u>Distribution</u> <u>list</u> <u>F</u>:
Distribution list A
Distribution list B

This is not a distribution list loop, but when distribution list F is fully expanded, it contains Susan Simmons and Howard Haskins twice. This is because they are directly included in distribution list B and indirectly included in distribution list A.

<u>Distribution</u> <u>list</u> <u>G</u>:
Donald Douglass
Distribution list H

<u>Distribution</u> <u>list</u> <u>H</u>:
Fran Fuller
Distribution list I

<u>Distribution</u> <u>list</u> <u>I</u>:
Steven Smith
Distribution list G

This is a distribution list loop because distribution list G contains itself indirectly. (Distribution list G contains distribution list H, which contains distribution list I, which contains distribution list G.)

Figure 1
Formation of distribution list loops

If a distribution list loop goes undetected, expanding it becomes an infinitely long operation. There are three ways to deal with this problem.

- When a distribution list is modified, check to make sure that there are no distribution lists inside it.

- Check for loop formation each time a distribution list definition is modified.

- Catch loops when distribution lists are expanded.

In the first case, it is an error to nest distribution lists. Without nesting, no loops can ever be formed. Making this check requires only reference access to the distribution list under scrutiny. The drawback to this method is that functionality is lost, because it often makes sense to nest distribution lists. For example, a company might have a distribution list for each department that contains the names of individual employees. A distribution list for the entire company would contain all the departmental distribution lists.

In the second case, the distribution list is fully expanded to check for loops when it is modified. It is an error if a loop is found. This procedure requires read and reference access to all distribution lists at each level of nesting. Therefore, it may not always be feasible to perform this check.

The third method, checking for loops as a distribution list is expanded, is similar to the second approach. The checks are performed by whatever entities would normally perform expansion, so there is no problem with having read access. As a distribution list is expanded, a record is kept of its name and the names of all the distribution lists that it has been found to contain, directly or indirectly. If, at some level, a distribution list that has already been expanded is encountered, it is passed over by the expansion process. Some small amount of storage and computation costs are associated with this method, but it will always work and does not place artificial restrictions on the use of distribution lists.

An undetected distribution list loop can bring a CBMS to its knees by exhausting storage and requiring infinite computation when it is expanded. Therefore, every CBMS that implements distribution lists should take some measures to guard against this problem.

4.2 Duplicate Suppression

Whenever a message is sent to more than one distribution list, or to some individual recipients and a distribution list, there is a potential for some recipient to get more than one copy. While this is not a fatal condition (as is the case with distribution list loops), suppressing duplicate messages can be a worthwhile design goal.

There are several approaches to duplicate suppression.

- Make the originating UA fully expand all distribution lists before it submits a message. If a duplicate is found, it can be eliminated or brought to the originator's attention for some action.

- Make the MTS take care of all distribution list expansions and elimination of any duplicates <u>before</u> it routes each copy of the message to its final destination.

- Make the MTS check for and eliminate duplicates as it expands each distribution list.

- o Have the MTS keep track of those messages it has delivered to a given recipient. Before a message is delivered, have it checked to make sure another copy has not already been delivered.

- o Make the recipient's UA responsible for discovering and discarding duplicate messages in its possession.

The first method puts the onus completely on the originating UA. For it to work, the UA must have sufficient read access to fully expand the distribution lists in question. Such access is not always available.

The second, third, and fourth methods rely on the MTS to suppress duplicates. The second method will work most of the time, at the expense of inefficient routing and potential delivery delays. It fails if there is no one MTA with read access to all the levels of all the distribution lists involved and if there is no way to route the message so that no MTA can discern the definition of a distribution list that it is not permitted to read. Allowing some potential duplicates may be acceptable in order to optimize routing or minimize delivery delays.

The third approach doesn't try to catch all the duplicates. If one is found, it is suppressed. This method is much cheaper to implement and run than the second approach, and can be nearly as effective if one MTA takes care of most of the expansion for a given message.

The fourth method, checking for duplication just before a message is delivered, can be completely effective. The overhead involved, however, can be considerable. It is necessary to keep a record of every message that has been delivered to a given recipient. (Presumably there is a way to identify a message unambiguously.) This record can get quite large; it may be desirable to restrict it to all the messages received within a certain amount of time.

The final alternative places the burden on the recipient's UA. It is otherwise identical to the fourth method.

As can be seen, duplicate suppression can become quite costly, depending on how thorough it must be. Deciding whether or not duplicates are to be suppressed, and the choice of method, requires careful weighing of costs and benefits.

4.3 Using UAs as Distribution Lists

It is possible to build a UA that, when it receives a message, turns around and sends a copy of the message to each member of a distribution list that it stores. With this approach, the only way to send messages to the distribution list is by sending them to the UA that stores it. The following paragraphs examine this approach to distribution list expansion.

This kind of UA is very useful in situations where it is desirable to have a central agency read or modify the contents of a message before it is delivered. The UA can maintain logs, create digests, or add to or reformat the contents of a message before it sends the individual copies out again. This arrangement can be valuable in teleconferences because the UA can maintain a transcript of the teleconference dialog, issue digests of the dialog, etc. Another use for such a UA is to create "form messages" by filling in blanks in the original message with the names of the individual message recipients.

There are several drawbacks to this paradigm. First of all, a directory cannot tell you if a given UA is of the garden variety or if it will send your message out to other recipients. Second, an originating UA cannot find out the contents of the distribution list. Both of these problems mean that an originator can be very surprised by what happens when a message is sent, either on purpose or inadvertently, to one of these special UAs.

A third difficulty is that this use of distribution lists can create severe bottlenecks in the flow of messages. Only the receiving UA can expand the distribution lists it stores. If one of these distribution lists is heavily used, or a distribution list is large, its UA can accumulate a vast backlog of messages to process. One way to overcome this problem is to insert a level of indirection in the definition of large distribution lists, which decomposes them into smaller distribution lists that can be expanded elsewhere, presumably closer to the ultimate destinations of the message.

Special care must be taken to detect distribution list loops when using this paradigm. In the contents of each message sent out by one of these UAs, it is necessary to maintain a record of each UA that has fanned it out. By doing this, a UA can discover whether or not it has already dealt with a given message.

Finally, there is the problem that UAs cannot always be expected to operate as correctly as the MTS is trusted to do. While the MTS is regulated and may have its individual components certified to work correctly, the same cannot be said of UAs. This aspect of UAs may be an important factor in some situations.

Given these problems, it is evident that any decision to expand distribution lists in receiving UAs should be carefully considered.

4.4 Housekeeping

Whenever a name is eliminated from the CBMS directory, it should be removed from the distribution lists that contain it. Without this maintenance, distribution lists could become cluttered with invalid names, causing errors and wasting computation and storage.

One way attack this problem is to try to keep track of all the distribution lists in which a given name is included. With this method, when the name is invalidated, it is known which distribution lists must be updated. Given modification access to the distribution lists, the invalid name is removed. This approach is inadequate in that unless all distribution lists are stored in the directory, there is no way for all the cross-correlation to be done, because access to distribution lists stored in UAs is so restricted. An entity in the MTS cannot reach into a UA and change a distribution list definition. An entity in the MTS cannot even be sure about which distribution lists are stored in a given UA. Furthermore, even if all distribution lists are stored in the directory, the cost of performing the necessary cross-correlation may make it impractical.

Another approach to housekeeping is to do nothing about updating a distribution list until there is an attempt made to expand it. In this paradigm, as part of the expansion process, all names contained in the distribution list are checked for validity. If any are found to be invalid, they are removed from the distribution list. Once again, this approach requires modification access to the distribution list definition.

The drawback to this method is that all distribution lists must be checked for validity every time they are expanded, which involves some measure of computational overhead.

A third method is to check names for validity as a distribution list is expanded, and send an error report to the individual responsible for maintaining the distribution list, instead of automatically modifying the definition of the distribution list when an invalid name is found. The responsible individual can be a user or a system administrator. He or she would be expected to take the necessary corrective action.

All things considered, the second and third approaches to housekeeping seem to be more generally useful and simpler to implement than the first.

4.5 Delivery Notifications and Error Reports

A delivery notification is a report to an originator saying that a given message was delivered to a given recipient at a given time. An error report from the MTS lets an originator know about some problem encountered while trying to transfer a specified message to a stated recipient. The handling of delivery notifications and error reports is affected by the use of distribution lists as destinations for messages.

The question is one of policy. What should happen when a message is sent to a distribution list and a delivery notification has been requested? Do all the delivery notifications go to the message originator? If so, the originator must have read access to the distribution list definition. Otherwise, the originator would be able to deduce at least a subset of the distribution list contents by keeping track of the delivery notifications it receives.

Another alternative is to have all the delivery notifications go to the entity that expanded the distribution list. There is no problem with access in this case. When all the delivery notifications are received by that entity, it can signal the entity that requested expansion that delivery was successful. The drawback is that a lot of bookkeeping is involved in this process. Entities that perform expansion must keep track of outstanding delivery notifications and the sources of expansion requests.

The problems are compounded when handling error reports. If an entity does not have read access to a distribution list, error reports should not allow the entity to discern anything about the list's contents. Laundering the error reports to meet that requirement can render them practically useless.

The issue of how best to handle delivery notifications and error reports in a CBMS that uses distribution lists requires further study.

5. Conclusions

The basic operations on distribution lists are easy to describe and understand. However, designing a CBMS that will store and process distribution lists is not a simple task.

The CBMS designer must first consider the problem of access to distribution list definitions. It may be desirable to be able to limit access selectively to distribution list definitions. In some systems, it may be necessary to insure that all definitions are accessible; in others such access may not be important. The designer must consider which parts of the CBMS should be able to expand distribution lists and how that choice will affect performance. On this basis, the designer can decide where distribution lists are to be stored. If they are to be stored in directories, access controls may have to be designed and built. If distribution lists are to be stored in UAs, the UAs must be designed to handle citation and expansion properly.

The designer must have a workable strategy to deal with distribution list loops. Measures may be needed to suppress duplication of messages when distribution lists are cited. The CBMS may include mechanisms to help keep distribution lists up-to-date. Finally, the designer must develop some way to handle return receipts and error reports for messages sent to distribution lists.

Distribution lists can be powerful tools or minor additions to a CBMS. The difference is in the care put into their design.

REFERENCES

[1] Birrel, A., Levin, R., Needham, R., and Schroeder, M., Grapevine: an exercise in distributed computing, Communications of the ACM 25 (1982) 260-274.

[2] CCITT Study Group VII/5, Message Handling Systems: System Model- Service Elements, Draft Recommendation X.400, International Telephone and Telegraph Consultative Committee (CCITT) (November 1983).

[3] IFIP WG 6.5, Naming, Addressing, and Directory Services for Message Handling Systems, Working Paper (Version 3), International Federation for Information Processing Working Group 6.5 (February 1983).

[4] ISO/TC 97/SC 18/WG 4, Information Processing - Functional Description of Message Oriented Text Interchange System, Technical Report N116, International Standards Organization (October 1983).

[5] Deutsch, D., Resnick, R., Vittal, J., and Walker, J., Specification for Message Format for Computer Based Message Systems, Federal Information Processing Standards Publication 98, US Department of Commerce / National Bureau of Standards (January 1983).

[6] Oppen, D. and Dalal, Y., The Clearinghouse: A Decentralized Agent for Locating Named Objects in a Distributed Environment, Technical Report OPD-T8103, Xerox Office Products Division (October 1981).

[7] Schicker, P., The Computer Based Mail Environment: An Overview, Technical Report, Bell-Northern Research Ltd., Ottawa, Ontario, Canada (December 1979).

[8] Schicker, P., Naming and Addressing in a Computer Based Mail Environment, IEEE Transactions on Communications 30 (1982) 46-52.

[9] Schroeder, M., Birrell, A. D., and Needham, R. M., Experience with Grapevine: the Growth of a Distributed System, Technical Report CSL-83-12, Xerox Palo Alto Research Center (August 1983). To appear in Transactions on Computer Systems.

[10] Solomon, M., Landweber, L. H., and Neuhengen, D., The CSNET Name Server, Computer Networks 6 (1982) 161-172.

Computer-Based Message Services
H.T. Smith (Editor)
Elsevier Science Publishers B.V. (North-Holland)

Naming and Directory Issues in Message Transfer Systems

Marvin A. Sirbu, Jr.
Juliet B. Sutherland

Laboratory for Computer Science
Massachusetts Institute of Technology
Cambridge, Massachusetts
U.S.A.

A message transfer system requires some means for users to determine the addresses of their correspondents. A *Directory Service* aids users in identifying a particular correspondent and the correspondent's address. In this paper we discuss the technical, economic, organizational and political requirements which must be satisfied by a directory service. We develop a language for describing alternative architectures for directory service borrowed from notions of hierarchical computer file system design. We propose a system of naming and directory services which meets the stated requirements based on names which specify a *path* through a sequence of directories. Finally, we compare our proposal to several alternative designs for directory service which have appeared in the literature.

1. Introduction

Technologies for sending mail have evolved considerably since early writers used clay tablets, papyrus or parchment for recording messages which took months to deliver by hand. Computer mail offers the possibility of near instantaneous delivery of messages in electronic form. A common problem in message systems, whatever the form, is specifying the recipient and his or her address. When there was no reliable postal service, messages were sent with anyone going in the correct direction and addresses consisted of an approximate description of where to find the person. One ancient Egyptian letter carrier, having arrived in the correct town, had to cope with the following:

> From Moon Gate [i.e., the particular gate of several in the town's defense wall that he was to enter by], walk as if toward the granaries ... and at the first street back of the baths turn left.... Then go west. Then go down the steps and up the other steps and turn right. After the temple precinct there is a seven-story house with a basket-weaving establishment. Inquire there or from the concierge.... Then give a shout. [2]

One wonders what would have happened if the letter writer had not known the town well enough to give directions.

As reliable postal systems became common and addresses became standardized, the problem shifted from providing a description of how to find the person to determining the person's standard address. Some towns published directories listing the streets and house numbers of residents. However, the generalized problem of finding postal addresses continues to this day. A similar problem was created in 1876 with the invention of the telephone. Prior to automatic switching, there was no standardized "address"—*e.g.* telephone number—for subscribers; nevertheless, written subscriber directories first appeared in 1878 [21]. In the mid 1960s, following the introduction in 1964 of the first convenience facsimile machines, Xerox published a directory of facsimile users. The practice was quickly abandoned when Xerox discovered that its competitors were using the directory as a list of prospects.

Although the directory problem of determining addresses exists in all communication systems, at present only the telephone system has explicit, widely available, printed directories and a service for obtaining telephone numbers. In the future, we believe that a worldwide electronic mail system, like the telephone system, will find some form of directory service indispensable.

Addressing and directory issues are just beginning to be addressed in world standards organizations such as the CCITT [14]. We have not seen, however, a comprehensive discussion of the many issues raised in the provision of directory services for electronic mail. Our purpose in this paper is to provide a starting point for such a discussion. To this end, we set forth some goals for a worldwide directory system, discuss naming issues as they pertain to directories, and present our views on a selection of architectural and usage issues. To provide some perspective, we conclude by examining several existing or proposed directory systems to see how they have addressed the issues we have raised.

2. Goals

The design of a directory system is complicated by the need to meet a number of different, and at times conflicting, goals. In order to facilitate design, and the comparison of alternative designs, we have identified the following goals or criteria for evaluating a proposed directory system and service.

1. *The directory service should be easy to use.* It should provide a simple means for users to find the addresses of their correspondents.

2. *The design must be scalable.* We are proposing a design for a world-wide directory service which should eventually grow to accommodate literally billions of correspondents. The design should allow for efficient operation at that scale. At the same time, it should be implementable at reasonable cost on a smaller scale so that getting started is not a large hurdle.

3. *The service should provide for a high degree of automation.* Economic operation at a scale of billions of users requires a high degree of automation.

4. *A directory service should always be available.* To insure that directory service is always available, the design should allow for replication of information and of service providers.

5. *Directory information should be correct and up to date.* A good design should make it easy to update directory information. It should also provide procedures which insure that the information is accurate.

6. *Personal privacy must be protected.* A directory is a database of information about an individual. As with all such databases, it must provide for the protection of individual privacy.

7. *Corporate or organizational privacy must be protected.* Organizations may also have privacy concerns separate from those of individuals. These concerns must also be respected in the design of a directory service.

8. *The design must provide for multiple unrelated organizations to both compete and cooperate in the provision of directory service.* This requirement expresses our belief that directory service is a business in which numerous unrelated organizations will engage, often in competition with each other. A directory service design must be capable of operation without assuming a level of cooperation among participating entities beyond that which can be expected in a competitive marketplace.

We are certain that other criteria could easily be added to this list. One of our goals in this paper is to begin to set down explicitly the design criteria behind alternative approaches to the directory service problem.

3. The IFIP Model of a Message Transfer System

Much recent work on electronic mail has adopted a model[1] first set forth by IFIP Working Group 6.5. [5, 14] In this model, the major components of a message system are the User Agent (UA) and the Message Transfer Agent (MTA). A user, known as an originator or a recipient depending on his or her role in the communication, sends or receives mail through the User Agent. A UA might provide a text editor, a file system, or other tools for preparing and storing messages. The Message Transfer System (MTS) is an interconnected network of UAs and MTAs which moves messages from one UA to another. A UA submits a message to an MTA, which either delivers it to the destination UA or relays it to another MTA nearer the final destination. All of these concepts are illustrated in Figure 3-1 which is adapted from Redell and White [14].

UA's and MTA's can be grouped together in any combination to form a Management Domain (MD). A management domain is an organizational unit that is distinct from the physical architecture, that is, the interconnection of MTAs and UAs. of the system. Within a management domain, MTA's and UA's may use protocols different from those prescribed in a message transfer standard. At the boundaries between all

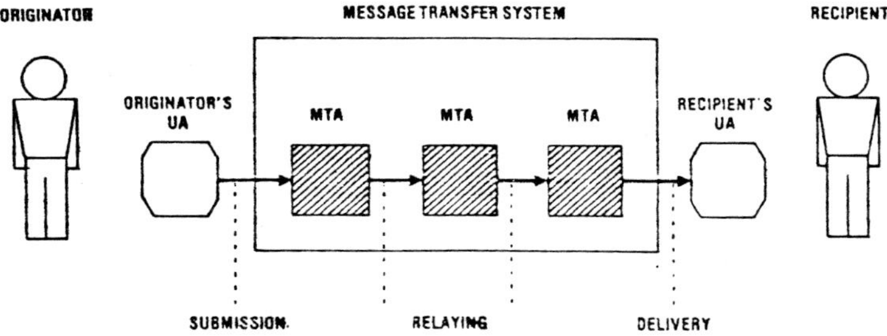

Figure 3-1: A model of an electronic mail system.

management domains, however, the standard protocol will be employed.

The conceptual model just described can also be expressed in terms of layers following the principles of Open Systems Interconnection [9]. The message system model has two layers, the User Agent Layer (UAL) encompassing the functions of the UA's, and the Message Transfer Layer (MTL), which contains the functionality of the MTS. These layers are shown in Figure 3-2. The layered model defines three entities within the two layers. The UA entity in the UAL and the MTA entity in the MTL have already been described. The Submission and Delivery Entity (SDE) is present only if there is no MTA entity colocated at the same site as the UA entity. The SDE does not provide transfer services but does provide the interface between the UA and the MTA. These entities are shown in Figure 3-2.

IFIP Working Group 6.5 has also provided some terminology for directories [8]. Directory services are provided by one or more *Directory Service Agents* (DSAs). A DSA can communicate with either a UA or an MTA and is outside of the UAL or MTL layers. The *client* is the entity which is requesting information from the DSA. We define further the *target* of the inquiry as the person or service about which information is being requested.

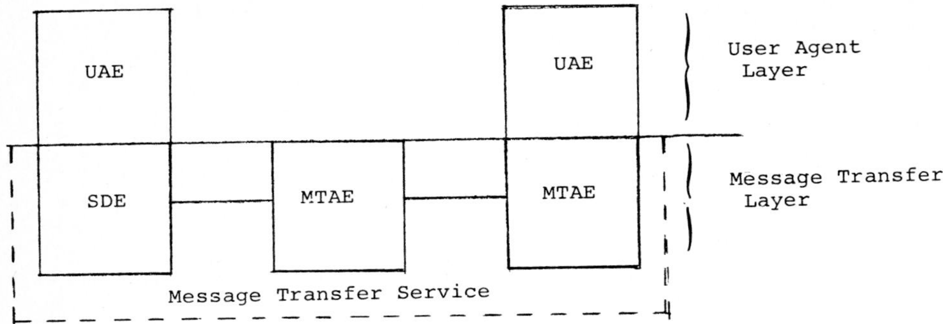

Figure 3-2: Alternate model showing layers, entities, and their relationships.

4. Naming and Binding

What's in a name? A rose by any other name would smell as sweet...

—William Shakespeare

Any discussion of a Directory Service must first begin by clarifying the meaning of the various terms to be used in the discussion, and most particularly the concept of a *name*.

IFIP Working Group 6.5 has described a *name* as

> "...a linguistic object that corresponds to a particular entity in some universe of discourse germane to the language in which the name is expressed. The correspondence between names (in the language) and entities (in the universe of discourse) is the relation of denoting. A name denotes or identifies the entity with which it is paired." [8]

Another view of naming is given by Saltzer who describes naming as the mapping or binding of a higher-level semantic construct into a lower-level construct. [16] This lower-level construct may be viewed as a name for a still lower level construct until the most fundamental physical constructs are identified.

For example, several mappings or bindings are required to access a service over a computer network: [17]

- Binding of a service to a computer node from which the service is available;
- Binding of a computer node to an attachment point on a computer network;
- Binding of an attachment point on a computer network to a route from the source to the attachment point.

A *context*, according to Saltzer is, abstractly, a particular set of bindings. A *name* is a character or bit-string identifier which is bound to a lower level construct in some context.

Key to Saltzer's notion of names, is that they do not exist apart from a "context" or abstract mechanism within which they are resolved. This "context" may be a piece of hardware—as in the computer circuits which map the "name" of a piece of data (its hardware address) to a particular data item in memory. More often, the context is a data table in which the name appears along with the lower level name to which it is bound.

The city at the geographic location 51° 32' N, 0° 5' E. is *named* London in the context of an English language Atlas. In a French Atlas, that location identifier is associated with the character string "Londres". Each name is valid only in the context of a particular Atlas.

More concretely, a *directory* is an object consisting of a table of bindings between names and objects; a directory is an example of a context. A *directory service* takes a *name* as input, and as output produces the lower level object to which the name is bound. For example, given the "name" of the user of a message handling system, a directory service might return the "name" of the User Agent to which mail for that person should be addressed. The entries in the table are the *names*, or identifiers, of instances of each type of object or construct of interest.

As with layering in protocol design, the purpose of multiple levels of binding is to allow higher levels to be oblivious to changes in lower levels. A binding allows users of higher level semantic constructs to use an unvarying name to refer to a construct, while allowing for changes in the lower level constructs to which the first construct is bound. Thus, one might want to specify that some mail is to be sent to the complaint department at the local department store without being concerned that the construct identified by "complaint department" might be mapped to different User Agents at different times.

Multiple levels of binding also facilitate sharing of information that may be used by more than one service. Thus, a binding of a host to a network attachment point may be used in the process of mapping a variety of different services to their network addresses.

One goal, then, in developing a system of names and bindings for use in electronic mail networks, is to allow parts of the system to use unvarying names while allowing the binding of those names to other, lower-level entities, to change.

If we examine the IFIP model for a message handling system, we can identify a number of entities that require names and bindings. These entities include:

1. *Users*

   Users are outside the message transfer system. The MTS serves the needs of users. A variety of different entities might be users of an MTS:

   a. *Person*

      A person is a particular human being. The human being may change jobs, change employer, change residence, even change names, but is still the same person. Frequently we wish to send a communication to a uniquely identified human being.

   b. *Roles*

      A role is a job title, or functional responsibility within an organization or social structure. Sales manager, affirmative action officer, parent or guardian, and mayor are examples of generic roles. A specific role generally requires further qualification such as "sales manager for Massachusetts for the ABC line of products from the XYZ corporation". Frequently we wish to address a communication to the person (or computer service) currently acting in a particular role. Roles are bound to one or more persons and the binding may change occasionally or at regular intervals (*e.g.* shift supervisor). Roles are created, altered and destroyed at intervals ranging from months to years. There is typically a many to many binding of Persons to Roles.

   c. *Personnae*

      Most working persons will receive mail — as they do today — at both the home and the office. We might view these as separate roles, but roles which are always bound to the same person. We define *personnae* as a set of roles which — though they may be created and destroyed — can never be bound to any other person. Thus "Marvin Sirbu at work" and "Marvin Sirbu at home" are different personnae. These personnae will generally correspond to different User Agents — one at the office paid for by the employer, and one at home, paid for by the household.

d. *Computer Service*
The originators or recipients of electronic mail may be computer services as well as persons. Thus, computer services may appear as entities in a directory service.

2. *Distribution List*
A Distribution List is a protocol entity which consists of a list of several users.

3. *User Agent*
A User Agent is a protocol entity which provides services to an individual user in reading and sending mail. A User Agent may be bound to a Personna, to a Role, or to a Computer Service.

4. *Message Transfer Agent*
Message Transfer Agents accept messages from and deliver messages to User Agents.

5. *Management Domain*
A management domain is a portion of the total Message System that is controlled by a particular organization or group of cooperating organizations. It may contain numerous Message Transfer Agents and User Agents. A management domain may or may not control other parts of the Message System.

This partial list of entities in a Message Transfer System illustrates the types of objects for which bindings might be found in a directory. As suggested above, a directory is a table of bindings from symbolic names to objects or other symbolic names.

In the context of a Message Transfer System there are at least three bindings of interest which should be provided by a directory service. [8] Users approaching a Message Transfer System may have in mind a particular person, a human user of the MTS, to whom they wish to direct mail. They may know some attributes about the person, such as his or her surname, given names, place of employment or home address, and whether they wish to reach the person at home or at work. A first level of binding provided by a directory service takes from a client a set of attributes of a personna and maps them into a particular form of identifier for that personna, which we shall call a PersonnaName.[2] A second binding maps a PersonnaName—the name of an object outside the Message Transfer Service, but necessarily part of the Directory Service—into the name of a User Agent, an object inside the MTS. Finally, a third binding maps a User Agent Name into a User Agent Address. We leave to section 4.5 a discussion of the latter two bindings, as well as other bindings which might be necessary in an MTS.

4.1. Names in a Message Transfer System

A PersonnaName is clearly a central object in a directory. What characteristics would we like this PersonnaName to possess? It is helpful to consider first some general choices in designing names, and then the specific requirements for a PersonnaName.

Human versus computational use. [16]

Names intended for use by human beings should consist of character strings as opposed to bit strings or numeric strings. They should be mnemonically useful. Ambiguity may be acceptable, if it can be resolved through interaction with a human being. In general, such names should be selected by human beings, not assigned by machines.

Names for computational use need not have mnemonic value. However, they must be absolutely unambiguous, so that they can be resolved by machines without human intervention.

Flat versus structured names.

Names can consist of arbitrary strings which provide no additional information. Or they can be structured from multiple components which can permit the directory to be logically or physically partitioned according to the components. This partitioning may be desirable for reasons of scalability, efficiency, or privacy (Cf Section 4.2).

Component values can be assigned by separate *naming authorities*. This allows delegation of naming to distributed authorities while assuring that all names are universally unique.

Characteristics of PersonnaNames

Of the general considerations described above, which are particularly applicable to PersonnaNames in a directory service?

1. A PersonnaName should uniquely identify an individual personna, so that a machine could automatically map a PersonnaName into a User Agent Name without further interaction with a human user.

2. The PersonnaName should not change even though various other attributes of the person, such as address, employer, or marital status should change. Thus, once we have found someone's PersonnaName, we can trust that that name will continue to identify the same person when we use the directory to find the current User Agent Name bound to that PersonnaName.

3. The PersonnaName should be a multi-component name which allows the directory to be logically or physically partitioned for reasons of efficiency, privacy, and decentralized naming authority.

4. If the PersonnaName could be easily remembered or guessed by human beings, users would not need to utilize the directory service to find the PersonnaName for a particular user.

In the real world, it is virtually impossible to meet all of these criteria simultaneously. Criteria 4 might suggest the use of Given Names plus Surnames as PersonnaNames. However, Given Names + Surnames do not, in general, uniquely identify an individual, violating requirement 1. Women often change their surnames when they marry, violating requirement 2. In addition, Given Names + Surnames do not provide for a natural partitioning of the name space among directories as specified in point 3.

The concatenation of {Surname} + {Given Name} + {Address} + {City} + {State} + {Residence|Office} is used by most telephone companies to provide a unique PersonnaName for deriving a telephone number from the telephone directory service. The problem with this approach is that since the binding between a Person and a StreetAddress changes over time, it is as if the unique identity of the individual were to change whenever he or she moved. Other solutions, involving "attributes" of a person such as Employer or Department also suffer from the same problem. Each of these attributes represents a (possibly temporary) binding. If the binding should change, we would have to update our tables showing the binding between Person and User Agent, not because that binding had changed, but because the way we identify the Person entry in the table had changed. Indeed it would make more sense to use an unvarying attribute, such as someone's city of birth, as opposed to their current residence, for constructing a unique PersonnaName [3]

The concatenation of {Country} + {National ID Number} would provide a unique name. but would fail to meet requirement 4. It would meet requirement 3 only if the ID number were itself structured into components. and even then. the partitioning of the name space implied by the use of ID number components is not natural in terms of directory management.[4]

Note that we do not require that a personna have only one PersonnaName. There can be many PersonnaNames which will reference the same User Agent Name. and thus can be considered synonyms of each other for the purpose of binding PersonnaNames to User Agents. In an environment in which multiple organizations will likely maintain directory services partitioned along different lines. we can expect clients to employ a variety of PersonnaNames, resolved through a variety of directory services, in order to map users into User Agents.

In practice. therefore, we have little choice but to use as PersonnaNames. names which depend on several attributes of the individual. even if these represent bindings subject to change. The key is to use attributes which change less frequently than the binding we are trying to determine.[5] By using a multiplicity of attributes, and particularly attributes which do not change (place of birth; graduated from MIT; etc.) we can improve our ability to reliably identify an instance of a Person.

4.2. Names and Partitions

In the simple case of a small network or community of users, it is feasible for a single DSA to store the entire database of users. We can expect, however. that the community of interconnected users—including persons, roles, and services—will eventually grow to be of the order of the number of telephones in the world, or even larger -- *e.g.* several billion users. Given our desire for reliable and economic operation, protection of privacy, and efficient management of updates, maintaining a single database of that size—even if service is provided through multiple servers each with copies of the database--is not a feasible option.

We can suppose, therefore. that there are multiple DSAs each with a fraction of the database. What might be strategies for partitioning the name space among DSA's? There are several principles of division.

Geographical The world telephone network partitions directory responsibility into geographic regions generally corresponding to recognized civil boundaries.

By Management Domain Each management domain will probably maintain a list of names of its users. In fact, if the management domain and naming authority are the same, the management domain must maintain such a list.

Organizational DSA's may be maintained by organizations independently of whether they constitute a management domain. Thus the IEEE maintains and publishes a directory of its members, although it is not likely to be the provider of mail service to them.

Hybrid Various combinations of the above divisions can also be imagined.

Indeed, it is likely that individual names will appear in multiple DSAs with overlapping partitions of the entire name space. In order to assure availability of the directory. it is also necessary that any given partition will be maintained on more than one service machine.

In order to take advantage of a partitioned directory, it must be possible by inspecting a name to determine in which directory to look. This implies that names are not arbitrary strings, but in fact have some structure, or components. which provide information about the partition structure of the database. There are two quite distinct alternatives for conceptualizing a multi-component name.

A "tuple-name" is a multi-component name which is regarded as a "tuple" in a relational database. Each component of the name corresponds to a particular field type of a *name-address record* (Figure 4-1).

<country>	<organization>	<personal name>	<org. discrim>	. . .	<mailbox>
.	.	.	.	.	.
USA	MIT	Marvin Sirbu	Lab for Comp Sci	. . .	<mailbox>
UK	Univ. of London	John Smith	Dept of Comp Sci	. . .	<mailbox>

Figure 4-1: Names as Tuples in a Relational Database

To use the directory service a client must supply sufficient field values to identify a unique tuple. When that tuple is retrieved from the database, the address field (User Agent Name) of the tuple is also retrieved.

The "tuple-name" requires that each field which might appear in the tuple be well defined. Multiple directories would presumably use the same record structure, i.e. the same fields, for the tuples in their portion of the name-address database. Having names for fields would allow the client to present components to the Directory Service in an unordered fashion; named fields would also facilitate guessing.[6]

An alternative view is to regard a multi-component name as a *path name*. Each component of a path name is an entry in a directory. Opposite the entry is either a User Agent Name, or the address of another directory in which the next component of the path name is resolved (Figure 4-2). This view of names is similar to that used in various computer filing systems. [16].

With path names, there is no *a priori* expectation that the component entries represent some "field" type with specific characteristics. A component simply represents an entry in *some* directory. It is reasonable to assume that the entries in a particular directory might have something in common — for example, the ITU might maintain a directory whose entries were official names of countries, and which pointed to national directories in each country.

However, such a meaning is not required. For example, one entry in the "Stanford" directory may be the component "MIT" and a pointer to the "MIT" directory. Thus persons at Stanford could query the local Stanford directory to resolve the path name (STANFORD)MIT.JULIET SUTHERLAND.[7]

As the above example makes clear, a path name can be resolved only if one knows the directory in which the first component of the path name is to be found. That is, a path name is not complete without specifying an initial directory. Traditionally, file systems use two approaches to resolving this problem. The first approach assumes the name is relevant to some default working directory, which may be different for each user. The second assumes that directories are organized not into an arbitrary *naming network*[8] but as a *naming hierarchy* or rooted tree. [16] The first component of the path name is always resolved in the root directory. The root directory itself can be found in one of two ways: either every directory contains a pointer back to the root directory; or, every directory contains a pointer to its parent in the hierarchy, and this chain can be traced back to find the root. [15] Once the root directory has been located, the path name — which for this specific case might also be called a *tree name* — is resolved starting with the root. A third alternative, used in the Clearinghouse design, assumes that there is a group of directories at the "top" level, all of which have pointers to each other. Thus, starting with any one of these "top level" directories it is possible to resolve any name.

For a universal MTS directory service, the use of tree names could require every name resolution to examine the root directory, which is clearly inefficient. An alternative, therefore, is used in the ARPA Domain Name proposals to reduce the load on the root directory. In this name/directory design, a

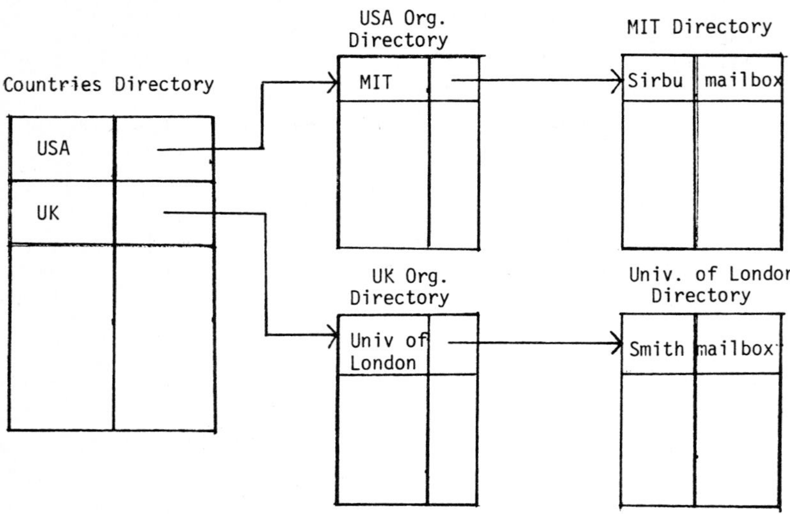

Figure 4-2: Multi-Component Names as Path Names

directory may contain a multi-component entry which allows some directories in the path to be bypassed. Thus, if a client looks in the Stanford directory to resolve the name (STANFORD)ROOT.USA.MASSACHUSETTS.MIT.JULIET SUTHERLAND the MIT directory might contain an entry for the multiple component string ROOT.USA.MASSACHUSETTS.MIT which points directly to the MIT directory. This would allow the tree name to be resolved without searching either the root directory for the entry USA or the directory thus pointed to for the entry MASSACHUSETTS. A similar technique is used in the telephone network where a switch in Manhattan might resolve the telephone number 415-473-1234 by mapping the six digit sequence 415-473 into a direct trunk to the appropriate downtown San Francisco exchange. [19].

Let us summarize the discussion thus far. The components of a multi-component PersonnaName may have two very different interpretations. In one interpretation they are values for well known and commonly understood attributes or fields in a name-address tuple. A directory database is a collection of tuples. In theory, no implication concerning the physical partitioning of the database is implied by the component structure In practice, all directory databases are required to support a common minimal set of fields which are used to partition the name space among DSAs.

A second interpretation views a multi-component name as a series of entries in a network of directories. Each component is resolved within a specific directory. The resolution of the component is either a pointer to another directory or the name of the User Agent pointed to by the path name. A path name cannot be resolved without specifying the initial directory for resolution of the first component. Tree names are a special case of path names in which the naming network is a rooted tree. The directory for the first component is then well-known and can be found either because every directory has a pointer to the root or because every directory has a pointer to its parent.

The path name model for PersonnaNames, without restriction to a hierarchical naming network, provides great generality in the organization and distribution of directory service. Any service which maintains a table of PersonnaNames to User Agents or PersonnaNames to directory pointers can be part of a PersonnaName path name. Corporations, non-profit groups, municipalities, and service providers may all be providers of directory service. The set of entries stored in a directory need not be defined in any common manner—the M.I.T. directory may contain entries which are names of persons or entries which point to other directories. Path names are always resolvable by a directory service without user interaction.

If PersonnaNames are path names, then it is possible, even likely that many PersonnaNames will map into the same User Agent. Thus,

(ITU)USA.UNIVERSITIES.MIT.MARVIN SIRBU-HOME ADDRESS

is a synonym for

(ITU)USA.MASSACHUSETTS.CAMBRIDGE.MARVIN SIRBU

The former "name" can still be used to find Sirbu's home User Agent, even if he changes his residence from Cambridge to Boston, while the latter cannot unless historic information is kept in geographic directories. Far better might be the path name

(ITU)USA.UNIVERSITIES.MIT.ALUMNI.MARVIN SIRBU-HOME ADDRESS

which is likely to be usable even if Sirbu changes jobs in the future.

Users will thus learn to rely on path names which are unlikely to change. They may also choose to use path names for which the intervening directories charge the lowest price (Cf Section 5.1.4).

4.3. Directories versus Directory Service Agents

Each component in a path name is resolved in some directory. A directory is simply a table of bindings between names and objects. In order to assure availability, this table, or directory should be maintained on multiple service hosts, or by multiple Directory Service Agents. Thus a directory, and a DSA are not the same. A DSA may provide service for multiple directories. Conversely, any given directory should be replicated among several DSAs. The Xerox Clearinghouse architecture distinguishes Registries from Registration Servers in order to assure availability, and to share the processing load of handling directory requests among multiple servers. [13, 18]

4.4. Finding a PersonnaName

Finding an unambiguous PersonnaName for a correspondent differs from mapping PersonnaNames into User Agents. We expect the latter operation to proceed, in most cases, automatically. The former is a more difficult task, and is assumed to require an interactive dialog.

Whereas a path name approach is suitable for resolving a PersonnaName, finding a PersonnaName from general information about a user more strongly resembles identifying a name-address tuple using various attribute values for well-known fields. Interaction with the DSA should resemble a database query in which attributes of the desired record are provided until it is uniquely identified. As with any query system, it must provide a number of capabilities.

The DSA must be able to provide the client with information from the data dictionary—*e.g.* the names of the attributes for which data values are available, and something about the nature of those attributes. Some of these attributes may be well known and commonly defined among DSAs. Common definition may imply a central source for the data dictionary, such as the CCITT, or it may imply agreements between organizations providing directory service. These are not mutually exclusive options.

- The DSA must be able to respond with the count of records which match a particular *attribute:value* query, and allow further searches on the subset thus obtained. Ideally, full boolean query support should be provided.

- If a limited thesaurus of values is defined for some attribute, this thesaurus must be obtainable.

- DSAs will have only part of the total name space of users. Most likely a DSA will have a partition corresponding to specified values of some attributes. The DSA should provide pointers to other DSAs which may have information on the desired set of records.

It is possible, of course, that clients will be able to guess a PersonnaName *a priori*. If you know that Marvin Sirbu graduated from MIT, you might guess that (MIT)ALUMNI.MARVIN SIRBU was a valid PersonnaName. However, this PersonnaName, is not resolvable unless you know where to access the MIT directory. The name of a directory is a multi-component name of the form *e.g.* (ROOT)USA.UNIVERSITIES.MIT. One might try several names such as (ROOT)USA.ORGANIZATIONS.MIT or (USA)MASSACHUSETTS.MIT until one locates the MIT directory.

4.5. User Agent Names and Addresses

We have suggested above that directories map PersonnaNames into User Agent Names. Is such a binding necessary? If the "name" of my User Agent is always the same as my PersonnaName, no directory service is required for this level of binding. As long as we are certain that we will never want to have more than one User Agent associated with the same Personna, then using the same name will not pose any difficulties.[9] We have already noted that several forms of a PersonnaName may map into the same UA Name; thus, an equivalence of PersonnaNames and UA Names implies that a UA may have numerous aliases.

A UA Name which has the same form as a PersonnaName provides no hints as to where such a UA is located. A third binding *is* needed from the directory service, therefore, which maps a UA Name into a UA Address. There are in fact two forms of UA Address. From the point of view of the originating MTA, a UA Address is simply the name of the Message Transfer Agent which currently accepts mail for the recipient UA. From the point of view of the recipient MTA, the UA Address is a network attachment point to which mail for that UA should be directed. This corresponds to the difference between the "address" of a UA from the point of view of CCITT protocol P1 versus protocol P3 [3]. In particular, such a binding must indicate which Message Transfer Agent currently accepts mail for this User Agent.

An MTA in turn can be regarded as a service which runs on some host. As noted at the beginning of Section 4, at least 3 additional bindings are needed to map this service into a route over the internetwork. Viewing an MTA as a service, as opposed to as a host allows for the service to migrate to a different host in the event of hardware difficulties. Alternatively, one can imagine that MTAs are permanently bound to a particular host. In that case, reliable mail delivery might require that the mapping from UA to MTA specify secondary MTAs to use in the event the primary MTA is out of service; this approach is used in the Grapevine system [18]. When MTAs are viewed as a service which can be provided on different hosts, there is no advantage in having multiple bindings from a UA to several MTAs.

5. Issues in Directory Service Design

In this section we attempt to provide a reasonably comprehensive list of directory design issues, both technical and organizational, which can be used as a starting point for further discussion. To this end, while we have much to say on some topics, others are included for completeness and are discussed only briefly.

5.1. Directory Operation

5.1.1. Direct vs Indirect

In obtaining a PersonnaName or an address, a client might interact with a directory service and the DSAs that implement it in either of two ways. One model puts the burden on the client. The client contacts a DSA; if its directory has all of the required information, the transaction is complete. If the directory has none, or only part, of the desired information, the client must contact another DSA. The name and address of the next DSA may be provided by the previous one or the client may determine them by other means. In any case, the client must establish direct contact with another DSA, and continue this pattern until a complete name or address is obtained. This approach is called "Direct Access" (Figure 5-1). [8]

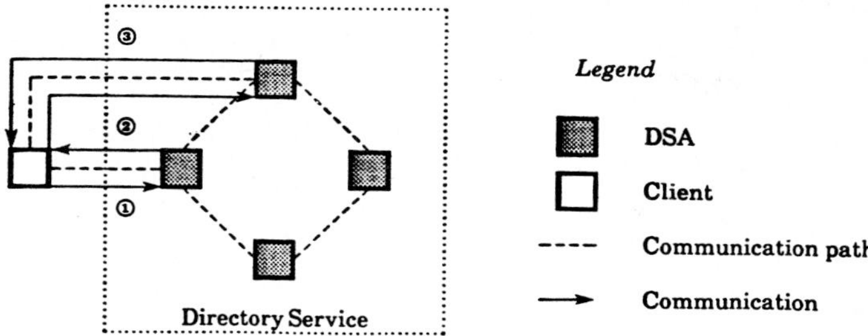

Figure 5-1: Direct Access to DSAs.

A second model has the first DSA making the contact with the next DSA, and so on, until the name is resolved. This model is known as "Indirect Access" (Figure 5-2). [8]

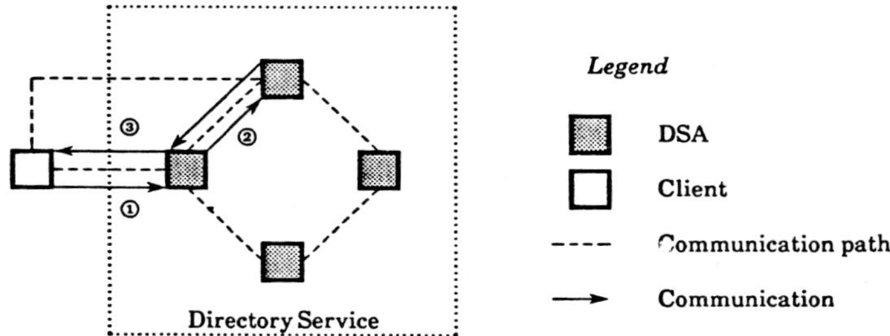

Figure 5-2: Indirect Access to DSAs.

Domestic telephone directory assistance in the U.S. is provided by direct access. If a local directory assistance operator doesn't have the right part of the database (e.g. the city of the person being called) the operator will usually provide the correct number for directory assistance in that city. The user must then make a new call to the correct directory assistance service. International directory assistance, however, is provided indirectly. The domestic operator establishes contact with the foreign directory assistance operator to resolve the query.

Direct access has the advantage that it allows the client to choose the communications network used to contact each DSA, thus permitting control over communication costs. In addition, if the client can communicate directly with every DSA, it reduces the processing load on DSAs acting as intermediaries.

Indirect access may offer economies of scale in communications if DSAs are in frequent contact. Billing may also be simplified through the use of a settlements process between DSAs. Direct connection requires direct billing to the client for DSA service.[10] Authentication may also be simpler with indirect access, since DSAs may have established procedures for authenticating themselves to each other and users would need to establish an initial authentication with only one DSA.

5.1.2. Incremental vs Absolute Name Resolution

There are two methods by which names can be resolved. One method specifies that the name-to-mailbox mapping must be performed completely before a message is sent. That is, the message must be sent with a complete address. The other method allows the mapping to take place in incremental steps. The sending entity resolves enough components of the name to determine an address of the next forwarding point. The next entity resolves some of the remaining components in order to send the message further. By the time the message is delivered to its destination, the name has been completely resolved. We refer to the first method as *absolute* name resolution, and to the second method as *incremental* name resolution.

Incremental resolution has the advantage that the name resolution and message transport can occur simultaneously. For absolute resolution, one might find the case where an expensive connection is required to perform the initial resolution and another expensive connection is required to send the message. CSNET[11] allows a form of incremental resolution to accommodate mail users who only connect to the network once a day. By using incremental resolution, these users avoid having to wait a day to receive the address before they can send the message. Incremental resolution may also be required if the sender cannot directly address the destination, for example due to differences in communications and addressing protocols.

One can argue, however, that caching—storing information locally—gives absolute resolution the advantage. With incremental resolution, one can only cache the first part of the name-to-mailbox mapping, and later parts of that mapping must be performed each time a message is sent. Caching, combined with absolute resolution allows the mapping to be performed only once with the cached address perhaps used many times before it is no longer valid.

A further problem with incremental resolution is that if the structure of the name and address are very different, incremental resolution may produce a very different route. In the worst case, incremental resolution of a name may send a message across the country and back, while the address might have shown that the physical destination of the message was nearby. In fact, incremental resolution may imply that the name and the route are related, while absolute resolution keeps the name and the route distinct.

If organizations are mutually suspicious, and if an address in some way reflects either the organization's network structure or organization chart, the organization may not want to divulge employees' complete addresses. The organization may choose instead to perform that part of the name to address mapping that occurs within its control. One can thus imagine a system whereby absolute resolution is used to contact the organization's gateway, which then performs any further mapping that may be required. Incremental resolution can also confine directory updating to within the organization.

These considerations, are more pertinant to the electronic mail system which uses the directory than to the directory itself. The mail system makes the choice between absolute and indirect name resolution, but this choice affects the directory service, as the discussion of the implications of caching shows. The issue of direct vs indirect DSA communication is only of concern if absolute name resolution is presumed.

5.1.3. Caching

Caching in directory systems has many permutations, depending on the answers to the following questions: *When* should caching occur? *Where* should caching occur? *What* should be cached? And *how* should the caching be performed? We will not answer the last question since a discussion of caching algorithms is beyond the scope of this paper.

By looking at the use of a directory service we can answer questions about when and what to cache. In obtaining an unknown name, a client will contact some directories and will make use of some attributes to describe the target of the query. Since the client will have obtained a unique name at the end of this process, the complete set of directory names and attributes should also uniquely identify the target. One might, therefore, consider caching the set of directory names and attributes. However, by the time that set is complete, one has also obtained a name. The only reason to save the information used to obtain the name would be to obtain the name again. Since names should change slowly, if at all, it seems unlikely that anyone would cache the information used to obtain the name. Having obtained a name, one might want to cache it to avoid having to get it again. Similarly, once an address has been obtained, one might want to cache it as well. We expect that different caching methods will be used for names and addresses since addresses will change more quickly than names.

Names and addresses can be cached at several locations. A directory might want to cache information from another directory. This would be particularly likely under the indirect model, since having information locally would save the cost of obtaining it from a remote directory.[12] Under the direct model, a directory might cache information, but it would be purely as a service to its clients. Names and addresses can be cached by a client or a client's UA. Caching at this point allows locally assigned nicknames and aliases. Finally, caching can be done by an MTA. An MTA might store the addresses for particularly common names, thereby saving the time and expense of using a directory to resolve them. Fortunately, all of these types of caching can coexist, since all are likely to be desirable, and each meets different needs.

There are two concepts within directories and mail systems that are strongly related to caching. The first concept is that of *authority*. Cached information, unlike information replicated for reliability purposes, is not guaranteed to be correct. There must be, however, a place where the information is always supposed to be correct. That is, there must be an authoritative directory to which one can refer. In addition to the concept of authority, there must be a way to determine that a cached item is, or may be, incorrect. This might be done via an error message, by a time out, or by some other method.

5.1.4. Accounting and Billing

There are three distinct models for how directory services will be financed: by the network, by the originator, and by the recipient. Examples of all three of these methods are in common use today.

1. Telephone Directory Assistance service has traditionally been furnished free by the communications network services provider. In theory, the cost of directory assistance is recovered from other telephone service charges.[13]

2. Recent studies by the phone company have shown that a small number of subscribers make large numbers of directory assistance calls. In order that these heavy users bear their appropriate share of Directory Assistance costs, phone companies have begun to charge subscribers explicitly for local calls to Directory Assistance above a specified maximum per month. Besides telephone callers, mailers frequently pay for address lists which resolve generalized directory queries such as "the addresses of all doctors in the Greater New York area".

3. The Yellow Pages is an example of a directory service paid for by the recipient of a communication. Also, the corporate telephone operator, who resolves requests for an individual's extension, is paid for by the receiving organization.

These examples suggest we should expect an equally diverse pattern of payments and billing in an electronic environment. Organizations which expect to benefit from making their members accessible will provide directory services for free. Network providers may also be expected to provide such services to their subscribers to induce additional network usage. Clients will be charged where the volume of queries is large, or a search is performed to retrieve a large set of addresses meeting specific criteria.

5.1.5. Update

Managing the addition, deletion, and change of directory entries, assuring the authenticity of update requests, and propagating changes to other directories storing the same information, are practical problems that must be addressed by any directory system. We will not discuss authentication methods, and have only one point to make regarding updates.

If an attribute or name component changes, it may have to change in several directories. Given multiple unaffiliated directory service providers, should it be the target's responsibility to see that the change is made in all relevant directories or should the update be propogated automatically by the directory service agents? Automatic propogation should lead to more reliable and consistent updating; however, such cooperation among directory service agents may be too much to expect in a competitve environment.

5.2. What Kind of Directory Information?

In its most basic form, a directory is simply a table matching names to addresses. As a minimum, then, a directory must contain names or components of names, and for each name component either an address or the name and/or address of a directory where that component can be resolved. In order to help a client find an unknown name, however, a directory may contain other kinds of information. Since this information is to be used to identify the name of the target, it will describe some aspect or *attribute* of the target. Different kinds of attributes will be used to identify different kinds of targets. For example, name, geographic location, and organization may be attributes associated with people, while name, topic, size, and membership may be attributes associated with distribution lists. As we have pointed out in Section 4.4, in order for attributes to be useful, a client must be able to determine what attributes a directory supports. This can be done by having all directories agree to support certain attributes, by having a protocol for obtaining attribute information, or by a combination of the two.

Issues of personal and organizational privacy become important in determining what types of attribute information to provide. Some of these issues are addressed in Section 5.3.

There are other kinds of information that a directory might provide as a service to its clients and because it seems a logical place within the message system to keep the information. Examples of this include tariff information, information about the capabilities of recipient's UAs, and authentication information. The scope of this type of information, and its relationship to names, addresses, and attributes are issues that have not been addressed by most directory efforts. Clearinghouse provides an arbitrary list of properties, values for which can be stored with each directory entry.

5.3. Types of Listing

In the US, most telephone directories distinguish between regular listings, unpublished listings, and unlisted telephone numbers. In a regular listing, a person's name, address, and telephone number appear in both the printed directory and the information operator's directory. For an unpublished listing, the information appears in the information operator's directory but not in the published directory. An unlisted telephone number does not appear in either the published directory or the information operator's directory, although the fact that the person has a telephone does appear in the information operator's directory. Similar distinctions will apply to electronic mail directories.

Given the complex attribute data that may be maintained in a directory, there will be many more types of restricted listings. A person might specify that the values of certain attributes be listed as null. A person may specify a list of people who are allowed access to that person's address. An organization that provides optional attributes in its directory might want to distinguish between permanent employees, temporary employees (including consultants), friendly outsiders, and competitors, making a different amount or kind of information available to each. All of these examples can be provided by a simple structure.

For each attribute there can be several kinds of listing:

Regular The value of this attribute is available to any client.

Restricted The value of this attribute is available to a specified list or class of clients.

Unlisted The value of this attribute is not available to any client and is always listed as null.

Verified The value of this attribute can be verified but not volunteered. That is, if the client specifies the correct value for the attribute, the DSA will confirm that the value is correct. For example, the DSA might confirm that there is a Joe Smith at 56 Broad St.

Volunteered The value of this attribute can be provided by the DSA as a choice to the client. For example, the DSA might ask if the client means the Joe Smith at 56 Broad St or the one at 21 Elm St.

Regular, restricted, and unlisted are mutually exclusive. The listing options for some attributes might be chosen by the person to whom the attribute refers or the options might be chosen by the organization maintaining the listing.

The difference between volunteered and verified information does not protect the privacy of the target from determined inquiry. A client who is willing to make a sufficient number of inquiries can obtain enough information in most cases to infer the values of attributes that can only be verified. This distinction, then, is useful to prevent everyone who makes a query from seeing certain information, but cannot protect against a client who is determined to obtain that information.

6. Existing Directory Systems

Having discussed a number of issues regarding the design of directory services and DSAs, we now examine some existing systems to see how they have resolved the questions we have raised. We will discuss three directory systems which are in various stages of design and implementation as well as the work done on models of directory service by IFIP Working Group 6.5.

Figure 6-1 summarizes our discussion of these systems and adds the telephone directory system for comparison. In the figure, the columns represent the answers to the following questions:

DSA Communication
What method is used to obtain information from several directories? The possible values are direct, indirect, and Not Applicable.

Discovery Is the directory service designed to support a client in determining an unknown name? In the telephone directory system the yellow pages provide such support while the white pages do not.

DSA Architecture Which architecture is used to provide the directory service? The possible answers are distributed or centralized.

Caching Does the directory service allow caching? In those systems where caching is allowed, the method and place are described in the section that describes that system.

Access Control Does the directory service allow restriction of access to some information? Note that this is for read access and is not the same as authorization for update.

Authoritative How much of the information obtainable from a DSA is authoritative?

Name Form What type of name does the directory assume? The possibilities are tuples or some type of tree.

6.1. Clearinghouse

The Clearinghouse name server was designed at Xerox and is described in [13]. This directory maps names of the form "Individual@Domain@Organization" into sets of properties. Properties have names, types, and values. Properties can range from, for a printer, its network address, to, for a user, the name of the mail server that stores that user's mail. The examples and terminology of the names suggest that the designers intended "organization" to refer to a corporate entity and "domain" to the corporation's parts. However, one can generalize this three level structure. An "Organization" might be a state such as Massachusetts and a "Domain" might be a city such as Cambridge. Whatever the interpretation of the levels of names, the clearinghouse is explicitly designed to be a distributed system composed of many local clearinghouse servers.

	DSA Comm.	Discovery	DSA Architecture	Caching	Access Control	Authoritative	Name Form
Clearinghouse	direct	no	distrib.	unspec.	yes	all	3-level tree
CSNET	N.A.	yes	central	yes	no	all	tuple
ARPA	direct	no	distrib.	yes	no	some	multi-level tree
IFIP	either	yes	distrib.	unspec.	unspec.	unspec.	unspec.
Telephone	both	yellow pages	distrib.	yes	yes	all	tuple

Figure 6-1: Comparison of existing directory systems.

From the structure of the names, and the requirement that complete names must be used, it is clear that Clearinghouse is primarily intended to map names into addresses although it does provide some facilities for discovering unknown names.[14] These services, however, do not address the problems of personal privacy or corporate privacy and are only the roughest tools for finding addresses based on partially known information.

Clearinghouse servers are structured hierarchically, going from organizations to domains to individual targets. Organizations and domains have clearinghouse servers which are logically the principal servers for that level of the structure and which are required to know about lower levels of the structure. In addition, "each clearinghouse server points 'upward' to *every* organization clearinghouse." While the organization/domain hierarchy follows many of the same ideas that we have suggested, this final requirement quickly becomes difficult to implement on a nationwide, much less an international, scale. Consider the number of businesses that might maintain clearinghouse servers, combined with service providers for small business, geographical clearinghouses for residential use, and clearinghouses maintained by professional and social organizations. Consider also the communication cost, not to mention the administrative nightmare, of having every clearinghouse, regardless of its level in the hierarchy, keep track of every organization clearinghouse. Thus, while Clearinghouse will work within a single organization or a group of organizations, the requirement that all servers must know about all organization servers prevents Clearinghouse from being scalable to a national level.

Clearinghouse uses the direct method of searching for information. The "clearinghouse stub" maintained by each user contacts successive clearinghouse servers until it finds one that has the desired information. Given the strict hierarchy and the upward pointers, the clearinghouse stub contacts at most three servers. The final server performs any authentication and access control that may be required. Access control is performed at the domain level and at the property level. This allows managers of domain level servers to restrict access to all of their data and allows individual users to restrict access to information about certain properties.

6.2. ARPA Name Server

The ARPA Internet is a network funded by the U.S. Department of Defense (DoD) which connects sites doing DoD research. These sites include universities, government contractors, and government agencies. A Request for Comment has recently been issued to the ARPA community regarding Domain Name Servers [10]. Through all of the following discussion, it should be remembered that these comments are based on a proposal which is still subject to change and which has not yet been implemented.

There will be many domain name servers, each knowing about a part of the total name space. The name space is defined to be a hierarchy of unlimited depth. The root of the tree is null and there is no discussion of how the first level will be defined. Initially, domain names and domain name servers will be used only for host names. Eventually information about users, such as mailbox names, will be added. There is optional provision for the completion of partially known host names. The intention appears to be to provide a simple name/address mapping service.

A client will access domain name servers via the direct method. "If a name server is presented with a query for a domain name that is not within its authority, it may have the desired information, but it will also return a response that points toward an authoritative name server." In actual fact, a client will talk to a resolver, located on the client's host, which will then perform the necessary interaction with the name servers.

The only form of access control is the restriction that authoritative name servers may prohibit copying of any part of their databases by other servers.

The Domain name server proposal does discuss caching. Resolvers may cache address information. To maintain current information, data for caching is provided with a time-to-live after which it is discarded. Name servers may also cache information, in that they may store information for which they are not the authoritative source. In providing this information, a name server must also provide the address of the authoritative name server. The resolver must then treat this non-authoritative information as a hint which may or may not be correct.

6.3. CSNET Name Server

The CSNET is a computer communications network designed to connect computer science departments in colleges and universities throughout the United States. One of the services that CSNET provides is electronic mail, and in support of that service there is a name server [20]. The CSNET name server is centralized, existing at a well known address on the network. Issues, such as direct vs indirect communication between DSAs, that apply only in distributed environments, are not relevant here.

The CSNET designers have not explicitly recognized that there are two levels of directory service. In discussing other work, they point out that a major difference between their work and the Clearinghouse project is the CSNET emphasis on facilitating lookup based on incomplete information. Since many of the CSNET name server goals involve user interaction, the design emphasis appears to be on providing a service to map attributes into names.

CSNET names, however, are not well defined. The CSNET name server makes provision for lookup based on a number of mandatory and optional attributes, known as "key words". Retrieval is based on string matching with partial strings permitted to allow for alternate spellings. Matching is done first on mandatory attributes, such as name and organization, with optional attributes used only to distinguish ambiguous results. The name server also provides a unique registration ID for each entry. The registration ID is used for "forwarding". That is, when a sender discovers that a recipient has moved, the sender's UA can use the registration ID to query the name server to obtain a new address.

The combination of mandatory and optional attributes that produces a unique result can be regarded as a name, as can the registration ID. The designers do not appear to distinguish between these types of names and, in fact, do not appear to regard the registration ID as a name at all. Since the registration ID is intended to be unvarying and can always be used to obtain an address, it most closely meets our definition of a name. The registration ID is neither easy to remember nor composed of multiple components, perhaps because it is intended only for machine use on a centralized server.

The CSNET name server does provide for caching of addresses by clients. How a client decides which addresses to keep is unspecified. When a message is returned as undeliverable, the client must query the directory to obtain the new address. This can be done automatically.

The CSNET name server provides for authentication for update but provides no access control for read-only operations. The designers assume that anyone providing information for the name server will provide only information that can be generally released. While this assumption may be valid in their environment of presumably friendly researchers, it does not generalize well to an environment of mutually suspicious organizations.

Unlike the other directory systems, the CSNET system allows the message to be sent with the query. If the query produces a unique result, the message is then sent to that address. If the query produces an ambiguous result, the message is returned with the request for clarification. This option was provided for the convenience of hosts which have access to the network only once a day (via telephone) so that users would not have to wait for the result of the query to send the message.

6.4. IFIP

IFIP Working Group 6.5 has been in the forefront of conceptual work on message systems. We have adopted their model and terminology for message systems and have been inspired by their work on directories. They have suggested the concept of the DSA, have recognized that any directory system must be distributed, and have started to explore some of the issues that we have discussed in this paper. In particular, [8][15] has an excellent discussion of direct vs indirect DSA access. Working Group 6.5 has recognized the two level of mapping, distinguishing between a service to get a name and a service to get an address but the implications of this distinction have not been fully explored. Since Working Group 6.5

is just starting to address directory questions, many practical problems, such as management, access control, and accounting and billing have yet to be discussed.

7. Conclusion

The design and operation of a directory service for electronic messaging must meet a variety of criteria, some of which we have enumerated in this paper. At present no existing or proposed directory system meets all of the desired criteria. In particular, the directory problem must be understood as two separate problems: finding an unambiguous name for a user and finding the mailbox which goes with that name. The structure and interpretation of user names is central to the design of a distributed directory service. The use of multi-component path names for users appears to allow many of the design objectives to be met. Further research is necessary on methods of updating directories, assuring availability through redundancy [18], and protection of personal and organizational privacy.

Acknowledgements

This work was supported in part by the Advanced Research Project Agency of the Department of Defense, monitored by the Office of Naval Research under contract N0014-83-K-0125.

References

1. Birrell, A.D., R. Levin, R.M. Needham, and M.D. Schroeder. Grapevine: an exercise in distributed computing. *Comm. ACM 25*. 4 (April 1982), 260-274.

2. Casson, Lionel. 'It would be very nice if you sent me 200 drachmas'. *Smithsonian 14*, 1 (April 1983), 116-131.

3. CCITT Study Group VII/5. Message Handling Systems: System Model- Service Elements. Draft Recommendation X.400. International Telephone and Telegraph Consultative Committee (CCITT), Nov., 1983.

4. CCITT Study Group VII/5. Message Handling Systems: Message Transfer Layer. Draft Recommendation X.411, International Telephone and Telegraph Consultative Committee (CCITT), Nov., 1983.

5. Cunningham, I. *et al.* Emerging Protocols for Global Message Exchange. Compcom '82, IEEE Computer Society, Sept., 1982, pp. 153-161.

6. Deutsch, Debra. International Standardization of Message Transfer Protocols: An Overview. Compcom '82, IEEE Computer Society, Sept., 1982, pp. 162-167.

7. Haas, C. W. et al. 800 Service Using SPC Network Capability--Network Implementation and Administrative Functions. *BSTJ* , 7, Part 3 (September 1982), 1745-1757". Special issue "Stored Program Controlled Network"

8. IFIP Working Group 6.5. Naming, Addressing, and Directory Service for Message Handling Systems. Working Paper N78, IFIP Technical Committee 6, Working Group 6.5, Feb., 1983. Version 3

9. ISO/TC97/SC16. Information Processing Systems - Open Systems Interconnection - Basic Reference Model. ISO 7498, ISO International Organization for Standardization Organization Internationale de Normalisation, 1983.

10. Mockapetris, P. Domain Names - Concepts and Facilities. RFC 882, University of Southern California, Information Sciences Institute, Nov., 1983.

11. Mockapetris, P. Domain Names - Implementation and Specification. RFC 883, University of Southern California, Information Sciences Institute, Nov., 1983.

12. Oppen, Derek C. and Yogen K. Dalal. The Clearinghouse: A Decentralized Agent for Locating Named Objects in a Distributed Environment. Tech. Rep. OPD-T8103, Xerox Corporation, Office Products Division, Oct., 1981.

13. Oppen, Derek C. and Yogen K. Dalal. The Clearinghouse: A Decentralized Agent for Locating Named Objects in a Distributed Environment. *ACM Transactions on Office Information Systems 1*, 3 (July 1983).

14. Redell, David D. and James E. White. Interconnecting Electronic Mail Systems. *Computer 16*, 9 (Sept. 1983), 55-63.

15. Ritchie, D.M., and K. Thompson. The UNIX Time-Sharing System. *Comm. ACM 17*, 7 (July 1974), 365-375.

16. Saltzer, J. H. Naming and Binding Objects. In *Lecture Notes in Computer Science 60,* Springer-Verlag, NY, 1978, ch. 3, pp. 99-208.

17. Saltzer, Jerome H. On the Naming and Binding of Network Destinations. *Local Computer Networks* (1982).

18. Schroeder, Michael D., Andrew D. Birrell, and Roger M. Needham. Experience with Grapevine: The Growth of a Distributed System. *ACM Transactions on Computer Systems 2*, 1 (Feb. 1984), 3-23.

19. Shoch, John F. Inter-Network Naming, Addressing, and Routing. Proceedings, COMPCON 78 Fall, IEEE, 1978, pp. 72-79.

20. Solomon, Marvin, Lawrence H. Landweber, and Donald Neuhengen. The CSNET Name Server. *Computer Networks 6*. 3 (July 1982), 161-172.

21. Stoffels, Bob. Turning Yellow into Gold. *Telephone Engineering and Management 87*, 19 (October 1 1983), 61-62. This article contains a reproduction of the 1878 New Haven District Telephone Co. Directory.

22. White, James A. and Jeanne Saddler. A.T.&T. Long-Distance Unit Offers Plan for $1.75 Billion of Rate Cuts Next Year. *Wall Street Journal CCII*, 66 (Oct. 1983), 4.

Notes

[1]The model described here is actually the IFIP model as adopted and changed by the CCITT and described in [3, 4].

[2]Similar arguments apply if the destination is a role or a service as opposed to a personna.

[3]As evidence that human beings have long since discovered this principle, we have only to note that a sentence such as "John of York is living in Kent" makes perfect sense.

[4]AT&T's *Expanded 800 Service* allows permanent "personal" phone numbers to be mapped into any physical number on the network. The distributed database is partitioned by the exchange code. [7]

[5]We would not want to identify John Brown as the person who gets his mail at JBROWN@MC in a table binding Persons to street addresses!

[6]Personnal communication from Debra Deutsch.

[7]The notation *(<first directory>)<name1>.<name2>...<nameN>* should be read: the first component, *<name1>* is resolved in directory *<first directory>*; subsequent componênts *<namei>* are each resolved in the directory pointed to by the previous component.

[8]*naming network:* a directory system in which a directory may contain the name of any object including another directory. An object is located by a multi-component path name relative to some arbitrary initial directory.

[9]The Xerox Ethernet standard uses the same 48 bit number for both host identifier and network attachment point identifier. This has led to problems when a host has more than one attachment point to the network (Cf. [17]).

[10]Consider the overhead involved in maintaining account information for each possible user of a DSA.

[11]Cf. Section 6.3.

[12]This presumes that communication costs are more significant that storage costs.

[13]AT&T has recently announced its intention to charge for the use of its network to gain direct access to remote Directory Assistance operators. [22]. The advent of competition means that AT&T cannot be assured of carrying the resultant call following a Directory Assistance inquiry.

[14]It is possible to ask about an individual via the *LookupIndividual* command and it is possible to list various types of information using the *LookupGeneric*, *EnumerateDomains* and *EnumerateOrganizations* commands. [12] The various lookup commands do simple string matching, while the enumerate commands simply provide complete lists of the domains and organizations known to the clearinghouse.

[15]The most recent subgroup meeting of WG 6.5 proposed numerous changes to this draft to be reflected in later versions.

Computer-Based Message Services
H.T. Smith (Editor)
Elsevier Science Publishers B.V. (North-Holland)

A User-friendly Naming Convention for Use in Communication Networks

James E. White

Office Systems Division
Xerox Corporation
Palo Alto, California
USA

Networking has created an environment in which many kinds of entities must be named. Standards bodies are apt to develop a single, widely applicable, user-friendly naming convention and the distributed directory system required to support it. The purpose of this paper is to facilitate that work by describing such a naming convention.

The ideas presented in this paper were developed by the European and North American Systems Environment Subgroups of IFIP Working Group 6.5, International Computer Message Systems, during the period from April 1982 through March 1984.

Introduction

1 The Role of Names

A *name* is a linguistic object that singles out a particular entity from among a collection of entities. For example, the name "Walter E. Jones" might identify a particular employee of the (fictitious) Conway Steel Corporation, distinguishing him from other Conway Steel employees. An entity's name need not indicate where the entity resides. Thus, for example, Walt Jones' name above does not reveal whether he works in Roanoke, Virginia; in Richmond, Virginia; or at some other Conway Steel site.

Names are unambiguous but not necessarily unique. A name must certainly be *unambiguous*, that is, denote just one entity; this follows from the definition of the term "name" given above. However, a name need not be *unique*, that is, be the *only* linguistic object that unambiguously denotes the entity. For example, Walt Jones might have (at least) the following four names in the Conway Steel context:

- "Walter E. Jones" — *his "signature" name*
- "Walter Edward Jones" — *his full, unabbreviated name*
- "L36N" — *his employee number*
- "Room 511, 42 Riverside Drive, Richmond, Virginia, USA" — *his geographical address*

The last two names above are different in character than the first two. The corporate personnel office might consider employee numbers ideal names, since its database is indexed by them. Similarly, the corporate mail system might like geographical addresses, since its routing system is based upon them. However, one's fellow employees would have trouble with either scheme. Employee numbers are too difficult to remember. Geographical addresses change too rapidly; for example, during his six years with Conway Steel, Walt Jones has occupied eight different offices. The last two name forms lack a quality that might be termed *user-friendliness*; they cater to the mechanism (the personnel office or mail system) that processes names, rather than to the human beings who use them.

2 Document Scope

This paper describes a user-friendly naming convention suitable for use in communication networks. While the most urgent need for such a convention arises in the context of public data networks, the convention could be used in private data networks and in public and private voice networks as well.

The naming convention is intended to govern the naming of many of the kinds of entities found in or made accessible by communication networks. Among these entities are people, roles, distribution lists, services, service users, service providers, hosts, and terminals.

The naming convention is intended to govern the naming of entities engaged in any or all of a wide range of applications. Among these applications are electronic mail, remote file storage and retrieval, remote job entry, and terminal emulation.

The naming convention is intended to govern the naming of entities in a variety of social environments. Among these are the business and residential environments.

The naming convention is assumed to be implemented by a *directory system*, a specialized database management system with which entities are registered and in which information about them is stored. The precise nature of the directory system–the services it provides, the protocols by which its components interwork (if it is distributed), and the kinds of information stored in its database–lies beyond the scope of this paper.

The paper is organized in two parts. Part I specifies the naming convention proper. Part II suggests how the naming convention might be applied to selected entities in the business environment. The manner in which the naming convention might be applied to other business entities or to entities in other environments is beyond the scope of the paper, but is briefly explored in an appendix.

3 Design Goals

Five principal goals guided the design of the naming convention described in this paper. These goals are identified and briefly discussed below.

3.1 Generality

Over a long period of time, the naming convention will be called upon to provide names for a wide variety of entities in a wide variety of environments. Not all of these entities or environments can be identified in advance. Therefore, the naming convention must provide a general framework in which *any* kind of entity can be named.

3.2 Specificity

Over a much shorter period of time, the naming convention will be called upon to provide names for a few known kinds of entities (for example, people and distribution lists) in just one or two known environments (for example, the business environment). Therefore, the naming convention should offer detailed guidelines for naming those particular kinds of entities in those environments.

3.3 Multiplicity

The naming convention must enable entities to be known by different names in different settings. For example, Walt Jones might require two intrinsically different names, one reflecting his employment by the Conway Steel Corporation, the other his membership in the United Steel Workers Union.

3.4 Distributability

In the case of public data networks, the directory system that implements the naming convention will be of international proportions. Its database, therefore, will be highly distributed. It is likely that this distribution will be predominantly (although not exclusively) hierarchical in nature. For example, the database might be distributed first by country, then by organization within country, etc. Thus the naming convention must facilitate a distributed and largely hierarchical implementation.

3.5 User-friendliness

The naming convention must be user-friendly. In some sense, this is its most important goal. A *user-friendly* naming convention is one that takes the human user's point of view, not the computer's (or, for example, even the corporate mail system's). It is one that yields names that are easy for people to deduce, remember, and understand, rather than ones that are easy for computers to interpret.

The goal of user-friendliness can be stated somewhat more precisely in terms of the following two principles:

- A human being usually should be able to correctly guess an entity's name on the basis of information about the entity that he naturally possesses. For example, one should be able to guess a business person's name given only the information on his business card.

- When an entity's name is guessed incorrectly, the directory system should recognize that fact rather than interpret the guess as the name of another entity. For example, where two people have the same last name, that last name alone should be considered inadequate identification of either party.

The following subgoals follow from the goal of user-friendliness:

1. The naming convention should not *artificially* remove natural ambiguities. For example, if two people share the last name "Jones", neither should be required to answer to "WJones" or "Jones2". Instead, the naming convention should provide a user-friendly means of discriminating between the entities. For example, it might require first name and middle initial in addition to last name.

2. The naming convention should admit common abbreviations and common variations in spelling. For example, if one is employed by the Conway Steel Corporation and the name of one's employer figures in the naming convention, any of the names "Conway Steel Corporation", "Conway Steel Corp.", "Conway Steel", and "CSC" should suffice to identify the organization in question.

3. If names are multi-part, both the number of mandatory parts and the number of optional parts should be relatively small and thus easy to remember.

4. If names are multi-part, the precise order in which those parts appear should be immaterial.

5. Names should not involve computer addresses.

"The *name* of a resource indicates what we seek,
an *address* indicates where it is,
and a *route* tells us how to get there."

–John Shoch, "Inter-network Naming, Addressing, and Routing",
COMPCON Proceedings, Fall 1978, IEEE Computer Society

Part I
The Naming Convention

Part I of this paper specifies the naming convention proper and is organized in two sections. Section 4 states the rules to which all names must adhere. Section 5 offers general guidelines for name assignment.

These sections apply to named entities of all kinds in all environments.

4 Naming Rules

All names subject to the naming convention have certain prescribed characteristics. These rules to which all names adhere are briefly summarized as follows. First, every name is an attribute list. This follows the practice of CCITT's Recommendations on message handling [6]. Second, every name is chosen from a global name space that is modeled as a directed graph. Third, every purported name is tested for validity–by comparison with the graph–by means of a single, prescribed algorithm.

This section specifies in detail the rules summarized above. It introduces the notions of attributes and attribute lists, reviews the mathematical concept of directed graphs, describes the particular directed graph that governs the naming convention, introduces some useful graphical shorthands, and finally specifies the algorithm by which purported names are tested for validity.

4.1 Attributes

The component parts of names are attributes. An *attribute* is a linguistic object that denotes a characteristic of the entity being named. In the case of a business person, for example, the particular attributes of interest might include the individual's personal name (for example, "Walter E. Jones") and the name of his employer (for example, "Conway Steel Corporation"). In the case of a business role, the title associated with the role (for example, "Foreman, Swing Shift") would probably be of importance.

An attribute is considered to have a type as well as a value. An *attribute type* is a class of information (for example, a country name or a telephone number). An *attribute value* is an instance of such a class (for example, "US", the name of a particular country, or "1-804-494-0674", a particular telephone number).

Examples of attributes appear throughout this paper. All of the examples are constructed using the standard attribute types specified for the business environment in Section 8. Each attribute type is denoted by one of the abbreviations found in Table 2 of that section. Each attribute value has the syntactic structure prescribed for the corresponding attribute type–either atomic or composite. An *atomic* value is a number or string. A *composite* value is an ordered sequence of numbers and strings. (Other atomic and composite structures are easily imagined but are beyond the scope of this paper.)

Note: The reason for drawing all of the examples from the business environment is pedagogic: the detailed discussion of that environment found in Part II of the paper makes such examples concrete and easy to understand. It should be clear, however, that examples pertaining to the residential environment (for example) could also have been given. Such additional attribute types as Street Name, Street Number, and Postal Code, however, would first have to have been defined. This subject is pursued a bit further in the appendix.

For both conciseness and precision, the examples are couched in a simple, formal notation. This notation is illustrative only and is not intended to suggest how attributes should appear at user interfaces or when transferred between two open systems. In particular, the transfer syntax for attributes is beyond the scope of this paper.

The formal notation is described by means of Backus-Naur Form (BNF) [4] as follows. The lexical order in which individual components of composite attribute values appear is significant:

```
Attribute           ::= AttributeType = AttributeValue

AttributeType       ::= string
AttributeValue      ::= AtomicValue | CompositeValue

AtomicValue         ::= Component
CompositeValue      ::= ( ) | ( ComponentSequence )

ComponentSequence   ::= Component | ComponentSequence , Component
Component           ::= number | " string "
```

Examples: C = "US" — *the entity's country*
GN = "Foremen" — *the name assigned to the entity, a group*

L = "Richmond"	*the entity's geographical locale*
O = "Conway Steel Corporation"	*the entity's organization*
OL = "Roanoke"	*the geographical locale of the entity's organization*
OTN = (1, 703, "923-0078")	*the telephone number of the entity's organization*
OU = "Manufacturing Division"	*the entity's organizational unit*
PN = ("Walter", "E.", "Jones")	*the personal name of the entity, a person*
TN = (1, 804, "494-0674")	*the telephone number of the entity, a person or role*
T = "Foreman, Swing Shift"	*the title of the entity, a person or role*

In figures the normal punctuation for attribute values, exemplified above and specified in Section 8 for business attributes, is either simplified or omitted to conserve space on the printed page.

4.2 Attribute Lists

The naming convention set forth in this paper specifies that names are attribute lists. An *attribute list* is a linguistic object that denotes any number of characteristics of the entity being named. In the case of a business person, for example, an attribute list might specify the individual's personal name, the name of his employer, and the name of his country. In the case of a business role, the title associated with the role might replace personal name.

An attribute list is an unordered set of zero or more attributes. The attributes that constitute the list must be distinct. That is, although several attributes may have the same type, no two attributes may have both the same type and the same value. For example, if telephone number is an attribute and one has both a primary and an alternate number, both numbers might appear in an attribute list; the two numbers would appear as separate attributes having the same type but different values.

Examples of attribute lists appear throughout this paper. For both conciseness and precision, the examples are couched in a simple, formal notation. This notation is illustrative only and is not intended to suggest how attribute lists should appear at user interfaces or when transferred between two open systems. In particular, the transfer syntax for attribute lists is beyond the scope of this paper.

The formal notation is described by means of Backus-Naur Form (BNF) [4] as follows. It makes use of the formal notation for attributes specified in Section 4.1. The lexical order in which individual attributes appear is insignificant, that is, conveys no information:

AttributeList ::= **( ) | (AttributeSet)**

AttributeSet ::= **Attribute | AttributeSet , Attribute**
Attribute ::= *defined in Section 4.1*

Examples:	(PN = ("Walter", "E.", "Jones"), O = "Conway Steel", C = "US")	*a person*
	(T = "Foreman, Swing Shift", O = "Conway Steel", C = "US")	*a role*
	(GN = "Foremen", O = "Conway Steel", C = "US")	*a group*

4.3 Directed Graphs

A useful tool for further describing the naming convention is the directed graph, an example of which appears in Figure 1. This section briefly reviews this important concept from mathematics [3].

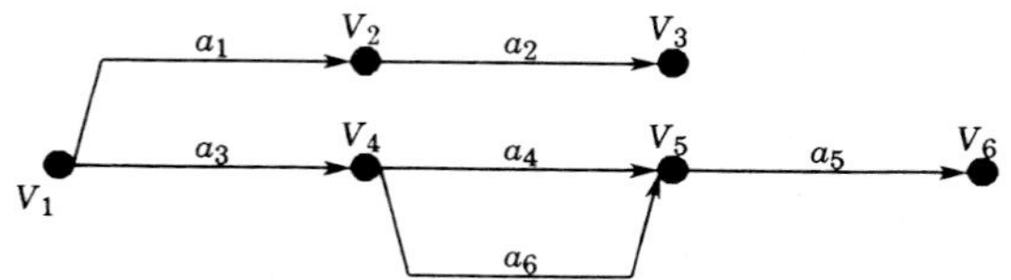

Figure 1. A Directed Graph

A *directed graph* is a set of points, called *verticies*, and a set of directed lines, called *arcs*; each arc a leads from a vertex V to a vertex V'. For example, the directed graph in the figure has six verticies, labeled V_1 through V_6, and (coincidentally) six arcs, labeled a_1 through a_6.

Two vertices V and V' are said to be the *initial* and *final* vertices, respectively, of an arc a from V to V'. For example, V_2 and V_3 are the initial and final vertices, respectively, of arc a_2. Several different arcs may have the same initial vertex, the same final vertex, or both. For example, arcs a_1 and a_3 have the same initial vertex, V_1, and arcs a_4 and a_6 have the same final vertex, V_5.

A vertex that is not the initial vertex of any arc is often referred to informally as a *leaf* vertex or, even more informally, as a "leaf" of the directed graph. For example, vertices V_3 and V_6 are leaves.

An *oriented path* from a vertex V to a vertex V' is a set of arcs $(a_1, a_2, ..., a_n)$ $(n \geq 1)$ such that V is the initial vertex of arc a_1, V' is the final vertex of arc a_n, and the final vertex of arc a_k is also the initial vertex of arc a_{k+1} for $1 \leq k < n$. A *simple oriented path* is an oriented path, no two of whose arcs have the same initial or final vertex. For example, one of the two simple oriented paths from vertex V_1 to vertex V_6 is the set of arcs (a_3, a_4, a_5).

A directed graph is said to be *rooted* if there is at least one vertex R, called the "root", such that there is an oriented path from R to V for all $V \neq R$. In Figure 1, there is one root ,vertex V_1.

The directed graphs of interest in the present context are those with a single root. Throughout the remainder of this paper, therefore, the term "graph" will be used to denote such a graph. The paths that figure in the naming convention are those from the root to a leaf vertex. Therefore, the term "path" should be understood henceforth to denote a simple oriented path from the root to a leaf.

4.4 The Global Naming Graph

For purposes of the naming convention, graphs are interpreted in a particular way. This interpretation is illustrated in Figure 2 and described below:

1. Each leaf vertex represents a single named entity. For example, in the figure, vertex V_3 represents the person commonly known as Ron Uhlig, and vertex V_6 represents Walt Jones.

2. Each arc represents an attribute of one or more named entities. The entities in question are those represented by leaf vertices that terminate paths involving the arc. For example, the two arcs that lead from vertex V_4 to vertex V_5 represent Walt Jones' employer.

   An arc is labeled by the attribute it represents. An unlabeled arc represents the *null attribute*, a fictitious attribute that is possessed by every named entity.

3. Each non-leaf vertex represents the naming authority responsible for assigning the attributes (both types and values) represented by all arcs emanating from that vertex. For example, vertex V_1, the root, represents the global naming authority responsible for assigning names to countries and international organizations. Vertex V_5 represents the corporate naming authority responsible for assigning names to Conway Steel employees.

   Note: One can imagine a naming authority with no subordinate naming authorities and no registered entities. Such a state of affairs is likely to be transient, for example, occurring just after the naming authority's creation and again just before its destruction. Although such situations are important in practice and, therefore, the directory system must take cognizance of them, they are not considered further in this paper.

   Note: In practice one naming authority may request cooperation from another. For example, the Canadian naming authority might insist that provincial naming authorities assign only Locale or Organization attributes. Such bilateral agreements lie outside the naming convention.

Each path through a graph interpreted as described above *determines* an attribute list, the elements of which are the attributes represented by the arcs that make up the path. (The null attribute does not contribute to the list even when it labels an arc in the path.) For example, referring again to the figure, the

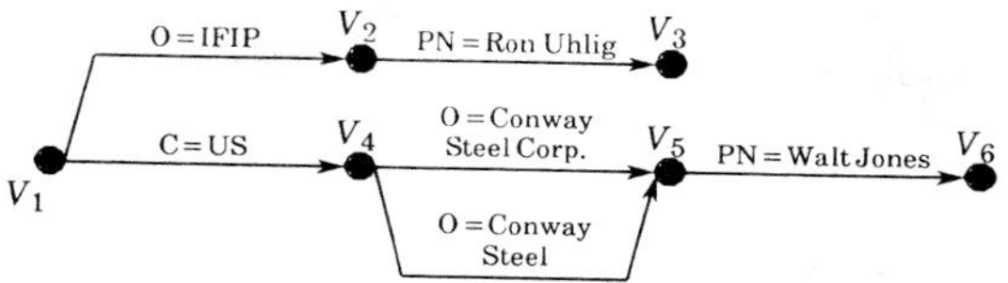

Figure 2. An Extremely Simple Global Naming Graph

path comprising one of the paths to vertex V_6 determines the attribute list (PN = ("Walt", "Jones"), O = "Conway Steel", C = "US"). The entity–in this case, Walt Jones–to which the attributes refer is that represented by the leaf at which the path terminates.

At the heart of the naming convention is the *Global Naming Graph* whose components are interpreted as indicated above. (In the case of public data networks, this graph is of international proportions.) The Graph will physically manifest itself as the directory database alluded to in Section 2. A major virtue of the graphical approach to specification of the naming convention is that it provides a powerful tool for expressing how this database is distributed. The use of this tool, however, is beyond the scope of this paper.

With all of the foregoing as background, the essence of the naming convention is now simply stated as follows. The attribute list determined by a path through the Global Naming Graph to a leaf vertex is a *name* for the entity represented by the leaf unless a path to another leaf vertex determines the same list. Thus, referring again to the figure, Walt Jones has the following two names:

- (PN = ("Walt", "Jones"), O = "Conway Steel Corp.", C = "US")

- (PN = ("Walt", "Jones"), O = "Conway Steel", C = "US")

The following attribute list, on the other hand, is *not* a name for Walt Jones because it is not determined by a path through the Global Naming Graph to the leaf representing him. This is the case even though the specified telephone number happens to unambiguously identify him. The fact that the Graph does not use telephone numbers in this way rules out this attribute list as a valid name:

- (PN = ("Walt", "Jones"), TN = (1, 804, "494-0674"), C = "US")

Note: The terms "primitive name" and "descriptive name" sometimes arise in discussions of naming. An attribute value is a primitive name. An attribute list is a descriptive name.

4.5 Graphical Shorthands

The task of naming entities is seen above to be that of designing the Global Naming Graph. In this graph, a few patterns will arise so frequently that the use of graphical "shorthands" for those patterns will yield a graph that is simpler and easier to understand. The three shorthands defined below and illustrated in Figure 3 are used throughout the remainder of this paper.

Two arcs in series represent a pair of attributes, both of which appear in the attribute list determined by any path involving the arcs. This situation can be represented more concisely, as shown in Figure 3a, by a single arc labeled by the conjunction (that is, the logical "and") of the two attributes. Note that the order in which the two arcs appear in series is insignificant.

Two arcs in parallel represent a pair of attributes, exactly one of which appears in the attribute list determined by any path involving the arcs. This situation can be represented more concisely, as shown in Figure 3b, by a single arc labeled by the disjunction (that is, the logical "exclusive or") of the two attributes.

A labeled and unlabeled arc in parallel represent an attribute that may, but need not, appear in the attribute list determined by any path involving the arcs. This situation can be represented more concisely,

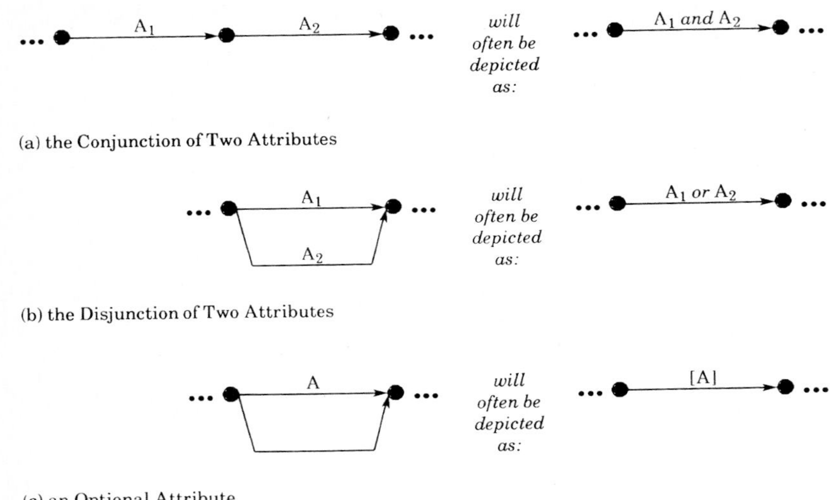

Figure 3. Graphical Shorthands

as shown in Figure 3c, by a single arc labeled by the optional attribute enclosed in square brackets ("[" and "]").

The above shorthands can be applied recursively, resulting in arbitrarily complex arc labels (and correspondingly simpler graphs) to which the ordinary laws of Boolean algebra apply.

4.6 The Name Verification Algorithm

Not every attribute list is a name. For example, the attribute list (PN=("Ronald", "Reagan"), O="Conway Steel Corporation", C="US") might well describe no one and thus be erroneous as a name (if no one with that personal name worked for Conway Steel). Similarly, the attribute list (PN="Smith", O="Conway Steel Corporation", C="US") might describe several people and thus be ambiguous as a name (if several Smiths worked for Conway Steel).

An important element of the naming convention is the algorithm by which attribute lists that purport to be names are verified to be names. The algorithm accepts a purported name as an argument, compares its component attributes to the Global Naming Graph described in Section 4.4, and returns one of four, mutually exclusive assessments of the purported name. The four possible assessments are defined below and in Table 1. In the definitions that follow, the phrase "a portion of the purported name" refers to an attribute list comprising a proper subset of the purported name's component attributes:

- *Valid*: Paths to exactly one leaf determine the purported name. The purported name is thus in fact a name, and the algorithm returns the identity of the leaf.

- *Valid-with-reservations*: No paths determine the purported name, but paths to exactly one leaf determine a portion of the purported name. The remaining attributes cannot be verified. Strictly speaking, the purported name is not in fact a name, but could be made a name by removing the unverified attributes. The algorithm returns the identity of the leaf and the unverified attributes.

- *Erroneous*: No paths through the Graph determine the purported name or any portion of it. The purported name is thus erroneous; attributes must be added or replaced to make it valid.

- *Ambiguous*: Paths to two or more leaves determine the purported name, or no paths determine the purported name but paths to two or more leaves determine a portion of it. The purported name is thus ambiguous; attributes must be added or replaced to make it valid.

Table 1. Purported Name Assessments

Portion of Purported Name[2] \ Number of Leaves (Purported Name[1])	*0*	*1*	*2 or more*
0	Erroneous	Valid	Ambiguous
1	Valid-with-reservations	Valid	Ambiguous
2 or more	Ambiguous	Valid	Ambiguous

[1] Each column of the table is labeled by the number of leaves terminating paths that determine the purported name.

[2] Each row of the table is labeled by the number of leaves terminating paths that determine a portion of the purported name.

Note: A purported name deemed *valid-with-reservations* contains attributes that the directory system cannot substantiate. The user will usually have supplied such attributes for one of two reasons: (1) to ensure that the directory system has all the information it needs to identify the intended entity, or (2) to ensure that the directory system does not identify an entity *other* than the one intended. In the first case, the user would be happy for the algorithm to accept the purported name as valid even though certain attributes cannot be verified; in the second case, however, he would prefer that the algorithm reject the purported name as invalid. By reporting that the purported name is *valid-with-reservations*, rather than *valid* or *erroneous*, the algorithm allows the *user* to decide the correct course of action.

The name verification algorithm is formally stated below using the Pascal programming language [2]. It comprises two procedures. The first procedure, *assess-purported-name*, represents the algorithm as a whole. The second, *assess-attribute-list*, is a subroutine called by the first procedure. Departures from the Pascal language are rendered in italic and are self-explanatory:

```
procedure assess-purported-name (
        purported-name: attribute list;
        var assessment: (valid, valid-with-reservations, erroneous, ambiguous);
        var leaf-vertex: vertex;
        var unverified-attributes: attribute list);
    var
        full-matches: set of vertices;
        partial-matches: set of vertices;
    begin
    full-matches ::= empty;
    partial-matches ::= empty;
    assess-attribute-list (purported-name, root of GNG,
        full-matches, partial-matches, leaf-vertex, unverified-attributes);
    if cardinality of full-matches = 1 then
        assessment ::= valid
    else
        if (cardinality of full-matches = 0) and (cardinality of partial-matches = 1) then
            assessment ::= valid-with-reservations
        else
            if (cardinality of full-matches = 0) and (cardinality of partial-matches = 0) then
```

```
            assessment ::= erroneous
        else
            assessment ::= ambiguous
    end

procedure assess-attribute-list (
        attribute-list: attribute list;
        vertex: vertex;
        var full-matches: set of vertices;
        var partial-matches: set of vertices;
        var leaf-vertex: vertex;
        var unverified-attributes: attribute list);
    label 1;
    var
        arc: arc;
        attribute: attribute;
        remaining-attributes: attribute list;
    begin
    if vertex is a leaf then
        begin
        if attribute-list is empty then
            full-matches ::= full-matches union vertex
        else
            begin
            partial-matches ::= partial-matches union vertex;
            unverified-attributes ::= attribute-list
            end;
        leaf-vertex ::= vertex
        end
    else
        for arc := first arc emanating from vertex to last arc emanating from vertex do
            begin
            attribute ::= label of arc;
            if (attribute is null) or (attribute is in attribute-list) then
                begin
                remaining-attributes ::= attribute-list;
                if attribute is not null then
                    remaining-attributes ::= remaining-attributes less attribute;
                assess-attribute-list (remaining-attributes, final vertex of arc,
                    full-matches, partial-matches, leaf-vertex, unverified-attributes);
                if cardinality of full-matches > 1 then goto 1
                end
            end;
    1:
    end
```

Note: This algorithm is not intended to fully describe the behavior of the directory service primitive that verifies purported names. For example, the primitive might return additional information with each of the four possible assessments. Such issues are beyond the scope of this paper.

Note: The implementation of this algorithm is apt to be highly distributed. The exact nature of that distribution is beyond the scope of the paper.

Note: As indicated by the presence of the *for* statement in the *assess-attribute-list* procedure, the verification algorithm must sometimes follow several paths through the Global Naming Graph. In practice, the paths are likely to be pursued concurrently, but this is beyond the scope of the paper.

5 Naming Guidelines

The naming convention as described thus far is very flexible. This flexibility is necessary to accommodate the variety of entities and environments that will eventually be served by the naming convention. However, it also has the potential to make names less predictable and thus less user-friendly. This potential problem is alleviated by specifying guidelines for name design.

This section specifies the general guidelines to be followed by the naming authorities represented by non-leaf nodes of the Global Naming Graph. A naming authority should follow the guidelines in general, but may disregard them in special cases. Users of the directory system are informed of the guidelines so that they can better predict the names of the entities with which they must deal.

Two sorts of guidelines are offered to naming authorities, those related primarily to the selection of individual attributes, and those related primarily to the structuring of the Graph as a whole.

5.1 Selecting Attributes

The following guidelines for selecting individual attributes are offered:

1. As far as possible, names should be constructed from a (perhaps environment-specific) set of standard attribute types. For example, the name forms recommended for the business environment in Section 7 are constructed from the standard attribute types defined in Section 8.

2. Non-standard attributes should meet the tests of user-friendliness given in Section 3.5. For example, an entity's transport-level address would be inappropriate as one of its attributes.

3. When an attribute value has several common abbreviations or spellings (for example, "Conway Steel Corporation", "Conway Steel Corp.", "Conway Steel", and "CSC"), all of those abbreviations or spellings should be reflected in the Graph as a disjunction of attributes (see Section 4.5) having the same type but different values.

5.2 Structuring the Graph

The following guidelines for structuring the graph as a whole are offered:

1. The dominant structure of the Graph should be hierarchical. The hypothetical graph of Figure 4, for example, adheres to this guideline.

2. In the case of public data networks, arcs emanating from the root should be labeled by attributes of type Country (see Section 8.1) or Organization (see Section 8.4), the latter corresponding to international organizations. The hypothetical Graph of Figure 4 adheres to this guideline as well.

3. A level should be added to the hierarchy only if it reflects a geographical, organizational, or similar partitioning that is well known to human users of the naming convention. For example, the Locale, Organizational Locale, and Organizational Unit attributes (see Sections 8.3, 8.5, and 8.7, respectively) lend themselves to this purpose.

4. When Guideline 3 above rules out the introduction of another hierarchical level as a means of reducing name conflicts, an arc representing an optional attribute should be introduced instead.

5. "Cross-over" arcs should be added to an otherwise hierarchal Graph where "synonyms" are required. For example, the vertex representing an organization that does business in two countries might be the final vertex for two arcs whose initial vertices represent those countries.

6. As few arcs as possible should separate a leaf from the root. As many of those arcs as possible should represent optional attributes, that is, be disjoined with arcs labeled by the null attribute.

"A good name is rather to be chosen than great riches."

–Proverbs 22:1

Part II
Application of the Naming Convention in the Business Environment

Part II of this paper suggests how the naming convention might be applied to selected entities in the business environment. It is organized in three sections. Section 6 defines the kinds of entities to be considered. Section 7 recommends particular name forms for those entity types. Section 8 defines the standard attribute types from which the recommended name forms are constructed.

These sections apply only to the business environment and only to the indicated entity types within that environment. In the present context, a *business* is any organization–for example, a company, an educational institution, or a government agency–that has local, national, multi-national, or international status. International organizations (for example, the Red Cross) lend themselves to, and benefit from, somewhat specialized treatment, as discussed in Section 7.4.

6 Named Entities

Name forms are recommended for three kinds of business entities: business people, business roles, and business groups. Recommended name forms for other kinds of entities are beyond the scope of the paper. However, this topic is briefly explored in the appendix.

6.1 Business People

A *business person* is a human being employed by, or in some other important way associated with, a business. For example, Walt Jones is a business person by virtue of his employment by the Conway Steel Corporation.

6.2 Business Roles

A *business role* is a function, position, or office within a business. For example, the Public Relations Office at Conway Steel, which is responsible for fielding questions about, and enhancing the public image of, Conway Steel, is a business role. A business role is always *filled* by a particular business person. Over its lifetime, however, a role may be filled by a number of different people in succession.

6.3 Business Groups

A *business group* is an unordered set of business people, business roles, or other business groups, each of which is designated by name. For example, the group of Conway Steel employees who are foremen is a business group. The *membership* of a group is static. That is, it is explicitly modified by administrative action, rather than dynamically determined each time the group is referred to.

Note: Groups have a number of uses, perhaps the most important of which is as distribution lists for the addressing of electronic mail. In this (and other) contexts, the membership of the group is reduced to a set of people and/or roles by replacing each group with its membership. This process is carried out recursively until the names of all constituent groups have been eliminated and only the names of people and roles remain.

Note: A set of entities whose membership is determined dynamically is sometimes called a *class*. Classes are beyond the scope of this paper.

7 Recommended Name Forms

The naming convention of Part I admits names of many forms. The names of business entities are made significantly more predictable by recommending a particular form of name for each kind.

This section specifies the *recommended name forms* for the kinds of business entities defined in Section 6. A naming authority should adhere to these recommended forms in general, but may disregard them in special cases. Users of the directory system are informed of the recommended forms so that they can better predict the names of the business entities with which they must deal. All of the recommended name forms are constructed from the standard attribute types defined in Section 8.

The examples that appear throughout this (and the following) section could arise in the context of many different Global Naming Graphs. The hypothetical graph shown in Figure 4 reflects one plausible physical distribution of the directory database. The real Graph, of course, will be much more complex than that in the figure, since it will provide names for many more entities

7.1 Mandatory Attributes

Each of the recommended name forms comprises a number of attributes that must be present in every name of that form, additional attributes that may be necessary to discriminate between similar organizations within a country, and yet additional attributes that may be required to discriminate between similar people, roles, or groups within an organization.

The name forms recommended for business people, roles, and groups contain three mandatory attributes. The first and second of these attributes are common to all three types of named entity, while the third varies with it:

- Country
- Organization
- Personal Name *or* Title *or* Group Name

Examples: (PN=("Walter", "E.", "Jones"), O="Conway Steel", C="US")
(T="Public Relations Office", O="Conway Steel", C="US")
(GN="Foremen", O="Conway Steel", C="US")

7.2 Conditional Organizational Attributes

If two or more organizations within the specified country share the specified organization name (for example, McDonald's Restaurant in Winchester, Virginia and McDonald's Restaurant in Norfolk, Virginia), one or both of the following attributes must be specified to discriminate between them:

- Organizational Locale (perhaps several occurrences)
- Organizational Telephone Number

Note: The Organizational Locale attribute may also be required if the relevant portion of the directory database is physically distributed on the basis of that attribute and cannot be searched cost-effectively without it.

If the country is hierarchically partitioned by locale (see Section 8.5), several occurrences of the Organizational Locale attribute may be required.

Example: (T="Manager", O="McDonald's Restaurant",
OL="Winchester", OL="Virginia", C="US")

7.3 Conditional Individual Attributes

If two or more people, roles, or groups within the specified organization share the specified personal name, title, or group name, respectively (for example, W. Jones in the Manufacturing Division of Conway Steel

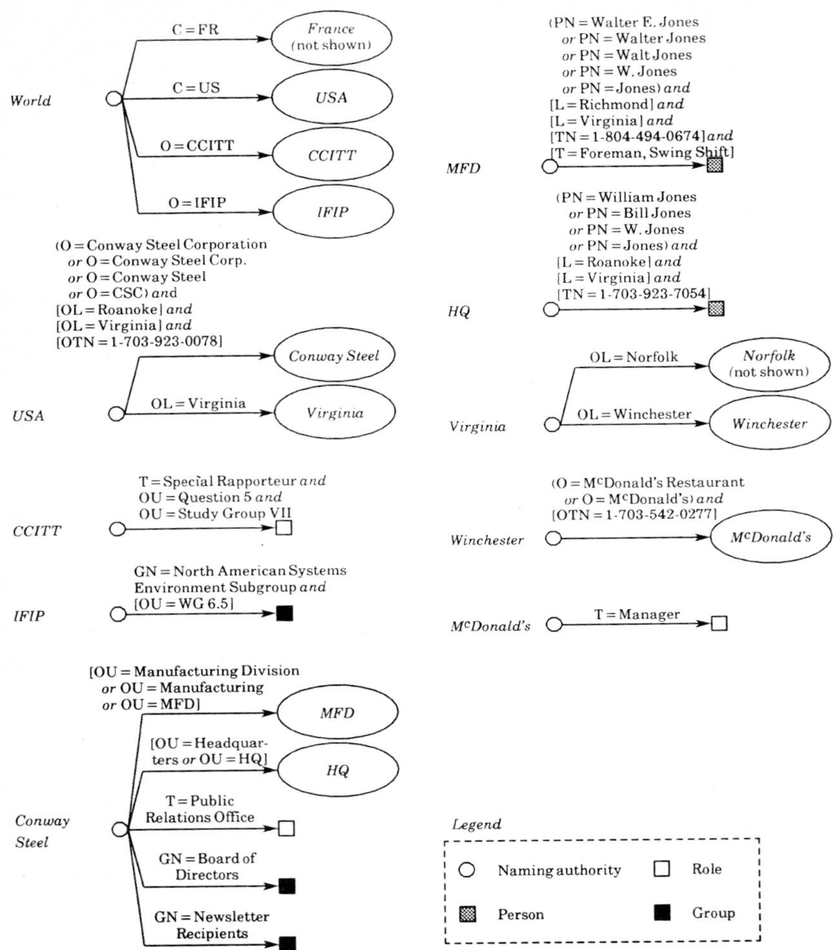

Figure 4. A Graph Illustrating the Recommended Business Name Forms

and W. Jones at Conway Steel's headquarters), either or both of the following attributes may be required to discriminate between them:

- Locale (perhaps several occurrences)
- Organizational Unit (perhaps several occurrences)

Note: The Locale or Organizational Unit attribute may also be required if the relevant portion of the directory database is physically distributed on the basis of that attribute and cannot be searched cost-effectively without it.

If the country is hierarchically partitioned by locale (see Section 8.3), several occurrences of the Locale attribute may be required. If the organization is hierarchically partitioned by organizational unit (see Section 8.7), several occurrences of the Organizational Unit attribute may be required.

Example: (PN=("W.", "Jones"), OU="MFD", O="Conway Steel", C="US")

If two or more people or roles within the specified organization share the specified personal name or title, respectively (for example, W. Jones at 1-804-494-0674 and W. Jones at 1-703-923-7054), the following attribute may be required to discriminate between them:

- Telephone Number

Example: (PN=("W.", "Jones"), TN=(1, 804, "494-0674"), O="Conway Steel", C="US")

If two or more people within the specified organization share the specified personal name (for example, the W. Jones who is the foreman of the swing shift and the W. Jones whose title is unknown), the following attribute may be required to discriminate between them:

- Title

Example: (PN=("W.", "Jones"), T="Foreman, Swing Shift", O="Conway Steel", C="US")

7.4 Special Rules for International Organizations

The recommended name forms for business entities within international organizations are those for the corresponding entities in the general business environment, as described above, with the following two exceptions:

1. The Country attribute is not specified.

2. No two international organizations are permitted to have the same organization name. This eliminates the need for the conditional attributes that discriminate between organizations with the same name. Hence neither the Organizational Locale nor the Organizational Telephone Number attribute is ever specified.

Example: (T="Special Rapporteur", OU="Question 5", OU="Study Group VII", O="CCITT")

8 Standard Attribute Types

Ten attribute types are used in the construction of the business name forms recommended in Section 7. This section describes those *standard attribute types* in detail.

The standard attribute types and the abbreviations used for them throughout this paper are listed in Table 2. The Country attribute identifies the country in which the named entity is located. The Group Name attribute identifies a group by stating its purpose or characterizing its members. The Locale attribute identifies a geographical area in which the named entity is located. The Organization attribute identifies an organization with which the named entity is affiliated. The Organizational Locale attribute identifies a geographical area in which the named entity's organization is located. The Organizational Telephone Number attribute specifies the telephone number of the named entity's organization. The Organizational Unit attribute identifies an organizational unit with which the named entity is affiliated. The Personal Name attribute identifies a person by name. The Telephone Number attribute specifies the telephone number of the named entity. The Title attribute specifies the position held by the named entity.

Note: A number of the attributes described in this section clearly have application in environments other than the business one. For example, the Telephone Number attribute is relevant to the residential environment as well.

The subsections that follow specify the semantics and general syntactic structure of each of the standard business attributes. The structure of attribute values is specified using Backus-Naur Form (BNF), and the examples given conform to the notational conventions set forth in Section 4.1. Comments are sometimes

Table 2. Standard Attribute Types
for the Business Environment

Standard Attribute Type	Abbreviation
Country	C
Group Name	GN
Locale	L
Organization	O
Organizational Locale	OL
Organizational Telephone Number	OTN
Organizational Unit	OU
Personal Name	PN
Telephone Number	TN
Title	T

embedded in the BNF. They are preceded by two hyphens ("-") and terminated by either two more hyphens or the end of the line.

8.1 Country

The *Country (C)* attribute identifies the country in which the named entity is physically located or with which it is associated in some other important way.

For a business person, the country identified is usually that in which his office is located. For a business role, it is usually the country in which its organization (see Section 8.4) or organizational unit (see Section 8.7) is headquartered. For a business group, it is usually the country in which the organization or organizational unit that maintains the list is headquartered.

An attribute value of this type is either a two-letter alphabetic country code defined by ISO International Standard 3166 [1] or a three-digit numeric country code defined by CCITT Recommendation X.121 [5]. This follows the practice of CCITT's Recommendations on message handling [7]:

Country :: = string -- *two letters specified by ISO 3166* -- |
number -- *three digits specified by CCITT Recommendation X.121*

Examples: C = "FR" *or* C = 208
C = "US" *or* C = 310

8.2 Group Name

The *Group Name (GN)* attribute identifies a group by stating its purpose or characterizing its members.

An attribute value of this type is a string chosen by the maintainer of the group. In such strings the distinction between upper- and lower-case letters is insignificant:

GroupName :: = string -- *chosen by the maintainer of the group*

Examples: GN = "North American Systems Environment Subgroup"
GN = "Newsletter Recipients"

8.3 Locale

The *Locale (L)* attribute identifies a geographical area or locale in which the named entity is physically located or with which it is associated in some other important way. The designated locale is understood to lie within the country designated by the Country attribute (see Section 8.1).

For a business person, the locale identified is usually that in which his office is located. For a business role, it is usually the locale in which its organization (see Section 8.4) or organizational unit (see Section 8.7) is headquartered. For a business group, it is usually the locale in which the organization or organizational unit that maintains it is headquartered.

An administrative body within each country decides whether recognized locales are provinces or states, shires or counties, cities, and/or other geographical entities. It also decides whether the country is partitioned hierarchically (for example, first by state and then by city) or nonhierarchically (for example, by city only). Hierarchical partitioning associates two or more attribute values of this type with a named entity.

An attribute value of this type is a string approved by the administrative body mentioned above, or its designee (for example, a country might delegate part of this responsibility to a state or province). In such strings the distinction between upper- and lower-case letters is insignificant:

Locale :: = **string** -- *approved by the country or its designee*

Examples: L="Virginia"
L="Richmond"

8.4 Organization

The *Organization (O)* attribute identifies an organization with which the named entity–a business person, role, or group–is affiliated.

For a business person, the organization identified may be that which employs him full time, that for which he consults, or that to which he contributes in some other way.

An attribute value of this type is a string chosen by the organization. In such strings the distinction between upper- and lower-case letters is insignificant. All variants (for example, abbreviations) of the organization's name should be associated with the named entity as separate and alternative attribute values:

Organization :: = **string** -- *chosen by the organization*

Examples: O="Conway Steel Corporation"
O="Conway Steel Corp."
O="Conway Steel"
O="CSC"

8.5 Organizational Locale

The *Organizational Locale (OL)* attribute identifies a geographical area or locale in which the organization designated by the Organization attribute (see Section 8.4) is physically located or with which it is associated in some other important way. The designated locale is understood to lie within the country designated by the Country attribute (see Section 8.1).

An administrative body within each country decides whether recognized locales are provinces or states, shires or counties, cities, and/or other geographical entities. It also decides whether the country is partitioned hierarchically (for example, first by state and then by city) or nonhierarchically (for example, by city only). Hierarchical partitioning associates two or more attribute values of this type with each named entity.

For a business person, role, or group, the locale identified is usually that in which the organization is headquartered. However, if the organization is geographically dispersed, it may be any of the locales in which the organization does business.

An attribute value of this type is a string approved by the administrative body mentioned above, or its designee (for example, a country might delegate part of this responsibility to a state or province). In such strings the distinction between upper- and lower-case letters is insignificant:

OrganizationalLocale :: = string -- *approved by the country or its designee*

Examples: OL="Virginia"
OL="Roanoke"

8.6 Organizational Telephone Number

The *Organizational Telephone Number (OTN)* attribute specifies the telephone number of the organization designated by the Organization attribute (see Section 8.4). The telephone number specified is that of the central switchboard of the organization's headquarters.

An attribute value of this type comprises two numbers and a string, which encode country code, city code, and local telephone number, respectively. Dashes may (but need not) punctuate the last of these for increased readability. In the presence of the Country attribute (see Section 8.1), the country code may be omitted and is taken to be the one implied by that attribute. In the presence of both the Country attribute and an Organizational Locale attribute (see Section 8.5) that designates a city, the country and city codes may be omitted and are taken to be the ones implied by those attributes:

```
OrganizationalTelephoneNumber  :: =  ( CountryCode , CityCode , LocalTelephoneNumber ) |
                                     ( CityCode , LocalTelephoneNumber ) |
                                     LocalTelephoneNumber

CountryCode                    :: =  number
CityCode                       :: =  number
LocalTelephoneNumber           :: =  string
```

Example: OTN=(1, 703, "923-0078")

Note: The detailed structure of telephone numbers is complex. The structure indicated above is meant to be suggestive only. The precise structure is beyond the scope of this paper and is likely to be dictated by CCITT Recommendations.

8.7 Organizational Unit

The *Organizational Unit (OU)* attribute identifies an organizational unit with which the named entity–a business person, role, or group–is affiliated. The designated organizational unit is understood to be part of the organization designated by the Organization attribute (see Section 8.4).

An administrative body within each organization decides whether recognized organizational units are divisions, departments, groups, and/or other organizational entities. It also decides whether the organization is partitioned hierarchically (for example, first by division and then by department) or nonhierarchically (for example, by division only). Hierarchical partitioning associates two or more attribute values of this type with each named entity.

An attribute value of this type is a string approved by the administrative body mentioned above, or its designee (for example, an organization might delegate part of this responsibility to an organizational unit). In such strings the distinction between upper- and lower-case letters is insignificant. All variants (for example, abbreviations) of the organizational unit's name should be associated with the named entity as separate and alternative attribute values:

OrganizationalUnit :: = string -- *approved by the organization or its designee*

Examples: OU="Manufacturing Division"
OU="Manufacturing"
OU="MFD"

8.8 Personal Name

The *Personal Name (PN)* attribute identifies a person by name. It is the name by which the person is commonly known, and conforms to the naming conventions of his country or culture. For example, the name of a typical person in an English-speaking country comprises his first name, middle name(s), and last name; a generational qualifier (for example, "Jr.") may also be present.

An attribute value of this type is a sequence of strings chosen by the person himself. In such strings the distinction between upper- and lower-case letters is insignificant. All variants (for example, abbreviations) of the person's name should be associated with him as separate and alternative attribute values:

PersonalName :: = **NamePart | (NamePartList)**

NamePartList :: = **NamePart | NamePartList , NamePart**
NamePart :: = **string** -- *chosen by the person*

Examples: PN=("Walter", "E.", "Jones")
PN=("Walter", "Jones")
PN=("Walt", "Jones")
PN=("W.", "Jones")
PN="Jones"

8.9 Telephone Number

The *Telephone Number (TN)* attribute specifies the telephone number of the named entity–a person or role.

For a business person, the telephone number specified is usually that of his office.

An attribute value of this type comprises two numbers and a string, which encode country code, city code, and local telephone number, respectively. Dashes may (but need not) punctuate the last of these for increased readability. In the presence of the Country attribute (see Section 8.1), the country code may be omitted and is taken to be the one implied by that attribute. In the presence of both the Country attribute and a Locale attribute (see Section 8.3) that designates a city, the country and city codes may be omitted and are taken to be the ones implied by those attributes:

TelephoneNumber :: = **(CountryCode , CityCode , LocalTelephoneNumber) |**
(CityCode , LocalTelephoneNumber) |
LocalTelephoneNumber

CountryCode :: = **number**
CityCode :: = **number**
LocalTelephoneNumber :: = **string**

Example: TN=(1, 804, "494-0674")

Note: The detailed structure of telephone numbers is complex. The structure indicated above is meant to be suggestive only. The precise structure is beyond the scope of this paper and is likely to be dictated by CCITT Recommendations.

8.10 Title

The *Title (T)* attribute specifies the position held by the named entity–a business person or role. The designated position is understood to exist within the organization and organizational units designated by the Organization and any Organizational Unit attributes (see Sections 8.4 and 8.7, respectively).

An administrative body within each organization or organizational unit assigns titles to people and roles.

An attribute value of this type is a string approved by the administrative body mentioned above. In such strings the distinction between upper- and lower-case letters is insignificant. All variants (for example, abbreviations) of the title should be associated with the named entity as separate and alternative attribute values:

Title :: = string -- *approved by the organization or organizational unit*

Example: T="Foreman, Swing Shift"

References

The following documents supplement this paper.

[1] International Standard 3166, Codes for the representation of names of countries (ISO, Geneva).

[2] Jensen, K. and Wirth, N., PASCAL User Manual and Report, 2nd Edition (Springer-Verlag, New York, 1974).

[3] Knuth, D. E., The Art of Computer Programming, 2nd Edition, Vol. 1: Fundamental Algorithms (Addison-Wesley, Reading, Massachusetts, 1973).

[4] Naur, P., Revised report on the algorithmic language ALGOL 60, Comm. ACM 1 (1963) 1-17.

[5] Recommendation X.121, International numbering plan for public data networks (CCITT, Geneva).

[6] Recommendation X.400, Message handling systems: system model–service elements (CCITT, Geneva).

[7] Recommendation X.411, Message handling systems: message transfer layer (CCITT, Geneva).

Appendix
Other Applications of the Naming Convention

Part II of this paper describes how the naming convention might be applied to three kinds of entities found in the business environment: people, roles, and groups. This appendix briefly discusses how the naming convention might be applied to other business entities and in other environments. What follows is intended to be suggestive rather than definitive.

Other Business Entities

The standard attribute types defined in Section 8 are adequate for naming a variety of additional types of business entities, including network-accessible hosts, file services, and workstations. The definition of the Title attribute (see Section 8.10) would have to be broadened slightly to accommodate the following uses.

The network-accessible host on which Conway Steel's payroll is processed each week might have the following name:

(T="Payroll Processing", OU="HQ", O="Conway Steel", C="US")

The network-accessible file service on which Manufacturing's engineering drawings are archived might have the following name:

(T = "Engineering Drawings Archive", OU = "MFD", O = "Conway Steel", C = "US")

The network-accessible workstation that sits in Walt Jones' office might have the following name:

(T = "IBM PC # 42", O = "Conway Steel", C = "US")

This is the forty-second workstation in Conway Steel's inventory, and the name above is that by which Facilities refers to the device. Walt Jones' directory entry might contain the name of his workstation, and the workstation's entry might contain the name of its owner (that is, Walt Jones).

Note: In general, an entity's type cannot be deduced from its name. (An entity's type is presumed to be determined from information in the entity's directory entry.) For example, one cannot reliably determine the types of the host and file service mentioned above by examining their names: the names comprise the same types of attributes, but the entities are of different types. (People are an exception to this rule, since their names can be distinguished by the presence of the Personal Name attribute.)

Note: An entity may have several names, each reflecting a different use of the entity. For example, the host and file service mentioned above might be one and the same computer.

Residential Entities

Standard attribute types beyond those described in Section 8 must be defined before people in the residential environment can be named. The example below makes use of three additional attribute types: (1) Delivery Point (DP), a location within a buiding; (2) Street Address (SA), a location within a city or town; and (3) Postal Code (PC), a small geographic area of significance to the postal system.

The private citizen who happens to be the foreman of the swing shift at Conway Steel might have the following name:

(
PN = ("Walt", "Jones"),
DP = "Apartment 7", SA = "541 Fallbrook Road",
L = "Richmond", L = "Virginia", C = "US",
PC = "22180")

Note: Certain attribute types will serve several entity types or environments, while others will be unique to them. For example, the Title attribute type figures in the names of most kinds of business entities, and the Locale attribute type figures in the names of both business and residential entities. On the other hand, the Postal Code attribute type might be relevant only in the residential environment.

Computer-Based Message Services
H.T. Smith (Editor)
Elsevier Science Publishers B.V. (North-Holland)

THE DOMAIN NAME SYSTEM

Paul V. Mockapetris

USC Information Sciences Institute
Marina del Rey, California
U.S.A.

.ne domain name system is a protocol and a set of servers which provides a uniform method for associating the names of resources (e.g., mailboxes, host names) to information about the resources (e.g., mail server addresses, network addresses). The name database is distributed among multiple name servers scattered though one or more internets. The protocol provides tools for controlling both the distribution of the database and the responsibility for maintenance of the distributed pieces of the database.

OVERVIEW

The problem

Most contemporary problems with naming in computer networks result from two trends: the first is the rapid expansion in the number of users, hosts, networks, and other resources to be named, and the second is the connection of more and more systems with different data formats and characteristics. The resulting problems include:

1. A large number of names as well as a large rate of growth in the number of names. Continual gradual growth occurs as users and hosts are added; large jumps can occur when networks or internets are connected. The size of this problem varies with the resource being named; for example, there is usually a difference of orders of magnitude between the number of hosts and the number of mailboxes on those hosts.

2. The need to distribute responsibility for naming. Organizations usually want to have authority for assigning names on their own hosts, networks, etc.

3. The need to accommodate varying classes of information associated with a name. For example, two different networks might have different formats for host addresses, yet have identical formats for mailboxes. Thus the information associated with a name may depend on what the named object represents and may also vary according to the network or internet in which the object resides. In general, we can hope for consistency in some resources (for example, mailboxes), but we expect inconsistency in other types of resources (for example, host addresses). The domain system enforces consistency for the formats of names, but allows variety in the uses of a name and the information associated with a name.

This research is supported by the Defense Advanced Research Projects Agency under Contract No. MDA903 81 C 0335. Views and conclusions contained in this paper are the author's and should not be interpreted as representing the official opinion or policy of DARPA, the U.S. Government, or any person or agency connected with them.

4. Variety in the capabilities of the hosts and networks that use names. Solutions that are appropriate for highly connected networks (e.g., the ARPANET) may be inappropriate for networks using once-a-day phone calls; similarly, solutions appropriate for large timeshared hosts may be inappropriate for personal computers.

The ARPA Internet illustrates several of these problems; it is a large system and is likely to grow much larger. Currently hosts in the ARPA Internet are registered with the Network Information Center (NIC) and listed in a global table [1]. The size of this table, and especially the frequency of updates to the table, are near the limit of manageability.

Mailbox names in the ARPA Internet are not distributed according to any network-wide scheme, although many organizations distribute mailbox lists for the organization to all hosts serving the organization. Inconsistency in the semantics of mailbox descriptions is a continuing source of problems; most of these problems arise from various ad hoc encodings of routes in the mailbox name.

Characteristics of the proposed solution

Several of our basic design assumptions for the domain name system evolved from the concerns outlined above:

1. The database must be distributed. The size and update rate of the database prohibit centralization. By distributing the database, we may also improve the performance and availability of the system.

2. From the user's point of view, the database should appear to be centralized. That is, measures to allow distribution, redundant copies, etc., should be transparent to the user.

3. The costs of implementing such a facility dictate that it be generally useful and not restricted to a single application. We should be able to add new resource types indefinitely.

4. The database must be hierarchical. Such an organization offers the opportunity for delegating responsibility for "subtrees" to separate organizations.

5. The hierarchy must be extensible. The spread of local networks will place the same pressures on organizations to allow partitioning of responsibility as are now apparent in long-haul networks. We would like the capability to partition the database whenever such a partition makes database management more convenient.

We also imposed restrictions on the initial domain system:

1. The domain system provides facilities for distributing the database and using redundant copies, but relies on local system administrators to configure the database so that it works properly. This responsibility includes change control, authentication, etc.

2. Rather than including a mechanism for performing atomic updates, the domain system periodically distributes updated data. Thus redundant copies of parts of the database may be incorrect for short periods. The system administrator who creates a particular piece of data also assigns a refresh interval for that data. The update interval can be made arbitrarily short, or the update problem can be avoided by prohibiting copies of particular data.

These restrictions simplify the initial implementation task, but may be changed in the future.

THE ABSTRACT DATABASE

Since the distribution of data is hidden from the typical user by the programs used to access the domain system's distributed database, the user is mainly concerned with the structure and contents of the abstract database (i.e., the database which would result if all of the distributed data were collected in a single database).

The domain name space

The domain system uses names that are hierarchical; conceptually, the name space is a tree with labels on the nodes of the tree. A node's domain name is the list of labels associated with the nodes on the path from the node to the root of the tree. By convention, we list the labels from left to right corresponding to the most specific node to the least specific (the root). With the exception of the root node, which has a null label, labels are not required to be unique. The root's unique label is a convenience which allows programs to easily recognize the end of a name.

Although the domain system does not require the name space's structure to correspond to any other structure, by convention we structure the majority of the domain name space to roughly correspond to the "nesting" of organizations that use the domain system, followed by other levels that correspond to the nesting of mailboxes, hosts, etc. within organizations. An example domain name space is illustrated below:

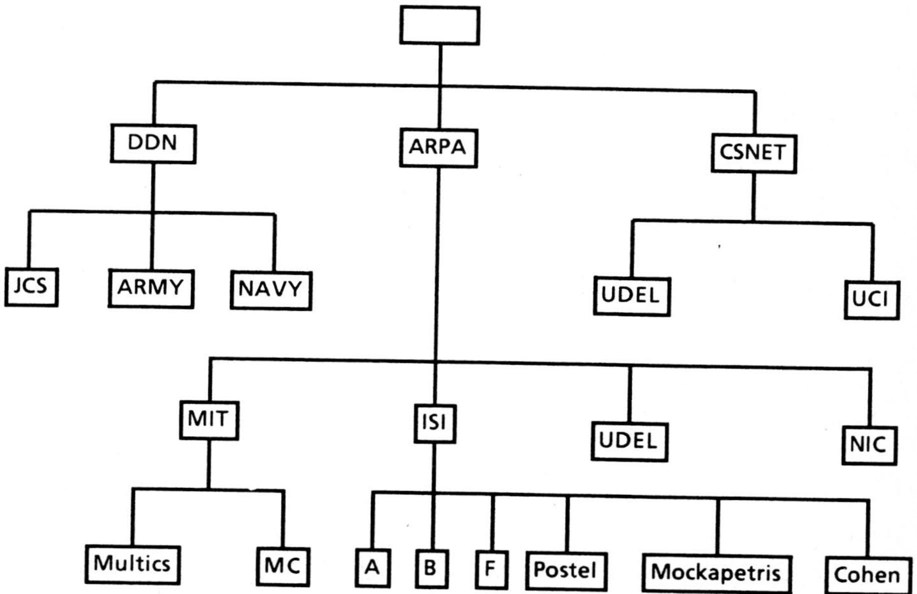

The tree is anchored at the root and is divided into three domains, DDN, ARPA, and CSNET, corresponding to the DDN network, the ARPA Internet, and the Computer Science Network. (The term domain is used to refer to any subtree of the abstract tree.) In the ARPA domain, the four subdomains MIT, ISI, UDEL, and NIC, are organizations that we have chosen to place in the ARPA domain. Each of these is its own domain for creating mailbox names, host names, etc.; the example diagram does not show this substructure, with the exception of a few example entries under ISI.ARPA.

The ISI domain shows a substructure for three hosts (A, B, and F) and three mailboxes (Postel, Mockapetris, and Cohen). Note that the name space itself does not imply this binding in any way; the correspondence is created using resource records.

Conventions

Internally, the domain system maintains names using a binary structure. However, many applications need methods for representing domain names as printable text. The default method is to list the labels from most specific to least specific, using dots to separate the labels. Since all domain names end in the root label, the root label and its preceding dot are omitted. A different method is used for mailboxes. A mailbox specification of the form local-part@global-part is mapped to a domain name whose most specific label is "local-part" and whose remaining labels are taken from "global-part", with dots representing label divisions. For example, the mailbox Mockapetris@ISI.ARPA maps to domain name Mockapetris.ISI.ARPA.

The domain system uses case-insensitive matching rules for comparing domain names, but retains the case of all data in the system. For example, if the system administrator defines a mailbox for Mockapetris@ISI.ARPA, that data will match queries for mockapetris@isi.arpa as well as queries for MOCKAPETRIS@ISI.ARPA; however, the returned answer will always be Mockapetris@ISI.ARPA.

Resources

In order to create a correspondence between a resource and its name, we associate resource records (RRs) with nodes. For example, to make the domain name Mockapetris.ISI.ARPA correspond to a mailbox, we store a mailbox resource record at that node; to make A.ISI.ARPA a host name, we store a host name resource record at the A.ISI.ARPA node.

We can associate as many RRs as we desire to a particular name. The most frequent use of this facility is to associate multiple host addresses to a single host or multiple mailbox names to a mailing list. However, we could also use a particular name to refer to both a host address and a mailbox name. Such multiple use is not forbidden by the domain system, but rather is avoided to spare users unnecessary confusion.

Each RR contains several standard fields, including a type and a class, as well as a variable-length resource data (RDATA) field, which contains type-and class-specific information describing the resource.

Type values are drawn from a set of well-known codes, and they refer to abstract resource types and include such types as "mailbox", "host address", and "mailing list".

Class values are drawn from a set of well-known codes and specify the system used to represent the data in the resource record. Class values usually identify an internet. For example, the ARPA Internet is one class, and RRs with type=A (host address) and class=IN (ARPA Internet) use 32-bit addresses, while another internet might use 10-digit phone numbers. Note that the class field does not represent protocol families per se; separate classes could be used for two private copies of a particular protocol, and there are cases such as the CSNET class, which uses ARPA Internet addresses as well as phone numbers and X.25 addresses in the RDATA field of its host address RRs.

Class definitions are orthogonal to domain structure. Thus, although all resources of a particular class may be organized into a specific domain, this type of organization is not required. For example, the CSNET domain and the CSNET class may happen to be related, but they are not constrained to be so.

In addition to defining data format, class information is used to guide the search process associated with queries. For example, a requestor looking for mailbox information might constrain the search to resource data of a class compatible with the requestor's machine; alternatively, the requestor might collect all of the resource information for the mailbox, regardless of class, and then decide which information to use.

The following is a partial listing of the RRs in the ISI section of the sample domain space:

Owner	Type	Class	RDATA
A.ISI.ARPA	A	IN	10.1.0.32
B.ISI.ARPA	A	IN	10.3.0.52
F.ISI.ARPA	A	IN	10.2.0.52
Postel.ISI.ARPA	MB	IN	F.ISI.ARPA
Mockapetris.ISI.ARPA	MB	IN	F.ISI.ARPA
Cohen.ISI.ARPA	MB	IN	B.ISI.ARPA

The RRs are attached to particular nodes; the node that "owns" a particular RR is shown in the owner column. The next two columns show the type and class of the RR; the two types shown here are host address (A) and mailbox (MB), the only class shown is ARPA Internet (IN). Host address RRs include the 4-octet ARPA Internet host address; this 32-bit quantity is shown here using the ARPA standard method of octets separated by dots (this is NOT a domain name). The RDATA section for mailbox records contains domain names, and points to a mail server for the particular mailbox. Thus the mailbox Postel@ISI.ARPA is bound to the mail server on F.ISI.ARPA, while Cohen@ISI.ARPA is bound to host B.ISI.ARPA.

QUERIES

From the user's point of view, the domain database is accessed though three kinds of query. The user interface to the query mechanism is typically through operating system calls, and hence depends on local conventions for details of the call, but the general form of the query follows one of these three kinds.

Simple queries

In a simple query the user presents a query which contains the domain name, the type, and the class of a resource. The system returns either the corresponding RR or an indication that the RR does not exist, or possibly a transient error indicating that the appropriate database cannot be accessed.

For example, the user could ask for the resource record with domain name=F.ISI.ARPA, type=A (host address), and class=IN (ARPA Internet). This would bind the host name F.ISI.ARPA to its address. A similar query for the domain name Mockapetris.ISI.ARPA would return a non-existent RR error, indicating that the appropriate type of RR was not found, but a type=MB (mailbox) query would return the Mockapetris mailbox RR.

Completion queries

Completion queries allow a user to identify a resource using a partial name specification. This feature can be used to create shorthand notation for local resources, or a completion facility similar to that of the TOPS-20 operating system. The arguments for a completion query include the partial domain name, a type and class, and a target domain name. The type and class specify the eligible resources; in addition, the answer must be contained in the domain specified by the target domain name.

For example, a user at ISI who wishes to send mail to Mockapetris.ISI.ARPA might use a mail program which used completion queries. When the user asked to send mail to "Moc", the mail program might create a completion query with a partial string of "Moc", type=MB, class=IN, and a target domain name of ISI.ARPA. This query would be interpreted as a request for a mailbox which begins with the text "Moc" and resides in the ISI.ARPA domain. Using our example, the program would receive the mailbox RR for Mockapetris.ISI.ARPA.

Such a query may well be ambiguous, especially if the target domain does not greatly restrict the search. To deal with this, and to allow user programs a chance to resolve the ambiguity if they choose, completion queries also specify whether the requestor wants all possible matches, or if the domain system is to resolve any ambiguities using simple rules based on the number of labels in the possible answers.

Implementation of this feature is optional, and hence it may be available for certain domains and not for others.

Inverse queries

Inverse queries allow a user to perform the inverse of simple query mappings, i.e., given a resource record, an inverse query returns the domain name or names that possess such a resource record.

Uniqueness is rarely a problem for most applications of this type of query. For example, the most frequent use is mapping a host address to a host name. In situations where ambiguity exists, the response to the query contains all domain names found.

Implementation of this feature is optional, and hence it may be available for certain domains and not for others.

DISTRIBUTION OF THE DATABASE

While the distributed nature of the domain system is hidden from the user program, a user query may cause activity in several processes, both on the local host and in foreign hosts. The possible interprocess communication is shown below:

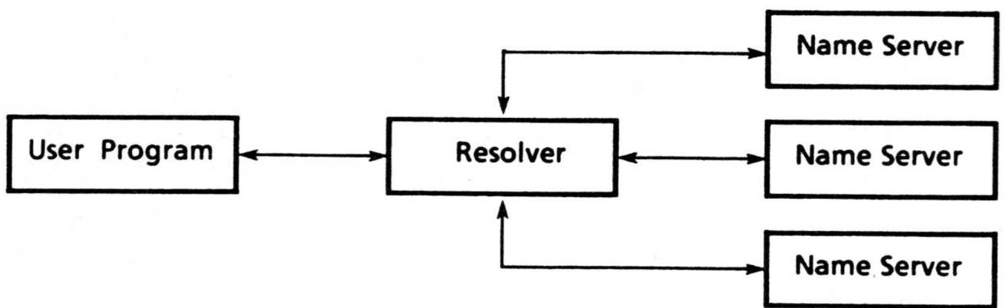

The user program issues a query via some sort of call to a local program called a resolver. This query is expressed according to local conventions, and the resolver is usually part of the host operating system. The resolver answers the query using information it acquires from one or more name servers. The transaction between the resolver and the name server is expressed using the domain protocol.

Name servers are repositories for sections of the domain database. A given name server will typically only have information for a small part of the abstract database. Nme servers internally break the abstract database into sections called zones. While name servers can be configured to treat each domain name as a separate zone, system administrators will usually configure name servers to group organizationally related domain names in a single zone. A particular zone may be replicated at several name servers to provide higher availability.

This section discusses the methods that are used to create the zones and the operations performed by name servers and resolvers to process user queries. Note that the division of responsibilities is often conceptual rather than actual; a host that possesses both a name server and a resolver will often mingle the functions to improve performance.

Zones

The abstract database is partitioned into zones by inserting zone boundaries on selected arcs of the abstract tree. A zone begins at the point where it is divided from its parent zone and ends at leaves in the abstract tree or at arcs where new children zones begin. Our example tree might be divided as follows:

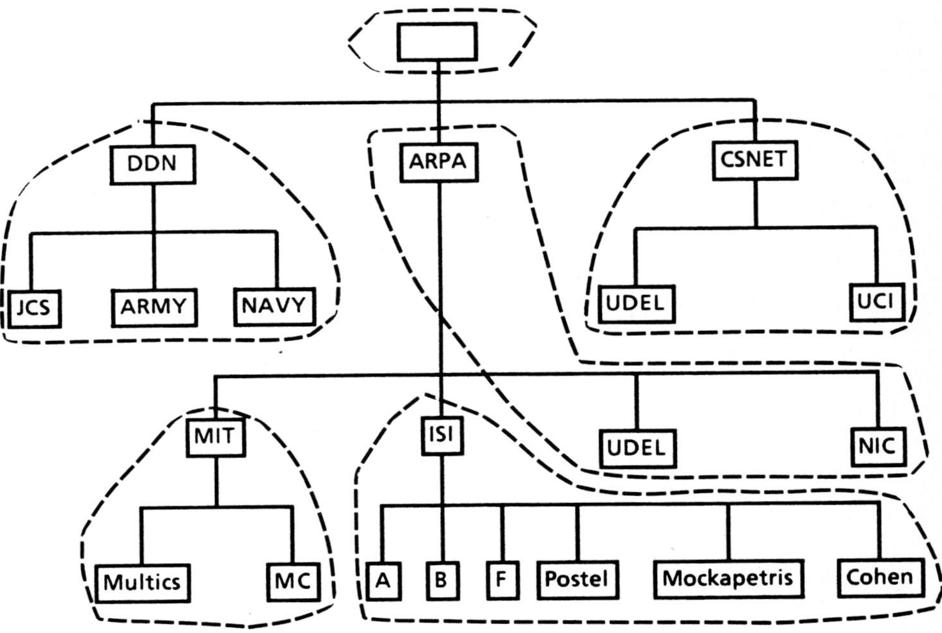

Here the root has delegated authority to three zones: DDN, ARPA, and CSNET. The ARPA zone has delegated authority to the MIT and ISI zones.

In addition to marking the delegation of naming authority, the zone boundaries also represent the distribution of the domain database. Thus the term zone is also used to refer to the complete data for the structure and the RRs for all nodes within a zone. An organization that has a zone is responsible for maintaining the zone's data on name servers that make it available to hosts both within and outside of the zone.

The domain name of a name server and the domain names of the zones the name server possesses need not be related. An organization can either provide name servers on hosts in its own zone, or contract for name service from other organizations. A name server can support multiple zones, as long as it internally remembers the boundaries. For example, the zones described in the previous example might be bound to name servers as follows:

```
Zone          Name servers

" " (root)    NIC.ARPA
DDN           JCS.DDN, B.ISI.ARPA
ARPA          NIC.ARPA, F.ISI.ARPA
MIT.ARPA      Multics.MIT.ARPA
ISI.ARPA      F.ISI.ARPA, B.ISI.ARPA
CSNET         UDEL.CSNET
```

Since zone boundaries provide the basis of redundant copy distribution, an organization may choose to partition its authority simply to separate the database and not to delegate authority. For example, the DDN zone might be partitioned into ARMY.DDN and NAVY.DDN subzones simply to split a large database between two name servers, rather than to actually split administrative control of the data.

Similarly, a name server can arrange to receive a zone copy simply to improve performance for local users. For example, the DDN zone might be supported on B.ISI.ARPA simply to provide direct access to the DDN zone's data for users on B.ISI.ARPA.

The data that makes up a zone consists of three kinds of RRs:

1. A comprehensive set of RRs to describe all of the resources attached to nodes in the zone.

2. Special RRs, associated with the top node of a zone, which enumerate name servers that have copies of the zone and describe the characteristics of the zone. The characteristics are contained in a single Start of Authority (SOA) RR; this record identifies a single master copy of the zone from which redundant copies receive updates. All name servers with copies of the zone are identified with Name Server (NS) RRs.

3. Special RRs which mark delegation of authority to subzones. These RRs are also NS RRs; they point to name servers which support the appropriate subzone.

For example, the data for the ARPA zone would include the following:

```
Owner         RR

ARPA          SOA  IN   NIC.ARPA
ARPA          NS   IN   NIC.ARPA
ARPA          NS   IN   F.ISI.ARPA
ISI.ARPA      NS   IN   B.ISI.ARPA
ISI.ARPA      NS   IN   A.ISI.ARPA
MIT.ARPA      NS   IN   Multics.MIT.ARPA
```

The SOA and NS RRs attached to node ARPA name NIC.ARPA as the holder of the master copy of the zone, while the two NS records at ARPA point to name servers for the ARPA zone as being on hosts F.ISI.ARPA and NIC.ARPA. The NS RRs attached to ISI.ARPA point to hosts B.ISI.ARPA and F.ISI.ARPA as holders of zones for ISI.ARPA.

The special RRs that delimit a zone also provide connectivity for searches throughout the name space. If a resolver knows the address of any root server, it can find any node in the abstract tree by retrieving the appropriate NS records from the root name server and iterating "down" to the name server which has the desired information. To guarantee connectivity, we can also put pointers to root servers in all name servers; if this is done, the resolver needs to know how to reach only one name server to be able to eventually access all of the domain data.

Resolvers

Resolvers are programs that process user queries and chain through name servers to find the specified data. A user program issues a query, which is passed to the resolver via an OS call or some other mechanism. The resolver then queries local and foreign name servers to acquire the specified information. Since a particular query may involve several network transmissions to a series of foreign name servers, resolver actions take an indeterminate amount of time.

Name servers

The action taken by a name server to process a query depends on the kind of query and the composition of the zones possessed by the name server. For simple queries, the name server checks to see if the domain name in the query is contained within any of the name server's zones. If it is, the name server returns either the requested RRs or an indication that the requested resource does not exist. Since all copies of a zone are assumed to be equivalent, such an answer is marked as being authoritative, so that the resolver that sent the query will know there is no point in attempting further queries at other name servers. If the query does not refer to a node in one of the name server's zones, the name server searches its database for NS RRs corresponding to zones that are parents of the query domain name. Since all name servers include pointers to a name server for the root, this search always succeeds. The name server then returns the NS RRs for zones "closest" to the domain name in the query. This type of response is called a referral.

For completion queries, the name server examines the target name for the query and decides whether it refers to a node in one of the name server's zones. If so, the name server performs the completion search and returns the results. If not, it returns a referral.

For inverse queries, the name server has no indication of the domain name that is the answer to the query. Hence inverse queries are processed using whatever zones are available, and the answer is returned.

A central feature of this functionality is that name servers do not need to be concerned with the location of non-local data; they simply answer queries based on their local zones. This allows for quite simple name server implementations.

DATABASE MAINTENANCE

Two types of database maintenance activity occur in the processes that implement the domain system: refreshing of zone copies, which occurs on a planned and regular basis, and caching, or demand-driven copying of data for one resolver request on the assumption that the data may be useful for subsequent queries. Although the mechanisms are quite different, both rely on the notion that the creator of a particular RR should be able to set a time-to-live (TTL) for the RR, describing the maximum time that a copy of the RR can be assumed to be correct before the creator should be consulted. This TTL is effectively the length of time before a change to the database is guaranteed to be effective throughout the system. Of course, the time intervals must also take into account the cost of too short an interval.

Refreshing discipline

The master copy of the data that makes up a particular zone is assumed to reside on a single host. That host's name server creates a zone by reading a file. Other name servers use the domain protocol to get a copy of the zone.

All name servers which have copies of a zone are responsible for checking periodically to see if the zone has been updated. The name server with the master file does this by checking to see if the file has been updated; name servers which acquired a copy of the zone can check for updates by requesting the serial number of the zone from the name server that has the master copy.

The identity of the name server with the master copy, the time intervals for checking for updates, etc., are contained as part of the zone data. In general, the timeouts are set up so that the check for update (refresh interval) occurs frequently and the copy is allowed to persist (expiration interval) for a very long time when the master copy is unavailable.

For zones, a single TTL value covers all of the data in the zone. If this were not the case, false non-existent RR errors could result.

Caching

Caching is performed as the result of resolver activities. The premise is that, if a resolver goes to the trouble of acquiring a particular RR, it should cache it for use in answering future queries. While this feature is optional in resolvers, and resolvers may use different cache sizes, etc., a resolver that caches RRs must also manage a TTL for each RR it caches.

The TTL for a particular RR is derived from a zone TTL when a name server supplies an RR to the resolver. Since the resolver does not have zone information, it times each RR out separately. The derived TTL will typically be much smaller than the TTL for the zone as a whole. The reason for this is that, while zone copies are tested periodically for updates, cache copies are not similarly protected.

Adequate performance probably dictates that resolvers should cache at least the referral RRs they acquire, to avoid repetitive chaining through name servers. Zone designers assist this process by assigning long TTLs to NS RRs whenever possible.

STATUS AND DIRECTION OF FUTURE WORK

Status

The domain system has been issued as a set of draft RFCs [11,12] and is currently being implemented according to a schedule described in [13]. After the experimental period, a final specification will be issued.

The experimental period is designed to allow operational experience with several features which are optional in the present design and to further refine the specification. This section discusses several of the optional features under study.

Connecting internets

The greatest challenge and least understood problem for the domain system is sharing information between different internets. The current system recognizes that such interconnection will require translation at some level, if only to forward queries over different transport protocols. The class notion is our mechanism for controlling routing to the appropriate translation process.

At the simplest level, each internet replicates its information for each possible class of requestor. For example, the ARPA internet information for mailboxes could be replicated in both the IN and CS classes, with separate zones on name servers for the respective classes.

In practice, we expect that each zone will be completely described in a single class corresponding to the system in use, but that in other classes the zone will consist of pointers to appropriate gateways. For example, while hosts in the IN class can acquire mailbox information for the ARPA domain, hosts in the CS class would receive a single forwarding RR regardless of the mailbox they name. This forwarding record directs the mail to a mail gateway. A slightly more powerful use of class directs the search to a name server which can perform translation between the RRs of one class and the RRs of another.

The most general system would create a universal class for data which could be represented in a class-insensitive way. In general, the only universally known data types would be domain names themselves, so this strategy implies a level of indirection in the binding. For example, a universal mapping might bind mailboxes to the domain names of mail agents, and then a class-sensitive binding could direct the mail sender to either the mail agent or a mail gateway capable of reaching the agent.

While these strategies all seem possible, the usual source of problems is interference with freedom at the lowest levels. For example, translation at the name server level implies variability in response time, and can make datagram name service difficult. Similarly, there are networks that will be connected to the domain system on an infrequent basis.

Our intuition is that the domain system will evolve to use a mixture of these strategies at the discretion of the clients of the domain system.

Update management

Although the refresh mechanism provides an adequate mechanism for distributing information that does not change with use, it is inadequate for applications that are intended to allocate names dynamically. Such applications might include dynamic creation of new names, and name binding that is a function of dynamic conditions (e.g., what is the name of an idle print server in the ISI domains). Such services are under study, but will not be added until the informational services described herein are stable.

ACKNOWLEDGMENTS

The author wishes to thank Jon Postel and Paul Kirton for their contributions to the domain name system, as well as Shelia Coyazo and Ruth Brungardt for their contributions in improving this paper.

REFERENCES and BIBLIOGRAPHY

[1] E. Feinler, K. Harrenstien, Z. Su, and V. White, "DOD Internet Host Table Specification", RFC 810, Network Information Center, SRI International, March 1982.

[2] K. Harrenstien and V. White, "NICNAME/WHOIS", RFC 812, Network Information Center, SRI International, March 1982.

[3] M. Solomon, L. Landweber, and D. Neuhengen, "The CSNET Name Server", Computer Networks, vol. 6, no. 3, July 1982.

[4] K. Harrenstien, "NAME/FINGER", RFC 742, Network Information Center, SRI International, December 1977.

[5] J. Postel, "Internet Name Server", IEN 116, USC/Information Sciences Institute, August 1979.

[6] K. Harrenstien, V. White, and E. Feinler, "Hostnames Server", RFC 811, Network Information Center, SRI International, March 1982.

[7] J. Postel, "Transmission Control Protocol", RFC 793, USC/Information Sciences Institute, September 1981.

[8] J. Postel, "User Datagram Protocol", RFC 768, USC/Information Sciences Institute, August 1980.

[9] J. Postel, "Simple Mail Transfer Protocol", RFC 821, USC/Information Sciences Institute, August 1980.

[10] J. Reynolds and J. Postel, "Assigned Numbers", RFC 870, USC/Information Sciences Institute, October 1983.

[11] P. Mockapetris, "Domain Names - Concepts and Facilities", RFC 882, USC/Information Sciences Institute, November 1983.

[12] P. Mockapetris, "Domain Names - Implementation and Specification", RFC 883, USC/Information Sciences Institute, November 1983.

[13] J. Postel, "Domain Name System Implementation Schedule", RFC 897, USC/Information Sciences Institute, February 1984.

PART 2:

MESSAGE ARCHITECTURE AND MULTIMEDIA SYSTEMS

Computer-Based Message Services
H.T. Smith (Editor)
Elsevier Science Publishers B.V. (North-Holland)

CURRENT ISO WORK ON DOCUMENT PROFILE

Joan M. Smith

Senior Consultant
National Computing Centre
Oxford Road
Manchester M1 7ED
U.K.

This paper is concerned with what is known within ISO/TC 97/SC 18/WG3 as 'Information Processing - Text Preparation and Interchange - Text Structures - Part 3 Document Profile'. Shortly to be presented to SC 18 as a draft proposal for a multi-part international standard, part 3 deals with the description of an interchanged document. The purpose and scope of the document profile are presented, the attributes explained and examples of usage given.

I INTRODUCTION

Document profile is that which precedes the document body to be interchanged, and is considered as an integral part of a document. The profile provides information by means of attributes relating to the document as a whole - its presentation, content, filing and retrieval. These attributes are meant for comprehension by both human and machine processes. Some are supplied by the sender of the document, others by the receiver. Attributes are basically of two categories: mandatory (such as overall length of the document, its title), and optional (such as information included for purposes of electronic filing, keywords, say); furthermore, private parameters may be supplied giving additional information. Thus the profile aspires to be all embracing, yet simple in its minimum form (there are just four mandatory attributes).

II ISO/TC 97/SC 18/WG3

Technical Committee 97 of the International Organization for Standardization (ISO) is that which deals with information processing, its Subcommittee 18 being charged with the area of text preparation and interchange, text structures being the remit of Working Group 3. This, then, is the group which is currently writing a multi-part standard for text structures that it plans to submit to SC18 as draft proposals at its next plenary session in May 1984. Four parts are proposed:

- part 1 general introduction,
- part 2 office document architecture,
- part 3 document profile,
- part 4 office document interchange format.

The purpose of the standard is to facilitate the interchange of office documents. 'It provides for their representation in such a way as to enable the documents to be reproduced as intended by the sender and to facilitate their processing by the recipient, where the interchange is by means of data communications or the exchange of storage media.'[1] In the context of the standard, office documents are considered to be items such as memoranda, letters, forms, and reports, where these may include pictures and tables. The graphic elements of which a document is composed can include character box, geometric, and photographic elements, the standard's design being extensible to encompass further types of elements such as voice. Potentially, all types may be in one document (mixed-mode).

III THE ROLE OF THE DOCUMENT PROFILE

Preceding the body of any office document which conforms to this standard there is to be a profile of the document. In fact it forms an integral part of the interchanged document. It provides information by means of attributes for the handling of the document as a whole, including that for its processing (for example formatting and editing), also for its filing and retrieval. Also included are those attributes which apply to its own rendition - how it can be displayed. Enveloping data is deemed to be a separate issue, although some items may be included in the document profile which appear on the envelope, as can others which are in the main body.

The attributes are intended to be comprehensible both to a human and to machine processes. Not all of those listed in the standard need to be completed before onwards transmission: some are mandatory; others are optional. Examples of the former category are title and length; examples of optional ones are author(s) and document date. Whilst some attributes are provided at the originating end, others may be added by the recipient who may also amend attributes to suit his or her particular needs.

Thus, for example, the secretariat, on receiving the note containing apologies for absence at the meeting, might add a filing reference, expiry information, and so on. All these aspects and many more are covered by the document profile. There is one important point to note here: amending the document and/or the document profile results in the creation of a new document.

In the context of open systems interconnection (OSI), this proposed multi-part international standard is at the application level and can interact directly with the OSI presentation service. Documents can be transferred using the message oriented text interchange system (MOTIS) as specified by ISO/TC 97/SC 18/WG4, or the message interchange distribution application standard (MIDAS) as specified by the European Computer Manufacturers' Association (ECMA).

There is a section on document description embedded in the proposed standard being written by ECMA on office document architecture, to be presented at the general assembly later this year (1984). It is expected that the ECMA work would be a subset of and certainly compatible with that of ISO. No specific work on document profile is currently being undertaken by the International Telegraph and Telephone Consultative Committee (CCITT), but it is expected to be a question for study in the next four-year study period, and will be announced at the forthcoming general assembly later this year. In this respect, the work of ISO on document profile leads that done by other standards-making bodies.

IV ATTRIBUTES OF THE DOCUMENT PROFILE

There are many and various attributes, the document profile being designed in such a way as to be all things to all men. Since it could not possibly contain all those items which may at sometime be required, the list of optional ones can be used as an aide-memoire, and any further (private) parameters may be given in a free-format field which follows the completed (mandatory and optional) attributes. It can thus be a short description or a relatively long one, depending on the usage to which the document is put. Figure 1 shows a list of the attributes for the document profile as it might be displayed for completion by the preparer of a document.

A Mandatory Attributes

There are just four basic attributes in this category which must be completed to form part of the interchanged document.

(1) Document profile graphic character set:
This specifies the graphic character set to be used for character data of the document profile. The character set used for the body of the document could well be Arabic, for example, but that used for the profile itself (including the title of the document) might be in ISO 646.[2] By default, this is the minimum subrepertoire of ISO 6937.[3]

(2) Content type(s):
Here is the method of encoding the content type(s) of the document, where this may be either implied by a particular service and/or specified by the type(s) of elements used. Examples of a service are Teletex and Videotex. Where content types are specified explicitly these could be character box, graphic, photographic, or voice. Character box elements might be in ISO 6937 (the full repertoire) and ISO registered set No. 59,[4] that for Arabic (CODAR-U). In the case of geometric elements the encoding method could be in VDM, the virtual device metafile language currently being specified by other ISO work. Photographic elements are specified in pixel arrays, the coding method for voice having yet to be specified. Furthermore, the document could be marked-up in accordance with SGML, the standard generalized mark-up language about to be the subject of another ISO draft proposal.

(3) Title:
A word or phrase is supplied by the author(s) or originating organization(s) of a document to identify it. Were a document profile completed for this paper, then the attribute for title would be 'Current ISO Work on Document Profile'. As another example, if a consumer were being invoiced for electricity by the Electricity Board's area office, the attribute might be 'Account for Electricity'.

(4) Length:
The length of a document, including that of the document profile, is expressed in 8-bit bytes. It may be either the actual length (and this could be system supplied before onwards transmission) or estimated, where this must not be less than the actual length. Thus, were a researcher to key in data at a library using a hand-held device, the estimated length of the document could be the capacity of the cassette tape.

B <u>Optional Attributes</u>

Those attributes which are optionally for completion could be likened to items on a menu which may be selected. Just as favourite items tend to be frequently, so it is to be expected that some will be specified by the majority of users, where such attributes could relate to electronic filing. Whilst others will doubtless be used for other specific purposes, which is why they have been included, I regard the provision of this list as an <u>aide-memoire</u> for the person who completes the profile. Completion could be at the transmitting end, perhaps the author of the paper, or the receiving end, maybe by the archivist of an on-line data bank. Whatever else needs to be added for present purposes may be supplied as ancillary information. Before we deal with that, let us look first at this (extensive) list of optional attributes.

(a) Further Basic Attributes

(1) Document class:
This attribute specifies the type of document be it a memorandum, letter, report, or paper, as in the present case.

(2) Required functional capability:
The functional capability of the receiving system required for the receiving device is specified here. This will be in accordance with ISO-defined 'levels'.

(3) Generic reference(s):
References to the generic structure and possibly generic content portions assumed to be already held at the receiving end are indicated here.[5] This obviates the necessity of retransmitting structure and/or information which is common to a type of document.

(4) Number of pages:
The number of pages currently occupied by the body of the document is inserted here. This version of my paper may take ten A-4 pages (printed), so '10' would go in that position.

(5) Copy list:
All the intended or actual recipients of the documents are listed here, depending on whether or not the document has actually been interchanged. In the case of my paper the list could be 'Dr T.D. Wells, Mr J.G. Cook, Mr P.J.E. Dyce' at a draft stage, for comment by representatives of ISO and BSI. Later I would expect to add that of 'Mr H. Smith'.

(6) ODA version date:
This is provided to state that this document has been prepared in accordance with ISO xxxx (date) where the data is that of the original version of the standard or its subsequent revision, 1985-11-14, say. It is expected that this would be supplied by the system.

(b) Document Filing and Recognition

(1) Reference:
Here is a unique reference assigned by the owner(s) of the document so that it may be identified within a document library (by man or machine) for further operations. In my system I might call the (now) current version of part 3 of the draft proposal 'ISO/TC 97/SC 18/WG3/N285' thus distinguishing it from other ISO and BSI documents of which I hold copies, N285 being the WG3 reference for the fourth working draft.

(2) Version number:
This is a code to distinguish the current version of the document (technically another document) from other versions. It might be 4, for example, the earlier being a proposed working draft that was accepted at the last WG3 meeting.

(3) Status:
The status of the document may be indicated here, be it a working draft, approved, issued, superseded or withdrawn.

(4) Superseded document(s):
Here may be the title, version number and/or reference of any document(s) superseded by the present version. I may put 'N209 Third Working Draft'.

(5) User-specific codes:
These codes are used at the discretion of the user to identify a contract number perhaps, a project number, or a budget code. That associated with my work when preparing another draft

proposal could well be '5589003'. It would be for my use, however, or use within NCC; it would not accompany the finished draft when transmitted to other WG3 members who are not concerned with local information of that nature (and that version would then technically constitute another document).

(6) Author(s):
The name(s) of the author(s) of the document go(es) here, for instance, 'Joan M. Smith'.

(7) Organization(s):
This attribute specifies the originating organization(s) associated with the document. In the case of this paper, I would have completed the author attribute and would now add 'The National Computing Centre Limited'. However, the bill for electricity would probably have no author attribute, and here could be 'Norweb'.

(8) Preparer:
This is the place for the name of the person who prepared or encoded the document, analogous in some respects to the initials of the secretary/typist that appear as part of a reference to a letter. It is often useful to have this information, as in the absence of the author this is the person who can often deal with queries which may arise.

(9) Owner(s):
Here is the name of the current administrator(s) or the document. The administrator for the proposed fourth working draft of document profile was myself; when it was approved by WG3 as the fourth working draft the ownership changed to that of the WG3 secretariat at NCC.

(10) Keyword(s):
The official description of this attribute is: 'One or more character strings, assigned by the suthor(s), originating organization(s), and/or recipient of the document, that permit logical associations to be made about the content of the document'.[1] Whilst I might put 'ISO/TC 97/SC 18/WG3, text preparation and interchange, standards, document profile, conference paper', Hugh Smith as local organizer may have deleted one or more of these for his purposes but added others, including 'IFIP 6.5'.

(11) Summary information:
This attribute is for internal reference(s) to summary or equivalent information within the document. In the case of the paper I could put 'Abstract page 1'. If documents do not have an abstract or summary per se, reference here could be to 'Introduction' or 'Conclusions', if appropriate. The attribute is seen as being of

particular value for data banks which may contain abstracted information only and pointers to the source document.

(12) External reference(s):
Reference(s) to other associated document(s) may be made here. In my paper I cite the most recent draft of document description and could put 'ISO/TC 97/SC 18/WG3/N285' at that point.

(13) Language(s):
This attribute is for the primary language(s) in which the main body of the document is written. I could put 'English' but would not bother; however, in the case of the report in Arabic, that would be indicated here. In the case of the document's being a computer program, COBOL or BASIC, say, could be specified.

(14) Document date:
This is the date associated with the document by its author(s) or originating organization(s), so here I might have '1984-05-01'.

(15) Creation date and time:
Here is put the date when the document was created. All dates and times are to be specified in accordance with the appropriate ISO standards, thus that for this paper could be '1983-11-11-10:30'.

(16) Expiry date:
The date here is that after which the document may be discarded. I could be interested in retaining this paper as a write-up on the project, parts of which may be incorporated in future documents. For this reason I might put a relatively long life on the paper and perhaps specify '1986-12-31'. However, should it be superseded by a more up-to-date version, the chances are that it would be erased long before then.

(17) Local filing reference(s):
It is here that filing information is given to identify where a copy of the document may be found. Since different media could be used, one might point to where hard copy is filed, another to a floppy disc, and the third give the system filestore details. So mine could be 'DP Presentations - drawer 4, disc no. 34 JMSIFIP, JMSIFIP'.

(18) Local filing date and time:
This attribute refers to the filestore copy of the document and could therefore be '1984-04-19-15:30'.

(19) Copyright:
This attribute specifies the name(s) of the legal party/parties in whom the copyright of the document is vested. On submission of this paper, I would wish to retain copyright, so 'Joan M. Smith' would appear at that stage; however, on publication of the proceedings the entry could read 'North-Holland'.

(c) Document Security Attributes

(1) Authorization:
The name(s) of the person(s) approving or authorizing the document may go here. My paper for IFIP would not require this to be completed for transmission from me to the organizer. However, since only selected papers are included in the proceedings, it could well be sent on to the publisher by the editor or chairman of the programme committee and that person's name would be in this position as the one responsible for having given approval.

(2) Security classification:
The security classification assigned by the document owner(s) is specified by means of this attribute, examples being secret or company confidential. These are seen as being similar to those printed currently on letters or other documents that are not meant for general information. This attribute relates to such aspects as its visibility, reproduction, storage, audit and destruction requirements.

(3) Access right(s):
Specific access right(s) to the document are spelt out here, including read, insert, replace, erase, extend, management.

(4) Encryption:
In the case of some secret documents, the main body could be encrypted. Specified in this attribute would be a sequence of up to eight a-characters (as defined in the ISO file transfer standard). Any further information is to be obtained by other means, thus not providing the complete key for certain types of encryption. Should the document profile itself also be encrypted, this attribute would be specified first, being positioned immediately before those attributes that are mandatory.

(d) Additional information:

This is effectively a free-form field for ancillary information, infra-company private parameters, and so on. In a company implementation, any such private parameters could be defined in much the same way as those above, prompting the document preparer to complete them before onwards transmission of the document. Prior to interchange, and in a way that could be transparent to the end-user, these private parameters would be preceded by 'additional information ='.

V IMPLEMENTATION CONSIDERATIONS

It has yet to be decided what bits will actually be interchanged. Where optional attributes are concerned, it would be sufficient to pass on only those which have been completed; that is, those with no value in the right-hand-side of the equation will be deleted. However, for equipment that conforms to this standard, even though most attributes are optional, there must exist the ability to display the entire list or menu for the preparer and/or recipient as the case may be. Figure 2 illustrates a completed document profile for this paper, as I might see it on my terminal equipment, prior to the interchange of the document.

VI CONCLUDING REMARKS

The document profile is the one part of this multi-part international standard that will be used regularly by many thousands of end-users. It must be able to be unambiguously understood, otherwise the document profile itself could fail to impart certain information; it must be user-friendly, otherwise it could fail in one of its important design criteria.

VII REFERENCES

[1] ISO/TC 97/SC 18/WG3/N285 ISO/DP xxxx/3, Information Processing - Text Preparation and Interchange - Text Structures - Part 3 Document Profile (first draft of DP).

[2] ISO 646, Information Processing - ISO 7-bit Coded Character Set for Information Interchange.

[3] ISO 6937, Information Processing - Coded Character Sets for Text Communication.

[4] ISO International Register of Coded Character Sets to be Used with Escape Sequences.

[5] ISO/TC 97/SC 18/WG3/N283 ISO/DP xxxx/2, Information Processing - Text Preparation and Interchange - Text Structures - Part 2 Office Document Architecture (first draft of DP).

DOCUMENT PROFILE

Note that items marked * must be completed. The others are optional.

Basic Attributes

* document profile graphic character set =
* content type(s) =
* title =

document class =
required functional capability =
generic reference(s) =
number of pages =
copy list =

Document Recognition and Filing

reference =
version number =
status =
superseded document(s) =
user-specific code(s) =
author(s) =
organization(s) =
preparer =
owner(s) =
keyword(s) =
summary information =
external reference(s) =
language(s) =
document date =
creation date and time =
expiry date =
local filing reference(s) =
local filing date and time =
copyright =

Document Security Attributes

authorization =
security classification =
access right(s) =
encryption =

Additional Information

additional information =

NOTE - It is assumed that the length and ODA version date attributes are system supplied in this instance.

Figure 1
Example Display

Basic Attributes

* document profile character set = ISO 646
* content type(s) = character box elements, ISO 646
* title = Current ISO Work on Document Profile

document class = paper
required functional capability =
generic reference(s) =
number of pages = 10
copy list = Dr T.D. Wells, Mr J.G. Cook, Mr P.J.E. Dyce, Mr H. Smith

Document Filing and Recognition

reference = JMSIFIP
version number = 2
status = approved
superseded document(s) = JMSIFIP/1
user-specific code(s) = 55894
author(s) = Joan M. Smith
organization(s) = The National Computing Centre Limited
preparer = Ann
owner(s) = Joan M. Smith
keyword(s) = ISO/TC 97/SC 18/WG3, text preparation and interchange, standards, document profile, conference paper
summary information = abstract page 1
external reference(s) = ISO/TC 97/SC 18/WG3/N209 ISO/DP xxxx/3 Information processing - Text preparation and interchange -Text structures - Part 3 Document profile; see also section VII of the document body
language(s) = English
document date = 1984-05-01
creation date and time = 1983-11-11-10:30
expiry date = 1986-12-31
local filing reference(s) = DP Presentations - drawer 4, disc no. 34 JMSIFIP, JMSIFIP
local filing date and time = 1984-04-19-15:30
copyright = Joan M. Smith

Document Security Attributes

authorization = IFIP programme committee
security classification =
copy protection(s) =
access right(s) = JMS all
TDW read
JGC read
PJED read
HS read, copy
encryption =

Additional Information

additional information =

Figure 2
Example of a Completed Document Profile

Computer-Based Message Services
H.T. Smith (Editor)
Elsevier Science Publishers B.V. (North-Holland)

MULTIMEDIA MESSAGE CONTENT PROTOCOLS FOR COMPUTER MAIL

J. J. Garcia Luna Aceves and A. Poggio

SRI International
Menlo Park, California 94025
U.S.A.

The electronic interchange of information represented in different forms is becoming increasingly important as computers are becoming a common tool in all sectors of society, and in office environments in particular.

This paper discusses technical issues associated with the design of the protocols necessary for the organization of multiple media (character encoded text, geometric graphics, stored speech, bitmap images) in messages exchanged through computer-based message systems. A specific protocol--the multimedia message content protocol (MMCP) is described as an example of such protocols. MMCP is being proposed for the organization of multimedia documents exchanged in the DARPA Internet.

1. INTRODUCTION

The key technology of the twentieth century has been information gathering, processing, and distribution. By now, telephone, radio, and broadcast television networks are ubiquitous in all developed countries. As we move towards the end of this century, computers are becoming a common tool in many sectors of society (military, industry, and household) in such nations. The recent advances in computer and communication technologies over the last two decades have made public and private computer networks economically affordable.

Whether civilian or military, scientific research or support of office environments, the user applications that will result from the computing power of the '90s will require "electronic highways" to enable users to orchestrate their efforts and take advantage of the wider distribution of machine intelligence. Hence, during the current decade, support of information flow and automation of office tasks by means of computer tools will become major foci of effort in research and development activities. Protocols and techniques will be needed to merge most of today's separately handled text, voice, geometric graphics, data, and bit-map image information into machine-processable messages that can be dealt with by computer processes and displayed as integrated presentations. Furthermore, a coherent set of standards will have to be agreed upon and implemented for the interconnection of different user messaging environments.

This paper addresses the design of protocols for the integration of multiple media into coherent messages exchanged through computer-based message systems (CBMS). In this paper, such protocols are called "multimedia message content protocols." First, an architectural framework is presented to show the role of multimedia content protocols in CBMSs (Sections 2 and 3). Then, the protocol being proposed for the DARPA Internet is discussed as a specific example of such protocols (Sections 4 and 5).

2. ARCHITECTURAL ELEMENTS OF A MULTIMEDIA CBMS

The services of a CBMS can be categorized as ***message processing*** (composing, deleting, filing, retrieval), or ***message transfer*** (to whom, where, through which route, when). For the purposes of modeling a CBMS, it can be viewed as formed by two different types of functional elements. According to the CCITT model for CBMS, these components are: *User agents (UA)*, dedicated to message processing functions, and the ***message transfer system (MTS)***, dedicated to message transfer functions. In turn, the MTS is formed by a number of ***message transfer agents (MTA)*** that serve one or more UAs. UAs interact with the MTAs on behalf of CBMS users.

The interaction among users of a multimedia CBMS is accomplished through the exchange of multimedia messages between their UAs. Messages transferred in a CBMS are formed by an envelope and a content. The envelope of a message contains the requisite information to transfer a message from one UA to another. The content contains the information to be conveyed to the message recipient and is not interpreted by the MTS. The ***meaning*** of the message content is not understood by UAs; however, UAs do require that such information be structured in a machine-processable form to provide a coherent presentation of the content meaning to the mesage recipients.

Messages are composed by the sender establishing a dialogue with his (her) UA. The sender specifies the recipient(s) of the message and any other parameter germane to the presentation of the message. The UA is responsible for formatting the multimedia message in a machine-processable form, and for asking the MTS to deliver the message.

The transfer of a message from one UA to another is a store-and-forward procedure in which the message may be handled by more than one MTA. The ultimate responsibility for the message rests on the originating MTA, and the confirmation of message deliveries is end-to-end, as opposed to hop-by-hop. Thus, relay MTAs limit their activity to forwarding end-to-end messages and acknowledgments between sender and recipient MTA.

A multimedia CBMS constitutes a very general messaging environment in which messages can be used for different CBMS user applications, such as database access and interpersonal communication.

3. PROTOCOLS FOR MULTIMEDIA CBMS

To interact with one another, MTAs and UAs need well defined communication protocols. We shall refer to such protocols as a ***multimedia message handling facility*** (MMHF) [4]. An MMHF constitutes the framework for implementing the mechanisms needed to distribute and present multimedia messages among CBMS users.

We call the protocol used for UA-to-UA communication the ***multimedia message content protocol*** (MMCP). In our model, MMCP specifies two main things: (a) the rules for the presentation of machine-processable, multimedia information in a standard format understood among UAs, and (b) the rules for the establishment of dialogues among UAs.

We call the protocol used for MTA-to-MTA communication the ***message transfer protocol*** (MTP). The main objective of MTP is to support a reliable store-and-forward environment for the delivery of multimedia messages among UAs. MTP defines a set of various ***transfer primitives*** that specify the procedures to be carried out by sender and receiver MTAs when they cooperate with one another. The content of a message is considered as an uninterpreted string of bits by MTP; hence the same MTP could be used for multimedia and text-oriented message systems. MTP assumes the existence of a two-way (virtual) transmission channel between a sender and a receiver MTA. This protocol layer of MMHF has received considerable attention. The CCITT and the U.S. National Bureau of Standards (NBS) have specified their own versions of the protocols required for the transfer of messages among MTAs [2], [6]. The first specification of an MTP was due to Postel [8]. In the rest of this paper, we shall be concerned only with multimedia message content protocols.

4. A MULTIMEDIA MESSAGE CONTENT PROTOCOL (MMCP)

In this section we describe a specific multimedia message content protocol, which we will simply call MMCP. This protocol is being proposed to structure multimedia messages in the DARPA Internet. The specification presented in this paper modifies the document structure specified by Postel [9], but uses the same basic building blocks.

4.1 ELEMENTS OF MMCP

There are two main elements of MMCP: (a) the mechanisms used to handle the dialogue among UAs, and (b) the mechanisms used to structure document objects (e.g., text paragraphs, images) into multimedia documents.

A message in MMCP is formed by a set of message fields that specify attributes of the message (e.g., who its author is, who the recipient is, when it was composed), and actions to be carried out at the recipient site upon reception of the message (e.g., reply to). Each message field is a name-value pair consisting of a keyword denoting the type of field, and a value component containing the value of the field. The value component of a field may contain data for user consumption, other document fields, or entire documents. The dialogue between UAs is handled by means of these message fields. Currently, however, a sender UA cannot make a receiver UA carry out a certain action. Messages are passive entities, and it is always a user who tells his UA what to do with a message. Hence, the concept of UA-to-UA dialogue is very rudimentary in MMCP.

The main purpose of sending a message is to transfer a document, which is sent as the value portion of an MMCP message field. The presentation of a multimedia document requires the specification of the organization of each document object (e.g., a text portion, a picture) and the organization among objects to form a document. The ultimate control over this presentation resides with the message recipients; however, the sender of the message has the prerogative of indicating how he (she) would prefer the message to be presented. In addition, in some cases, it may be necessary to preserve the form in which the objects of a document are organized when they are transferred from the sender to the recipient UAs. An example of this case is when a user obtains from a database a portion of a document that contains sections, subsections, pictures, and footnotes, and the user's query refers to such document objects. MMCP specifies a standard document format defined between UAs that specifies: (a) the form in which different document objects are combined in a document, (b) the presentation parameters of each such object, and (c) the data in each object intended for user consumption.

Every component of an MMCP message contains information of a certain class (e.g., textual, binary, boolean) that we call ***data type***. For instance, the message field "FROM: Joe" is formed by two textual data types. MMCP defines an encoding procedure to represent data types in a standard, machine-processable form among UAs. Each data type is represented by means of a ***data element***, and data elements are combined to form fields and entire MMCP messages. We call such an encoding procedure the ***presentation*** *transfer syntax* of MMCP.

4.2 GRAMMAR CONVENTIONS

Throughout this section, we describe the structure of MMCP messages using the Backus-Naur Form (BNF) presented here. We shall refer to the BNF description of a protocol as its *grammar*. The conventions that we shall observe in the formal specification of MMCP are the following:

a) Nonterminals are delimited between the bracket symbols "< >". Thus, <y> means that y is a nonterminal in the grammar.

b) "::=" is the equivalence operator, and assigns a value to a nonterminal. It separates the name of a nonterminal from its definition.

c) "|" is the alternative operator. It indicates that one or the other of the symbols it separates are to be included in the definition of a nonterminal. For instance, <x> ::= <y> | <z> means that the nonterminal <x> can be defined as equivalent to either <y> or <z>.

d) "[ ]" encloses one or more optional symbols. That is, the symbol or symbols enclosed between brackets may or may not appear as part of the definition of the nonterminal being defined. For instance, <x> ::= [<y>] <z> means that <x> can be either "<y> <z>" or "<z>".

e) "<x>*" denotes the possible repetition of the preceding symbol class one or more times and following an ordered sequence. More precisely, " <x> ::= <y>* " is a shorter form for the recursive rule: " <x> ::= <y> | <x><y> ".

f) "l{ }" encloses the repetition of a symbol class, i.e., a nonempty, ordered list of elements.

g) "p{ }" denotes an unordered set formed with the ***name-value pairs*** enclosed in the braces of p{ }. We shall refer to such sets of pairs as ***property lists***. A name-value pair consists of two consecutive symbols. The first symbol must be a nonterminal, and the second symbol can be any type of symbol. The name-value pair formed by the symbols <x> and <y> will be denoted " <x> . <y> ". This specifies that <x> must appear immediately before <y> in the definition of a property list.

h) "..." denotes item(s) currently undefined in the grammar.

i) ";" precedes a comment that does not form part of the grammar.

4.3 MULTIMEDIA MESSAGE STRUCTURE

MMCP defines a set of required document fields that every document must include, and an open-ended list of optional document fields. The minimum document consists of four fields: "date: value", "from: value", "subject: value", "body: value". Many other optional fields can be added to this basic set. In terms of our BNF we have:

```
<document> ::= p{
                    DATE . <date>
                    FROM . l{ <mailbox> * }
                    SUBJECT . <subject>
                    [ <optional document-field> ]
                    BODY  .  <document-body>
                  }

<date>                  ; the date when document was posted
<subject>               ; a text string describing the subject of the message
<document-body>         ; a data structure with the body of the document
<mailbox>               ; defined in Section 6.2.3

<optional document-field> ::=  BCC . l{ <mailbox> * }
                             | CC . l{ <mailbox> * }
                             | TO  . l{ <mailbox> * }
                             | SENDER  . l{ <mailbox> * }
                             | REPLY-TO  . l{ <mailbox> * } .
                             | COMMENTS . <comment string>
                             | KEYWORDS . <keywords>
                             | MESSAGE-ID . <message identifier>
                             | IN-REPLY-TO . <message identifier>
                             | REFERENCES  . l{ <message identifier> * }
                             |  ...

<keywords>          ; a text structure specifying key terms used
                      in the message

<message identifier>  ; a text structure specifying an identifier
                        assigned to the message

<comment string>      ; a text structure containing comments on the message
```

With the exception of the syntactic unit <document-body> and <mailbox>, the syntactic units specified above have the same meaning as in hard-copy text messages.

A <mailbox> is simply a property list containing name-value pairs that denote a destination (person or process). The <document-body> unit is the subject of the next subsection.

4.4 MULTIMEDIA DOCUMENT BODY

The document body of a message in MMCP may assume different forms. It may consist of a short textual memo (e.g., "Çan you have lunch with me today?"), or it may consist of a long and complex audiovisual presentation including stored speech, graphics, and text.

There are two main types of relations among the components of a document: presentation relations and logical relations. Logical relations determine the logical structure of a document, e.g., whether it contains sections, subsections, footnotes, etc. Presentation relations determine the form in which the components of a document are presented to the user in time and space. Spatial presentation relations could be used to specify parameters such as size, priority of presentation, and position on the display. In terms of their temporal relationships, document components could be presented to a user independently from one another, sequentially, or simultaneously.

In MMCP, a document is a tree-structured body of media information together with presentation control information that describes the ***intended*** presentation of the media as specified by the sender of the message. While the need to specify logical relations and spatial presentation relations among document objects is clear, MMCP only incorporates *temporal presentation control* among document components.

Each portion of the document body that contains a single medium is structured into a name-value pair, called a ***presentation element*** (or ***pe***). Its name portion is a keyword that specifies the type of medium (e.g., TEXT, GRAPHICS). Its value portion contains the medium data as well as the control information used to specify the presentation parameters for such data. There are five different types of media currently defined for multimedia messages in the Internet: text, voice, facsimile, graphics, and images. Protocol support is, at least in part, already available for these media. Other media could be introduced in the future.

Presentation elements are assembled into what constitutes a document body by means of ***presentation descriptors (pd)***. There are five different types of presentation descriptors currently defined in MMCP for the following types of temporal presentation control:

a) Sequential presentation of various media: Sequential data items are presented one at a time in the order listed. The order specified in the ***pd*** is left to right.

b) Simultaneous presentation of media: Simultaneous data are intended for synchronous presentation. That is, simultaneous data items are presented at the same time and the presentation is not considered to be complete until all data items of the simultaneous presentation have been presented.

c) Independent presentation of media: Independent data are intended for asynchronous presentation. That is, data items can be presented in any time order and the independent presentation of a given medium (e.g., facsimile) need not be completed before another presentation starts, as long as no conflict exists with the allocation of I/O resources (e.g., a facsimile terminal, a loudspeaker). This option is included to accommodate the use of slow output devices (e.g., a facsimile terminal), together with fast output devices.

d) Presentation of a single medium: A presentation element can be considered as a presentation descriptor used to control a single medium.

e) Presentation of a single document: A whole document (in machine-processable form) may be included as part of another document. Such an embedded document can be considered as a presentation descriptor used to indicate the document's position within the larger document.

A presentation descriptor ***(pd)*** is a name-value pair that constitutes a document component. Its name portion, a keyword, denotes the type of presentation control that applies to the information contained in its value portion. The ***pd's*** used for sequential, simultaneous, and independent control have the same structure. Their keywords specify the preferred order in which the nonempty sequence of ***pd's*** (i.e., smaller document components) in the value portion should be presented. The ***pd*** used for the presentation of embedded documents consists of a keyword followed by the document being presented.

Using the BNF notation introduced above, we can specify the structure of the <document body> unit defined in MMCP recursively as follows:

<document body> ::= ***<pd>***
<pd> ::= ***<pe>*** | ***<doc-pair>*** | ***<seq-pair>*** | ***<sim-pair>*** | ***<ind-pair>***

<seq-pair> ::= ***p***{ *SEQUENTIAL* . ***l***{ ***<pd>*** * } }
<sim-pair> ::= ***p***{ *SIMULTANEOUS* . ***l***{ ***<pd>*** * } }
<ind-pair> ::= ***p***{ *INDEPENDENT* . ***l***{ ***<pd>*** * } }
<doc-pair> ::= ***p***{ *DOC* . ***<document>*** }
<pe> ::= ***<tx-pair>*** | ***<vx-pair>*** | ***<fx-pair>*** | ***<ix-pair>*** | ***<gx-pair>*** |...

<tx-pair> ::= ***p***{ *TEXT* . ***<text structure>*** }

<vx-pair> ::= *p*{ *VOICE* . ***<voice structure>*** }
<fx-pair> ::= *p*{ *FACSIMILE* . ***<facsimile structure>*** }
<gx-pair> ::= *p*{ *GRAPHICS* . ***<graphics structure>*** }
<ix-pair> ::= *p*{ *IMAGE* . ***<image structure>*** }

The above grammar for the document body of multimedia messages has very nice properties that should be pointed out. First, the only form to stop recursion in a document body that does not contain itself, which is the case in all real documents, is by the introduction of presentation elements. Thus, only documents that contain some media (voice, text, etc.) are correct structures in MMCP. Second, note that a document containing a single medium simply consists of the ***pe*** of that medium. Third, there is no restriction as to what ***pd***'s can be included in the value portion of another ***pd***.

4.5 THE MEDIA

As we have stated, five different media are currently supported in MMCP. Each such medium is presented in a document by means of a "medium structure," which is a property list of name-value pairs that specify: (a) the data to be presented, (b) the medium-dependent presentation protocol being used, (c) the version of the protocol, and (d) spatial control (as yet unspecified). The use of medium structures is particularly important given the existing incompatibility among input/output devices and medium-dependent protocols.

4.6 PRESENTATION TRANSFER SYNTAX OF MMCP

The presentation transfer syntax assumed in MMCP corresponds to the encoding procedure proposed by Postel [7], [8]. According to this presentation syntax, each data element is formed with a sequence of one or more octets, and can be organized into a tag and a value component. The tag component specifies the data type being represented, as well as the size of the value component (either implicitly or explicitly). The value component contains the information that the data element is intended to present. The data elements included in the presentation transfer syntax can be classified in two categories, ***base data elements*** and ***structured data elements***. A base data element is self contained, while a structured data element is formed with various other (structured and/or base) data elements. The base data elements are: *NOP*, *PAD*, *BOOLEAN*, *INDEX*, *INTEGER*, *EPI*, *BITSTR*, *NAME*, *TEXT*, *ENDLIST*, *SHARE-TAG*, and *SHARE-REF*. The structured data elements are: *LIST*, *PROPLIST*, and *ENCRYPT*. Here we only describe the data elements used in the examples. These data elements are:

INDEX is a 16-bit unsigned integer datum. Its element code is 3, and it occupies only 3 octets, one for the code and two for the datum.

INTEGER is a signed 32-bit integer datum represented in two's complement arithmetic. This data element occupies five octets; one contains its element code, which equals 4, and the other four contain the value component containing the integer.

NAME has element code 7, and is used for the representation of character string names (or other short strings). The tag component of the data element consists of a one-octet element code followed by a one-octet count of the number of characters (one per octet) to follow. Seven bit ASCII characters are used, right justified in the octet. The high order bit in the octet is zero.

TEXT has element code 8, and is used for the representation of text. The one-octet element code of the tag is followed by a three-octet count of the number of characters (one per octet) to follow. Seven bit ASCII characters are used, right justified in the octet. The high order bit in the octet is zero.

ENDLIST is a one-octet data element used to permit the transfer of lists whose total length is not determined before their transmission. The element code of this data element is 11. A list of undetermined length is transmitted with the octet count cleared to zero, and the item count cleared to zero. A null or empty list, one with no elements, has an octet count of two (2) and an item count of zero (0). The ENDLIST element always follows a LIST, even when the length is determined.

LIST can be used to create structures composed of other elements. The tag component of this data element consists of three items. The one-octet element code, which equals 9, a three-octet octet count, which specifies the number of octets in the whole list (i.e., the number of octets following this count field to the end of the list, not including the ENDLIST octet), and the two-octet item count, which contains the number of elements that follow. Any element may be contained in the value component of this data element, including LIST itself.

PROPLIST is the property list element. It consists of a set of ***unordered*** <name, value> pairs. Each pair is composed of two consecutive data elements. The first element in the pair ***must*** be a NAME element; this element is used to specify the name of the pair. The second data element specifies the value of the pair and can be any data element. The pairs contained in a property list are distinguished from one another using their name portion. Thus, the name of a <name,value> pair is to be unique within the property list, i.e., there shall be, at most, one occurrence of any particular name in one property list. The element code of the PROPLIST is 10.

5. EXAMPLES

5.1 NOTATION

In this section we present two examples that illustrate MMCP. As we have stated in Section 4, each syntactic unit of MMCP is encoded using a data element. Here we are interested in describing the type and value of the data elements used to encode MMCP messages. We shall indicate the use of data elements grammatically as follows:

a) All identifying names of data elements are written in capital letters followed by a colon (e.g., LIST:).

b) Optional data elements in the structure of a primitive are delimited between brackets "[ ]".

c) Terminals of MMCP are written in capital letters enclosed in quotes (e.g., "OPERATION").

d) ";" precedes a comment

e) Any other data are specified between the symbols "< >"

As an example, assume that we want to specify that the syntactic unit IDENTIFIER is presented using the data element NAME. Then we would write:

NAME: "IDENTIFIER"

On the other hand, if we want to indicate that an arbitrary string of text is to be presented by the data element TEXT, we would write:

TEXT: < whatever..... >

5.2 EXAMPLE 1--A SIMPLE TEXT MESSAGE

Assume that the following message is to be sent from one UA to another:

Date: 1983-10-20-10:30-07:00
From: Jose Garcia-Luna <garcia@SRI-TSC.ARPA>
Subject: MMCP Format
To: Andy Poggio <poggio@SRI-TSC.ARPA>

Andy:

This is how the format of MMCP
looks like in a text-only document!

Jose.

The form in which this message would be encoded in MMCP is shown in Figure 1. In the figure, all information that pertains to a medium-dependent protocol is enclosed between the symbols "<< >>". The control information that pertains to MMTP, which was not specified in this paper, is indicated in lower-case letters, and only the document portion of the message is expanded.

5.3 EXAMPLE 2--A COMPLEX MULTIMEDIA MESSAGE

This example starts with various presentations in parallel, each of these presentations consists of smaller sequential presentations that could in turn consist of even smaller presentations. The resulting format is shown in Figure 2. The figure shows only the format of the document body and expands it up to the point where the first medium-dependent structures appear. The numbers in parentheses adjacent to PROPLISTs in Figure 2 indicate the level in the hierarchy of that data element.

6. CONCLUSIONS

A multimedia CBMS can be used for person-to-person, human-to-machine, and machine-to-machine communications. Protocols are used in such a system for the communication among the processes in charge of message distribution (MTAs) and for the communication among the processes in charge of message processing (UAs). A multimedia message content protocol specifies the rules for UA-to-UA interaction and the mechanisms for the representation of multimedia documents.

Recently, there have been a number of efforts related to the development of multimedia document protocols. Three organizations, the U.S. National Bureau of Standards, the International Telephone and Telegraph Consultative Committee (CCITT), and the International Standards Organization (ISO),, are working towards the development of standards for commercial CBMSs, and such standards include message content protocols.

This paper described the MMCP defined for the DARPA Internet. MMCP evolved from the pioneering effort by Postel [7], and experimental systems are now being implemented in various research centers in the DARPA research community. MMCP supports the presentation of very sophisticated multimedia documents, and permits different protocols to be used for a particular medium. However, MMCP supports only temporal presentation control of document objects. Spatial control (e.g., the size of objects) and logical relations among document objects (e.g., sections, subsections, footnotes) are not specified explicitly.

More studies and experiments are needed to understand the issues associated with the presentation and manipulation of multimedia documents. Accordingly, MMCP is expected to evolve in the future to include more document presentation features and dialogue control features.

ACKNOWLEDGEMENTS

The authors wish to thank Dr. Jon Postel and Greg Finn of USC-Information Sciences Institute for many helpful discussions on the structure of multimedia documents.

Preparation of this paper was supported by SRI IR&D funds. Portions of the work reported in this paper were supported under DARPA contract N00039-80-C-0658 with the Naval Electronic Systems Command.

REFERENCES

[1] CCITT Study Group VII/5, Draft Recommendation X.400: Message Handling Systems: System Model-Service Elements, 1984.

[2] CCITT Study Group VII/5, Draft Recommendation X.411: Message Handling Systems: Message Transfer Layer, 1984.

[3] Draft Recommendation X.409: Message Handling Systems: Presentation Transfer Syntax and Notation, 1984.

[4] J.J. Garcia-Luna-Aceves, A. Poggio, and D. Elliott, Research into Multimedia Message System Architecture, Final Report, Contract No. N00039-80-C-0658, SRI Proj. 5363, SRI International, Menlo Park, CA 94025, February 1984.

[5] U.S. National Bureau of Standards, "Specification for Message Format for Computer Based Message Systems," proposed federal information processing standard, National Bureau of Standards, Gaithersburg, Maryland, September 1981.

[6] U.S. National Bureau of Standards, "Specification of the Message Transfer Protocol", Draft Report No. ICST/CBOS-83-1, National Bureau of Standards, Gaithersburg, Maryland, July 1983.

[7] J. Postel, "An Internetwork Message Structure," Proc. Sixth Data Communications Symposium, Pacific Grove, California, November 1979, pp. 1-7.

[8] J. Postel, "Internet Multimedia Mail Transfer Protocol," Draft RFC 759-revised, Information Sciences Institute, Marina del Rey, California, 1982.

[9] J. Postel, "Internet Multimedia Mail Distribution Facility," Draft RFC 767-revised, Information Science Institute, Marina del Rey, California, 1982.

```
proplist:                          ;starts DELIVER primitive
   <identification unit>
   <command unit>
   name: "DOC",
------------------
          PROPLIST:                          ;starts document
               NAME: "DATE", NAME: <1983-10-20-10:30-07:00>
               NAME: "FROM",
                 LIST:
                   PROPLIST:
                          NAME: "HOST",   NAME: <SRI-TSC.ARPA>
                          NAME: "PORT",   NAME: [0.45]
                          NAME: "USER",   NAME: <garcia>
                          NAME: "PERSON", NAME: <Jose Garcia-Luna>
                   ENDLIST
                 ENDLIST
               NAME: "SUBJECT", TEXT: <MMCP format>
               NAME: "TO"
                  LIST:
                       PROPLIST:
                          NAME: "HOST",   NAME: <SRI-TSC.ARPA>
                          NAME: "PORT",   NAME: [0.45]
                          NAME: "USER",   NAME: <poggio>
                          NAME: "PERSON", NAME: <Andy Poggio>
                       ENDLIST
                  ENDLIST,
               NAME: "BODY",
                 PROPLIST:                          ; starts body
                   NAME: "TEXT",
                        PROPLIST:                   ; begins text
                          NAME: "PROTOCOL", NAME: "PARAGRAPH"
                          NAME: "VERSION", INDEX: <1>
                          NAME: "DATA",
                                LIST: <<  ; encoded with paragraph protocol

                                       Andy:

                                       This is how the format of MMCP
                                       looks like in a text-only document!

                                       Jose.
                                       >>
                                ENDLIST
                        ENDLIST                     ; ends text
                 ENDLIST                          ;ends body
          ENDLIST                               ; ends document

-----------------
endlist                            ; ends DELIVER primitive
```

Figure 1. Format of Example 1

```
PROPLIST (1):
   NAME: "SIMULTANEOUS",
        LIST:
           PROPLIST (2):
               NAME: "SEQUENTIAL",
                  LIST:
                        PROPLIST (3):
                             NAME: "SIMULTANEOUS",
                                LIST:
                                     PROPLIST (4):
                                       NAME: "VOICE", <voice structure>
                                     ENDLIST
                                     PROPLIST (4):
                                       NAME: "GRAPHICS", <graphic structure>
                                     ENDLIST
                                ENDLIST
                        ENDLIST
                        PROPLIST (3):
                             NAME: "SIMULTANEOUS",
                                LIST:
                                     PROPLIST (4):
                                       NAME: "VOICE", <voice structure>
                                     ENDLIST
                                     PROPLIST (4):
                                       NAME: "GRAPHICS", <graphic structure>
                                     ENDLIST
                                ENDLIST
                       ENDLIST
                        .
                        .
                  ENDLIST
           ENDLIST
           PROPLIST (2):
               NAME: "SEQUENTIAL",
                  LIST:
                        PROPLIST (3):
                             NAME: "SIMULTANEOUS",
                                LIST:
                                     PROPLIST (4):
                                       NAME: "VOICE", <voice structure>
                                     ENDLIST
                                     PROPLIST (4):
                                       NAME: "GRAPHICS", <graphic structure>
                                     ENDLIST
                                ENDLIST
                       ENDLIST
                       PROPLIST (3):
                             NAME: "SIMULTANEOUS",
                                LIST:
                                     PROPLIST (4):
                                       NAME: "VOICE", <voice structure>
                                     ENDLIST
                                     PROPLIST (4):
                                       NAME: "GRAPHICS", <graphic structure>
                                     ENDLIST
                                ENDLIST
                       ENDLIST


                  ENDLIST
           ENDLIST


        ENDLIST
ENDLIST
```

Figure 2. Format of Example 2

Computer-Based Message Services
H.T. Smith (Editor)
Elsevier Science Publishers B.V. (North-Holland)

Initial Experience with Multimedia Documents in Diamond[1]

Harry Forsdick, Robert Thomas,
George Robertson and Virginia Travers

Bolt Beranek and Newman, Inc.

Multimedia documents are collections of text, graphics, images, voice and other computer originated data presented on a single display surface such as a piece of paper or a computer display window. This paper describes experience gained in the design and implementation of the multimedia document model used in the initial implementation of Diamond, a distributed multimedia document system. Three different evolving document models are described and compared.

1. Introduction

Diamond is a system for creating, editing, filing, transmitting, and printing multimedia documents[2]. A Diamond document may contain text, graphics, images and speech as well as other types of objects such as electonic spread-sheets[3].

This paper describes three models for multimedia documents that we explored during the development of the initial implementation of Diamond. Each of the models is based on the premise that a multimedia document is a structured composition of objects of possibly different media types that is to be presented in a coordinated way. The three models are:

1. An Experimental model. This model was developed to experiment with ideas about how different types of media might be combined into a single document.

2. The evolving DARPA Internet model [4]. This model is being developed by several groups in the DARPA research community investigating the problem of transmitting multimedia documents between dissimilar computer systems.

3. The model supported by the initial implementation of Diamond. The Diamond model is based on experience with both the Experimental model and the DARPA Internet model, and in that sense represents improvements on them. We expect the document model used in Diamond to evolve as experience is gained with its use.

In order to provide a context for discussing these models, we first briefly describe Diamond. A more detailed description of the Diamond system is presented in another paper [3].

Several important goals have influenced the Diamond design:

- Diamond should handle multimedia documents.

- Diamond should be built upon a distributed architecture.

- The principal user access to Diamond should be supported by very powerful single user workstation computers[4].

- o Diamond should accommodate user access from devices with less capabilities than powerful single user workstation computers.

- o Diamond should be able to accommodate a variety of users with different interaction styles.

- o Diamond should operate in a fashion which ensures the security and privacy of users' messages and documents.

- o Diamond should operate in the DARPA Internet environment.

- o The Diamond implementation should be portable.

For the initial version of Diamond we have chosen to focus on the first three goals:

- o The ability to handle multimedia documents.

- o Use of a distributed architecture to support Diamond.

- o Use of powerful single user workstation computers to provide an advanced user interface to Diamond.

While important, the other goals have not been the primary initial focus of the Diamond effort. In particular, advancing the state-of-the-art in message processing systems, except as required to handle multimedia messages, has not been a primary goal.

Diamond is implemented as a distributed system. Documents and folders, which are used to hold collections of documents and other folders, are stored in a distributed data base. Information about users, such as passwords and usage preferences, is maintained in a registry data base managed by Diamond. Users access Diamond through user interface components. The user interface components, which typically run on powerful workstations computers, interact with the distributed components of Diamond to make the services provided by Diamond accessible to users.

An initial implementation of Diamond is operational, and work is progressing to enhance it in a variety of areas.

2. Experimental Document Model

The Experimental document model and the software that supports it was developed as a vehicle for exploring techniques for combining different types of objects into a single integrated document. The software evolved to a level that permitted the construction and transmission of multimedia documents as messages. This facility proved to be useful both as the experimental vehicle it was intended to be and as a means for demonstrating the concept of multimedia mail. However, it was never intended to be an operational system for managing multimedia documents. Experience with the experimental facility suggested a number of extensions, both to the model and the supporting software, that should be incorporated into an operational multimedia system.

Figure 1 is an example of the type of document that can be composed using this model. For this model, the position of an object is specified by its (pixel)

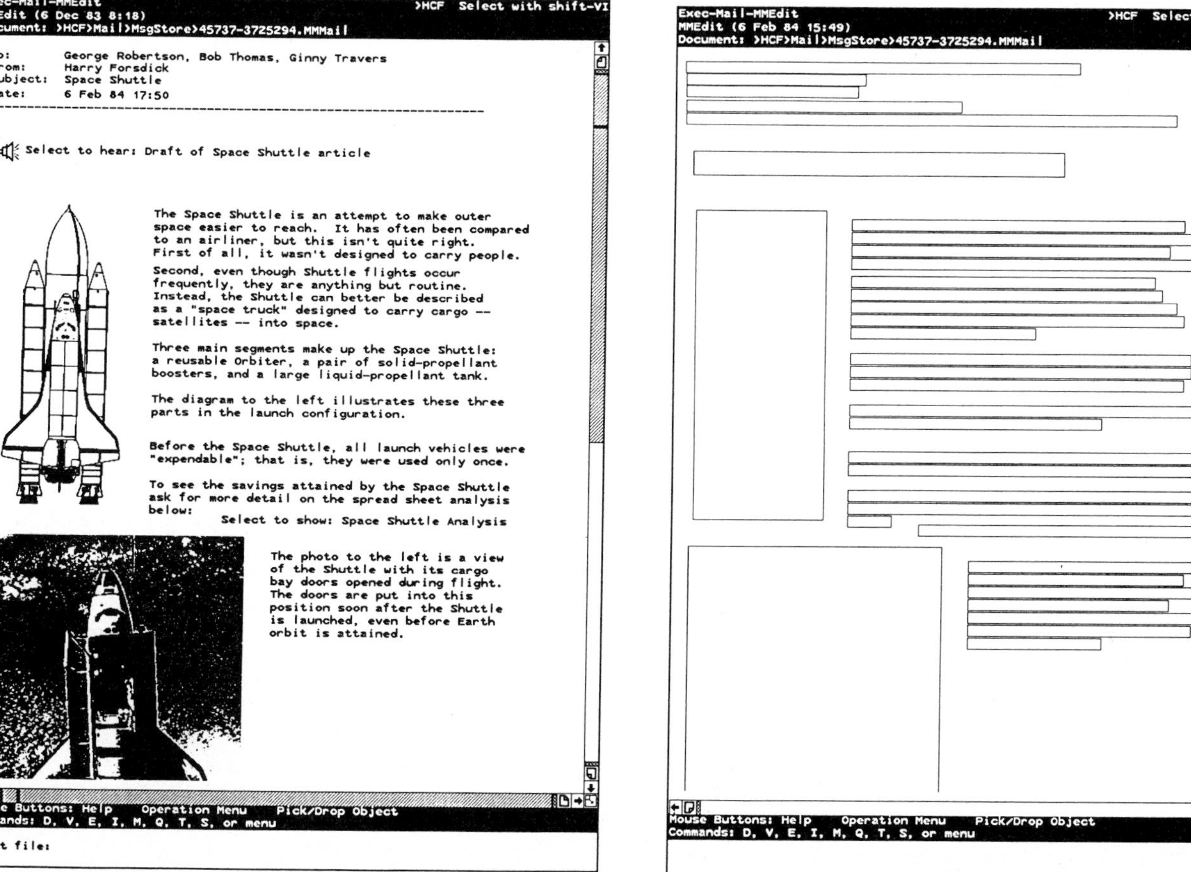

Figure 1: Document represented in Experimental Model

Figure 2: Underlying structure of the document in figure 1.

coordinates in a quarter plane. Every object has a width and a height, which are expressed in pixels. The underlying structure of the document in figure 1 is presented in figure 2. The types of objects that may be included in such a document are:

- Text: A line of text.

  Each line is a separate object which may be independently positioned. During text entry, the initial position of the pointing device (e.g., a mouse or trackball) determines the left margin. The right margin is determined by the width of the display window in which the document is being composed. New text objects (i.e., single lines of text) are created when the right margin is reached. The notion of collections of text objects grouped together, for example as in paragraphs, is not directly supported by the model, although the visual effect of such grouping can be achieved by carefully positioning the text objects.

- Scanned image: A picture or drawing which has been digitized on a facsimile scanner.

- Voice: A spoken passage encoded by a vocoder.

  Since voice objects cannot be displayed directly, an icon and a caption are used to indicate the presence of voice. The voice can be played back by pointing to the icon that represents it and invoking the "MoreDetail" operation.

- General Object: An object that is a collection of data, whose presentation is performed by a companion program corresponding to the type of data.

  General objects represent a mechanism for extending the types of objects which may be included in multimedia documents. A general object is represented by a caption which indicates the presence of the object. For example, in figure 1 the caption "Select to show: Space Shuttle Analysis" indicates a general object. A general object may be fully displayed by pointing to its caption and invoking the "MoreDetail" operation.

Figure 3 illustrates the manner in which general objects are displayed. When the user requests "MoreDetail" while pointing at a general object[5], a new window is created which, in general, overlaps the window used to display the document itself. The program corresponding to the general object is run within the new window to display the object. Examples of data types that are handled as general objects and that can be included in documents include electronic spread-sheets, graphical line drawings, and graphs generated from tabular data. The advantage of this approach is that the document system does not need to know the details of how a general object object is represented. All that it must know is the type of the object and the name of a program used to present that objects of that type. A difficulty with this approach is that the visual integrity of the document is destroyed by having to display the object in a separate window from that used for the main document. Consider, for example, a document that contains an electronic spread-sheet and an explanation, in text, of the spread-sheet; the explanation (a text object) cannot be viewed simultaneously with the spread-sheet itself (a general object).

Many of the difficulties with the Experimental model of multimedia documents are due to the fact that the implementation maintains relatively little

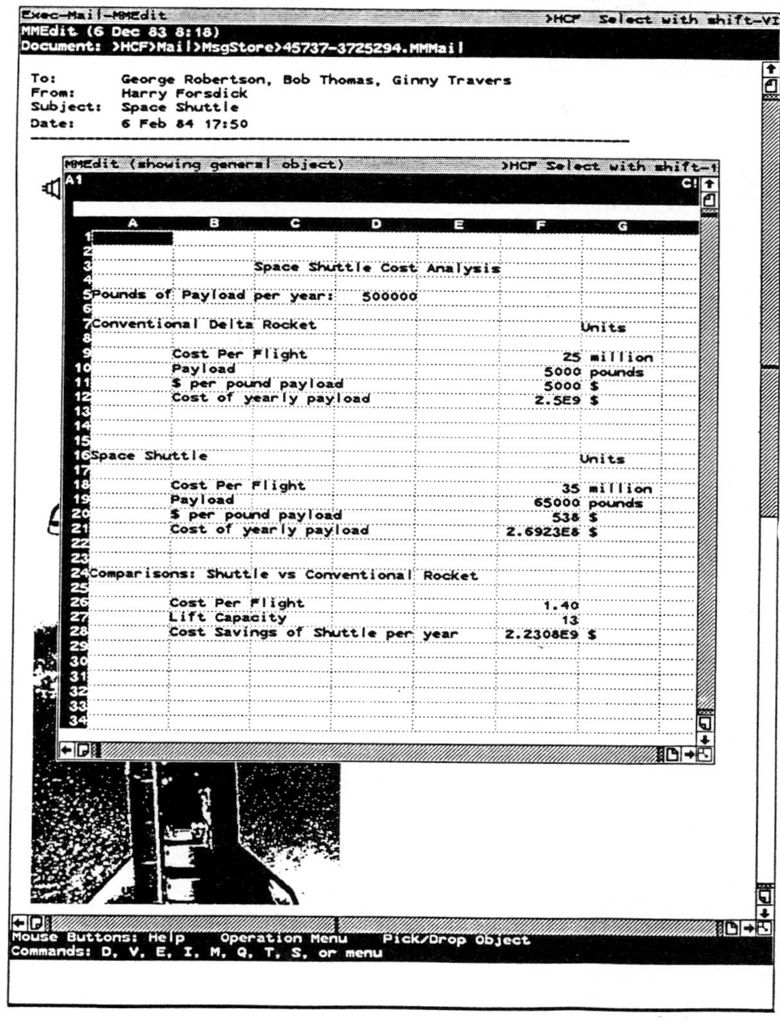

Figure 3: The presentation of a spread-sheet general object

information about the objects that make up a document and the interrelationships among them. This manifests itself in several ways. For text, it is difficult to change or reformat blocks of text once they have been entered into the document. After text is entered there is no provision for grouping lines into blocks which may be subsequently formatted or edited. For images, the symptoms resulting from maintaining insufficient information about objects are somewhat different. A variety of editing operations are provided including cropping, rotating, and scaling (reducing and enlarging). These operations are information lossy in the sense that when an image object is reduced and then enlarged by the same scale factor the result is loss of resolution. Another problem is there is no convenient mechanism for controlling the overlapping or grouping of objects and so, unusual and unpredictable interactions between objects on the display can occur.

The deficiencies of the Experimental model and its implementation are most evident by the difficulties of editing partially completed documents. However, as simple as it is, complex and sophisticated documents can be expressed using this model.

3. DARPA Internet Model

The DARPA Internet model [4] is the basis of a standard for representing multimedia documents in a machine independent manner for purposes of exchange among machines and document systems of possibly dissimilar architecture. In this model, objects, called "Presentation Elements", are organized hierarchically into a single composite document. The types of objects currently supported by the model include Text, Scanned Images, and Voice although there are plans for adding several additional types including Graphical Line Drawings.

To preserve the machine and device independence in the representation standard, certain attributes of documents are abstracted from their concrete (usually machine dependent) representations. As a result, the specification for these attributes tend to be qualitative or relative in nature as opposed to quantitative or absolute. For example, the positions of the objects that comprise a document are not specified explicitly. Instead, the objects are organized into groups, and the presentation of objects within a group is specified as being "sequential", "simultaneous" or "independent". The interpretation of these descriptions is left imprecise in order to permit a wide variety of implementations. A possible implementation of "sequential" is to divide the display surface into horizontal bands and to present the objects in sequence, one per band. A possible implementation of "simultaneous" is to present the objects side-by-side within one horizontal band. Figure 4 is an example of a document that could be encoded in this model. The underlying structure of the document in figure 4 for the DARPA Internet Model is shown in figure 5.

Work to refine this model [2] has produced conventions for expressing common formatting styles for text, such as paragraph, enumeration, and itemization as well as for unformatted text (i.e., formatted explicitly by the user).

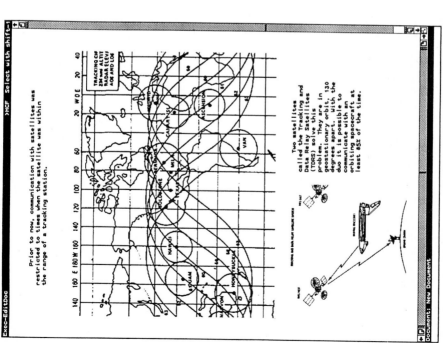

Figure 4: A Document expressed in DARPA Internet Model

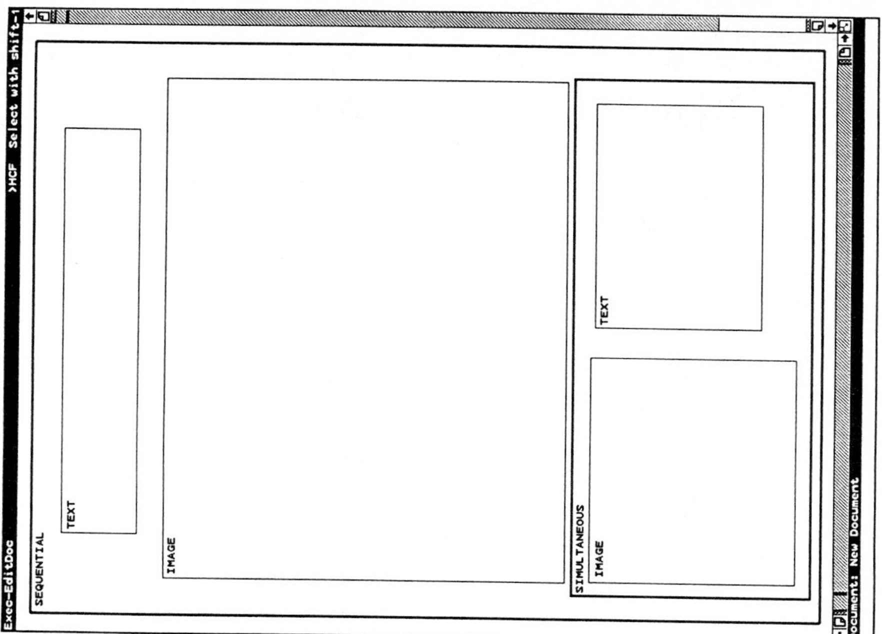

Figure 5: Underlying structure of the document presented in figure 4

4. Diamond Multimedia Documents

Based on experience with the Experimental and DARPA Internet models, we developed a model of multimedia documents for the initial version of Diamond. The major differences between the Diamond model and the other two are:

- o There are several alternative means of positioning objects in the document including absolute and relative positioning.
- o Graphical drawings are supported as an explicit object type rather than through extension mechanisms (such as general objects).
- o Color is supported in a general way for all object types.

This model represents an improvement over the Experimental model and an extension of the ideas in the current DARPA Internet model.

In practice, the expressive power that can be attained by a document model is largely determined by the software (e.g., the editor) used to produce documents according to the model. The current document editor for Diamond limits certain degrees of freedom possible in the model. It also automatically performs certain operations not addressed in the model in order to achieve a balance between expressive power and simplicity. These restrictions and additions include:

- o Different objects cannot overlap. This makes it easier for users to edit documents. Since objects don't overlap, there can be no ambiguity when a user points to an object as part of an editing operation as to which object is to be manipulated. Interrelations between objects can be represented explicitly by a linking connection (represented by an arrow) from a feature in one object to a feature in another object.
- o All objects that have a meaningful visual representation are displayed directly on the display surface. The distraction and confusion that is caused when some objects are directly displayed and others need additional action by the user to be seen (as was the case with the Experimental Model) has been eliminated.
- o Automatic formatting in several different styles is provided for text objects.
- o Assistance is provided for automatically formatting a composite multimedia document by adjusting the positions of objects so that they conform to standard margins and pre-determined inter-object spacings.

The style of a Diamond document (see figure 6) is similar to documents that appear as published books and journal articles, with a few significant differences. These differences include:

- o Voice: Books and journals have no means of incorporating voice. When displaying documents that contain voice, Diamond represents the voice passages by icons on the display screen, and provides means to playback the vocal passages.
- o Annotations: Footnotes provide a means for an author to annotate a

book or journal article. With formal publications however, there are no convenient means for readers to share their comments about a document with each other and with the author. Shared annotations to a document are feasible with electronic documents. Diamond supports annotations by allowing users to "attach" comments (which are themselves documents) to a document. In the initial version of Diamond annotations are represented by icons displayed in the margin of the original document. The user must explicitly request to see the contents of an annotation by pointing to its icon and requesting "MoreDetail".

- o Document Layout: Document formatting in publishing is a fine art involving a large amount of human judgement in the way the parts of a document are laid out. Early versions of Diamond will not be able to automatically generate document layouts of the sophistication that a graphic artist can produce. However, Diamond provides means for users to control the layout of documents.

- o Resolution of Displays and Printers: The devices currently used in Diamond for displaying and printing documents have relatively low resolution (in terms of the quality of lines, characters and images they can represent) compared to the devices used for high quality published material.

A Diamond document is a collection of objects which may be represented either directly (e.g., text, images, graphics) or indirectly by means of icons (e.g., non-visual objects such as voice) on a two-dimensional surface such, as a window of a display device or a piece of paper. The types of objects that may appear in a Diamond document include:

- o Text: ASCII text passages similar to the contents of current electronic text messages [1]. In addition, Diamond supports multiple text fonts, and a variety of styles of formatted text, including paragraphs, itemization (indented, marked lists of points), enumeration (indented, numbered lists of points), and verbatim.

- o Graphics: Drawings including lines, geometric figures (rectangles, circles, ellipses, etc.), and text strings. Closed regions may be shaded with arbitrary textures (regular bit patterns that fill the regions). Groups of objects may be formed to provide a macro capability. The drawings in this paper were produced using Diamond.

- o Images: Digitized images of drawings, maps, photographs, and other pictures. Images may be represented in black and white as well as shades of gray and color. Although it is possible to send text and graphics as image data, because conversion of text or graphics to image form generally results in loss of information and expansion of data, image data is most suitable for visual information that cannot be represented in any of the other forms.

- o Voice: Voice passages encoded by a vocoder. The most natural use of vocal objects in a document will be as a comment or as an annotation to other objects in the message. However, because Diamond places no restrictions on the use of voice in documents, the major information content of a document may be one or more voice objects. Currently, Diamond uses LPC algorithms [5] for vocoding.

- o Connections: Linkages, represented by lines with arrows, that connect a point within one object to a point within another. For example, it is possible to compose a comment about a small feature of an image using speech and have a line drawn from the comment to point at the feature.

The Diamond software and the internal representation used for documents are designed to permit introduction of new media types. Support for additional types, such as electronic spread-sheets will be added to Diamond in the future.

A Diamond document is structured in the sense that information about the individual parts of the document (paragraphs, captions, labeled fields, line drawings, images, vocal passages, etc.) is preserved in the document. This structural information facilitates the standard presentation of documents (e.g., on different types and sizes of display surfaces) as well as editing evolving documents. The underlying structure of the document in figure 6 is presented in figure 7.

For composition, editing and viewing purposes, a Diamond document is organized as a set of non-overlapping boxes, each of which can contain source material of a given media type, plus connections that relate a point in one box to a point in another box. The boxes are positioned on a quarter plane, although to conform with established standards, the width is usually bounded to a standard width for sheets of paper. A box is specified by its width and height as well as its position[6].

The positions of boxes can be specified in absolute or relative terms. In absolute positioning, the coordinates of the upper left corner of the box are described. For relative positioning, the relationship between box A and box B is described in terms of sets of positioning descriptors such as Above, Below, Right Of, Left Of, Top Aligned, Bottom Aligned, Centered On, etc. Relative positioning is used to facilitate formatting of a document so that it can be shown on display surfaces with different shapes and sizes, a common need in current bitmap display window systems. For example, in Figure 8 a document whose objects are laid out in relative positioning is shown as it would be displayed in two different shaped windows. The relative sizes of objects whose presentation is flexible (such as text or graphics laid out or scaled to fit into a box) can be adjusted so that the presentation of the composite document is roughly the same, regardless of the shape of the display surface.

Boxes are also used to group objects into collections of source material of diverse media types[7]. The purpose of grouping the contents of a document in boxes is to help the author distinguish one piece of a document from another and to bind two distinct objects together so that they behave as one object for the purposes of positioning and editing. The reader sees minimal evidence of the box structure of a document. For example, in figure 6, some boxes appear in the document, primarily for the visual appeal of showing the reader the boundaries of a graphical object. Figure 9 shows the view seen by the author when editing the same document. In this case, the boxes are shown, although an attempt is made to minimize the clutter and confusion by showing only the most relevant ones. For example, in this document there are three text boxes grouped together (paragraph, enumeration, paragraph) although only the outer grouping box and the inner text enumeration box are shown explicitly. Displaying the enumeration box shows its extent and helps the author position the cursor if, for example, an additional point is to be added.

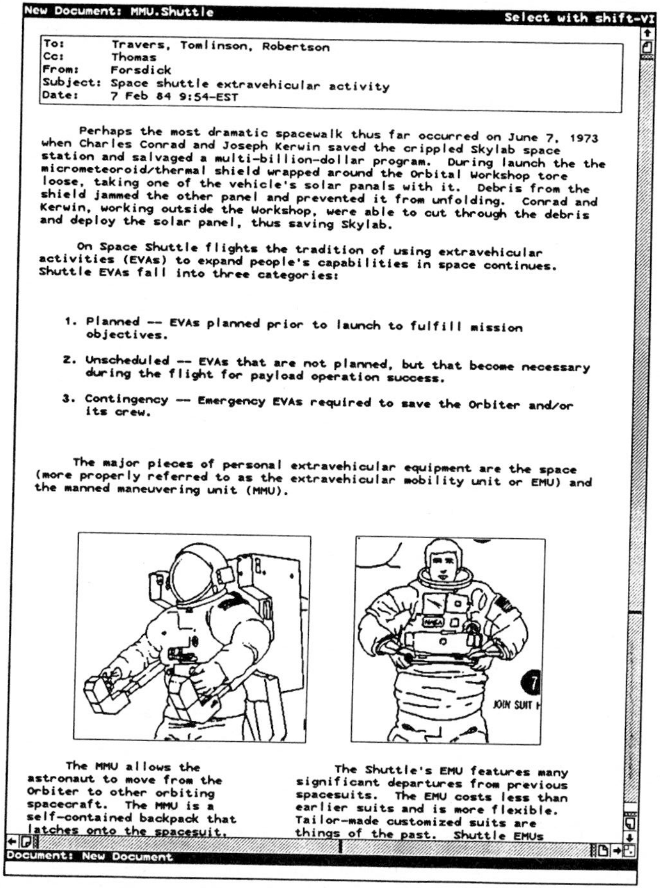

Figure 6: A Reader's view of a Diamond Document

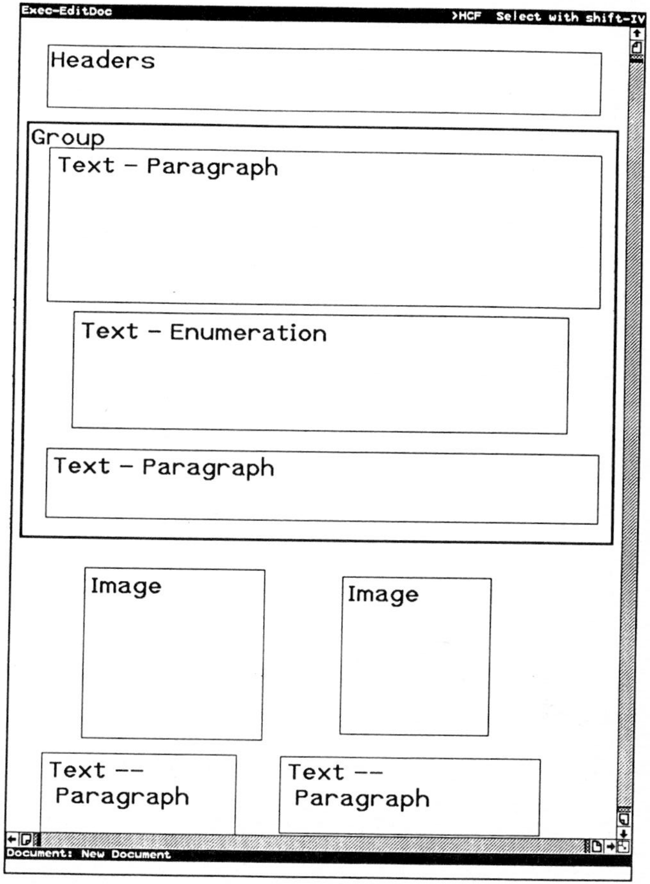

Figure 7: Underlying structure of the document presented in figure 6

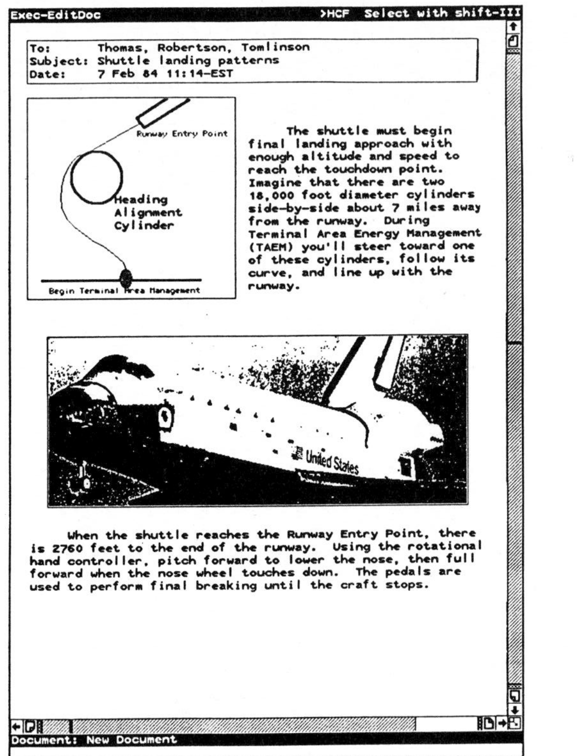

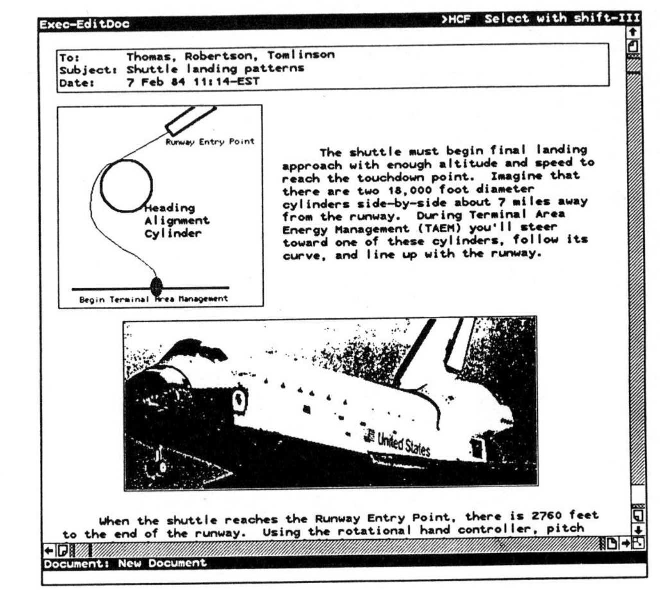

Figure 8: The same document displayed in different shaped windows

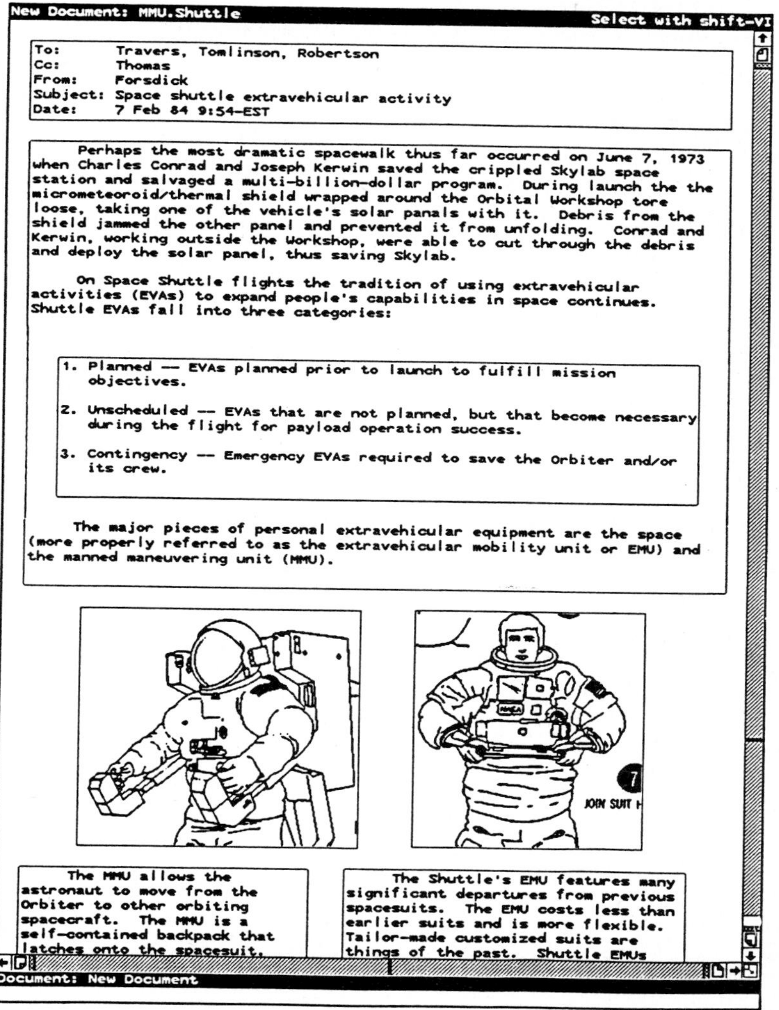

New Document: MMU.Shuttle   Select with shift-VI

To: Travers, Tomlinson, Robertson
Cc: Thomas
From: Forsdick
Subject: Space shuttle extravehicular activity
Date: 7 Feb 84 9:54-EST

Perhaps the most dramatic spacewalk thus far occurred on June 7, 1973 when Charles Conrad and Joseph Kerwin saved the crippled Skylab space station and salvaged a multi-billion-dollar program. During launch the the micrometeoroid/thermal shield wrapped around the Orbital Workshop tore loose, taking one of the vehicle's solar panals with it. Debris from the shield jammed the other panel and prevented it from unfolding. Conrad and Kerwin, working outside the Workshop, were able to cut through the debris and deploy the solar panel, thus saving Skylab.

On Space Shuttle flights the tradition of using extravehicular activities (EVAs) to expand people's capabilities in space continues. Shuttle EVAs fall into three categories:

1. Planned — EVAs planned prior to launch to fulfill mission objectives.
2. Unscheduled — EVAs that are not planned, but that become necessary during the flight for payload operation success.
3. Contingency — Emergency EVAs required to save the Orbiter and/or its crew.

The major pieces of personal extravehicular equipment are the space (more properly referred to as the extravehicular mobility unit or EMU) and the manned maneuvering unit (MMU).

The MMU allows the astronaut to move from the Orbiter to other orbiting spacecraft. The MMU is a self-contained backpack that latches onto the spacesuit.

The Shuttle's EMU features many significant departures from previous spacesuits. The EMU costs less than earlier suits and is more flexible. Tailor-made customized suits are things of the past. Shuttle EMUs

Document: New Document

Figure 9: The Author's view of a Diamond Document

5. Conclusion

This paper has described three models for multimedia documents that were investigated during the initial development of the Diamond multimedia document system. The Experimental model is adequate for expressing the appearance of multimedia documents laid out on a fixed size display surface. It [8] does not maintain sufficient information about the structure of a document to permit documents to be edited in a convenient way. Some of the more experimental features of this model (e.g., extensible object types) were omitted from the initial Diamond model in favor of a simplified style of presenting documents. The DARPA Internet document model is successful in recording structural information about objects in a document, although in an effort to be machine independent, some important layout characteristics, such as object positioning, are left loosely specified. The initial Diamond model, which combines features from the Experimental and DARPA Internet models, extends the previous models in ways that facilitate editing and object layout for presentation purposes.

All three models are relatively simplistic, and must be regarded as initial attempts to deal with multimedia electronic documents. More sophisticated models will evolve as experience with such documents is acquired. We plan to extend both the DARPA Internet model and the model currently supported by Diamond based on experience with the Diamond system.

NOTES

1. This work was sponsored by the Defense Advanced Research Projects Agency (DARPA) under Contract No. F30602-81-C-0256 which is monitored by the Rome Air Development Center (RADC). Views and conclusions contained in this report are the authors' and should not be interpreted as representing the official opinion or policy of DARPA, the U.S. Government, or any agency connected with them. This paper has been approved for public release and distribution is unlimited.

2. Throughout this paper we speak of Diamond as a system which handles "documents" rather than as a system which only handles "messages". In our view, a message is a document that has been sent from one user to another. The more general term, "document", has been chosen because only part of what a modern message system does is concerned with message transmission; much is concerned with the preparation, storage, management and processing of documents which may or may not be sent as messages.

3. Rows and columns of interrelated numeric data of the sort manipulated by programs such as VisiCalc.

4. A workstation in this class includes a powerful processor, high resolution graphics, a substantial amount of main memory (1-2 MByte), an interface to a high performance local area network, and possibly secondary storage, and it would be configured with a graphical pointing device and voice I/O equipment.

5. In this case, the object labeled "Select to show: Space Shuttle Analysis"

6. Positions and distances are expressed in pixels, and every document contains the resolution of the environment in which it was created in

pixels per inch.

7. In this special case, the enclosing box completely overlaps the boxes it groups together.

8. More precisely, the software that implements it.

REFERENCES

[1] Crocker, D. H.
Standard for the Format of ARPA Internet Text Messages.
Technical Report RFC 822, DARPA Network Working Group, August, 1982.

[2] Finn, G. G., Katz, A. R., Postel, J., Forsdick, H. C.
Proposal for the Body Item for a Multimedia Message.
Technical Report, USC Information Sciences Institute and Bolt Beranek and Newman, Inc., April, 1983.

[3] Forsdick, H. C, Thomas, R. H., Crowley, T. R., Robertson, G. G., Schaaf, R. W., Tomlinson, R. S., Travers, V. M.
Diamond: A Distributed Multimedia Document System.
Technical Report 5568, Bolt Beranek and Newman, Inc., February, 1984.

[4] Postel, J.
Internet Multimedia Mail Document Format.
Technical Report RFC 767, DARPA Network Working Group, March, 1982.

[5] Tremain, T. E.
The Government Standard Linear Predictive Coding Algorithm: LPC-10.
Speech Technology :40-49, April, 1982.

Computer-Based Message Services
H.T. Smith (Editor)
Elsevier Science Publishers B.V. (North-Holland)

An Experimental Internetwork Multimedia Mail System

Alan R. Katz

Information Sciences Institute
University of Southern California
Marina Del Rey, California
U.S.A.

Abstract:

A description is given of an of an experimental multimedia mail system which operates within the DoD. Internet Environment. The system runs on a PERQ personal computer and allows the user to compose, send, receive, read, and edit multimedia messages which contain text, image (bitmap), and voice data.

I. Introduction

This paper describes the implementation and use of an experimental multimedia mail system, in particular the user interface program called MMM. Using MMM, it is possible for a user to create a multimedia message which may contain various types of text, image, and voice data and to then send the message to other hosts within the Department of Defense (DoD) Internet Environment (the Internet).

MMM is written in Pascal and runs on a PERQ personal computer equipped with a large bitmap display, a local hard disk, and a connection to a 3 Mbit Ethernet. A CHI-5 LPC speech box connected to the PERQ's RS-232 port provides voice input and output.

Hardcopy pictures may be scanned by a Rapicom Facsimile machine, then translated into bitmaps for inclusion in multimedia messages. These bitmaps may be edited, or others created using a bitmap sketching program (which is also a part of MMM).

Section II of this paper briefly describes the DoD Internet and the family of protocols used in this environment. The physical data connections between the PERQ running MMM and the various networks used are also discussed. Section III describes the specific protocol used. This protocol allows general types of structured data to be transfered within the Internet. Section IV describes the subset of this protocol implemented in MMM and gives a detailed account of how MMM works and how one would use it to compose, send, and receive messages. Section V discusses our experience with this system and the problems encountered. Finally, Section VI outlines our plans for the future.

II. The DoD Internet Environment

For the past several years, the DoD's Defense Advanced Research Projects Agency (DARPA) has sponsored research on various types of computer networks, including the ARPANET, digital packet radio networks, and digital packet satellite networks. A family of protocols was developed to allow all hosts in the interconnected set of these networks (refered to as the Internet) to communicate with one another. (An interconnected set of networks such as this as been termed a *Catenet* [1].) In particular, the Internet Protocol (IP) [2] and the Transmission Control Protocol (TCP) [3] were developed.

This research is supported by the Defense Advanced Research Projects Agency under Contract No. MDA903 81 C 0335. Views and conclusions contained in this report are the author's and should not be interpreted as representing the official opinion or policy of DARPA, the U.S. Government, or any person or agency connected with them.

Hosts in the Internet range from very small personal computers on local area networks to large mainframes with many users on long distance networks such as the ARPANET. Data communication between these hosts is built upon IP datagrams. Data transfer via datagrams is unreliable, and higher level protocols (such as TCP) are necessary to ensure reliable communication. Networks within the Internet are connected to one another via gateways which route datagrams through the various networks, from gateway to gateway, until they arrive at their destination. (More information on the model of the Internet may be found in reference [4].)

In addition to IP and TCP, the User Datagram Protocol (UDP) [5] allows users to send IP datagrams. A simple file transfer protocol called the Trivial File Transfer Protocol (TFTP) [6] has been developed to allow the transmission of files using UDP.

At USC/Information Sciences Institute (ISI), we have three PERQ personal computers which are connected to a 3 Mbit Ethernet. We also have six TOPS-20 PDP-10 KL computers which are on the ARPANET. Multimedia messages created on the PERQs are transfered to the TOPS-20 system using TFTP through a PDP-11 gateway. These machines and networks are shown in figure 1.

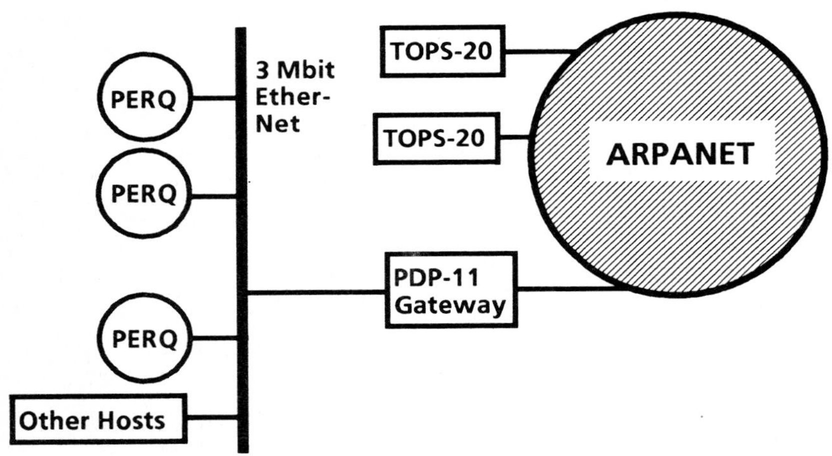

Figure 1:
Connection of PERQs to ARPANET at ISI

III. The Internet Message System

An Internet Multimedia Mail Transfer Protocol [7,8] has been developed at ISI which defines a mechanism for the transfer of messages through the Internet. These messages may contain very general types of data including text, voice, image, facsimile, and graphics. The protocol is general enough to allow additional types of data to be added in the future.

The protocol is implemented in a process called a Message Processing Module (MPM). The MPMs are responsible for the routing, transmission, and delivery of messages. Multimedia messages are created by a user with a User Interface Program (UIP). Messages so created are then submitted to an MPM for delivery. At ISI, MMM is our UIP and runs on the PERQs. The MPMs, written in BLISS and some Macro10, run on PDP-10 TOPS-20 machines.

The Multimedia Mail Transfer Protocol assumes a reliable method of data transmission within the Internet and is therefore built upon TCP. The place of this protocol in the normal hierarchy of Internet protocols is depicted in figure 2.

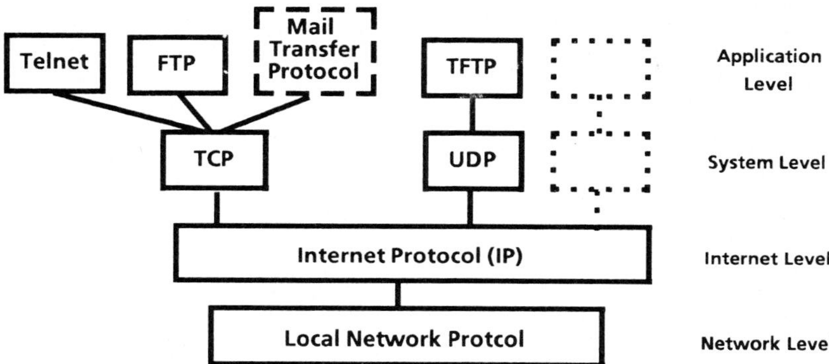

Figure 2:
Relationships of Internet Protocols

The basic unit transfered between MPMs, called a message, consists of three parts: a transaction identifier, which uniquely identifies the message, a command part, and the document. The document contains a header and a body.

The command part of the message contains information used by the MPM to route the message. Some of this information is supplied by the UIP. The document is not looked at by the MPM, but is displayed to the user by the UIP.

The header portion of the document corresponds to the date, to, from, etc., fields of a typical letter or inter-office memo. The body of the document contains the actual data of the message. This data is a structure of basic data types (as defined in reference [7]). There are types for exactly representing integers, strings, booleans, etc. Two other elements are used for building data structures: the list and the property list. Lists are simple lists of elements (which may include other lists). Property lists are lists of pairs of elements, where the first element of each pair names the pair. The names of the name/value pairs in a property list are required to be unique.

References [9] and [10] describe the format of the document of a multimedia message. The body of the document may be a simple character string or a complex structure of lists and property lists. It may be encrypted in part or in whole. Possible data structures allowed in the body include voice, paragraphs of text, and graphics.

The presentation of information in the message body can be compared to a seminar, where the speaker displays slides and other visual aids while providing a running commentary. The time coordination of such a presentation is captured in the body structure. There are three types of time ordered control possible within the document. They are: SEQUENTIAL, SIMULTANEOUS, and INDEPENDENT.

Sequential data items are presented one at a time, in the order listed. Simultaneous data is intended for synchronous viewing, and independent data can be presented in any time order. For example, one could have a text item displayed alone, then have graphics displayed while simultaneously listening to a voice description of the graphics.

Because of the very wide range of possible items within a document, we realized that in order to implement a UIP it would be necessary, at least at first, to limit this range. This is described in the next section.

IV. The UIP Implementation: MMM

Introduction

In the summer of 1982, a first attempt was made at limiting the possible data types allowed in a document body for the purpose of demonstrating the Multimedia Message System [11]. It was decided that, for the intial series of experiments, the only media allowed would be TEXT, VOICE, and IMAGE. The only time control allowed would be SEQUENTIAL.

TEXT data would be structured as a list of paragraphs only. (This was later extended to allow four types of TEXT data: Paragraph, Enumerate, Itemize, and Verbatim; roughly corresponding to commands in the text formatting system Scribe [12]). VOICE data would be LPC (Linear Predictive Coding, a way of digitizing voice [13,14]) only. The LPC data would be represented by a bitstream data type which represents a stream of speech data at 2400 bps. IMAGE data would be represented by raw bitmaps only (not compressed or encoded). It was suggested that these bitmaps not exceed 512 pels horizontally by 663 pels vertically (which is the same aspect ratio as 8 1/2 by 11).

It was expected that there would be at least two ways messages could be presented to the user. In the first way, there would be separate bitmap and text windows which would scroll separately. In the second way, both bitmap and text would be displayed in the same window in the order given and would scroll or page as necessary. In either case, voice data would not take up any space on the screen, and if a voice element appeared after an image element, it would be intended that the image be displayed while the voice was played.

The first approach was taken in the PERQ implementation, MMM, at ISI. The following subsections describe the program in detail.

Hardware

MMM is implemented on a PERQ Systems (previously Three Rivers Computer Corporation) PERQ personal computer. The PERQ has a 16-bit microprogrammed processor, a high resolution 1024 by 768 bit mapped raster display, a 12 megabyte Winchester hard disk, a megabyte of memory, and a tablet. It is also equipped with a standard RS-232 I/O interface.

The PERQ is optimized to be programmed in Pascal. Software is provided to make it easy to access the display (which is very fast) and for multiple window management.

Voice functions are provided by connecting the PERQ's RS-232 port to a CHI-5 Voicebox. The CHI-5 is a programmable array processor. It needs to be downloaded with a program before it is able to perform voice I/O. The CHI-5 is connected to a speaker and a microphone. Later, we also used a Lincoln Labs voicebox, which does not need to be downloaded.

The PERQ is connected to a 3 Mbit Ethernet as described in Section II. Using TFTP, it can send multimedia messages to the MPM running on the TOPS-20 systems. The interconnection of the MMM hardware is shown in figure 3.

Data Representation

In general, a message can be very large. One reason for this is that there can be a very large amount of data in a bitmap or voice data element. Thus, an entire bitmap may not fit into the availible PERQ memory and must therefore be stored in a file.

In MMM, the various parts of a message are stored in seperate files. The message structure, which contains pointers to the bitmap and voice data files, is itself stored in a file. This internal representation differs from the standard message representation, in which the entire message (including bitmaps and voice data) consists of one continuous stream of bits. MMM must therefore convert messages to and from the standard representation in order to send or receive messages using the MPM. This conversion process is transparent to the user, although reading in or sending out messages might take longer than the user would expect.

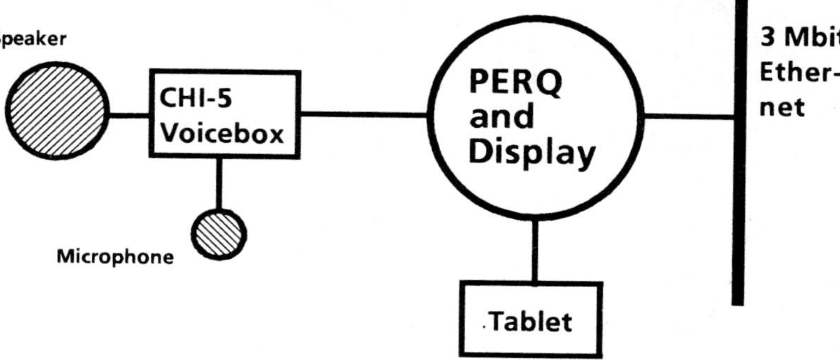

Figure 3:
Hardware Connections to the PERQ

Because bitmaps and voice data are stored in separate files, programs other than MMM may access and operate on them without knowing anything about the Multimedia Mail Protocol. For example, it is possible to display and edit a stored bitmap using the bitmap editor.

Bitmaps

There are two ways to create a bitmap for inclusion in a multimedia message. The first is to scan an existing image with a facsimile machine, and the second is to create a bitmap with a bitmap editor. The bitmap editor (which is a greatly modified version of a program supplied with the PERQ) can be run separately or under MMM.

At ISI, we use a Rapicom 450 facsimile machine. Programs exists both on the TOPS-20 systems and on the PERQ to store and send facsimile images from the Rapicom into a file and to convert that file into a standard bitmap [15,16] which can then be edited or viewed with the bitmap editor. The bitmap editor allows the user to view part or all of a bitmap, to draw an image using various brushes (analogous to using pens with differently shaped points), and to copy, move, or erase portions of the bitmap. It is also possible for a user to enter text in various fonts into the bitmap. If the bitmap is too large to fit into the display, the user can edit parts of it at a time.

A standard Rapicom 450 (8 1/2 by 11 inch) fascimile page, converted to a bitmap is 1726 by approximately 2200 bits (corresponding to 200 bits per inch). Since the display on the PERQ is 768 by 1024 bits, this page cannot be fully displayed unless it is compressed. The bitmap editor can perform this function.

Voice-related functions

If the CHI-5 Voicebox is used for voice I/O, the user must first download it with a special program. This takes a few minutes. Then, to enter voice, the user gives the appropriate command to MMM and simply speaks into the microphone. When finished speaking, the user types control-C to terminate input. Similarly, to listen to voice data, the user gives the command to MMM and the speech data is heard from the CHI-5 speaker.

Because of the time it takes for the PERQ disk to access a page, all voice data must be read into memory before being sent to the CHI-5. Thus, there is a delay of a few seconds before voice output and after voice input while the file is being read or written.

How MMM looks to the User

When the user firsts runs MMM, four windows are displayed: the bitmap window, the information window, the command window, and the text window (see Figure 4). Commands are entered by *bugging* with the tablet in a menu in the command window, with additional information being provided with the keyboard. MMM can be in three Modes: Top Level, Outline Mode, and Create Mode. Each of these modes has its own list of possible commands, which are displayed in the command window.

Headers (each containing a brief summary of a message) are displayed in the information window. Whenever a new message is received or created, a new header for that message is displayed.

It is possible to Play a message by using the Play command and pointing to the header of the message to be played. When a message is played, information such as the To and From fields of the message is displayed in the bitmap window. Descriptions of the various entities (text, bitmap, or voice) are displayed in the information window. After the user has read this and has hit a carriage return, the text entities in the message are displayed in the text window, bitmaps are displayed in the bitmap window, and voice entities are played on the CHI-5. If the bitmap is too large to fit into the window, the user has the option of specifying which portion to view, the default being the middle portion. When the text fills up the text window, it is scrolled.

If the user wants to look at particular entities in the message out of order, he can go into Outline Mode, which allows the user to view particular entities and to edit or store them.

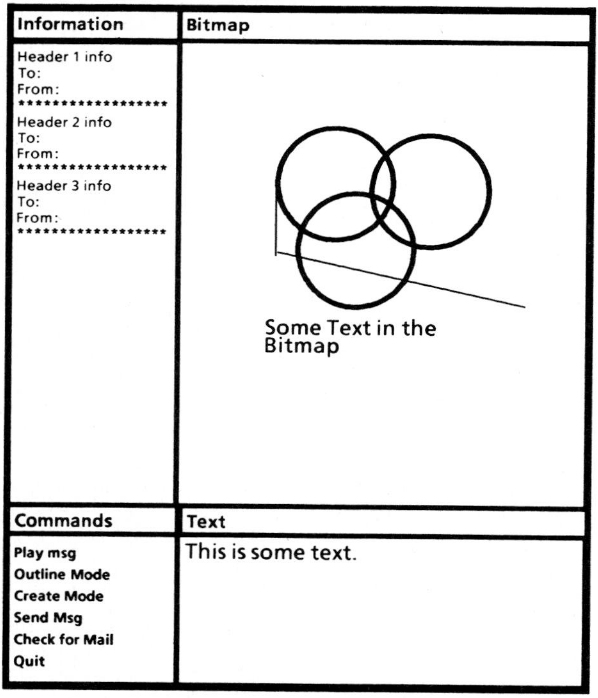

Figure 4:
The MMM Display

Messages may be created via Create Mode. In this mode, the user may enter the names and addresses of receipients, enter a subject field, and enter bitmaps, voice, or text data. Bitmaps may come from a file (which was created earlier with the bitmap editor or from the fascimile machine) or may be created on the spot. The same is true for voice or text data. When the user is satisfied with the composition of the multimedia message, he may leave Create Mode and the message is then created and stored. A header for that message will appear in the information window when the user is in Top Level Mode.

Sending and Receiving Messages: Communication with the MPM

In order to read in new messages which may be waiting, the user must explicitly tell MMM to read them in using the Check for New Mail command. The PERQ cannot continually check for new messages since the operating system does not provide for parallel processes to be run.

As was mentioned previously, the MPM at ISI runs on a TOPS-20 system on the ARPANET. Each MMM user must have a directory on that system into which the MPM will place new mail and from which the MPM will read messages to be sent. When the user uses the Check for New Mail command, MMM attempts to TFTP (see section II) a file containing that user's incoming mail. If the TFTP is successful, MMM converts the message into it's internal representation and then displays a header for that message in the information window. If the TFTP is unsuccessful, MMM notifies the user that no new mail exists. If a new message is read in, the user may outline or read the message as described in the previous subsection.

Similarly, after creating a message, the user must use the Send command to actually send the message. Then, MMM converts from the MMM internal format for the message and TFTPs the message to the TOPS-20 host, where the MPM will pick it up and send it on its way. MMM also sends a UDP datagram to a server on the TOPS-20 system which tells the MPM to look for new mail in the specified directory for that user (the MPM also checks all directories for new mail by itself at specific intervals).

V. Experience and Results

In October 1982, we demonstrated the MMM/MPM system by composing multimedia messages containing various types of text, bitmaps, and voice data; sending them to our MPM which then delivered them to their destinations; and receiving and displaying the multimedia replies. We were able to send messages to Bolt Beranek and Newman, Inc. (BBN) and the Massachusetts Institute of Technology (MIT) in Cambridge, Massachusetts, and to receive replies from BBN (MIT was able to view our messages but was unable, at the time, to create messages of its own). In one particular message, we sent a bitmap and some voice data to BBN and they replied with a bitmap depicting how our bitmap looked as displayed on their system.

We have recently been running MPMs on two TOPS-20 hosts and have been sending multimedia mail routinely using both of them to and from the three PERQs at ISI.

A number of problems were encountered with the PERQ, in particular with the RS-232 interface. When one alternates between sending and receiving data through the RS-232 port (as one must do to interface with the CHI-5 Voicebox), the port will sometimes stop sending data, and will send out many ASCII nulls. This destroys the downloaded program in the CHI-5 and the user must stop and redownload. Even when this does not happen, other problems with the RS-232 port cause voice I/O to be somewhat tricky and unreliable.

Also, while it is possible to perform both speech input and output using a special program separate from MMM, when the program was incorporated into MMM (which is a rather large program), the processor became too slow to keep up with incoming voice. Thus one may listen to voice in MMM, but one must use a separate program to create a voice data file.

On the other hand, the bitmap display and editing parts of MMM work extremely well. The display is very fast, considering its high resolution. Other than the problems encountered with voice, MMM seems to work well and is regularly used in the Internet Project at ISI.

VI. Future Plans

Because of the problems encountered with the PERQ and because ISI plans to utilize personal workstations (probably Xerox 8010 processors) to a much greater extent in the future, we have decided to implement the next version of a UIP on a Xerox 8010. The Xerox system allows multiple processes, and presumably we will not encounter the RS-232 problems that have plagued us on the PERQ.

The MPM continues to run on our TOPS-20 systems and at several other sites on the ARPANET. This makes it possible to exchange multimedia messages with other organizations that implement UIPs.

Recently, a system has been written to use a Packet Voice Terminal (PVT), connected to the Internet, as a voice server. When this system is incorporated into MMM, the PERQ will be able to send packets containing voice data to the PVT. The PVT will then call the user on his telephone and play the voice through the receiver. A similar chain of events will allow the user to enter voice data. This system will eliminate the need for each PERQ to have its own voicebox and will improve performance, as we will be able to bypass the RS-232 port.

VI. Acknowledgements

This research was done as a part of the ISI Internetwork Concepts Research Project and grateful acknowledgement is made to Jon Postel for his guidance and suggestions concerning this work. The MPM was programmed by Greg Finn.

References

[1] Pouzin, L., "A Proposal for Interconnecting Packet Switching Networks, " Proceedings of EUROCOMP, Bronel University, May 1974.

[2] Postel, J.,"Internet Protocol", RFC 791, USC Information Sciences Intitute, September 1981.

[3] Postel, J., "Transmission Control Protocol", RFC 793, USC Information Sciences Intitute, September 1981.

[4] Cerf, V. "The Catenet Model for Internetworking", IEN 48, Defense Advanced Research Projects Agency, July 1978.

[5] Postel, J., "User Datagram Protocol", RFC 768, USC Information Sciences Intitute, August 1980.

[6] Sollins, K., "The TFTP Protocol", RFC 783, MIT Laboratory for Computer Science, June 1981.

[7] Postel, J., "Internet Multimedia Mail Transfer Protocol", RFC 759-revised, USC Information Sciences Intitute, March 1982.

[8] Postel, J., "An Internetwork Message Structure", Sixth Data Communication Symposium, November 1979.

[9] Postel, J., "Internet Multimedia Mail Document Format", RFC 767-revised, USC Information Sciences Intitute, March 1982.

[10] Finn, G. and Postel, J., "Data Structures and Presentation Control for Multimedia Computer Mail", Proceedings of EASTCON, November 1981.

[11] Katz, A., "Proposal for the Document Format for a Multimedia Message Experiment", ISI Internal Memo, July 1982.

[12] Reid, B. and Walker, J., "Scribe - Introductory User's Manual", Unilogic Ltd., May 1980.

[13] Hofstetter, E., Tierney, J., and Wheeler, O. "Microprocessor Realization of a Linear Predictive Vocoder", IEEE Transactions on Acoustics, Speech, and Signal Processing, Vol. ASSP-25, Number 5, October 1977.

[14] Malpass, M. and Feldma, J. "A User's Guide for the Lincoln LPC Speech Processing Peripheral", MIT Lincoln Laboratory Project Report PSST-2, April 1983.

[15] Katz, A., "Decoding Facsimile Data from the Rapicom 450", RFC 798, USC Information Sciences Intitute, September 1981.

[16] Katz, A., "Format for Bitmap Files", RFC 797, USC Information Sciences Intitute, September 1981.

NOTE: *In the above references, the term RFC refers to papers in the ARPA "Request for Comments" series and IEN refers to ARPA "Internet Experiment Notes." These notes may be obtained from the Network Information Center, SRI International, Menlo Park, California, or from the author.*

PART 3:

USER INTERFACE ARCHITECTURE

Computer-Based Message Services
H.T. Smith (Editor)
Elsevier Science Publishers B.V. (North-Holland)

A USER AGENT FOR MULTIPLE COMPUTER-BASED MESSAGE SERVICES

A. Roger Kaye
Systems and Computer Engineering Department
Carleton University, Ottawa, Canada, K1S 5B6

and

Russell McDowell
Dept. 2X11, Bell-Northern Research
P.O. Box 3511, Stn. C, Ottawa, Canada, K1Y 4H7

A user agent, for computer-based message systems, is described of a type which could reside within either a professional workstation or a server on a local-area network. It is capable of accessing multiple, external CBMS of both the conventional and the UA/MTA type. It provides the user with a single UA which can be integrated with his local document creation and storage facilities and mediates his interaction with the external CBMS.

1. INTRODUCTION

The work reported in this paper is part of a program concerned with the needs of the office principal, (manager or professional) for technological support in the office. It approaches the need for enhanced communication facilities, in the form of CBMS, in the context of other needs and of the current environment of the many existing public and private CBMS together with the promise of new, CCITT-standard CBMS in the near future.

It is assumed, in this work, that the office principal will have a need for technological support by a multiplicity of different services of which CBMS is only one. Furthermore he will use each of these services on an intermittent basis, will have minimal time available for training and no interest in learning the multiple command sets of different systems when they involve similar functions or subfunctions. These needs can only be met by providing access to all services through a single workstation with effectively integrated software and consistent command sets. Where use is made of services which originate externally to the local facilities, it may be necessary for the local facility to mediate the user's access to the external service in order to maintain consistency of the interface.

CBMS is a specific, and important, example of the above situation. For some time to come many office principals will need access to several different CBMS in order to reach all their correspondents. In many cases they will need access to a corporate CBMS and to at least one public CBMS. Many corporations already make use of more than one internal CBMS.

In such a situation, one problem is the necessity of repeated dialling and logging on and off various CBMS. Another, equally serious, problem is that each of them provides editing and filing systems despite the fact that anyone who uses an integrated workstation facility will undoubtedly already have editing and filing capabilities with which he is familiar. Thus the user is forced to learn a number of different, and entirely redundant, command sets. Furthermore, his filing system becomes fragmented and consequently ineffective.

In the medium to long term, these problems may be averted by the introduction of public and private CBMS built according to the proposed new CCITT standards based on the User Agent (UA)-Message Transfer Agent (MTA) architecture [1]. In this case the UA may be fully integrated with local software and will communicate with an MTA according to a standard protocol. Nevertheless, in the short to medium term, the user will need to use CBMS which are not constructed in this way.

This paper describes an initial attempt at designing and building a UA capable of mediating access to multiple, external CBMS of the non-standardized type. Adding the capability to access CCITT standard MTAs would be a relatively straightforward undertaking. The UA described is of a type which could reside within either a professional workstation or a special server on a local-area network. It could also be the basis of a special facility associated with an MTA enabling it to intercommunicate with other non-CCITT-type MTAs.

The paper reviews the difficulties encountered in an initial implementation, the solutions which have been tried and the design approach used. It concentrates on those difficulties which would be encountered in any implementation: those which are associated with communicating with the external CBMS. The initial implementation was carried out on a 8080-based micro-computer running CP/M. It was recognized at the outset that this was far from an ideal environment but it was available. The software was structured for portability and written in the C language with the intention of porting it to other systems later [2].

2. FUNCTIONAL SPECIFICATION

The following functions are implemented in the experimental UA. The message handling features were selected in order to implement the basic features offered by most CBMS but they are only a subset of the functions specified in the CCITT standards.

Specify external CBMS hosts.
Identify external CBMS to be used and enter the necessary log-on/off and command profile.

Construct or maintain directory of known correspondents. Enter, delete or correct names of correspondents with identification of their CBMS and their address or identifier within it.

GET mail
Log-on to the external CBMS.
Retrieve mail from in-box.
Transfer to UA in-box.
Log-off the external CBMS.
Repeat for all CBMS unless single CBMS access is requested.

Review incoming mail
- List contents of in-box.
- Read specified messages.

Create and address messages.
- Reply to incoming message with automatic creation of reply header, including address.
- Annotate and forward incoming messages.
- Forward message to a new recipient with or without annotation.
- Originate a message.
- Create copies for multiple recipients.

In conjunction with last three sub-functions:
- Address mail by specifying the name of the recipient whose address is in a directory of known correspondents.

Send mail.
- Log-on to required external CBMS.
- Transfer appropriate contents of out-box.
- Log-off external CBMS.
- Repeat until out-box empty.

File messages.
- Store copies of incoming or outgoing messages in the UA file system.

3. DESIGN APPROACH

3.1 User's Conceptual View

The conceptual view of the UA, presented to the user, is based on the familiar model of an office environment. The user has an inbox in which he finds all incoming mail. There is a "desktop", or workspace, area where incoming messages are located for reading and subsequent action and where the user creates an outgoing message. Outgoing mail, to be sent via external CBMS, is stored temporarily in an outbox until the end of the user's session, when it is forwarded. Finally, there is a "filing cabinet" where the user may save copies of any messages that have been received or created. This model is common to many CBMS.

In addition, the user, or a technical support person, must be aware of the need to specify the means of accessing and controlling the various external CBMS to be used.

At the beginning of, or prior to, a session of dealing with mail, a user issues a single command which causes the UA to access all known CBMS in turn, or a specific one if preferred, and to retrieve all messages from it. The user then proceeds to deal with this mail and to initiate new messages using only the command set and facilities of the UA. At the end of a session the UA automatically accesses the necessary CBMS in order to send all messages and copies.

3.2 Architecture and File Structure

Figure 1 depicts the inter-relationship of the various UA components. The user interacts only with the UA process itself. When an external CBMS has to be accessed, it is done automatically by the UA. The information necessary for the UA to gain access to the various CBMS is contained in the CBMS-commands file. In addition to the syntax of the commands and of the expected responses from the CBMS, the UA requires information that is peculiar to each user, such as his userid and login passwords for each of the CBMS. This information is kept in a separate "user data" file which would be protected by encryption in a full development of the UA. Thus within an organization each user would have the same copy of the commands file, but the user data file would be modified for each user.

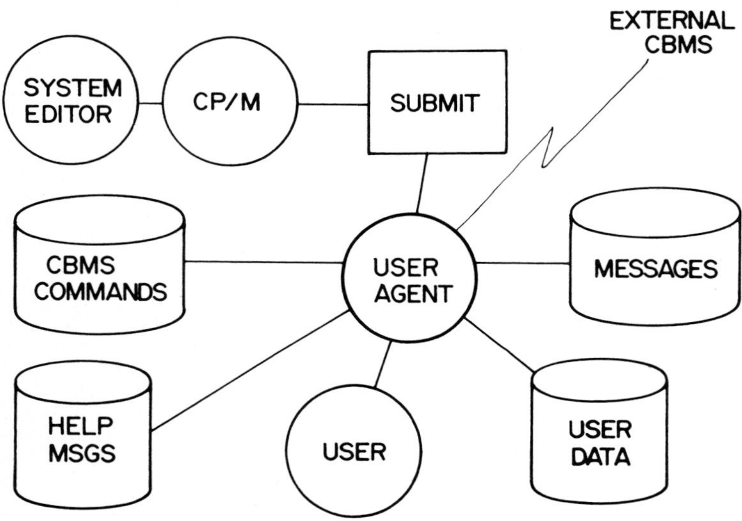

Figure 1: Interactions Between System Elements

Messages, in the various stages of their processing, are stored in message files which include the in- and out-boxes.

There is a "help" file which contains information on the error messages and on-line help facilities that are provided to the user. Whenever an error occurs or the user requests help, the UA uses a code number to find the appropriate message to display to the user. In this way a context-dependent help facility is provided.

As discussed in the introduction, it was a design objective to use the local system tools whenever common functions, such as editing, are required. Therefore the diagram shows that the UA will access the system editor whenever the user is editing messages. This is done through facilities provided by the operating system. Currently the only system tool that is used by the UA is the system editor although there are no fundamental restrictions on using other facilities as well.

4. IMPLEMENTATION

An experimental version of the above architecture was implemented on an 8080, CP/M-based microcomputer. The following paragraphs outline the techniques that were used.

The experiment was conducted using three different CBMS. The first was Envoy-100, a public CBMS offered by the major telephone companies of Canada. Envoy-100 is accessible only through Datapac, a national, public, packet switching network. The dial-up access ports to Datapac support virtually every common, low-level, terminal protocol. The second was COCOS, a private, corporate CBMS running on an IBM mainframe, operating in half-duplex mode over local, dial-up ports. The third was the CBMS offered by The Source, a public information utility oriented primarily to the hobbyist market and accessed via Datapac.

4.1 CBMS-Commands File

The CBMS-commands file contains the data necessary for accessing the various external CBMS and for communicating with them without the use of a high-level protocol.

The experimental UA was developed using the concept of various facilities based on macro instructions. These facilities do not necessarily have a one-to-one correspondence with commands on the external CBMS as can be seen from the explanation below.

For each external CBMS, the CBMS-commands file contains a separate section containing the information necessary for the following UA facilities:

Logon - number to dial
- Datapac network commands
- host login sequence
- access to the CBMS

Logout - reverse procedure of logon, including dropping of the network and telephone connections

Checkmail - determine whether there is mail to be collected from the CBMS

Read - collect mail for deposit in the UA inbox

Send - send mail from the UA outbox via the CBMS

Endsend - exits from the input mode of the CBMS

Analyse - analyse the header of all incoming messages so as to reformat the information into the internal message header format of the UA

Checkend - determine whether any additional mail is present in the CBMS

Currently new CBMS sections are added to this file using an editor but, in a more fully developed UA, a utility could be written which would prompt the user for the necessary information.

4.2 The Communication Process

Assuming that the communication lines between UA and CBMS are in a stable state, the process whereby the UA replaces a human user in communicating with the CBMS breaks down into two major components: determining when the CBMS is ready for the next input and sending the right command or data. The first of these presents some difficulties which are discussed in Section 5.1.

The UA obtains the appropriate command from the sequence in the CBMS-command file and sends it. Certain commands contain parameters which must be substituted with data related to the current transaction. This data is drawn from either the outbox or the user-data file as appropriate.

The major problem in the UA - CBMS communications lies not in sending commands to the CBMS but in interpreting the responses from it. In order to retrieve a message from the CBMS, the UA issues a read command and then collects all responses into a temporary data file. No attempt is made to analyse the data as it is being received as such processing could potentially cause the UA to lose characters being transmitted from the CBMS. Once the entire message has been saved, the UA draws the analysis data from the CBMS-commands file. This is essentially a mask of how it expects the received message to appear.

There are two commands following which the UA must analyse the message received from the CBMS. The first occurs when it is checking to see if there is any mail to read. In this case the UA compares the received message with the one it expects to receive if there is no mail. From the results of this the UA knows whether or not to attempt reading a message.

The second command requiring UA analysis occurs when a message has been read. The UA must decode the envelope data from the format provided in the command file given and convert it to the required internal envelope. For this purpose the CBMS-commands file contains data for the fields that are required for the internal envelope. The first item is the number of the field for the internal envelope (i.e., 1 - to, 2 - from, 3 - cc, 4 - subject). The next data item in the file is the literal string that will prefix the line in the message displayed to the user (i.e., "To:", "From:", "cc:", "Subject"). The next line of data indicates how many tokens and which ones are required to compose the envelope field (e.g., "To" data may consist of 2 tokens, first name and last name). Once all fields have been determined, the module opens the inbox file, transfers the envelope data it has just obtained and then copies the rest of the message to the inbox.

4.3 Local System Tools

In order for the UA to incorporate various local system tools, such as the editor, it is envisaged that interaction with the operating system would normally be required. In the case of the experimental UA, this was done through the use of the Submit facility of the CP/M. In this implementation the UA instructs the command interpreter to execute a submit file and passes it two parameters which are necessary to re-enter the UA process once editing is complete. The first is the user's password and the second is the command to be executed after invoking the UA. The submit file has two lines. The first invokes the editor and the second invokes the UA and passes back appropriate parameters so that it will automatically transfer the modified file to the outbox. This is a rather cumbersome procedure which would be simplified under a mere sophisticated operating system.

4.4 Portability and Hardware

The experimental UA has been written in as portable a manner as possible. However, there are some basic hardware dependencies which could not be avoided. The first concerned the use of an autodial modem and the protocol established between it and the UA. The second concerned the type and address of the I/O port used for serial communications, and its ability to handle the DTR line to the modem. Finally, the existence of two disk drives was assumed because of the small disks used in the experimental implementation. All of these hardware dependencies are well isolated and can be easily modified for different hardware environments.

While the UA makes use of the system editor, no assumptions are made about it and any editor could be used. The UA should be able to run under any CP/M environment with the hardware exceptions mentioned above. If the UA were to be ported to a different operating system, then the following areas should be considered:

- How the UA gets parameters from the command line;
- A facility to replace the submit invocation of the editor.

5. PROBLEMS AND SOLUTIONS

In this section we discuss some of the problems experienced in designing a UA to work with multiple, non-CCITT-standard CBMS and some of the solutions that were devised.

5.1 Communications Problems

A major problem with the design of the UA is the method of communication between the UA and the external CBMS.

In the case of the CCITT UA/MTA model, this problem is, of course, dealt with by a protocol to which both entities adhere. In the non-CCITT case, an alternative has to be devised from the one-sided point of view of the UA since the external CBMS assumes it is dealing with a human operator.

The UA should be capable of telling when the CBMS host is ready to accept input. On some hosts, such as IBM main frames, this can quite easily be done by detecting the X-ON character that is sent whenever the host has finished transmitting. However, this is not a standard feature and therefore can not be used for other hosts in general. Another alternative is to encode the various prompts, emitted by the host, within the CBMS-commands file. Thus by matching the CBMS output received against the file, the UA would know when the CBMS was ready for its next line of input. There are several problems with this solution. The first is the number of different prompts that may be involved. The UA would not only need to know the main prompt for each CBMS but also the prompts for logging on and off the host, and possibly those for the various subsystems such as editing text or reading mail. Another problem associated with such an approach is that there would be very tight coupling between the two computers. If the host changed its prompt then the UA would have to be modified to reflect the change. Such a problem could occur as either a new system release on the host or just by the upgrading of a user's sophistication setting on the host CBMS.

In order to avoid the above problems, the approach taken in the experimental UA was to use a timeout technique. A delay time is associated with every command that is sent to a CBMS. The delay is determined, for each CBMS, by estimating the maximum time which is expected to elapse either between sending a command and receiving the first character of the response or between successive characters of the total response. Thus when a command is sent, the UA waits in a delay loop. Each character of the response from the host resets the delay count. This technique is an improvement over the previous one in that it does not rely on specific responses from the host. However, it does presume that the commands are entered in the right sequence. It also implies that the UA will be slower in that it now must timeout on every command that it sends rather than the immediate response a local user would give. The technique also has the problem that the timeouts must be of a sufficient duration that a heavily loaded mainframe will have had enough time to respond to the input. This is especially a problem on such hobby systems as the SOURCE where the number of users can be quite high.

A problem was encountered in dealing with different communications facilities, including the Datapac network. For obvious reasons, the UA should not rely on the order in which the external CBMS are used. Therefore, when using an external CBMS the UA assumes that its modem is not dialled into the sytstem. However, when a user logs off a CBMS which he has accessed via Datapac, the line is not automatically dropped. In addition, there is no way to instruct Datapac through software commands to drop the telephone line. The network holds the line for a minimum of two minutes on the assumption that the user may want to use the network to access the next system. Therefore, the only way to drop the telephone line is to be able to control the DTR signal to the modem from software. This implies a hardware dependency which would have to be taken into account in porting the UA software from one computer to another.

There is also a potential problem of flow control in the communications of the two systems. When the host has a particularly long message, it may cause the UA to write to disk. An ideal system would use a multi-tasking program which would permit the UA to have an interrupt service routine which would be able to buffer the I/O activity with the CBMS. Unfortunately, the CP/M system, on which the UA was developed, does not have this capability.

A second alternative would be to use X-ON, X-OFF handshake signals. Most full-duplex systems have this capability built in to their I/O to allow a user to temporarily suspend output to the terminal. In the case of the UA, the program would send an X-OFF byte to the host whenever it was about to do file output and send the X-ON when it was ready again. Unfortunately, this simple handshake does not exist in the terminal I/O of IBM hosts, which operate in a half-duplex mode. There are two possible alternatives to emulate a similar technique with IBM hosts. The first would be for the UA to send an ASCII "Break" character to stop output and a "resume typing" command when ready to start accepting output again. However, this technique would still be prone to losing characters that were sent before the host receives the break signal. The other alternative would be to use a public network, such as Datapac, to access the host. Such a network usually enables a user to send X-OFF to a half duplex system. One of the disadvantages of this technique would be that the hosts would then all have to be accessible via such public networks.

The approach taken in the experimental UA is to allocate sufficiently large buffers to accommodate most messages without any disk activity. It is assumed, however, that a UA implementation would normally be on an operating system that had multi-processing capability.

In a standard UA/MTA environment there would be a protocol which would be able to check for such problems as an error in transmission and to request a resend. A much more serious problem is recovery from a host crash. How does the UA determine that the host is no longer responding and what sort of recovery mechanism should it try to invoke? A solution to this problem was deemed to be beyond the scope of the present work and was not attempted.

5.1 Problems with CBMS Functions

A basic problem is the question of how to tell when there is mail to be read on the CBMS host. When an interactive user logs onto a host, it normally informs him when mail is waiting for him and this can be checked by the UA. However, this is not of use for determining the existence of additional mail once the UA has already read one message. In the case of an interactive approach, one possible approach is to send a read command. The host response is either a message stating that there is no mail to be read or the text of the first message. This is the approach that was first attempted in the experimental UA. The UA sends a read command and then compares the results with the expected host response when there is no more mail. If the two do not match, then the UA decides it is a message and puts it into the in-box. If the two match, then it decides there is no more mail to be read and logs off the host.

Unfortunately, this technique does not work on The Source mail system. The commands required by The Source when there is mail will cause the system to become confused when there is no mail. As a result, it is necessary to have the UA check for mail first, before it attempts to read any messages. This has several implications for performance however. The first is that the UA must now issue two sets of commands whenever it wishes to read a message. The second implication is on how it checks for mail. On The Source, for example, there is no command within the mail subsystem to check for the existence of mail. Therefore the UA must get out of the mail environment, issue the mail check command and then reenter the mail subsystem on The Source. Fortunately, the majority of CBMS do not exhibit this type of behaviour.

A rather fundamental problem occurs in connection with sending copies of messages. The UA has the capability to send messages to people on various CBMS. When all the recipients are on a CBMS, sending a copy is no problem. The UA includes the copy names in the header of the message and the CBMS will insure that they are delivered. However, a CBMS will not normally allow a user to send a copy of a message without sending an original. This is a problem when the person to whom the message is addressed is located on a different CBMS from those receiving copies. One possible solution to this would be to send a message to the copy recipient as though he was the original receiver. A problem with this approach is that he may not realize that the message he received is a copy and may respond in a different manner than he would otherwise have done. Another problem is that he would not be aware of the identity of others who received the memo and might forward it to another recipient. The experimental UA gets around this problem by automatically including a list of the original receiver and copy list as part of the text of the message. This seems likely to be a price that will have to be paid in any UA which uses external, non-CCITT-type CBMS as an MTA.

6. CONCLUSION

Building a UA to acess a variety of non-CCITT-standard CBMS is possible but is fraught with a number of problems, some of which seem likely to prove difficult to overcome completely at reasonable cost. Nevertheless, the advantages to the user of having mediated access through a UA integrated with his personal workstation facilities seem to be well worth pursuing.

Although an 8080, CP/M microcomputer is by no means an ideal environment for a project of this type, the results demonstrate that it is possible to build a fairly sophisticated user-aid despite the system limitations.

REFERENCES

1. CCITT, SG VII, Draft Recommendations X.MHSO-7, Message Handling Systems, March 1983.

2. McDowell, R., A User-Agent for Multiple Computer-Based Message Systems, M.Eng. Thesis, Carleton University, Ottawa, April 1984.

Computer-Based Message Services
H.T. Smith (Editor)
Elsevier Science Publishers B.V. (North-Holland)
IFIP, 1984

The Active Mailbox - your on-line Secretary

P A Wilson, T I Maude, C J Marshall and N O Heaton

Paul Wilson, Office Systems Division, National Computing Centre, Oxford Rd, Manchester, M1 7ED, UK.
Tim Maude, Centre for Computing and Computer Science, University of Birmingham, Edgbaston, Birmingham, B15 2TT, UK.
Chris Marshall/Nigel Heaton, GEC Hirst Reseach Centre, East Lane, Wembley, HA9 7PP, UK.

As electronic mailbox systems proliferate, users of more than one system will need help to overcome the inconvenience of logging into several systems and to avoid information overload. This paper proposes that such help is provided by a split mailbox: a Passive function responsible for the collection and posting of mail to and from the Message Transfer System; and an Active function interfacing between the user and the Passive mailbox. This paper examines the functions that an Active mailbox might carry out, and how such a concept fits in with ECMA, CCITT and ISO proposals for messaging standards. Three recommendations are made.

1 Background

1.1 How the paper was produced

This paper is the product of a teleconference held between 3rd May 83 and 31st Oct 83 over an electronic network. The network in question was the BLEND system (Birmingham and Loughborough Electronic Network Development) established from 1st Jan 1981 under the auspices of the British Library Research and Development Department. The precise configuration of this system has been described in detail elsewhere (1). BLEND provided the vehicle for the teleconference but the discussion could have occurred, in similar vein, through any functional mailbox system and is therefore relevant to mailbox systems in general.

A total of 12 people contributed to the teleconference (see authors and acknowledgements) from 11 sites on the BLEND network. The active sites can be seen in figure 1.

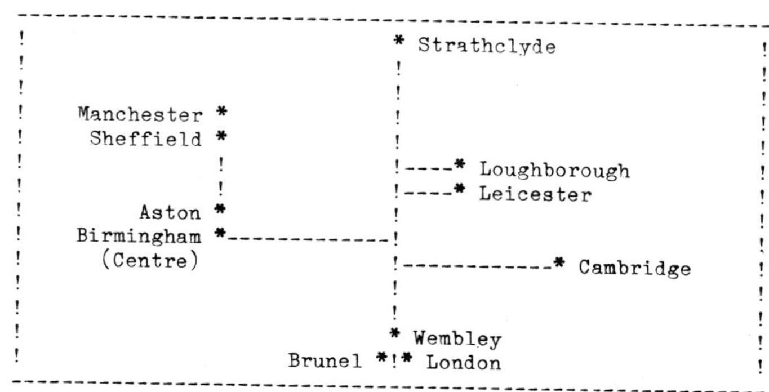

Figure 1 Active sites in this teleconference

In the course of the discussion, over 470 public messages were posted by teleconference members, with countless private messages adding to the general background level of interaction.

The writing of this paper commenced on the 1st Nov 83, and involved 5 of the original teleconference members. All writing took place over the network. Such distributed authoring requires a novel approach and functional control structures. It also raises interesting conceptual problems for the writers. A further paper has been produced (10) which deals specifically with the problems and processes of producing a structured document via a computer based mailbox system.

This paper is intended to contribute in several ways to the future design of mailbox systems, and as such, it is first necessary to briefly examine emerging international standards which will have a significant impact on the evolution and use of mailbox systems.

1.2 Existing standards

Few standards are specifically intended for mailbox systems; most being concerned with the wider field of text communication in general. Such standards can be divided into those which address "direct" communication between simultaneously linked terminals eg. Telex and more recently Teletex; and those which relate to "store and forward" communication in which machines send messages into the network where they may reside until directed to a receiving machine ie. direct machine/machine connection is not a prerequisite for communication. Standards for store and forward messaging will start to emerge from 1984 onwards.

Neither category of standard requires that a user should have a mailbox and for this reason the standards are not specifically oriented towards mailbox systems. "However, there are many facilities being defined in the standards which mailbox systems also make use of. Hence, many elements of the standards being developed will be directly applicable to mailbox systems" (2).

It is likely that mailbox systems will at least use elements of these standards to communicate with each other and with other text communication systems. The standards therefore, hold information pertinent to the design of mailbox systems.

Before examining the relevant text communication standards, mention should be made of a fundamental set of standards which influence the formulation and definition of the former. This fundamental set is concerned with Open Systems Interconnection (OSI). OSI standards allow any conforming systems to talk to each other. Basically this is achieved by matching interworking systems to the OSI model, which is made up of layers of hierarchical and complementary functions (9). These layers can be briefly described as follows - see Figure 2.

Element	Layer	Description
Major element 1:	7	The Applications layer
Communication	6	The Presentation layer
Management	5	The Session layer
Major element 2:	4	The Transport layer
Transmission or	3	The Network layer
Transfer	2	The Data link layer
	1	The Physical layer

Figure 2 The OSI model

The Transmission Element is concerned mostly with the task of physically moving information between network nodes, whilst the Communication management element is more concerned with the format, presentation and preparation of text. Hence, this latter element relates more to the human component of the system.

Many bodies will introduce standards in some part or form before the end of 1984. They are likely to have a large influence on the shape and growth of mailbox systems. In section 2 of this paper, we will examine models proposed by these standards; pointing out their similarities and differences.

Mailbox systems which ignore the standards are likely to become extinct within a short period of time, since they will not be able to communicate freely with other systems (including other mailbox systems). The standards themselves are likely to increase the number of mailbox systems and their users. Mailboxes implemented as applications on todays personal computers will begin to form nodes in tomorrows networks. Messages addressed and left in the system will, thanks to the standards, be guaranteed to reach any registered user's mailbox anywhere. As the ownership of, or access to, computer terminals increases, the potentially vital mailbox function which they carry will proliferate. Thus, within the foreseeable future, ownership of an electronic mailbox will be as important to "being in touch" as owning a letter box, telephone, pigeon hole etc. is today.

It is not difficult to imagine users with several mailboxes linked to various networks and services. With such a scenario, the most important human factors considerations are likely to centre around the questions of cognitive complexity in dealing with the multiple elements and nuances of the systems and with the information overload in dealing with the volume of messages and message types. Already, such problems are evident in current systems, where a few days absence can mean hours of sifting through incoming mail (much of it junk) to capture relevant information.

With this in mind, it is important that future systems adhere to a design philosophy which tailors mailboxes, and the information they deal with, to user needs. To quote once again from Wilson - "To cope with the increased quantity of messages relating to a variety of different aspects of an individual's life, the mailbox of the future is likely to be a powerful, intelligent tool performing many complex sorting, monitoring, reminding and general purpose assistance type functions." (3).

1.3 Rationale for the paper

Such a portrait of the future mailbox allows us to speculate about the way in which it should be constructed. It is the function of this paper to discuss such design questions by introducing the concept of Passive and Active Mailboxes. By proposing a model for this concept, it is hoped that a contribution can be made towards the formulation of standards concerned with Open Systems Interconnection management - the higher level layers defined in the OSI standard.

Within this framework, aspects of future systems will be explored in greater depth and suggestions and recommendations pertinent to future mailbox design will be made.

A subsidiary reason for producing this paper over a mailbox system was to explore the use of such a system for teleconferencing and distributed authoring.

To summarise: the rationale for the paper pertains to the following:
- introduce the concept of Active and Passive Mailboxes
- examine future scenarios for mailbox systems and make recommendations
- explore the problems and processes involved in distributed authoring.

2 Active and Passive Mailboxes

2.1 Existing messaging models

The models described here have been produced by ISO, CCITT and ECMA. Despite the fact that several different standards are emerging, the various bodies concerned do profess to want to merge their standards. The current feeling is that ISO will want to combine the CCITT and ECMA standards eventually to produce a universal long term standard. This will not emerge for a few years and meanwhile the other standards will be implemented. We must not ignore the corporate standards either; IBM have produced Document Interchange and Content Architecture standards. Xerox has also produced its own standard. These may become de facto standards which, like Fortran, will remain because of the heavy backing from their parent companies.

2.1.1 Description of existing models

ISO Model

A functional view of the ISO Text Preparation and Interchange reference model (ISO March 1983) is shown in Figure 3.

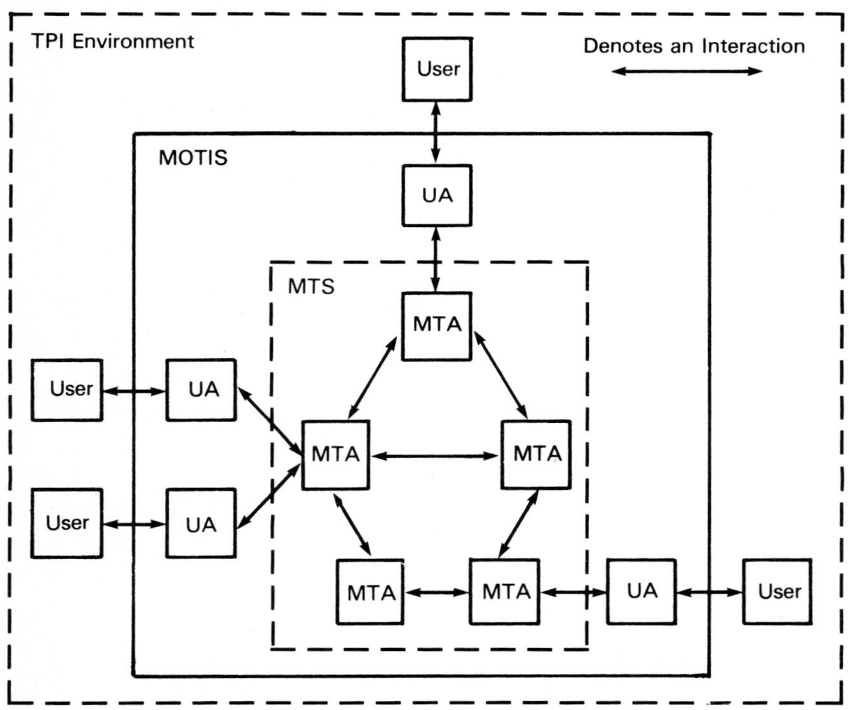

Figure 3 Functional view of the ISO Text Preparation and Interchange model

The users' view of the system is through a User Agent, each user having one Agent to work through. This is the process which allows him/her to prepare the text and then to give the commands to send it on to its ultimate destination. The User Agent then passes the message on to the Message Transfer System which consists of a network of Message Transfer Agents. The message will first be given to the Message Transfer Agent associated with the User Agent and then on through the network to the destination. Here it is passed to the recipient's User Agent. This presents him/her with the message in the way in which it is designed to. Although the Message Transfer System is shown as a network of interlinked Message Transfer Agents, it does not necessarily mean that this is a computer network, it could be a single machine on which the Message Transfer Agents exist.

CCITT Model

The functional view of the CCITT Message Handling System model (4) is shown in Figure 4. The diagram is very similar to that of the ISO model.

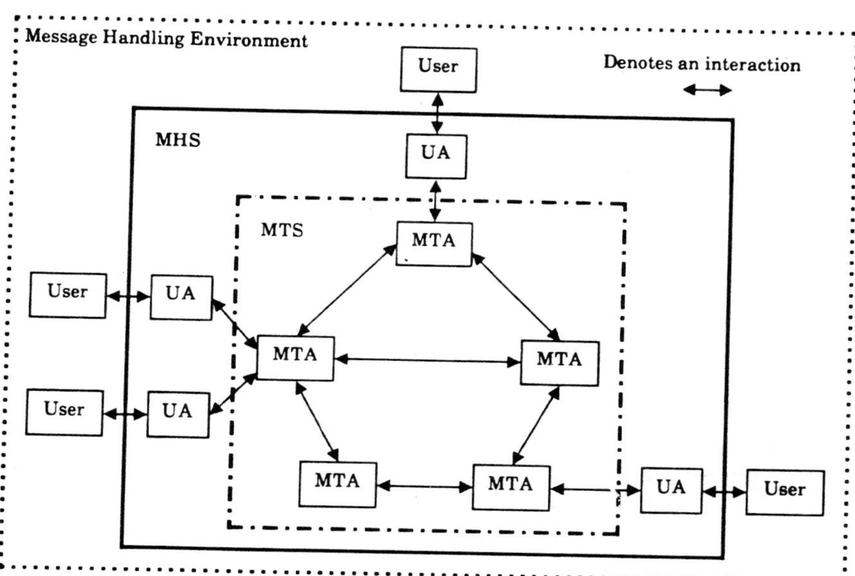

Figure 4 Functional view of the CCITT Message Handling System model

MIDA Model by ECMA

The MIDA model produced by ECMA (5) is shown in terms of the ISO Open Systems Interconnection reference model. Here the Applications layer is shown split into four sublayers which communicate through layers 1-6 described as a 'communication service' (See figure 5).

2.1.2 Differences between the existing models

The most obvious difference between the ECMA MIDA model and the other two is that it is expressed in terms of the ISO OSI model whereas the other two are expressed in terms of block diagrams showing communication between different processes.

The Message Transfer System is described by ECMA MIDA as a Reliable Transfer Sublayer together with the other layers of the ISO OSI model. This part of the model is left as communicating arrows on the block diagrams.

The terminology of the three models is overlapping but not identical. The terms 'User', 'User Agent' and 'Message Transfer Agent' are the same in all three models. The terms 'Text Preparation and Interchange Environment' (ISO), 'Message Handling Environment' (CCITT) and 'Application Layer' (ECMA MIDA) may

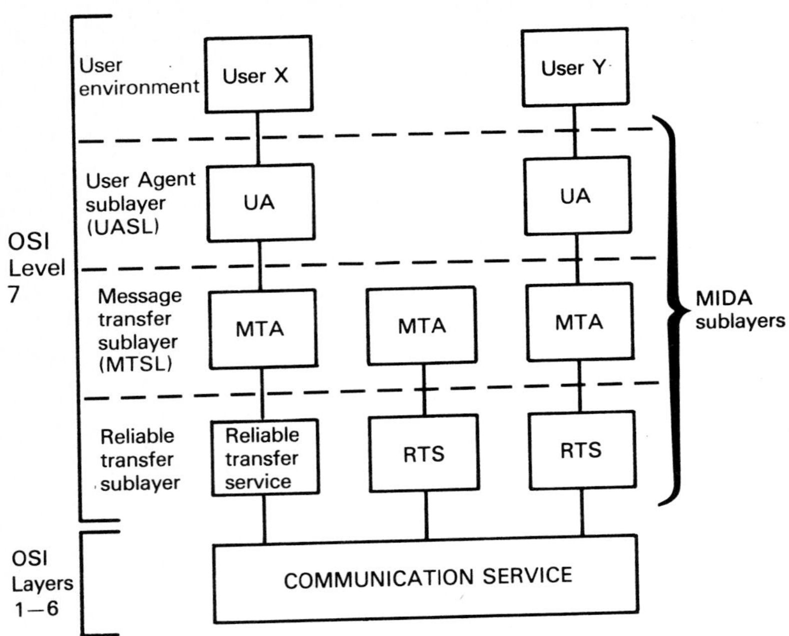

Figure 5 Functional view of the ECMA MIDA model

be equated. The terms 'Message Oriented Text Interchange System' (ISO), 'Message Handling System' (CCITT) and 'MIDA Sublayers' (ECMA MIDA) may be equated. Finally, the terms 'Message Transfer System' (ISO and CCITT) and 'Message Transfer Sublayers' (ECMA MIDA) may be equated.

2.1.3 Shortcomings of current models

The models are intended to show the working of a single mailbox system; thus the user communicates with a single User Agent which, in turn communicates with a single Message Transfer System. This is an inadequate view of such an environment as people often need to communicate with several such systems. Thus the user should be shown in the models as also being involved in other systems. Thus, in CCITT terms, the Message Handling Environment should consist of a number of Message Handling Systems each of which has many users communicating with it, and each user communicating with one or more systems. Again this is inadequate as we will undoubtedly see the User Agents taking on a more active role by communicating with several Message Transfer Systems. Thus the user could communicate with one User Agent and it could communicate with a number of systems providing different services or a different user group.

Secondly the models do not show how the User Agent can take on a further active role of sorting mail from the different Message Handling Systems for presentation to the user in his/her desired manner. This is important to include in the model as such an active function may include rejecting mail and not passing it on to the user (eg unsolicited and unwanted mail - 'junk' mail).

2.2 Proposed Active/Passive Mailbox Model

The various shortcomings of the current models can be removed by introducing the Active/Passive Mailbox concept. With this the functions of the User Agent are split between those of passively collecting and delivering mail and those of actively searching and sorting mail from various Passive Mailboxes.

2.2.1 Definition of Active and Passive Mailboxes

A Passive Mailbox is that part of the User Agent which monitors the Message Transfer System and collects mail addressed to the user to whom it is assigned.

An Active Mailbox is that part of a User Agent which collects messages from one or more Passive Mailboxes and performs various functions on them before they are collected by the user. These functions may perform transformations on the mail or they may effect the presentation of the mail to the user. It also performs various functions on the user's outgoing mail before passing it to the Passive Mailbox for sending.

2.2.2 Including Active Mailboxes in existing models

In the ISO and CCITT models the User Agent can be split into two - the active and passive parts (see figure 6). Part of the Active Mailbox is included in the user environment.

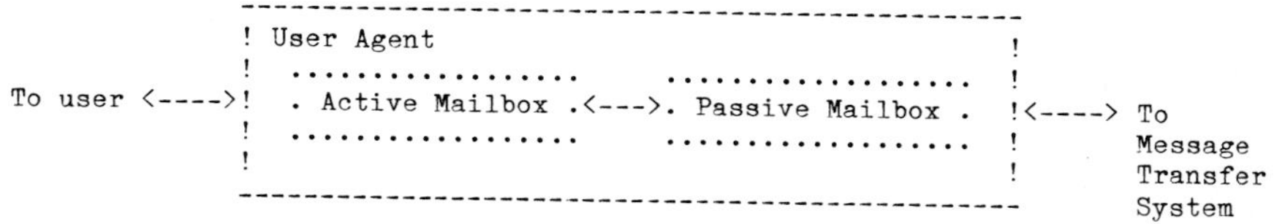

Figure 6 Active and Passive mailboxes in the User Agent

In the ECMA MIDA model the User Agent sublayer can be split into two further layers, the Active User Agent sublayer which is above the Passive User Agent sublayer.

2.3 Implications of the Active and Passive Mailbox concept

2.3.1 General implications

An Active Mailbox can take on a secretarial role in such a system. Some of the jobs that a secretary might perform on conventional mail might well be taken on by an Active Mailbox. It is, thus, a very personalised process, each individual requiring different functions of an Active Mailbox.

One function of a secretary handling incoming mail is to deliver mail from a variety of sources such as external post, internal post, telephone messages or circulars so that the recipient gets them together without going through a variety of access methods. In an electronic mailbox the Active Mailbox should be able to handle this sort of job by receiving messages from a variety of different Passive Mailboxes. People who use a variety of different computer systems may have many mailboxes at present. This gives rise to the overheads of learning many different user interfaces and accessing many different machines regularly. By using an Active Mailbox which is connected to all these Passive Mailboxes it would be possible to provide the user with a single user interface and a single machine to work with.

Another secretarial job is to sort the incoming mail. Thus mail which is urgent may be presented first or may be labelled as urgent, whereas circulars and junk mail may be kept aside or simply thrown away without even presenting them to the addressee. This function is one which could be taken on by the Active Mailbox. It would need some criteria for deciding how to classify incoming mail. This would be set by the user according to his/her personal tastes, for instance mail might be classified as urgent if

(i) It was marked URGENT (if such a field existed in the mail) OR
(ii) It was from the higher management OR
(iii) It was from the administration office AND NOT sent to all staff.

A classification of junk mail could be:

(i) It was sent to more than 40 people AND
(ii) It was not sent by one of a given list of people (eg. higher management, their secretaries, friends) AND
(iii) It is not urgent.

Clearly such classifications need to be thought about carefully and will be modified as it is realised that some mail is not being classified correctly. The problem of junk mail in an electronic mailbox is one which will need serious thought. At the Xerox Palo Alto Research Center a mailbox user interface called Laurel is used to access the Message Transport System Grapevine (6). There are over 2000 users of the system. Brotz describes the various social problems that occur when a relatively large group such as this uses a mailbox system. High on the list of anti-social behaviour is the sending of junk mail. This is partly due to the ease and lack of expense to the sender who wishes to send mail to a large number of people. It is, therefore, important that an Active Mailbox should be able to have a method of distinguishing junk mail so that it can be presented separately or thrown away completely.

A third secretarial job is that of sending the outgoing mail to various people by different methods. He/she has to know how it is to be sent (eg. internal or external mail, telephone, note on desk) in order to reach the destination. This can be achieved by an Active Mailbox in an electronic environment. The Active Mailbox must know the details of the structure of the destination systems.

The idea of accessing a variety of Computer Based Message Systems from one 'home' system has been explored in the GILT project (7). It is important to realise that the sorts of functions described above and those examined by GILT will be very important in the future and therefore it is important to put these active functions into the models that are being developed.

2.3.2 Passive Mailbox Functions within the User Agent

The first role of the Passive Mailbox is the collection of mail from the Message Transfer System. This may be a single computer system or a network. Only mail addressed to the user associated with the Passive Mailbox will be collected. It must then deliver the mail on to the Active Mailbox when it is requested.

The Passive Mailbox must pass messages from the Active Mailbox into the Message Transfer System. It must also do various tasks associated with the Message Transfer System which are routine. These include acknowledging receipt of mail as required and answering probes. A probe is a message sent to the mailbox to see if a given message can be delivered.

2.3.3 Active Mailbox Functions within the User Agent

The Active Mailbox must collect mail from one or more Passive Mailboxes. Since each Passive Mailbox will have a different structure of mail, with different fields meaning different things, it must then decode it according to its knowledge of the structure of that mail system. This means that a variety of messages from a variety of systems can be presented to the user in the same way. The user can use a single system to discover if he/she has any mail and if so, read it.

It must also be capable of sending mail to different people who use different systems in a uniform way. To achieve this the Active Mailbox must not only know which person is available through which mailbox system, but also the structure of that system. For instance if the remote mailbox has a number of distinct activities such as the Notepad Computer Conferencing System (Infomedia Corp., Palo Alto, California), then the Active Mailbox needs to understand that in order to send it to the right Activity. This is not a passive function since the Active Mailbox needs some information from the user to discover which Activity it would have to be put in and therefore may need some communication with the user.

This leads onto the next function of an active mailbox, that of maintainance of the structure rules of other mailbox systems. This will include information about Activity structures as well as information such as which mailboxes have a priority indicator associated with messages or which have a confidentiality rating. The actual Activity/Topic structure of each mailbox system is dynamic ie. it may change from day to day, thus the Active Mailbox must send out probes enquiring aout the current structure on occasions and answer probes coming to it. Probes may either be sent out to the destination mailbox or may be obtained through a communal structure server.

As a message may be sent to large groups of people, the Active Mailbox may need to maintain and use distribution lists, possibly obtained from a distribution list server.

A major function of an Active Mailbox will be to sort mail. Mail may be sorted into different categories according to the individual user's preference. This will classify the mail into a set of categories established by the individual user. For instance the mail may be classified as urgent, standard or junk; or it may be classified as administration, chit-chat or work. Clearly the Active Mailbox will have to have some procedure for the classification of mail. These procedures will examine the fields presented in the mail and deduce the classification according to some system of rules, thus it may be regarded as a simple expert system. To obtain an error free classification without the ability to understand the body of text may turn out to be quite a difficult problem.

2.3.4 Implications for CCITT-defined Service Elements

CCITT has set out a list of Message Handling System model Service Elements (4). These are elements which are included in the message as it is transferred and are included in the Message Transfer System and the User Agent. Service Elements handled by the Passive Mailbox are usually those that are routine enough for each Passive Mailbox in the system to handle in a similar way. Those handled by the Active Mailbox are either specific to the individual user or involved in handling a number of Passive Mailboxes.

The 'User-message identification' is a unique identification for the message used for cross reference. The originating Active Mailbox must supply this. The Passive Mailbox may also add a message-user identification which will be stripped off by the receiving Passive Mailbox. The receiving Active Mailbox must also receive an indication of which Passive Mailbox the message came from.

The 'original encoded information type' element describes any encoding used for the body of the message (eg. text, facsimile, encoded voice). This must be added by the Active Mailbox as it knows how the message was input. The receiving active mailbox uses it to decode the message.

'Multi-recipient designation', 'blind copy designation' and 'authorising user designation' are to do with sending multiple copies and signing the message with multiple names. These must be handled by the Active Mailbox as the multiple addresses will be in the form of a mailing list held by it. The receiving Active Mailbox must know about these factors in order to sort the incoming mail.

'Receipt notification' can be dealt with by the Passive Mailbox, being a routine event which is not specific to the individual user. There may be good reason to include various classes of this indicator such as 'received by

Passive Mailbox', 'collected by Active Mailbox' and 'read by user', the last of these being supplied by the Active Mailbox.

'Auto-forwarding designator' indicates that the message has been automatically forwarded and must be handled by the Active Mailbox. It must make the decision as to whether to forward a message or not (possibly by direction from the user), and then pass the message on through the appropriate Passive Mailbox (this is not necessarily the same one that it was received from).

The 'cross reference indication' gives a reference to previously sent messages and must be handled by the Active Mailbox in order that it can sort out any replies.

'Expiry date designation' indicates when the sender considers the message to be out of date. This should be dealt with by the Active Mailbox. Different users may choose to have their Active Mailboxes do different things with old messages eg. file or throw away. Similarly with the 'obsoleting indicator'.

The 'importance indicator' and 'sensitivity indicator' give an idea of the importance and sensitivity of the message and so can be used by the Active Mailbox when sorting mail. It may be necessary to include a further class of importance which the Passive Mailbox deals with. This occurs when there is great urgency and it may send a message to the Active Mailbox to say that an important message has arrived without waiting for the Active Mailbox to contact it.

'Subject indication' must be examined by the Active Mailbox so that it can be sorted.

'Forwarded user-message indicator' tells the user that the message has been forwarded by some person, not automatically. This information can be inserted by the Active Mailbox when the user forwards it.

The 'replying user-message designation' indicates a reply to a previous message and must be used by the Active Mailbox in order to sort the mail, likewise with the 'reply request indicator'. These must be set up by the originating Active Mailbox.

The 'body encryption indicator' may be handled by either Active or Passive Mailbox or both. The Passive Mailbox system may be designed to encrypt the message at all times, the receiving Passive Mailbox will then decrypt it. The Active Mailbox can make a decision on whether or not to encrypt depending on such matters as security or at a request from the user.

The 'query service element' lets the user start a query as to whether a message would get through to a certain address if sent. This can be set up and replied to by the Passive Mailboxes.

As well as the Interpersonal Message Service Elements, some of the Message Transfer Service Elements may also be required by the receiving Active Mailbox so that it can sort the mail.

3 Discussion

The concept of an Active Mailbox is perhaps a new one: it is not mentioned in the standards which are being developed by ECMA, CCITT or ISO. Nevertheless we are convinced that there is a real need for such a facility today and that this need will grow as the number of messaging services increases and their mail volumes grow. It is essentially a user need, for without it individuals will have to waste time and effort accessing a variety of different systems. Indeed there are many people who are having this problem today.

Although the concept may be new, in fact many systems do already incorporate such a facility without it being recognised as such. For example the ability to receive and send telex messages in a mailbox system means that there must be somewhere in the system some of the functions that we are prescribing for the Active Mailbox. Another example concerns mailbox systems such as Bell-Northern Research's COCOS, which "provides the user with an extensive set of tailoring options, which allow for both individual preferences and for terminal variations" (8).

The Active Mailbox we are proposing could form one part of what the standards currently being developed describe as the User Agent, though it is not clear how feasible it would be to standardise the functions of an Active Mailbox. The examination of the effect an Active Mailbox might have on the CCITT Interpersonal Messaging System Service Elements in section 2.3.4, indicates that some further facilities may have to be incorporated into the standards at some later date. In the meantime however it is thought that Active Mailboxes can be developed around the standards - they will simply have to be designed to act exactly as if it is the end user accessing the mailbox rather than his active agent.

The features of an Active Mailbox will be mainly defined by end user requirements. It will be a largely invisible facility which will perform functions not dissimilar to those that a personal secretary might carry out. It will present a constant interface to the user regardless of the variety of different systems it is interfacing with. Furthermore this interface will be user definable - possibly even automatically adaptive if the principles of Intelligent Knowledge Based Systems (IKBS) are incorporated. In future years, when electronic messaging has become a key communication media, the potential for severe information overload from ease of communication and junk mail will probably become a real threat. In such an environment the Active Mailbox will be required to sift the incoming mails, to present summary information to the user and even to deal with certain messages at its own discretion. Like a good secretary today an individual's Active Mailbox will be indispensable.

All indications point to a period of rapid growth for mailbox and messaging systems. The implementation of standards seems sure to fuel this process. By the turn of the century mailbox systems may rival the telephone as a communication media. Like the telephone, use will not be restricted to business. Indeed even today the prices of personal computers and modems are so low that there is a significant community of individuals exchanging messages on their micros at home. When an individual has access to many messaging systems, both at home and at work, his Active Mailbox will become a very personal tool which will belong to him (not the organisation) and which he will wish to carry around with him (or at least have possession of it at some location and access to it over the networks). This is the future for which Active Mailboxes must be developed and designed.

4 Recommendations for future work

Three items of future work seem indicated by this paper:

- The functions that an Active Mailbox is to carry out need to be categorised and defined
- A prototype Active Mailbox needs to be built and experimented with
- A detailed examination needs to be made of the implications of Active Mailboxes for the messaging standards which are currently being developed by ECMA, CCITT and ISO.

References

(1) Shackel B, 'The BLEND system - programme for the study of electronic journals', The Computer Journal, 25(2), pp 161-168, Ergonomics 25(4), pp 269-284, and the Journal of the American Society for Information Science, 34 (1), 1982, pp 22-30

(2) Wilson P A, 'Standards and the Electronic Mailbox', NCC Publications, 1984.

(3) Wilson P A, 'Introducing the Electronic Mailbox', NCC Publications, 1983.

(4) 'Draft recommendation X.MHS1; Message Handling Systems; Systems Model - Service Elements (Version 4)', Special Rapporteur on Message Handling (I M Cunningham) Study Group 7, June 1983.

(5) ECMA, 'Message interchange distributed application standard', ECMA working document, 5th draft, July 1983.

(6) Brotz D K, 'Message System Mores: Etiquette in Laurel', ACM transactions on office information system, 1(2), April 1983, pp 179-192.

(7) Fergus E, 'The GILT project - connecting computer based message systems via public data networks', in 'Pathways to the Information Society', (Proceedings 6th conference on computer communication, London 7th-10th Sept 1982) North Holland Publishing Company, Sep 1982, pp 407-411.

(8) Dawes N W, Harris S J, Magoon, M I Maveety S J, Petty D J, 'The design and service of COCOS, an electronic office system', in 'Computer Message Systems' edited by R P Uhlig, North Holland Publishing Company, 1981.

(9) Tanenbaum A S, 'Network Protocols', Computing.Surveys, 13(4), Dec 1983, pp 453-489.

(10) Maude T I, Heaton N O, Gilbert G N, Wilson P A, Marshall C J, 'An experiment in group working on mailbox systems', Proceedings of the IFIP INTERACT 84 conference, London, North Holland Publications, 1984.

Acknowledgements

The authors would like to acknowledge the contribution of the following to the BLEND teleconference in which the ideas and planning of this work were first developed:

Pat Wright	Brian Shackel	Julian Newman	Thomas Green
Elwyn Edwards	Peter Innocent	Chris Reynolds	

and especially to Steven Tagg who helped a lot in the production of this paper.

Computer-Based Message Services
H.T. Smith (Editor)
Elsevier Science Publishers B.V. (North-Holland)

Structures for Mailbox System Applications

Paul Wilson

Senior Consultant, Office Systems Division,
National Computing Centre, Oxford Rd,
Manchester M1 7ED

Standard Mailbox system facilities provide excellent informal communications. However, more formal applications can also be carried out via mailbox systems if extra facilities - mailbox structures - are provided. This paper describes the results of a study in which a generic classification of structures was identified as well as 13 different mailbox applications. A matrix relating structures to applications is provided. The paper concludes that much work remains to be done in identifying and designing mailbox structures for specific applications; and suggests that both users and suppliers need to upgrade their views of how these systems can be used. The studies 5 recommendations are included as an Appendix.

1 What are Electronic Mailbox Systems?

Electronic mailbox systems, like Facsimile, Telex and other message systems, allow people to send messages to each other electronically. However it is the MAILBOX facility that distinguishes these systems from other electronic message systems. An electronic mailbox will look after your messages until you wish to access them at the time and place of your own choosing. In many ways a mailbox can act as your own personal assistant - sorting your mail into different categories, telling you what needs to be dealt with urgently, helping you to deal with the messages, taking care of all the associated filing, and searching for and retrieving messages at your request (1).

1.1 Terminology

You may now be wondering about the relationship between mailbox systems and several other terms such as Electronic Mail, Computer Based Message Systems, Electronic Message Systems, Computer Conferencing Systems and Computer Mediated Message Systems. In fact, different people use each of these other terms to mean different things, so it is not possible to give clear cut, commonly accepted definitions for them. Another problem is that the technology is moving so fast that the concepts and terminology have to change quite often just to keep pace. However, in order to place some of these terms in context I will refer to the classification of Office Automation Systems I am currently using (see figure 1).

Taking each of the terms mentioned previously; Electronic Message Systems in the classification in Figure 1 is used to describe all electronic communication systems. However some people do use it to mean specifically mailbox systems. Electronic Mail is usually used to describe a simple mailbox system, though, on a number of occassions, I have seen it used to refer to the totality of electronic communication systems. Computer Based Message Systems, Computer Mediated Message Systems and Computer Conferencing Systems usually refer to mailbox systems which have special facilities, or structures, built into them. A typical facility of this type allows users to send and recieve

Office Automation Systems

- Electronic Message Systems
  - Image
    - Facsimile
    - Video Conferencing
  - Voice
    - PABX-based telephone systems
    - Voice Mailbox Systems.
  - Text
    - Telex
    - Teletex
    - Communicating Word Processors
    - Text Mailbox Systems
- Information Management Systems
  - External Information
  - Operational Information
  - Administrative Information
  - Personal Information Systems
- Decision Support Systems
  - Expert Systems
  - Business Graphics
  - Spread Sheets
- Document Preparation Systems
  - Text Creation
  - Text Formatting
  - Document Production

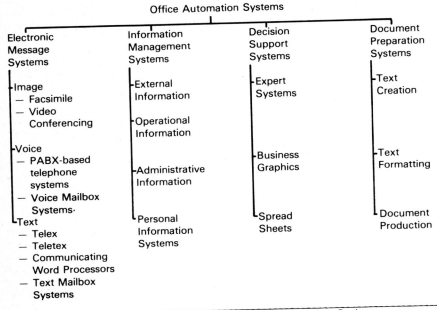

Figure 1 A classification of Office Automation Systems

messages only in certain pre-determined categories, and files them permanently so that they can be referred back to. In this paper, however, only the terms that are shown in figure 1 will be used.

1.2 Voice, image and text mailbox systems

Although the vast majority of mailbox systems around at present are text based systems, a range of voice mailbox systems (often referred to as Voice Message Systems) are now becoming commercially available. Voice message Systems can do most of the things that a text mailbox system can ie. messages can be read, pended, answered, filed in categories etc. In view of the fact that any ordinary telephone handset can be used to access a voice mailbox system these are likely to become widespread. Image mailbox systems (in which you would see a recorded picture of the sender actually speaking a message to you) are still too expensive a luxury and I do not know of any existing systems. However, all types of mailbox systems possess the same basic features and it is likely that, as the technologies of voice, image and text converge, so we shall see mailbox systems designed to handle the full range of text, voice and image messages.

1.3 Basic mailbox facilities

All mailbox systems have a range of basic facilities. Such facilities can be categorised as follows (2):

Message preparation: eg. word processing; notebook facilities; annotation of messages received prior to forwarding or filing.
Sending messages: eg. timed delivery; directory services; multiple addressing; distribution lists; abbreviated addressing; message priorities; automatic route selection; message status information; links to other networks.

Receiving messages: eg. mailbox scanning; selection of messages; replying to messages; forwarding messages; rerouting of messages; notification of new messages; message filtering.
Security and reliability: eg. system security; protecting against message loss; passwords; security software; encryption; inhibiting hard copy.
Message filing and retrieval: eg. storage capacity; retrieval facilities; archiving.
Message logging: eg. accounting reports; management reports.

Such basic facilities provide for excellent informal communications in much the same way as the telephone is used. Most of the systems in use today are of this type and are being used primarily for informal communications between people separated by geographical distance and/or time zone differences (3). This can benefit the individual by saving time, reducing interruptions and improving communications. However such benefits are intangible, difficult to measure and do not make a direct impact on an organisations profitability. Hence, there are probably many organisations today which would like to try out a mailbox system but are unable to cost-justify the investment.

2 Mailbox structuring

One way around this problem is to implement a mailbox system to support formal applications and processes which can be cost-justified. Such applications require that the mailbox communication is STRUCTURED so that specific tasks can be undertaken.

2.1 What are Mailbox Structures?

Mailbox structuring is equivalent to the structuring that is imposed on certain types of face-to-face communication; for example, face-to-face meetings often have a Chairman, an agenda, minutes and fixed procedures for conducting the meeting. Meetings that are disorderly and unstructured often achieve nothing and leave the participants feeling frustrated and angry that they have wasted their time. Communication using a mailbox system is no different: some structure is required if the 'meeting' of the participants is to be orderly and purposeful. However, whereas face-to-face structures must rely on the compliance of the individual and the memorising or recording of the communication that has taken place, mailbox structures can be easily controlled and no communication need be lost or forgotten. Consequently Mailbox structures have far greater scope and constitute a powerful new form of communication.

Structuring does not imply any reduction or change in the basic mailbox facilities. Structuring is added onto basic facilities to provide additional facilities for specific applications. Hiltz and Turoff have described structuring as tailoring the computer mediated communication process around the particular group and the application (4). Structuring has also been termed 'Groupware' by Johnson and Lenz (5).

The concept of mailbox structuring was not widely understood in the UK at the time of writing. This is hardly surprising since many people had not even heard about mailbox systems, and those who had were largely influenced by the products they had seen or were using. A survey of mailbox products on the UK market in May 1983 (6) established that the vast majority of the products identified provided only basic mailbox facilities, and there was no evidence that the manufacturers and suppliers appreciated what structuring was - or even the need for it.

I suspect the position is little better elsewhere in the world. Despite this however, enough progress has been made - mainly in the USA - to be able to get a picture of the range of possible structures. In general terms they seem to fall into three major categories (3):

- Structures for organising the information generated
- Structures for getting things done
- Structures for controlling who does what

Before expanding on these categories it is important to understand that structures can be implemented in two different ways: through software or through management.

2.2 Software and Management Structuring

Since all mailbox communication is performed via computers, it is quite feasible to program in any structures that are required (eg copies of all messages are to be sent to the chairman). This is **SOFTWARE STRUCTURING.** It has the advantage that the structures are imposed and policed quite impartially by the system, though its rigidity and inflexibility may be regarded as a drawback in some circumstances.

MANAGEMENT STRUCTURING, on the other hand, involves the application and policing of rules by users of the system. This is similar to the way in which we control face to face communication, and relies heavily on the degree of committment to the rules that the individuals concerned have, and their ability to perform those roles that the rules demand of them. However management structures do have the advantage of being flexible and requiring no software to be written or changed.

There is no reason why a mixture of software and management structuring cannot be used for a particular application. In many cases it may be advantageous to have a combination of rigid policing and a degree of flexibility. Each approach, and a combination of the two, should always be considered when designing new structures for a specific application.

2.3 Structure hierarchies

Structures themselves can be selected by software built into the system. Hiltz and Turoff describe one such example whereby a user is restricted in the contributions that he can make to a discussion on a particular topic, if that user's contribution to date has been more than a certain percentage of the contributions made by the whole group (4). In many respects this can be thought of as defining a hierarchy of structures - the upper level structure controlling which lower level structures to apply. Little is known about what such higher levels of structures might consist of, nor how useful they might be.

2.4 Structures for organising the information generated

Figure 2 shows a summary of the structures that are in this category.

- **Message classification:** Structures to achieve this include subject headings for messages; distribution lists with easily distinguishable titles; separating all communication into 'activities' such that you have to log into an activity to get any new mail that has been sent within it; and linking messages together so that it is possible to browse back through old messages on a particular subject.

- **Message formats:** In some circumstances it can be useful to place restrictions on the format of the messages that can be sent. For example, in the Politechs/Topics system, users decided to initiate a software structure which would allow them only 3 lines of text to request other users for information on any particular topic. Message formats are also essential when a mailbox system is used as a medium for form filling and transaction processing.

- **Message storage:** Most mailbox systems provide a filing facility in which the user may file any messages he wishes to refer to later. However it can be difficult for a user to know which messages to file: at one extreme he may delete most messages but then need some of those he has disposed of at a later date; and at the other extreme he may keep most messages and end up with an overloaded, under indexed, filing system. A structure which files all messages in a central file, and which provides good search and retrieval facilities,

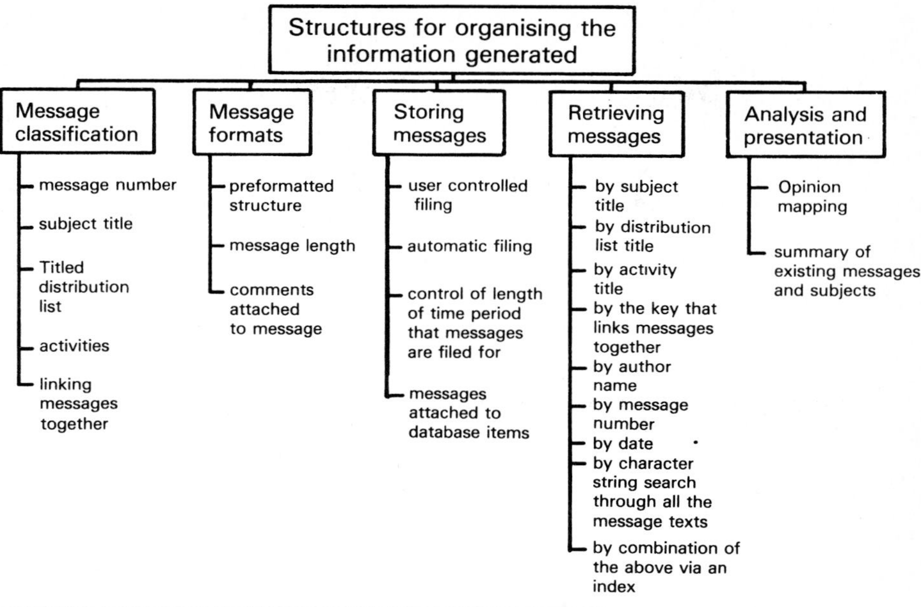

Figure 2 Mailbox structures for organising the information generated

can overcome these problems as well as allowing activity and linking structures to be introduced.

- **Retrieving messages:** It is an advantage to be able to search for messages using classification keys such as the names of distribution lists, activities and subject headings. Other search and retrieval structures are also possible: for example, in the NOTEPAD system messages can be searched for by author name, by message number or range of numbers, by last n messages, by date or by character string search through all the text of all, or some of, the messages in a particular activity.

- **Analysis and presentation of message content:** This category of structures is important in two respects: First it helps the individual to cope with information overload, and secondly they it plays a vital role in helping people who are working together, either as adversaries or as colleagues, to understand the other points of view that exist. Few structures exist in this category yet, and those that do tend to be of the management type. For example in a recent teleconference on the BLEND system (a British Library sponsored experiment to produce a scientific journal electronically (7)) the conference initiator took it upon himself to occassionally categorise the messages and present the results in summary form.

2.5 Structures for getting things done

Figure 3 shows a summary of the structures in this category.

- **Controlling the process:** Just as in a face to face environment, people who are using a mailbox system for a particular purpose need to know what roles they and the other participants have, and what responsibilities goes with those roles. Some typical roles include Leader, Chairman, Organiser and User

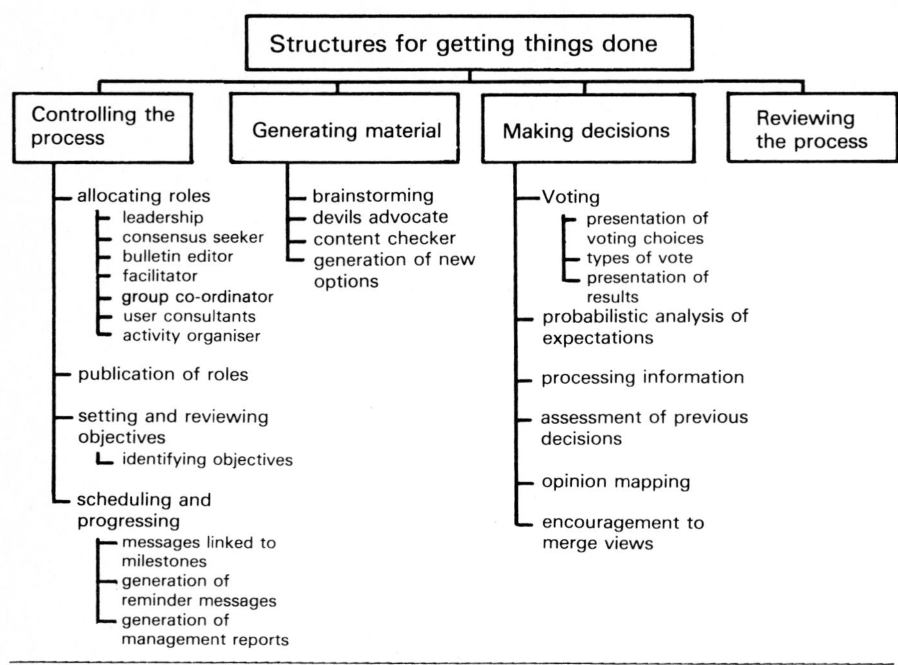

Figure 3 Mailbox structures for getting things done

Consultant. However different circumstances will undoubtedly demand different roles and responsibilities implemented by different combinations of software or management structures. For example, it may be decided to have an Organiser, rather than a Chairman, for exploratory talks between two organisations, and that a management structure, rather than a software structure, be initiated whereby the people involved are requested to send copies of all messages to the Organiser. Other types of structure that are often essential to control the work process include structures for setting and reviewing objectives, and for scheduling and progressing.

- **Generating material:** A variety of face to face structures (including Brainstorming and Synectics) have been devised to encourage the free flow of ideas and their subsequent synthesis into realistic proposals. There is considerable scope for translating these techniques (and perhaps devising others) into structures for use in a mailbox environment, thereby eliminating much of the tedious clerical work associated with recording and synthesising large numbers of ideas in a paper environment.

- **Making decisions:** Many of the more sophisticated mailbox systems in current use have voting facilities which can assist in the decision making process. For example, in the NOTEPAD system four types of responses can be illicited from participants: VOTE (Yes/No/Abstain), ESSAY (any text response), NUMBER (any positive number thereby enabling items to be ranked) and RANGE (a range of positive numbers allowing participants to indicate a degree of certainty/uncertainty). Various analysis and result presentation facilities can also be associated with voting structures. Robert Bittlestone's Metaconferencing system provides an example of how voting patterns can be analysed to inform users of who else is most in agreement or disagreement with their views in general or with their views on particular votes (8).

2.6 Structures for controlling who does what

Figure 4 shows a summary of the structures in this category.

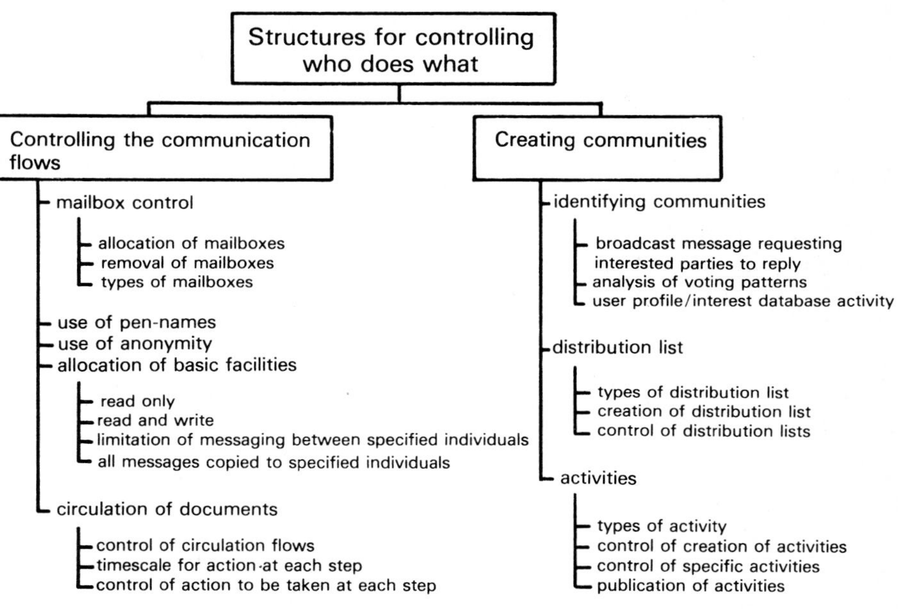

Figure 4 Mailbox structures for controlling who does what.

- **Control of the communication flows:** In many systems, management structures are in place for allocating and removing mailboxes. However, in the COM system a software structure does the same job, effectively allowing any member of the organisation to acquire a mailbox by logging on and answering some questions. The same system automatically removes those users who have not entered the system for a certain time period (9). Other structures associated with the provision of mailboxes include allocation of basic facilities (eg it is possible to specify an individual as a 'read only' member of an activity enabling them to observe the proceedings but not to contribute to them); and the use of pen names or anonymity eg the EIES system allows users to sign messages with either their real name, a pen name or anonymously as they so wish. Hiltz and Turoff report that experience in EIES has shown that pen names enable people to play a different role in a discussion whilst anonymity seems to be used to avoid embarrassment (4).

- **Control over the creation of mailbox communities:** Mailbox communities can be identified by using general mailbox facilities and structures such as sending a simple message to a large proportion of the user community asking for replies from interested parties, or using a voting facility. However some structures have been designed specifically for this purpose. For instance a data base of user interests and profiles can be maintained and searched by the system at the users request. Mailbox communities can be maintained by using Distribution Lists or Activities. In some systems two types of distribution list are held - private lists (created and maintained by individuals for their own purposes) and public distribution lists which are available to all users. Structures for maintaining who is on public distribution lists and their size and number are also beginning to appear.

Activity membership is often controlled by management structures. For instance, in the COM system there are 'open' activities, 'closed' activities and 'restricted activities. Any user can join an open activity, while only selected people can join a closed activity. Restricted activities are open to some but closed to others. An activity organiser, and only the activity organiser, has the right to add participants, exclude participants or change the activity organisor (9). However software structures which allow anybody to join if they wish and which exclude people automatically if they don't participate for a fixed length of time, are also possible.

3 Applications

The purpose of implementing the sort of structures described above is to enable mailbox systems to be applied to specific communication tasks and to solve specific communication problems. Only limited knowledge is currently available of the sort of applications that are feasible and of the associated structures that are required. However current useage seems to indicate the following categories of application:

- **Controlling branches:** Mailbox communication can reduce travel between an HQ and its branches and speed the flow of information. This results in the branches having greater autonomy while acting in a more uniform fashion (4)(10).

- **Transaction processing:** Any process that involves documents being passed through a chain of people, each taking some kind of action on them, can benefit from a structured mailbox approach. The system will control the route that the documents take, the time it takes to complete their passages and what information is added or changed. Informal communications relating to the transactions can be made through the system and attached to the transactions for subsequent referral. Detailed management information relating to current status is always available and the system can be programmed to issue warning messages when serious problems occur (5)(11).

- **Planning and progressing:** Mailbox systems can be used to control the achievement of targets. For example, in a project with several people responsible for achieving various goals throughout the project, informal communication relating to progress can be attached to specific milestones so that the history of that milestone can be easily reviewed. The system can also keep a check on timescales and issue reminder messages accordingly (5).

- **Distributing information:** Mailbox Systems can distribute most kinds of information - administrative, weekly or monthly reports, internal memos, updates of manuals or price lists, newsletters etc - faster and cheaper than the paper equivalent (3)(5)(7)(12).

- **Educational activities:** Business personnel currently have to take several days at a time out of the office to go on courses. With mailbox systems however the training can be done over a period of weeks or months and at the times most convenient to the individual. Furthurmore, discussion with fellow students and with the tutor is not constrained by time or numbers, and experts in the field can be hired to take part in the exercise no matter where in the world they happen to be located. The implications for the way schools, universities and colleges operate are clearly enormous. Already one USA Institution - The New Jersey Institute of Technology - has offered a range of 16 different continuing education participatory seminars via 'computer telecommunications' in its Spring 1983 program (13).

- **Communicating with suppliers and customers:** Two organisations that trade regularly with each other can benefit from a mailbox link. Information such as order status, delivery details and complaints can be requested by customers as required, without having to phone through to busy customer service departments and talk to someone who is not familiar with the background or details of the order. The supplier can deal with each request thoroughly and provide a well researched and complete answer within a specified turnaround time. Order placement and invoicing are logical extensions to this application (3).

- **Bringing like-minded people together:** Establishing contact between people who have the same interests, or who wish to share their knowledge, is an ideal application for mailbox systems. There are often occassions when it is likely that some valuable information is available somewhere in an organisation but it is impractical to go round everybody trying to find it. For example, if a job is to be subcontracted, the responsible manager might wish that the rest of the organisation could be asked if anyone has had any prior contact with the subcontracting company. Another example might be to provide a channel through which the users of a particular computer system can discuss problems and share the benefits of their experience (3).

- **Buying and selling:** Mailbox systems are commonly used on an informal basis for distributing, and getting responses to, small advertisments. However at the New Jersey Institute of Technology a set of structures, collectively called MARKETPLACE, have been specifically designed to facilitate an electronic market environment within the EIES system. To use these facilities an account must first be opened with a minimum deposit of $25. The MARKETPLACE structures subsequently take care of all billing. People who have purchased a particular item are allowed to add a qualitative review of the product they have purchased to the relevant advert and this cannot be tampered with or removed by the advertiser. In addition the system automatically logs and displays the number of people who have purchased from a particular advert. These facilities are being used to sell not only unwanted possessions but also consultancy over the system, computer programs, and subscriptions to ongoing discussions in closed membership activities (14). Such a system might be very useful in any organisation which wishes to promote internal efficiency and competitiveness; for example organisations which are split up into separate business units and in which internal services are cross charged. There would also seem to be a role for such systems in inter-company advertising and trading.

- **Joint working arrangements:** Mailbox systems can facilitate the preparation of documents by several co-authors. They can also provide communication facilities between people who work closely together, for example managers and secretarys or people who are sharing the same job (3).

- **Meetings:** Much of the time taken up by meetings is spent dealing with routine, non-immediate matters. These can be more effectively dealt with by appropriately structured mailbox systems thereby removing a significant administrative overhead. For example a weekly branch managers meeting might be held only once every two months if augmented by a structured mailbox system. Meetings held over a mailbox system give each individual a greater chance to contribute, and allow greater thought to be given to suggestions and opinions. Appropriate structuring can ensure better controlled meetings which emerge with clear decisions within a specified time scale. Actions can also be automatically progressed (15)(16).

- **Project teams and working parties:** In organisations that make extensive use of mailbox systems there is a tendency for cross company, cross location, project teams to emerge. This is because a mailbox system removes geographical constraints and makes it easy to talk to people in other parts of the organisation. Hence it makes sense to choose the most appropriate personnel for particular projects. No relocation is required and management can be easily kept informed of additional activities through the system. In effect this is Matrix Management under which individuals can have more than one boss and sets of responsibilities (16)(17)(18)(19).

- **Managing people:** The excellent communications afforded by a mailbox system can put managers in much closer contact with their staff. Not only can they talk more often to individuals but they can be kept informed of conversations among their staff by simply being included on a messages distribution list. Planning and progressing structures can be applied to aid the management of individual staff. Mailbox Systems also make Matrix Management a realistic and practical approach to the problem of deploying human resources (3).

- **Booking and control of facilities:** Resources such as meeting rooms, overhead projectors, company cars, dictating machines etc can all be controlled through the use of a mailbox system thereby eliminating an administrative overhead. For example if a message is sent out to a number of individuals to try and arrange a meeting, it can also be sent to 'meeting room'. The system, which maintains the record of bookings, will then automatically check its availability against the dates specified and send a message back to the originator saying if the room is available or not (3).

4 Structures for specific applications

The structures and applications descibed in this paper were identified in the course of a study of mailbox systems conducted in 1982/83 (20). In order to assess which structures are appropriate for which applications, a matrix was drawn up with Applications along the top and Structures down the side (see Appendix A). Entries were made in the matrix boxes for those systems that were known to exist or have been proposed. As can be seen in Appendix A the vast majority of the matrix is somewhat empty. This does not necessarily mean that the matrix as it stands is incomplete. However a number of reasons lead me to believe that this is the case: first of all, the list of applications is almost certainly incomplete since it represents only those applications in use today when the medium is only at a very early stage of development and use. As useage grows and understanding of its potential for formal and semi-formal communications increases, so too will the number of applications increase.

Secondly, the very concept of structuring, let alone the detailed design of specific structures, is not widely known or understood. Consequently the full range of generic structures has not yet been identified. This was demonstrated in the drawing up of the structure category diagrams shown in Figures 2,3 and 4: several structures were identified and included by myself simply to fill in obvious gaps.

However, perhaps the main reason that the matrix is empty is that users are not yet identifying application requirements and then systematically defining comprehensive ranges of structures to meet those requirements. In many cases users are happy to use mailbox systems simply as informal communication tools. However, even in those cases where users do percieve an application opportunity they usually view it as a way of making use of facilities they already have rather than appreciating that each application requires a particular brand of order and control if its goals are to be met. Those users who have identified an application requirement before they purchase a system, unfortunately find only a range of rather similar, inflexible products on the market, and consequently never become aware of what the possibilities are.

The implications for organisations about to obtain a mailbox system are clear: establish what applications you will be using it for and what associated structures you will require. Then ensure that the system you purchase can provide these facilities. However even this will not solve all the problems: inevitably users will identify new applications and will require new structures to implement them. Hence, for a mailbox system to be truly useful to an organisation, it needs to be easy to modify so that new structures can be built on demand - preferably by the users themselves. This requires an easy to use, communication-oriented, programming language. Unfortunately no such purpose-built language exists today. Hence one of the recommendations (3) of the study in which this work was conducted, encouraged the development of such a language (see Appendix B, item 3).

5 Summary

In summary, mailbox systems need not only be used for informal communications: major benefits can be obtained by using them for formal and semi-formal applications in conjunction with the appropriate mailbox structures. However for this potential to be realised an intensive research and development effort is needed, and users and suppliers must upgrade their view of what these systems are and how they can be used. Suppliers must offer products that are flexible enough to accomodate new structures as and when they are required; and users must start to implement mailbox systems for specific applications.

Bibliography

(1) Wilson P A, Maude T I, Marshall C J & Heaton N O "The Active Mailbox - your on-line Secretary', Proceedings of the IFIP 6.5 Working Conference on Computer-Based Message Services, Nottingham, 1-4th May 1984, North Holland Publications, 1984.

(2) Welch J A & Wilson P A, "Electronic Mail Systems - A Practical Evaluation Guide", NCC/Wiley Publications, 1981.

(3) Wilson P A, "Introducing the Electronic Mailbox", NCC/Wiley Publications, 1984.

(4) Hiltz S R & Turoff M, "The Network Nation", Addison-Wesley Publishing Company, 1978.

(5) Turoff M, "Management issues in Human Communication via computer" In 'Emerging Office Systems' edited by Landau R & Bair H J & Siegman H J, Ablex Publishing Corporation, 1982.

(6) Wilson P A, "Commercial electronic mailbox systems", NCC/Wiley Publications, 1983.

(7) Shackel B, Pullinger D J, Maude T I & Dodd W P, "The BLEND-LINC Project on 'Electronic Journals' after two years" In The Computer Journal Vol 26 No 3, 1983.

(8) Bittlestone R G A, "The 1982 Operational Research Society Metaconference", Company document issued by Metapraxis Ltd, 26 Barham Road, London SW20 OET, July 1983.

(9) Palme J, "The COM Teleconferencing system functional specification", Swedish National Defence Research Institute (Box 27322, S-102 54, Stockholm, Sweden), November 1981.

(10) Wilson P A, "Mailbox message systems", Limited circulation report for NCC Office Technology Circle Subscribers only, April 1984.

(11) Palme J, "Transaction-based management information systems", Swedish National Defence Research Institute (Box 27322, S-102 54, Stockholm, Sweden), March 1979.

(12) Infosystems, "Interactive computer system defuses information explosion", In Infosystems 6, 1982.

(13) NJIT Division of Continuing Education, "Continuing education participatory seminars via computer telecommunications", New Jersey Institute of Technology, Division of Continuing Education, Spring 1983.

(14) Turoff M & Chinai S, "An electronic information marketplace", Revised draft of a paper (subsequently submitted for publication to 'Computer Networking'), July 1982.

(15) Sharp I P & Perkins F J, "The impact of effective person-to-person telecoms on established management structures", In 'Business Telecoms' Conference Proceedings, September 1981.

(16) Turoff M & Hiltz S R, "Exploring the future of Human Communication via computer", In Computer Compacts Vol 1 No 2, April 1983.

(17) Wickstrom N, "College scholarships post big benefits with Telemail", In Edunet News No 24 in EDUCOM Vol 17 No 2/Summer 1982.

(18) Edunet News, "Mailnet project reaches significant milestone" In Edunet News No 25 in EDUCOM Vol 17 No 3/Fall 1982.

(19) Ferson L M, "ISA stepping up communications over EIES", In Edunet News No ppp 25 in EDUCOM Vol 17 No(;'Nidd 1982.

(20) Wilson P A, "Applications and structures for mailbox systems", in State of the Art Report 11:8iii 'The Wired Society', Pergamon Infotech Limited, 1983

Appendices A and B follow.

Appendix A (1): Application/Structure matrix

Structures for organising the information generated	Controlling branches	Transaction processing	Planning & progressing	Distributing information	Educational activities	Communicating with customers	Bringing like-minded people together	Buying & selling	Joint working arrangements	Meetings	Project teams & working parties	Managing people	Booking & control of facilities
Message classification													
• message number								1					
• subject title													
• titled distribution list	2												
• activities				3	4	5		6	7		8		9
• linking messages together				10								11	
Message formats													
• preformatted structure		12	13	14									15
• message length							16						
• comments attached to message									17				
Storing messages													
• user controlled filing													
• automatic filing									18				
• control of length of time period that messages are filed for				19									
• messages attached to database items				20		21							
Retrieving messages													
• by subject title													
• by distribution list title													
• by activity title													
• by the key that links messages together													
• by author													
• by message number													
• by date													
• by character string search through the message text													
• by combination of the above													
• via an index								22					
Analysis and presentation													
• opinion mapping													
• summary of existing messages and subjects				23									
Structures for getting things done													
Controlling the process													
• allocating roles													
– leadership													
election of leader										24			
responsibilities of leader													
setting of responsibilities													
set by group being led imposed on group being led													
control over structuring													
control over structures for organising the info. generated													
control over structures for getting things done													
control over structures for controlling who does what											25		
– consensus seeker										26			
responsibilities for consensus seeker													
establish where views differ													
try to move people towards consensus													
– bulletin editor													
responsibilities													
control over contents													
appointment of contributors/editors													

NB The numbers in the matrix refer to entries on the final page of Appendix A.

Appendix A (2): Application/Structure matrix

Controlling the process (Continued)	Controlling branches	Transaction processing	Planning & progressing	Distributing information	Educational activities	Communicating with customers	Bringing like-minded people together	Buying & selling	Joint working arrangements	Meetings	Project teams & working parties	Managing people	Booking & control of facilities
– facilitater										27			
responsibilities													
ensure debate doesn't flag and remains constructive													
– group coordinators													
responsibilities													
provision of assistance to members													
sending messages of general interest													
interface with other groups													
– user consultants													
responsibilities													
answer questions about the use of the system													
– activity organisor													
responsibilities													
control over membership of activity													
control over deletion of messages													
• publication of roles and responsibilities													
• setting and reviewing objectives													
– identifying objectives													
suggested by participants										28			
evaluation of proposed objectives										29			
by vote													
by leader													
• scheduling and progressing													
– messages linked to project plans/ milestones			30										
– generation of reminder messages			31			32				33			
– generation of management reports						34							
Generating material													
• brainstorming													
• devil's advocate													
• content checker										35			
• generation of new options										36	37		
Making decisions													
• voting													
– presentation of voting choices													
one per message													
several per message													
– types of vote													
yes/no/abstain													
any text response													
ranking													
range selection													
– presentation of results													
secret or open voting													
in summary form													
in detail													
as a group													
as a bar chart													
as a pie chart													
putting like voters in touch with each other													
• probabilistic analysis of expectations										38			
• processing of information		39	40					41					42
• assessment of previous decisions								43					
• opinion mapping							44			45			
• encouragement to merge views										46			
Reviewing the process													

NB The numbers in the matrix refer to entries on the final page of Appendix A.

Appendix A (3): Application/Structure matrix

Structures for controlling who does what	Controlling branches	Transaction processing	Planning & progressing	Distributing information	Educational activities	Communicating with customers	Bringing like-minded people together	Buying & selling	Joint working arrangements	Meetings	Project teams & working parties	Managing people	Booking & control of facilities
Controlling the communication flows													
• mailbox control													
– allocation of mailboxes													
under user control													
not under user control													
– removal of mailboxes													
by non-use criteria													
– types of mailbox													47
• use of pen names													
• use of anonymity													
• allocation of basic facilities													
– read only													
– read and write				48									
– limitation of messaging between specified individuals													
– all messages copied to specified individuals													
• circulation of documents		49											
– control of circulation flow				50									
– timescale for action at each step													
– control of action to be taken at each step													
Creating communities													
• identifying communities													
– broadcast message requesting interested parties to reply													
– analysis of voting patterns													
– user profile/interest database activity				51				52					
• distribution lists				53			54			55			
– types of distribution list													
public													
private													
– creation of distribution list													
created from result of broadcast message							56						
created from result of vote													
created from search of user interest database													
– control of distribution lists													
control of contents													
control of use													
Activities					57		58						
• types of activity													
– open													
– closed													
– restricted													
• control of creation of activities													
– uncontrolled													
– by number of existing activities													
– by topic of activity													
• control of specific activities													
– control of membership													
– by the wish of the user													
– controlled													
by number of current users													
by mix of current users													
by departmental representation													
by sex													
by qualifications													
by ability of potential members													
by test													
by qualification													
by interest taken in the activity													
expulsion for not reading messages in the activity													
expulsion for not contributing to the activity													
• publication of activities													
– simple listing													
– subject index													
– graphic display													

NB The numbers in the matrix refer to entries on the final page of Appendix A.

Appendix A (4): Application/Structure matrix (number references)

1 System tracks all adverts by their message no.
2 Distribution list containing all branch managers.
3 Special activities for topics, databases or newsletters.
4 Special activity for specific school/college/university courses.
5 Activity for communication between computer system's users and its maintainers.
6 Activity for adverts.
7 For joint authorship each message in an activity can be a section of text. An activity can also be used by a manager/secretary team.
8 Project teams/working parties can use an activity to discuss text being prepared in a separate file.
9 Records of bookings can be kept in an activity.
10 Newsletter items on the same topic can be linked.
11 A manager can link all messages between himself and one of his staff.
12 A preformatted message structure can be used for entering information at each stage on a transaction.
13 Preformatted message structure for reporting progress.
14 Database-type information held and distributed in preformatted messages.
15 Preformatted messages for making booking requests.
16 Requests for information limited to, say, 3 lines and replies limited to, say, 1 line.
17 Ability for joint workers to add comments to messages; comments perhaps to be displayed only on request.
18 All versions of text being jointly authorised are automatically filed.
19 Old newsletter items moved to another activity after a specified time period.
20 Messages attached to database items are presented to the user only when accessing that item of data.
21 Messages linked to orders or to customers/suppliers.
22 Index of advert messages so potential purchasers can identify those they are interested in.
23 Summary of existing messages and subjects for the assembly of a newsletter contents list.
24 Election of chairman for a meeting.
25 Chairman can decide what and how often to send hard copy versions of working party proceedings to those members who have no access to the mailbox system.
26 Consensus seeker can be appointed by meeting chairman.
27 Facilitater uses intervention tools when there is deterioration in the debate at a meeting.
28 Agenda items put forward by individuals.
29 Agenda items accepted or rejected as either mailbox topics or face-to-face topics.
30 All project-related messages attached to appropriate project milestones.
31 Reminder message automatically produced when the date of an action message is exceeded.
32 Reminder messages automatically generated to ensure that answers to customer queries are sent within a specified turnaround time.
33 Reminder messages generated in meetings to ensure that agenda items are discussed and that action items are reported back on.
34 Management reports automatically generated to summarise the turnaround time for replying to customer queries and to pinpoint significantly overdue queries.
35 A content checker could identify emotionally-charged terms etc in meetings.
36 New options could be inserted into a meeting discussion.
37 A specific individual generates a document, para. by para. in a separate file, making changes according to the discussion on the text generated in a separate activity by members of the working party/project team.
38 Analysis of message content could identify those options with the greatest group consensus.
39 Information entered in a transaction processing application can be processed (eg verification or totalling).
40 Diaries can be searched to set up meetings requested in messages.
41 The system can ensure there is sufficient money in a purchaser's account before allowing him to buy from an advert.
42 The system can search a booking list to see when a facility is free, make the booking and send back a reply to the user.
43 The attachment of a purchaser's comment and the no. of purchasers, onto the end of an advert.
44 The assessment of voting patterns to match like-minded people.
45 Mapping of the views of attendees at meetings for comparison.
46 Metaconference encourages participants to produce a 'focus of concern'.
47 Mailboxes can be allocated to particular facilities so that messages can be sent to, for example, 'meeting rooms'.
48 The specification of who is authorised to enter or change values in a database.
49 Control of transaction messages as they go round a series of people.
50 Distribution of social event messages to those who have said they are prepared to receive such information.
51 Record of user interests can be used to distribute social event messages.
52 Record of user interests can help advertisers to identify potential purchasers.
53 Distribution lists can be used by teachers to communicate with course students.
54 Distribution lists can maintain communication between like-minded people.
55 Distribution lists can be used to assemble and run *ad-hoc* meetings.
56 Users elect to receive all communications on a topic and are consequently put on a distribution list.
57 Activities can be used for communication between students and teachers on specific courses.
58 Activities can maintain communication between like-minded people.

Appendix B: Requirements for the effective deployment of Mailbox Systems.

1 The strategic application of mailbox systems will result in a significant improvement in the profitability and competitiveness of UK organisations, though the full impact will not become apparent until organisations have developed new cultures that take advantage of the new medium.

Recommendation: UK organisations should be encouraged to implement mailbox systems and to implement them quickly.

2 Despite the importance of the concept of structuring to the effective deployment of mailbox systems, the current level of knowledge of this subject is very low. Most of the work in this area is currently being done at a few centres in the US. The NCC project has identified very little work of this nature being undertaken in the UK at the present time.

Recommendation: A UK mailbox structuring research programme should be initiated immediately. This should concentrate on applied research with the results being transferred rapidly to industry and commerce, preferably via a mailbox communication channel.

3 Mailbox systems need to be written in flexible, high-level, communication-oriented programming languages so that they can be easily written and modified at will. Existing languages do not possess such features and consequently they slow down the development of mailbox systems and, more damagingly, constrain the addition of new structures.

Recommendation: Research should be done to establish what features are required of a high-level, mailbox-oriented language. This should take the form of first establishing the many requirements that have already been recorded in the literature and then building on those. Once a definitive set of requirements has been established, an appropriate language for use in the UK and elsewhere should then be developed.

4 Very few of the mailbox systems currently on the market have any structuring facilities or the flexibility to allow new structures to be incorporated.

Recommendation: Suppliers should be encouraged to develop new products which provide structuring capabilities.

Recommendation: The UK Government's Software Products Scheme should take this requirement into account when considering applications for funding the development of proposed mailbox systems.

5 The power of a communication system lies in the number of people that can be contacted through it. Consequently, the interconnection of mailbox systems is crucial to the development of the medium and must, in turn, rely on the development and adoption of standards. At the international level, bodies such as ECMA, CCITT and ISO are working on such standards and the UK is supporting these efforts. Within the UK itself a consortium led by the Department of Industry is working on international work and recommending standards which will stimulate the interconnection of mailbox and other message systems in the short term.

Recommendation: Consideration should be given to the funding of demonstration projects which utilise the messaging intercept standards.

Computer-Based Message Services
H.T. Smith (Editor)
Elsevier Science Publishers B.V. (North-Holland)

USER FRIENDLY INTERFACE FOR MESSAGING SYSTEMS

Liane Margarida Rockenbach Tarouco

Data Processing Center
Federal University of "Rio Grande do Sul"
Porto Alegre, RS
BRAZIL

This paper discusses a number of broad considerations for messaging systems design in order to achieve a good system. What constitutes a "good" design from a human factor point of view is presented, as well as experiences arising from developments at the University Federal of "Rio Grande do Sul".

1. INTRODUCTION

Anyone who has been involved in producing an interactive program is painfully aware that it is not a matter of developing a batch program and then slapping on a terminal interface, not even just a matter of designing good screen layout; a program can have an excellent screen layout and still be unsuitable (1).

The root of the problem is that dialog design is a job not only with technical but also with psychological, social, and even political implications.

On the psychological side, more attention has been given to response times. What reactions can be predicted if the user has to wait five seconds for a change of screen content? Or fifteen seconds? Or fifty?

The social aspects are less studied, more difficult, and much more important. They include questions such as what should a computer be used for, how does it affect the job content of users - and nonusers - and its effect on relations between people.

Social questions take on a political aspect when the use of the computer is compulsory rather than discretionary - when the user must switch to use specified programs from a terminal, or else lose his/her job. The fear of automation is related to the social impact of the new technology. Users are concerned about personal privacy and job security.

Computer Based Message Systems represent a new technology in a new area. Its success depends on research and experimentation in several areas determining the ideal characteristics of a system having only beneficial effects to society.

Such experiences are necessary because individual characteristics must be respected, adjusting systems to them or developing systems specially oriented to them, instead of trying to force the use of new technologies unfamiliar to their culture. Without this care, there are two risks; non-assimilation of the technology, however great the effort of training used, or the loss of cultural values, generating the cultural colonialism.

A computer mail system runs the risk of lying idle unless it is well-matched to its operational environment, if its use is not forced by a corporate management, Bruder (2).

A good example is provided by an experience at the Federal University of Rio Grande do Sul - UFRGS a few years ago (3). At that time the design and the implementation of a messaging system named CONFERENCE had started. A first version of CONFERENCE was developed in a very short period of time and it was installed on the computer B-6700 of UFRGS.

Its major characteristics were:

a. a menu driven user interface;
b. messages could be up to a limited size, and could be sent to only one receiver;
c. the only editing available was modification to the typed text before transmission of the message. The local editing capabilities of the terminal were used to insert or delete characters, on screen;
d. automatic notification of receipt of mail was not implemented and to receive messages the user had to answer YES to the display question "Do you wish to receive messages?";
e. Once read messages were automatically purged without any instructions from the user;
f. passwords were associated with individual users.

As soon as users start to try out the system, some complaints arose:

- a non-destructive feature with retrieval of messages when required by user;
- message length was too severe;
- a better man-machine dialog.

The last compliant was the major one and it demanded a complete redesign of the structure of the dialog. The studies and the solutions implemented are the main contents of the paper.

2. PREPARING THE USER FOR THE SYSTEM

Before realising that a user interface is unsuitable, one can plan to prepare the users for a new on-line system.

Several strategies have been used to prepare users to interact with an on-line system. The most frequently found are on-the-job training and self-paced programs.

a. ON-THE-JOB TRAINING

Although classroom instruction has been the most common

method of training the first system operators, on-the-job training has been the usual method of training additional operators. Managers have been reluctant to part with operators for a three-day classroom training. Furthermore, capable operators, recalling their own experiences, are often convinced they can do a better job training new operators themselves.

Usually on-the-job training enables a new user to perform basic tasks more quickly than classroom training; in a short time the operator can send a message. The operator is only marginally productive, however, and he will make frequent requests for assistance. In addition contradictory guidelines may be provided by the different people performing the training. Quite often, on-the-job training is tantamount to no training at all. Because exclusive time for training is not set aside, training becomes random. There is no planned curriculum, instruction in underlying concepts, or schedule of checkpoints to indicate mastery of certain procedures. The user can usually perform a task only one way, often not the preferred way. The result is a low level of user proficiency and underutilization of the system.

b. SELF-PACED PROGRAMS

Because of growing dissatisfaction with classroom and on-the-job training, an increasing number of vendors of on-line systems are offering self-paced programs. Sometimes these are the only available training methods. In any event, more users are opting for the self-paced programs.

A good program teaches concepts and applications information as well as step-by-step procedures. Self-paced programs also allow learners to work at their own speed. Materials can be reviewed as often as necessary, which is reassuring for many operators and instills self-confidence. A good self-paced program is also modular, allowing learners to complete segments of information in two-or three-hours blocks of time. Because they do not have to be completed in sequence, the modules can be selected on an as-needed basis, thereby increasing immediate productivity and providing learned reinforcement.

However, despite all efforts on preparing the user for any new on-line system, if the user-interface design is bad, some problems soon arise.

One of the symptons of usability defects is likely to be a demand for more documentation than originally planned. Some design faults can be overcome by good documentation, but in the case of messaging systems, people hope not to have to study too much to use it. The system should be as easy to use as the telephone set.

The next symptom may well be demands for program changes. Many requests for changing should be taken as a warning. Requests for new options, and other message sizes are examples of these kind of requests.

A more serious problem arises when projected improvements in productivity don't materialise. With a messaging system we expect:

- to provide more access to individuals and their work;
- to create more opportunities for information exchange;
- to eliminate partially the travel need or time waste in those situations in which face-to-face meetings can be

substituted by computer-based conferences;
- to favour co-authorship of joint work or research by geographically spread groups;
- to enable idea exchange for decision making or training at the most adequate time and place for everyone.

Since the user of a messaging system may be a laymen in computing, the man-machine interface must be humanized, the technical jargon be controlled, and different access strategies be implemented and tested. Thus, beginners have to use tutorial or menu-based dailogues. For more skilled users, mnemonics or parameters may be used to make the interaction more rapid and efficient. In any case, it is absolutely necessary that an error recovery structure exists, and the graphic character set used in communication must include all those forms normally used by users (lower case, accents, special letters as "cedilla", etc.).

The success of a computing system designed to intermediate human communication depends strongly on human factor or ergonomics issues. The goal of responding to human needs becomes increasingly important for automated offices in which people and computers share the same work space. The interface between them is critical because the success of automation ultimately depends on how easy the technology is to learn and how comfortable the users become with it (4).

In order to design better interfaces for messaging systems it was decided to start an intensive study of software ergonomics and the results (4) were used in designing the user interface.

3. DESIGNING THE USER-INTERFACE

A portion of each system must be devoted to communication with the user, to such activities as accepting and translating user commands, communicating results back to him or her, and informing him of any error conditions that arise. This portion of the system is known as its user interface. This is the combination of hardware and software that allows a user to communicate with and control thehe underlying functional aspects of the system.

User interfaces are thus of vital importance. Unless a user can communicate naturally, flexibly, efficiently, and robustly with a system, the usefulness of that system is diminished. Only recently has user interface design received the attention demanded by its importance. Specific benefits of good user interfaces include reduced training time, increased user satisfaction, increased speed of use, reduced error rate, and availability to casual users. This is an important point in a developing country where the lack of equipment results in a lower grade of utilization by each user.

One of the biggest complaints with the old system was the time required to use the system (i.e., to send or receive messages). Where users have easy access to terminals, the computer-mediated communication is more dynamic. In a developing country the availability of equipment is not enough, but users still consider the message system to be effective in environments with several users for each terminal. However, in such a situation, the time to use a system becomes more critical, since lots of people wish to use the same terminal.

On the other hand, currently available user interfaces fall short of the ideal of natural, flexible and robust communications:

there are however, considerable differences in quality among the various interfaces. These differences can be characterized in terms of several user interface features that have been shown to be important:

- Interactive interfaces

The most natural way for a human to communicate with a computer is an interactive conversation in which the user gives a command and the system immediately performs it and presents the results.

- Rapid response

A system should respond rapidly to user commands. Otherwise, the user will become frustrated, his performance will be degraded, and his time will be wasted. Experience shows that the user does not use a very slow system, because it is possible to execute the work faster without the help of the computer.

- Feedback

An interface should provide immediate feedback to its user about the effect his commands have had. If such feedback is not given the user may be uncertain whether his command has been carried out. In this case the user could repeat the last command (causing it to be executed twice) or simply leave the system.

- Error is recoverable

An interface should, as far as possible, protect the user against his own errors. In particular, it should permit destructive commands to be reversed, at least for a limited time after they are issued. For instance, if the user had commanded a deletion of a message and changes his mind, it could be possible to catch the message again.

- Help facilities

An interface should be able to explain how to use its underlying system. This often takes the form of a HELP command, which can give canned explanations of the other available commands.

- Multiple contexts

A user should be able to perform more than one task at a time. In an electronic mail system it is often convenient to refer to other, already filed messages, while composing a new one. The user should be free to consult this information without interrupting composition of his new message. The most natural way to do this is through a split display screen in which different parts of the same physical screen act as independent windows onto different tasks, as was done with the APPLE LISA system.

Then the question becomes how large a part of the various system resources (both hardware and software) should be devoted to making their user interfaces as efficient, effective, and as friendly as possible. But without good interfaces, sophisticated systems cannot be used to their full potential, and the total benefit from such systems might actually be less than from systems with less sophisticated capabilities but better interfaces.

A good and helpful interface is accessible to casual users. Essentially for the reasons mentioned in regard to the reduction of training time, a user need not be an expert to make an effective use of a system with a good interface. Instead he should be able to use it on a casual or occasional basis without the need to remember a lot of complicated procedures. This means, for example, that a manager might sometimes deal with his own mail through an electronic mail system. He would be freed from relying on his secretary as an operator to mediate between him and the machine.

Initially, in designing the system at UFRGS a great deal of effort was put into making the system as straightforward to use as possible for the casual user (with such techniques as extensive prompting, and menu selection by letters typed from the keyboard). This kind of approach, a menu driven interface, was appropriate to naive users but too dull for regular ones. Evaluation of the prototype showed that more frequent users didn't like it. The system was implemented in a centralizated facility, sharing a very busy machine with a lot of other on-line systems. So, the response-time was very bad and it demanded too much time to search inumerable menus. Furthermore, in this kind of approach, where the system has the initiative, the only thing the user can do is answer the questions of the system. The more serious user is likely to become frustrated with the inherent rigidity of this approach to interface design.

Another alternative could be a system in which the user has the initiative in the interaction. An interface allowing the user initiative requires, for instance, a command language to express wishes in the form of entire commands, complete with parameters. Although restricted, a command language should be a real language in the sense that it has consistent syntax and semantics that allow the meaning of a command to be built up out of the meanings of its parts. Consistency is particularly important. Inconsistencies can make it difficult for the user to remember what can be used and when and this will lead to considerable frustation and inefficiency on his part.

In a developing country, the most common problem faced when a new system is being designed is the lack of equipment (machine capacity) and, in the case of a messaging system, the fact that users are naive or casual.

So, in designing the new messaging system at UFRGS, it was decided to start with two new approaches: a hybrid menu and natural language based interface.

a. The hybrid menu and command language interface

The first alternative, the hybrid menu and command language interface, is being implemented on a microcomputer. In this way, the response time can be improved because the micro, the brazilian COBRA-305, operates as a dedicated User Agent when a user wishes to submit or receive messages.

The recommendations being developed by CCITT on messaging were used as model for the system. The annex present a brief summary on it (5). Only after the User Agent has all the elements to understand what the user really wishes, does it start the interaction between the User Agent and the Message Transfer System. The Message Transfer System runs in a COBRA-530, a medium brazilian computer system. The user originator of the message prepares messages with the assistance of his User Agent. The User Agent is an application process (a MUMPS program running in the COBRA-305 microcomputer) that interacts with the Message Transfer System (another MUMPS program running at the COBRA-530 computer) to submit messages. The Message Transfer System delivers to one or more recipient User Agents (only when they connect) the messages submitted to it.

The user interface to access the User Agent Services was designed with a menu prompting for a list of commands. The user selects an entry and provides additional parameters. If he does not add them, the system asks specifically for the parameters needed. So, the naive user can be lead by the system, and the more frequent user can have more initiative and be more efficient.

b. The natural language interface

Another approach to improving the user interface is to imlement a natural language processing system, where the user may command the system using Portuguese as command language.

This approach was tested initially on a DEC system, at LNEC-Laboratório Nacional de Engenharia Civil, in Portugal. The language used to implement the recognizer of Portuguese language is PROLOG. The implementation was done by Rosa Maria Viccari from UFRGS, with the orientation of Dr. Helder Coelho from LNEC based on a previous work he has developed in this field and using Artificial Intelligence techniques (6). The first step was finished in March '84 with a complete query system about a specific data base. The system is able to understand questions and affirmatives in natural language (Portuguese) and react to the commands issued, answering the questions.

The next step will be the implementation of this Portuguese understanding system on a microcomputer and then it will be used as a man-machine interface for another system (a CAI-Computer Aided System and the CONFERENCE system).

We believe that this interface will be the best alternative because it allows not only the naive but also the frequent user to interact in a very natural way. The naive user does not need to remember a command language or codes, and the frequent user does not need to proceed through innumerable tedious menus.

An important point that will not be evaluated until this step is concluded is the minimum amount of system resources (hardware and software) requested for the efficiency and effectiveness of the system.

4. CONCLUSIONS

Messaging systems are expected to become an important means for domestic and international exchange of technical and scientific information. They represent the synthesis of telecommunications and information systems, and can offer the ability to organize and structure the access and location so as to enable optimization of resource and manpower use, mainly the specialized one (not necessarily in computing), which is the most critical in developing countries.

But it is important, as stated before, that the man-machine interface must be humanized. With the approaches at UFRGS, it is expected that eventually, the interface to each user or class of user may be personalized according to his degree of knowledge and experience with the system. The interaction way may vary from menus showing the possibilities of the system and parameters provided or requested to the user, to a natural language based interface, in which any user will be free to communicate his requests to the computer.

Computer-Based Message Services
H.T. Smith (Editor)
Elsevier Science Publishers B.V. (North-Holland)

You Have 134 Unread Mail! Do You Want To Read Them Now?

Jacob Palme
QZ Computer Center
Box 27322, 102 54 Stockholm
Sweden

Electronic mail system can, if used by many people, cause severe information overload problems. The cause of this problem is that it is so easy to send a message to a large number of people, and that systems are often designed to give the sender too much control of the communication process, and the receiver too little control. The solution to the problem must be too increase the control of the receiver. To do this, structure is needed on the set of messages. Electronic mail systems thus need to be more data base oriented, like some computer conference systems already are.

The problem

In many large computer message systems or networks, one of the major problems already is that people get too many messages, which they do not have time to read. This also means that the really important messages are difficult to find in a large flow of less important messages.

In the future, when we get larger and larger message systems, and these systems get more and more interconnected, this will be a problem for almost all users of these systems.

If electronic message systems are to succeed, we must find a way of overcoming this problem. This paper discusses the problem, and ways of overcoming it in different existing electronic message systems.

The cause

In order to handle this problem, we must first understand its cause.

The average time of writing a message (accourding to statistics on our COM system, see Palme [6]) is 3.6 minutes, and the average time of reading a message is 0.47 minutes. Thus, if every written message was sent to one receiver, people would spend eight times more writing messages than reading them. Some very few very popular people would in such a situation get too many messages, but the average user would certainly not be overloaded with messages.

If, however, the message system allows the sender of a message to send copies of the same message to many receivers, the odds will change. In many systems, the time to write a message to one hundred receivers is not any longer than the time to write a message to one single receiver. Thus, with only 3.6 minutes of work to write a message, its author can cause 0.47 minutes of reading time for one hundred receivers, or a total of 47 minutes of reading time for all its receivers. Obviously, this will easily mean that receivers get more messages than they can cope with.

Thus, the problem of people getting too many messages is closely connected with the facilities of message systems to easily distribute the same message to a large number of receivers. In ARPANET and CSNET, for example, this problem is severe because these networks have a large number of distribution lists where a message sent to a distribution will be sent to all people on the distribution list. USENET has the same problems for its distributed conferences.

Another way of explaining the problem is to say that many mail systems give too much control over the communication to the senders of messages, too little control to the receivers:

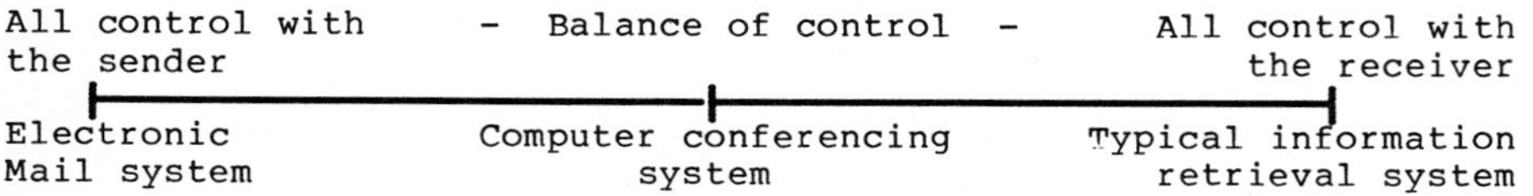

By designing CBMS-es to shift the control more to receivers, less to the senders, the information overload problem can be overcome.

Do not forbid multi-receiver messages

Since the cause of the problem is that it is so easy to send messages to many receivers, one solution might be to forbid messages to many receivers. This is however a bad solution. There is a need for messages sent to many receivers. Many systems have a facility called "distribution list" or "bulletin board" or "computer conference", through which the sender only needs to give the name of a group of receivers, in order to get a message sent to all members of the group. In the rest of this paper, the word "group communication" will be used for this facility. It is very is popular and widely used.

By sending messages to many receivers, a communication process involving many people is created. And computer message systems can, with better design, be very useful for communication between many people.

Suppose you have a need to communicate in a group of 12 people. The total time for all 12 participants is shown below (Turoff [2], Palme [6]):

Computer message system: Longer writing time but shorter reading time

Writing	Reading	Total time
3.6 min.	11 times 0.47 = 5.2 minutes.	3.6 + 5.2 = 8.8 minutes.

Face-to face or telephone/video meeting: You talk faster than you write, but you listen slower than you read:

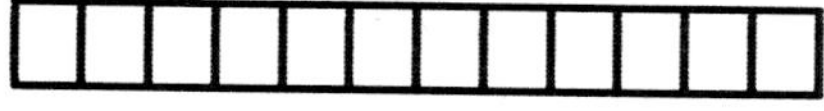

Total time for talking and listening: 12 times 1.7 = 20.4 minutes.

Communication through a computer message system is thus more efficient with time, and this will be more pronounced as the group size increases. If the time and cost of travel is included, the message system is of course even more efficient.

The reason why the reading time is shorter in the computer message system is not only because people read faster than they listen, but also because a computer message system allows every participant to decide how much time to spend on each message. You can read carefully items of importance and skip items with information you already know or which is of no interest to you.

This difference is not only an efficiency factor. It is also important psychologically. With twelve participants, as in the example above, every person uses about a third of his/her time giving information and about two thirds of the time receiving information, in the computer message system. In an ordinary face-to-face meeting with 12 participants, they would on average talk 8 % of the time and listen 92 % of the time (Palme [6]). Communication can work psychologically better with computer message systems, because you are not forced to be a passive listener as much as in face-to-face meetings. This also means that computer message systems can work well even in group sizes of 30-100 people which would be very difficult to manage in face-to-face meetings, provided the problem with information overload can be solved.

A typical situation in a face-to-face meeting with 12 participants is that one person is talking. Some other persons are listening very impatiently, saying to themselves: "Does he have to say the same things I have heard ten times before. The meeting is already late, and I have other things to do." But at the same time, other participants at the same meeting may find the same presentation very valuable - they have not heard it before.

Another side of the same coin is that a talker may not say what he wants to say, because he knows that some participants have heard it before and want to go somewhere else. But this may mean that other participants do not get information which is important to them and which they have not heard before.

Very common in face-to-face meetings is that time is not enough to take up all you want to discuss, and people have to supress comments which might have been very valuable. This seldom happens in computer communication systems.

Thus, because of the shorter reading time and that you easily can skip messages you are not interested in, computer message systems can be very efficient media in larger groups.

Compare the following times to communicate the same amount of information to all the participants in a group (Palme [6]):

To 5 people in a face-to-face meeting: 9 minutes

To 33 people in a face-to-face meeting: 56 minutes

To 33 people with a computer message system: 18 minutes

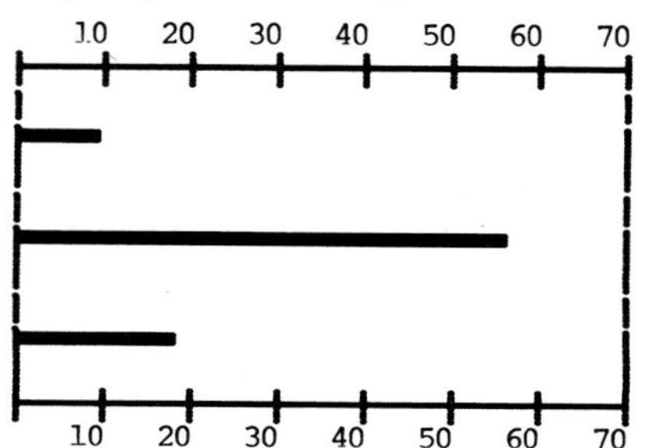

Increasing the group size to 33 people becomes prohibitively ineffecient with a face-to-face meeting, but not so with a computer message system - if we can solve the information overload problem.

This table shows how much of the communication in a large research institute using the COM computer conference system which went between people who were close and distant in the organization (Palme [6]):

	Using the mail facility	Using the conference facility
Communication between people within one department	77 %	38 %
Communicatin between people in different departments	23 %	62 %

These result shows that there is a difference between who communicates with whom using the mail and the conference facility in the system. The mail facility gives more communication between people who are close geographically or organizationally and who know each other well. The group communication facility gives more communication between people who are far away and do not know each other. The reason for this is that the sender of a conference entry does not have to think of the names of all the people who are to receive the entry.

A CBMS with a group communication facility provides an environment where people can "meet" and exchange ideas much more freely than in a pure mail system (Hiltz [2]). Contacts between people who did not know each other before are much easier to establish with a group communication facility than in a pure mail system. A system with group communication facilities will much more easily provide cooperation and a feeling of togetherness between widely dispersed people. People who regularly use computer conferencing say that a whole new dimension of contacts and communication has opened up for them, and that they cannot understand how they were able to live in the seclusion before they started using the system.

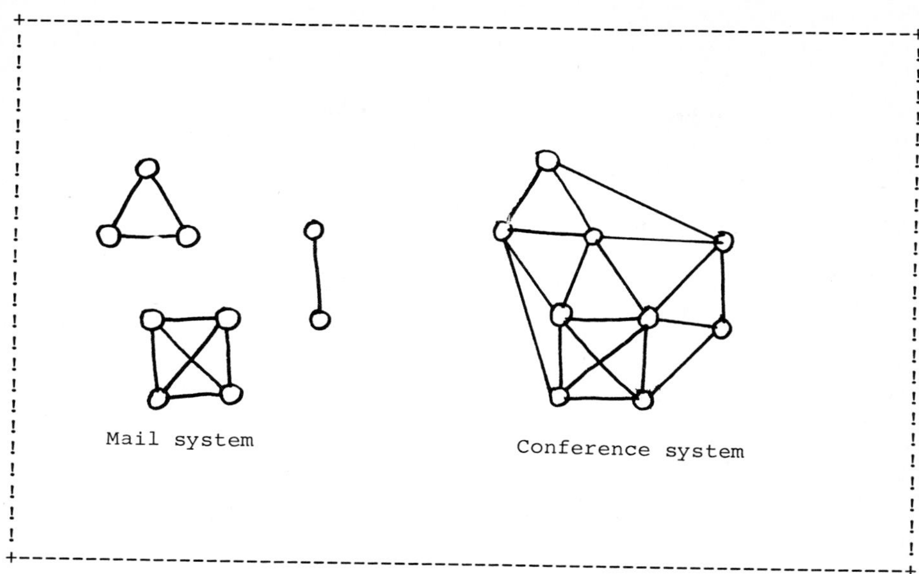

What then, is the effect of the increased number of contacts at large organizational and geographical distances, which systems with group communication facilities give. This has been studied in sociological research (Allen [1]). This research shows that people having such contacts are more successful. They tend to be less conservative, they will easier accept new ideas and they are less prone to get stuck with bad or suboptimal solutions to their problems.

Thus, even though sending the same message to many receivers can cause information overload problems, it is also a very valuable and useful facility. We should find ways of overcoming the overload problems but still permitting larger groups.

Control by conferences

One solution to the information overload problem is to put a structure on the set of incoming messages. Instead of delivering an unordered heap of messages, the system should deliver a neatly structured data base of incoming messages. The structure of this data base should be such that the reader can easily find those messages he finds important. It should allow the reader to decide which messages to read immediately, which to save to another time, and which not to read at all. It should be easy for a user to change these decisions as new information comes in.

Here is an example of how a user of the COM computer conference system is greeted by the system (Palme [7]):

```
You have 5 unseen letters
You have 2 unseen entries in GILT open meeting
You have 13 unseen entries in Supercomputers
You have 5 unseen entries in English language
You have 6 unseen entries in Announcement (of new) conferences
```

```
You have 19 unseen entries in Speakers corner
You have 19 unseen entries in Presentation (of new) COM users
You have 1 unseen entries in Fifth generation computer project
You have 18 unseen entries in Packet-switched network use
You have 11 unseen entries in Microcomputers
You have 5 unseen entries in TeX inter-network mailing list
You have 1 unseen entries in KERMIT experience
You have 34 unseen entries in TOPS-10/20 SIG

You have 134 unseen entries
```

Every message which was sent to the user via a computer conference (distribution list, bulletin board) is also delivered to him as an entry in that conference. The user normally will read one conference at a time. The users decide themselves in which order to read the conferences, and they can save some conferences to read at a later time. If they get too much information, they can also withdraw completely from conferences they are not interested in, or skip part of the discussion in that conference but still stay as a member.

A computer conference system also allows messages which are not sent as conference entries. But the systems usually intentionally are designed to make it difficult to send such a message to more than a few receivers. Thus, the amount of messages which are not sorted into conferences is kept small. Instead, the systems make it easy to create new conferences as the need arises.

A computer conference has an organizer, who can remove messages which do not fit to the subject of the conference. Thus, the organizer helps the participants to control what they receive by ensuring that they get messages on the subject they have choosen when participating in the conference. In the COM system, the organizer can not delete text entries. The organizer can only remove the link between the entry and the conference, and optionally add a link to another conference more suitable to the contents of the entry.

Control by comment trees

Another way of structuring messages is by comment trees. A system can be designed to store relations between messages, where one of them can be a comment or a reply to another message. Thus, a set of messages which refer to each other directly or indirectly can be identified automatically by the system. Such a set of related messages can be called a "comment tree". It is a grouping of messages, just as a computer conference. And in the same way, the receivers of messages can be given the facility of choosing in which order to read the different comment trees, and to skip messages in a comment tree of less interest.

In the COM computer conference system (Palme [7]), comment trees are used to structure those messages which do not belong to conferences, and comment trees are also used as a sub-structure within conferences.

Control by keywords

Yet another solution is to affix keywords to messages. The system can then be told to deliver messages according to their keywords, thus giving the reader more control of what to read and not to read. A problem with this solution is that it can be difficult to get the senders of messages to assign well-chosen keywords to their messages.

Note that keywords and computer conferences are very similar concepts. This is especially so in the COM and PortaCOM computer conference systems, since in those systems one and the same entry can be linked to more than one conference (Palme [7]). Thus, the set of conferences for a COM message is very similar to the set of keywords in a keyword-based system. In other systems, like the EIES system, keywords and conferences are kept as two separate concepts which can both be used by readers to select which messages they want to read.

Control by subject

Another way of controlling communication is to select messages by subject. Again, this is rather similar to computer conferencing, where all messages with a certain subject can be seen as a kind of conference. Just like in conference systems, it would be valuable to be able to read all messages on a certain subject before continuing with a new subject.

In the EIES computer conference system, there is a facility called TOPICS in which every new subject taken up in a conference becomes a new sub-conference on that subject. Every member of the main conference decides whether or not to participate in the subconference.

The experience from EIES is that this facility is very efficient in reducing communication. In fact, it is so efficient that it can easily kill a conference by splitting the participants into too many small subconferences, and thus reducing communication so much that people stop participating in the main conference. Thus, the people behind EIES recommend use of the TOPICS facility for very large and too active conferences where too much is written for each member, but they do not recommend this facility normally for normal-size conferences.

In COM, comment trees as sub-conferences work in a similar manner, but every member of the main conference becomes a "member" of the subconference unless they explicitly give a command to skip that subconference. This design will not reduce communication so much as the TOPICS facility in EIES.

Control by selection

One way of controlling communication is to have some people select messages. Other people can then read only the selected messages. This is thus similar to editors in magazines who select what to publish.

In the COM computer conference system we have write-protected conferences, where only certain people can link entries to the conference. Other people must thus first send their entries to one of the editors, or to a conference for submitted papers. The editors then decide which messages can be linked to the write-protected conference.

Write-protected conferences can also be used to contain a selection of the most important entries from ordinary open conferences. COM also has a special kind of conference to which no one can send messages directly, but anyone can link messages indirectly. Anyone can link a message s/he reads which is especially interesting to such a conference. They have been very useful.

Both these kinds of conferences get very few messages compared to ordinary open conferences, and are thus a good selection criteria for those who only want to read a small selection of the most important items.

Control by author

Finally, messages can be selected by author. This can be done in several ways. One crude way would be to allow a person to tell his system "I do not want to read any more messages written by John Smith".

Other ways of selecting by author is to divide the user population into groups, so that a reader can select only messages by authors within certain groups. The write-protected conference, as described above, can be seen as such a facility, since the editors can write directly to the conference, but no other users.

In COM, a comment on an entry in a write-protected conference is automatically furthered to a specially designated super-conference which is not write-protected.

Group selection can also be used so that only experts in a certain field can write in a conference, but other people may read their discussions and comment on them in a super-conference. COM has such a facility. Or one might select by CBMS. For example, ARPANET-CSNET might for some of their mailing list allow people outside ARPANET-CSNET to read, but not to enter messages to that particular mailing list.

Instead of just skipping messages by certain authors, it is better to further these messages to special structures, so that those who want to read them can read them there. For example, the so-called "postmaster" conference often gets many messages, which can automatically be sorted by categories and sent along to different conferences depending on who is interested in reading them.

Selection by abstract writing

Finally, some people could abstract the discussions in volumnious open conferences into write-protected conferences containing only the abstracts. Such abstracts have been very useful in the ARPANET-CSNET community. In the EIES TOPICS system, an abstract of each subconference is meant to be entered into the main conference.

User interface aspects

To reduce information overload, we need structuring on the message set. This structuring must be based on information input by the writer of the messages, by someone else (e.g. assigning keywords) or automatically by the system. Having special people assigning keywords to all messages in a large mail system is not practical.

Important is therefore to use such information which we can easily get the writers of message to input in a reliable manner. Useful is also if someone else can correct mistakes by the writers, like the conference organizer who moves entries to another conference when needed.

The COM system is intentionally designed to make it easier to input a comment on a previous entry than to input a non-comment, just because the comment link is useful structuring information. This is an example of how the user interface can be designed to further structuring.

Future development

In the future, we can expect larger and larger systems and networks of systems. New structuring facilities will then be needed. Probably what will have to be introduced is a facility to divide large discussion groups into subgroups, where only selected messages or abstracts of the discussions in the subgroups are made available to all participants in all groups.

Conclusion

Computer-based message systems are especially good for communication in large groups, where they can widen horizons and give more people more information and contacts. Efficient methods of allowing the readers of messages to control what they get will actually enable communication in larger groups than without such methods, and will thus make the message systems more valuable.

References

[1] Allen, Thomas J.: Managing the Flow of Technology. MIT Press 1977.

[2] Hiltz, Starr Roxanne and Turoff, Murray: The Network Nation: Human Communication via Computer. Addison-Wesley 1978.

[3] Hiltz, Starr Roxanne and Kerr, Elaine B.: Studies of computer mediated communications systems: A syntehis of the findings, New Jersey Institute of Technology, August 1981.

[4] Hiltz, Starr Roxanne, Johnson, K., Aronovitch, C., Turoff, M.: Face-to-face vs. computerized conference: A controlled experiment. New Jersey Institute of Technology, 1980.

[5] Kerr, Elaine . and Hiltz, Starr Roxanne: Computer-Mediated Communication Systems. Academic Press 1982.

[6] Palme, Jacob 1981: Experience with the Use of the COM Computerized Conferencing System. Swedish National Defense Research Institute, Box 27322, S-102 54 Stockholm, Sweden, 1981.

[7] Palme, Jacob 1983: COM/PortaCOM conference system: Design goals and principles. QZ Computer Centre, Box 27322, S-102 54 Stockholm, Sweden, 1983.

[8] Palme, Jacob 1983: Computer Conferencing is More than Electronic Mail. Transcripts of the EUTECO, European Teleinformatics Conference, North-Holland, 1983.

[9] Palme, Jacob 1984: Survey of computer-based message systems. Transcripts of the INTERACT '84 first IFIP conference on human-computer interaction. North-Holland, 1984.

Computer-Based Message Services
H.T. Smith (Editor)
Elsevier Science Publishers B.V. (North-Holland)

A REFERENCE MODEL FOR COMMAND AND RESPONSE LANGUAGES

David Beech

Computer Research Centre
Hewlett-Packard Company
Palo Alto
California 94304, USA

The nature and role of command and response languages, and of reference models, are discussed. It is claimed that there is an urgent need for improvement in command and response languages, and that a reference model can help achieve this.

An overview is provided of the reference model being developed by IFIP Working Group 2.7. The unifying concept of data abstraction is shown to give the model the desired characteristic of modularity. The model defines an architecture for customisation and help facilities for users, and for naming and protection schemes to be used by command and response languages.

INTRODUCTION

The time has come to rescue command languages from their customary mediocrity. The number of people using them will grow enormously (even allowing for the availability of other interfaces which conceal the command language from the user), and these people will not generally take kindly to struggling with inferior languages. Moreover, the proliferation of small computers and the spread of networks cry out for a high-quality standard command language to be developed.

The IFIP Working Group 2.7 on Operating System Interfaces has, since its inception in 1976, been largely concerned with the command language level of interface to a system. In January, 1982, the results of these studies began to crystallise in the form of a document entitled "The IFIP WG 2.7 Reference Model for Operating System Command and Response Languages" [1], which has now grown to substantial proportions. This represents perhaps the first attempt to provide a general basis for the design of command languages. Since it is concerned with the nature of certain components of a system which could support such languages, it can also be thought of as a user-orientated view of some of the requirements to be satisfied by an operating system design.

The concept of a *reference model* is essentially that of an architectural model of a system (or part thereof) at a high level of abstraction, intended to serve as a point of reference for designers of more concrete realisations of the model. Even these realisations may still be somewhat abstract, for example involving languages or protocols with certain specified syntax and semantics, but not describing how they are implemented on any particular hardware and software configuration. Thus the Reference Model for Command and Response Languages (CRL) does not describe any specific language, but provides a partial definition that could be completed by adding further definitional material, such as a syntax for particular commands and a description of their semantics in terms of the operations of the model. The intention is to help improve the quality and, where desirable, the uniformity of future command and response languages.

Reference models show signs of becoming deservedly popular. The best known is that for the Open Systems Interconnection (OSI) architecture [2], and one is also being developed by the Data Base Systems Study Group of the American National Standards Institute committee X3. Their goals and methods and levels of abstraction may differ, but they share the vision that the world needs systems which are designed to fit together within some well-conceived framework if we are to make the most of their potential.

In embarking on the construction of a reference model for command languages, one of the hardest problems is to identify its subject matter - what is a command language exactly (or what should it be in the future)? In particular, how extensive should be the function that it embraces, and how should it differ from a programming language?

My personal perspective on this has evolved over the years. When I was engaged in the design of PL/I, the idea of an eventual unification of command languages and programming languages seemed appealing. Here was a programming language which already included much more system function than usual - file manipulation, dynamic storage allocation, asynchronous processing - with semantics more abstract than those of a particular operating system, and with quite a civilised syntax. If it were extended with a few more capabilities for job specification and file definition, would not an interactive subset of it then be superior to the dreaded Job Control Language, while at the same time leading naturally to the ability to invoke the JCL actions from programs when needed?

For various pragmatic reasons, this unification never took place, and it is easy to see now that a monolithic approach to languages could not have lasted indefinitely- for example, if some users of Cobol now want to access network databases, others hierarchical, and yet others relational (quite apart from future models which may improve on all of these), does that mean that Cobol should itself cater for all of them, or does the language force its users to choose only one? Therefore, it becomes desirable to introduce modularity into language design, such that different languages and sublanguages can be combined as desired. This is already beginning to happen in practice, and the technical basis for it has been discussed at some length elsewhere [3].

If we adopt the definition that "A Command and Response Language is a computer language whose primary concern is to invoke system functions, and to convey system responses" [4], then a command language is seen to be a classic case of a language that needs modularity. The situation is very much like that for data bases described above, where there is too much function to be included in a single language, and provision must be made for alternative approaches, especially if we hope to have a system-independent command language that could be used on many different computers or across a network.

If a command language thus comes to be regarded as a framework for interfacing to various other languages, how much is left for it to do? My own view is that this should be very little, and indeed that a command language must be kept very small if it is to have a chance of being widely adopted and beginning to provide an escape from the tiresome minor differences confronting users of different systems at present. Occam's razor is wielded in [5] with such enthusiasm that the scope of functions recommended for inclusion in a standard command language is limited to the ability to login and logout, to ask for help, to invoke operations on objects of arbitrary type (using data abstraction as a conceptual model), and to perform in a uniform way certain operations common to all or most types of object, such as those concerned with creation and destruction, naming, and protection. This would lead to having about 15 commands in the language, with "invoke" providing the power to perform in a modular way any other available operations, which might themselves be the subject of other standards, such as for data base query.

Without prejudging the question as to whether a command language should in fact be limited to these capabilities, IFIP Working Group 2.7 has concentrated on modelling the fundamental operations in developing its reference model.

THE MODEL

The unifying concept of the model is that of the *object*, in the sense used in data abstraction [5-9] - see fig. 1. At the highest level of abstraction, a complete system can be thought of as a single object with which users may communicate, by issuing commands and receiving responses. The behaviour of this object can be elucidated at the next level of abstraction by considering it to be populated by interior objects which are of different types - a *type* defines the operations which are permissible on objects which are instances of that type.

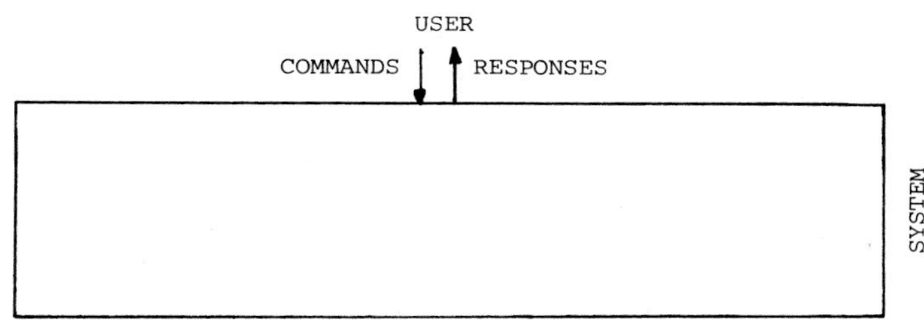

Fig. 1. A system viewed as a single object

It is worth mentioning that this not only provides a strong theoretical framework, but also corresponds to the attractively anthropomorphic view which may be taken of many existing systems [3,4]. The user "converses with" different objects inside a system as though they are people of different background and character who have to be addressed appropriately, and it is important to remember with whom one is conversing, especially when misunderstandings seem to be creeping in.

The precise description of the reference model consists of a set of abstract type definitions, including the semantic specification of each of their operations. There is always English text to describe each type and operation, supplementing the formal definitions provided.

The outline structure of the type definitions is quite conventional, including the names of other types which need to be imported, the declarations of the operations which form the interfaces to the type, and the error signals which may be returned.

This still allows some freedom of choice in the method of semantic specification of operations - they could, for example, be in deathless prose, or an operational or an axiomatic formalism. We have mostly employed the metalanguage of the Vienna Definition Method [10].

Overall Structure

The outermost view of the model is that of a system capable of supporting multiple user conversations simultaneously, where a user may or may not be human. Thus another system connected to this one in a network can be modelled as a user if there are reasons to emphasise the separation of the systems; on the other hand, to describe the behaviour of commands to which the network is transparent, the whole network can be modelled as one system for simplicity.

Besides this interactive usage of a system, we have taken it as a requirement that the model should accommodate programming usage of the functions provided, and that commands can be grouped into collections, and that the CRL should be able to invoke arbitrary operations, such as those provided by user-written programs. Other functional needs to be addressed include the storing and protection of information in general, and sharing and communication between users, although the last two have not yet received detailed attention.

The main components of the present model are illustrated in fig. 2.

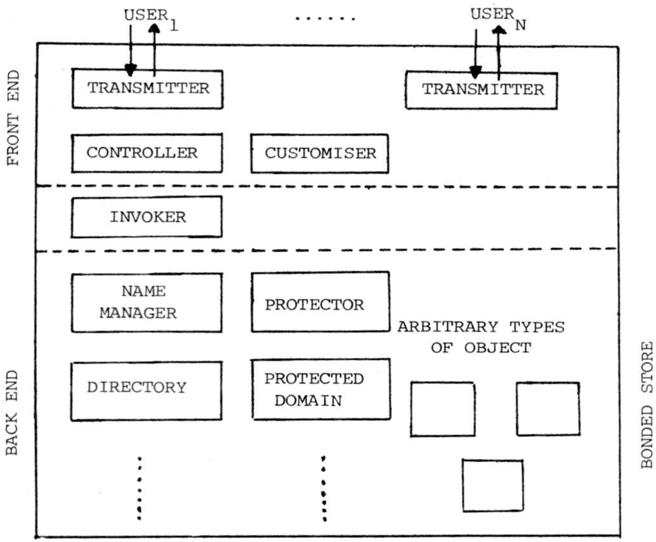

Fig. 2. Main components of the reference model

The objects that transmit and massage the commands and responses constitute the "front end" of the model relative to the user. The "back end" contains the objects that do the real work of the system, both those that are defined by the model, and those that are arbitrary objects within the system, of which the command language has no special knowledge.

Intermediate between the front and back ends is the Invoker, whose role is to apply the protection mechanisms defined by the model before passing on an operation to the intended object. It also models a potentially useful internal interface at which programs could access the function provided, rather than using an outer customised interface.

The model defines a minimal initial state that must exist when a user approaches an access port to the system, i.e. the objects that must be present and related to each other in order for a *session* to proceed. For systems requiring an authenticated login, the initial anonymous session would have a protection structure that permitted little other than login to be performed (but some requests, e.g. for help, or for the time of day, might be honoured freely). A successful login results in a new session structure being constructed, with protection appropriate to that user, and the new Controller is put in charge while the old session is stacked.

Front end

Let us concentrate on one user who is issuing commands to, and receiving responses from, the system. The object with which that user is communicating directly is called a Transmitter, and is modelled as analogous to a "virtual"terminal such as is being studied in the Open Systems Interconnection world [11]. Indeed, in a spirit of modular cooperation, we hope to achieve compatibility of the OSI and CRL reference models here.

Beyond the Transmitter is a Controller which has been established to take charge of affairs on the system's side of the interface, and essentially loops on requesting input from the Transmitter and sending responses to it.

The model allows for customisation of commands and responses, and the Controller makes use of operations on a Customiser object and various ancillary objects to achieve this. Note that between the user input and the eventual response of each iteration at this outer level, the model does not prevent other operations from dealing with this Transmitter, so that, for example, the Customiser may engage in dialogue with the user to help construct the desired command.

The customisation envisaged is of two main kinds, being either device-oriented or user-oriented. Devices may allow for one-dimensional or two-dimensional representation, or for possibilities such as audible input and output, touch-tone signals, sensors to aid the handicapped, or network message formats. Users may want commands and certainly responses, expressible in their own native languages; and will generally be glad to be able to tailor their working environments, for example to use their own abbreviations for common tasks. There is another side to this coin: customisation can also be imposed as a discipline on a user, say by a system administrator, rather than offered as a total freedom, since part of the customisation is to establish an initial protection structure that might limit the amount of subsequent customisation the user could perform.

The main outline of the customisation structure is as follows. When a Customiser is created at the start of a session, an AuthorisedUserTable object is searched and should yield Profile and History objects for the user (even for the anonymous user prior to a login). These are used to initialise a Context object whose lifetime will be that of the session only. The Context may be changed to reflect temporary changes in the customisation, and information about the session will be accumulated in the History. The user may also be able to make changes to the persistent Profile. The model lists some functional requirements to be considered in offering customisation facilities, but does not go into detail in specifying exactly what information these objects might use in a particular command and response language.

Closely connected with the Context and History objects are the help facilities envisaged within the model. The value of high quality help still tends to be underestimated by system designers, and the reference model therefore proposes an ambitious list of requirements and an architectural framework within which these can be satisfied. The requirements cover many aspects of the comprehensiveness, consistency, appropriateness and timeliness of the help provided, and the first stage of satisfying them might be largely user-independent. However, it is easy to see that, in the long term, genuinely helpful information should take note of much more than the native language of the user and the customised form of the interface that is being used. This is where the Context and the History lend themselves to much more powerful reasoning as to what help the user really needs.

Session creation may involve authentication of the user, so that AuthorisedUserTable will carry the necessary control information, such as passwords or fingerprints. It also allows for actions specified in the Profile to be carried out implicitly at this time. Session termination will likewise allow for implicit actions determined by the Context, and will then return control to the initiator of the session, who can destroy its ephemeral objects.

Invoker

Any operation can enforce protection checking in its semantics by passing the desired operation, complete with its parameters, as an argument to the Invoke operation of the Invoker. Of course, the metalanguage also allows operations to be applied directly to objects - for example, the Invoke operation itself must be directly accessible, and it must have the ability to make direct application of operations passed to it, after successfully checking them.

To appreciate how the Invoker performs its checking, it is necessary to understand the protection scheme, and we shall say something about the Protector and related object types shortly. Although the Invoker relies upon querying them, they are back-end objects that may be created and modified by operations which are protected and have to be applied via the Invoker.

Back end

The back-end operations defined within the model are principally concerned with naming and protection. These are quite substantial mechanisms which deserve fuller exposition than space allows here, so we will give only the briefest indication of their nature.

The naming structure provided by the Name Manager and Directory types adopts a form of the widely accepted model which has hierarchial naming and the possibility of additional aliasing links between directories. The Name Manager is the focal point for the name resolution for a user - it knows from the Context what is the current search path for that user, and it deals with composite qualified names by operating on the appropriate directories. A Directory object itself provides only operations which are local to that directory, searching or updating it.

The protection scheme considers every object to be held in a Bonded Store, accessible only through the good offices of a Protector that knows the Protected Domains of the user. A Protected Domain is a mapping between object references and the Protections associated with them, where a Protection object contains both type information and a set of Permissions. When an operation is passed to the Invoker, the object reference to both the operation and its operands have Access Right tokens. These are compared with the Permissions required for these objects in the user's Protected Domains, and have to be sufficient (in a defined sense) for execution of the operation to be allowed to proceed.

CONCLUSION

There is a pressing need for high-quality user interfaces, and for greater uniformity to spare both users and vendors the agonies of proliferation. Yet the pace cannot be altogether dictated - it is necessary to be sensitive to the realities of migration from existing systems and interfaces, and to the needs to accommodate new developments and to allow for practical experience to play its part in arriving at consensus as to reasonable ways of instructing computing systems. Nor are these problems ones that can be avoided by claiming that the reference model is not for this transitory stage, but only for the long term - they will be perennially with us.

Therefore the model was designed from the start to be evolutionary, relying on the assistance provided by the modularity of data abstraction. Certain of the types are already quite fully specified, as in the treatment of naming, because it was judged that a wide consensus could be reached on this. The protection model is also well developed, because of the natural fit offered between protection and the definition of types of object in a system in terms of the permissible operations on them.

Other parts of the model are left open where there is still room for experiment and research - some of which will fall within the future program of Working Group 2.7, while topics such as psychological study of human factors will have to be treated by others. One aspect of the work so far has been to try to lay the foundations for a field of study which deserves to attract more talent around the world.

The point of view that the reference model has something to say about the design of operating systems is also germane to the consideration of future work. Since the title of Working Group 2.7 is "Operating System Interfaces", a natural development would be to examine more closely and pragmatically the internal interfaces and the implementation aspects of the model.

An interesting observation on the use of data abstraction is that it has been very successful in focussing discussion and producing constructive results. Its introduction may have been merely coincidental with the point in the work of the group where this was about to happen anyway. Nevertheless, it is undeniable that the clarity of the model, and the terminology which can be associated with it, are particularly valuable in debate between people from different technical and linguistic backgrounds.

Finally, we might look to the possible utility of this reference model, not merely for the designers of individual languages and systems, but at an international level. The recently constituted Command and Response Language working group (ISO TC97/SC5/WG7) of the International Organisation for Standardisation is faced with a daunting task in even knowing how to start, and the model may perhaps provide some helpful clues.

ACKNOWLEDGEMENT

Thanks are due to all members of IFIP WG 2.7 who participated in this work, and especially to Christian Gram and Hans-Juergen Kugler who have made major contributions to the Reference Model document. I am grateful also to Samuel Feldman and Mark Scott Johnson for comments which helped to clarify this paper.

REFERENCES

[1] D. Beech and H.-J. Kugler ed., The IFIP WG 2.7 reference model for command and response languages, (in draft), Palo Alto, (1982).

[2] ISO TC97/SC16, Information processing systems - open systems interconnection - basic reference model, Draft proposal ISO/DP 7498, American National Standards Institute, New York, (1982).

[3] D. Beech, Modularity of computer languages, *Software Practice and Experience*, 12 (1982), 10.

[4] D. Beech, What is a command Language?, in Beech, ed., Command language directions, (North-Holland, Amsterdam, 1980).

[5] D. Beech, Criteria for a standard command language based on data abstraction, *Proceedings of the 1982 National Computer Conference, AFIPS Vol.51*, (AFIPS Press, Arlington, 1982).

[6] O.-J. Dahl, K. Nygaard and B. Myhrhaug, The SIMULA 67 common base language, Norwegian Computing Center, Oslo, (1968).

[7] B. Liskov, R. Atkinson, T. Bloom, E. Moss, C. Schaffert, R. Scheifler and A. Snyder, CLU reference manual, Lecture notes in computer science, 114, (Springer-Verlag, Berlin, 1981).

[8] W.A. Wulf, R.L. London and M. Shaw, An introduction to the construction and verification of Alphard programs, *IEEE Transactions on Software Engineering*, SE-2 (1976), 4.

[9] A.I. Wasserman, D.D. Sheretz, M.L. Kersten, R.P.van de Riet and M.D. Dippé, Revised report on the programming language PLAIN, *ACM SIGPLAN Notices*, 16 (1981), 5.

[10] D. Bjørner and C.B. Jones, The Vienna development method - the metalanguage, Lecture notes in computer science, 61, (Springer-Verlag, Berlin, 1978).

[11] ISO TC97/SC16 , OSI - Virtual terminal service and model - generic description, N713, American National Standards Institute, New York, (1982).

Computer-Based Message Services
H.T. Smith (Editor)
Elsevier Science Publishers B.V. (North-Holland)

EXPERIENCES WITH THE KOMEX SYSTEM AS AN INHOUSE CBMS

Uta Pankoke
Institute for Applied Information Technology
Gesellschaft für Mathematik und Datenverarbeitung
St.Augustin W-Germany

The following paper tries to give some hints of how to avoid acceptance problems when intr ducing a CBMS into an organisation. Some results of the evaluation of KOMEX use as inhouse c mmunication system within GMD are presented. Finally some proposals are given of which new concepts are required from user's point of view to improve CBMS technologies.

Computer conferencing systems are computer-based message systems with some special features to support communication within groups. The KOMEX system developed and used in the GMD is such a computer conferencing system.

An initial configuration of the KOMEX system was presented to a broader public at the Hanover Trade Fair in 1979. In 1980/81 a first field trial of KOMEX was carried out with external university institutes. Since the beginning of 1982 a network of three KOMEX systems (on different computers) has been installed and used by GMD people as inhouse CBMS.

Practical CBMS introduction has shown that - despite of an existing demand - great problems arise in the acceptance of these new media by their possible users. The first field trial disclosed possible reasons for acceptance problems. On the one hand, these problems are based on technical factors, on the other on communication-specific factors. When introducing KOMEX we tried to consider these barriers to acceptance from the very beginning. First, this was realised by improving the technical design of KOMEX and by taking some promoting measures.

Technical Factors

The technical factors can be compared to those observed, for example, in the introduction of word processors, namely:

- availability of display terminals and printers;
- system reliability and availability;
- easy and transparent handling;
- small processing effort.

Of course, each user should have his own terminal and easy access to a printer, furthermore, a 24 hours' operation of the system is absolutely necessary. System reliability requires much from the developers since messages shall never go lost, be 'jammed' or even delivered to the wrong address.

The operation of a CBMS has to be such easy and transparent that even the DP beginner will be able to familiarise with it within very short time.

The computer conferencing system KOMEX discussed here secures an easy handling by means of the menu technique that allows the user to know at any time what he is doing and which further steps he can take. Even DP beginners did not require more than 1-2 hours to familiarise with system operation and handling.

KOMEX considerably reduces the effort required for processing texts and messages if compared with conventional office processing. For this purpose KOMEX provides the following facilities:

- text processing including text editing, formatting and filing;
- mailing and receipt facilities for texts (i.e. messages) with simple addressing (just specify family name), automatic addition of sender's name, generation of reference identification etc. and automatic archiving;
- reply facility with automatic addressing and reference chaining;
- automatic archiving of incoming and outgoing messages;
- support of user-specific filing (file catalog etc.);
- retrieval from user archive;
- automatic distribution and copying of messages.

Furthermore, KOMEX provides so-called conferences which enable the user to structure communication flows. In general, conferences are mailing lists which can be inspected by any user and which define the authorisations of mailing and receiving for each conference participant.

For the acceptance of KOMEX within the management area it is of special importance that independence and privacy of KOMEX users are secured by providing each user with his own local archives which can only be accessed by this very user.

Several user agents each are connected to a so-called KOMEX message agent that secures distribution and copying of messages. By means of the public packet switching network DATEX-P some agents are connected to a KOMEX network. (Message and user agents are implemented on SIEMENS computers of the 7000 series running under BS2000.)

Communication-specific Aspects

In the new installation of a CBMS the basic problem of acceptance is that one user alone would never be able to discover the innovative benefits of such a system, i.e. those benefits going beyond the facilities provided by a word processor. These will only appear if a sufficient number of partners use the system. Important prerequisites for acceptance are therefore:

- integration into the every days work processes of the participants;
- reachability of participants;
- adequate communication needs and volumes;
- experiences in system use and ability to assess the reactions of communication partners;
- suitable organisation of communication.

With respect to reachability it is important that messages are inspected by the recipients as soon as possible. Problems, in particular, use to appear with participants who receive only a small number of messages but who should not be excluded in order to secure a maximum number of participants. Furthermore, it should be possible to reach people as 'passive' participants who neither use actively a terminal. KOMEX supports the reachability of those people by providing the facility to print messages automatically if requested so by the recipient. The print-outs can then be distributed within the GMD by messengers. The passive participants are however not able to mail themselves messages via KOMEX. Passive participants are mainly those people who do not expect to receive many messages or who have only a limited access to terminals etc..

Reachability also means that as many participants as possible can be reached via the system. Furthermore, the system will become especially attractive if it enables the user to contact people who are hardly reachable by other media. Therefore, system use should start with as many users as possible.

The inhouse use of KOMEX was started with about 120 participants. Thus, from the very beginning most participants were able to reach interesting partners by means of KOMEX.

During a training period of several weeks we daily distributed by KOMEX exercises which had to be performed by the participants. This secured a sufficient amount of messages from the very beginning and accustomed the participants to a regular use of the system. This training provided an adequate communication volume and simultaneously helped the participants to gain experiences in the habits of use, thus allowing them to assess the practicability of the system after a short time. Simultaneously it was possible to indicate forms of organisation and rules of behaviour. In the course of use these could and should be advanced by the participants themselves.

Furthermore, the provision of personal advice on possible facilities is an important measure which should permanently accompany the use of the system.

Acceptance of KOMEX

Within the last two years the group of KOMEX participants has considerably been extended. In particular, since KOMEX has provided the possibility of accessing the system via a so-called line interface by means of any display terminal, external cooperation partners of the GMD are able to join the KOMEX group without great effort.

Furthermore, reorganisation within the GMD and the foundation of GMD research groups at German universities have most recently led to an increase of the number of participants and to an increasing usage of KOMEX.

The success of KOMEX introduction is best illustrated by the statistics presented in the following. After the completion of training communication was continued, though to a somewhat reduced extent, even during the period of summer vacation. Of course, vacation and holidays always lead to a reduced amount of messages since a considerably smaller number of participants can be reached in those periods. However, from the very beginning the number of

KOMEX participants was sufficient to survive such critical periods.

This is confirmed by the following figures of KOMEX statistics:

- The number of reachable KOMEX participants has presently increased to more than 300, about 150 of them use the system regularly and actively.
- About 120 conferences are currently defined.
- In September 1983 nearly 2500 messages were mailed in about 2800 sessions and nearly 3500 messages were received.

Furthermore, the reaction of the KOMEX participants was investigated by questionnaire surveys and in group discussions. In the takeoff period, i.e. in the first two to four months, the participants expressed rather extreme statements reaching from almost euphoric views to very sceptical comments. After a 10 months' use these evaluations have turned to 'normal', i.e. they have become altogether more positive, extreme views are hardly occurring. (60 % are content, previously 45 % were content, the rest assumes a neutral attitude.)

User Groups

Three user groups can be distinguished in the GMD:

- management (board of directors, heads of institutes and departments);
- administration;
- research area.

In general, the organisation of the research area secures that project members mainly communicate within the project and that they sit in nearby rooms. Most communication is done by personal talks. Further important communication partners are working in external organisations. Therefore, this area shows a demand for new communication media only in those cases where external organisations can be reached by these media. This is the reason why KOMEX has so far been used by such GMD members to a small extent only.

The members of the administrative areas have frequent contacts with other organisational units, especially with people from the management. Form-oriented procedures, however, cannot be handled by KOMEX as yet which means a restriction of its benefit within this area.

The most important and active users of KOMEX are the people in the management area. Frequently the communication partners cannot be reached simultaneously (they are out for travels, meetings etc.). Mostly the whole KOMEX correspondence is directly handled by the managers themselves and becomes, therefore, much more efficient (e.g. even the GMD directors use to keyboard short replies themselves). KOMEX also allows direct contacts with those GMD members whose contacts are usually handled by their secretaries. Furthermore, KOMEX is often used to communicate with one's own secretary. Beyond that, the secretary should also read incoming messages to keep the same level of information and, if required, keyboard and mail longer messages on behalf of the 'boss'.

The possibility of answering messages spontaneously and personally is felt by managers to be more agreable and direct than the former delegation to the secretary. The GMD managers constitute about 8 % of the active KOMEX users, produce nearly 35 % of the messages and receive about 30 % of all messages(as of October 1983).

The Benefits Provided by KOMEX

Measuring the benefits of computer-based communication systems only by possibly saved transport costs would mean to underestimate these systems. Furthermore, one should not consider these systems to be substitutes for conventional media, but they have to be seen in the overall context and must be regarded as completion of these media.

The main benefit of using a computer-based communication system is the improvement of information flow and easier distribution, archiving and retrieval of information. Such a system is especially suitable in those cases where information has quickly to be distributed to several persons who should answer quickly.

Therefore, the most important statement of the KOMEX participants is in our opinion that they feel better informed than before.

The KOMEX users participating in the survey listed the following benefits:

- wider distribution of information; nobody is forgotten by error; no information is lost by error;
- additional information is distributed (e.g. small comments, suggestions or recommendations);
- messages are processed more quickly and more frequently answered personally;
- no disturbance or interruption as in case of a telephone call and, therefore, a greater willingness to transmit information;
- no simultaneous presence required, messages can be processed on any display at any time (e.g. even at places reached during a mission);
- messages are formulated in a more spontaneous, personal way than other written information;
- the efforts required for copying, filing, addressing and mailing are reduced;
- meetings are better prepared, agendas and records are coordinated outside the meetings;
- most bits of paper on your desk are no longer required since short requests are immediately mailed, answered and archived by KOMEX and can be retrieved at any time;
- for regionally separated working groups KOMEX facilitates the maintenance of personal contacts. Joint sessions can thus be limited to discussions of contents. The important ideas which - as everybody knows - use to come into one's mind only after the session can be distributed by KOMEX.

By its spontaneity and directness of communication KOMEX is more comparable to the telephone than to conventional letter writing. Sometimes it is used for replacing telephone calls, e.g. if the partner cannot be reached by repeated calls. Where and how to use KOMEX for work facilitation, depends on the specific tasks of the user.

Problems of information pollution as they are sometimes reported by CBMS users in the USA have so far not yet occurred with KOMEX. We assume that the possibility of defining in KOMEX specific closed communication groups, so-called conferences, and the discipline of the users have contributed to a restriction of distributed information to really relevant messages.

Problems of KOMEX Use

The greatest problem of KOMEX use is that of 'double-entry bookkeeping', i.e. apart from the usual in-tray with conventional letters or internally distributed correspondence, the user must also regularly inspect the messages received via KOMEX. In addition, there are two filing systems: that of paper files and that of KOMEX. Especially in the takeoff period the use of the respective file is less based on individual user considerations but rather on general conditions, e.g. on the fact that only some of the people involved in a specific process are KOMEX users.

Therefore, the KOMEX participants would appreciate if more people joined their group so that, for example, all GMD members and external cooperation partners could be reached via KOMEX.

In our opinion, the last point is of particular importance to further developments. Just in the scientific area projects are often carried out in cooperation with external partners. In such projects it is rather difficult to maintain an adequate information flow in the periods between joint project sessions. However, on long term the required considerable increase of the group of reachable participants can only be achieved by advancing and introducing international standards.

Future Developments

The user agent's local functions will be advanced. From the user point of view this would mainly mean to improve the retrieval facilities, such as full text retrieval. Furthermore, all improvements known from word processing would also be appreciated in this context (e.g. integration of graphics, voice annotations). The complexity of requirements differing from user agent to user agent require individually tailored systems.

The recent developments in the field of single-user and multi-user computers will in future consider these aspects to a much greater extent. The continuous cost reduction and the improvement of performance with respect to minicomputers and storage systems (laser disk) will lead to a wide-spread use of comfortable communication-supporting single-user computers.

Furthermore development and implementation of Messagehandling standards are heavily required.

Beyond the existing concepts users require more sophisticated support in organising communication flows as proposed in the following.

New Concepts of Organisational Support

The detailed analyses of user surveys, discussions as well as requests and suggestions sent to the consultants show that the user mainly require the support of the following two aspects:

- improved facilities to support the mapping of relationships between persons (organisational contexts);
- improved facilities to support producing relations between informations and to process them within these relations (subject contexts).

Relations between Information Items

KOMEX differentiates between messages (including transport information) and the actual information content (without transport information) the so-called document. The latter is uniquely identifiable throughout the system. Copies of documents have the same identifier unless they have been updated. References (e.g. revision of, answer to) can be established between documents (not between messages since references must be independent of transport information).

This construct allows to establish relations, e.g. relations between units of information.

Processing such relations is supported by KOMEX. For example, references can automatically be produced by means of the reply function or in text updating, and local retrieval supports the selection of documents belonging together etc.

KOMEX users are accustomed to these facilities and call for further support in processing information bodies. For example, they would like to transmit a document with all references and all pertinent transport information, specified so far, by a single operation or they want to file the latter simultaneously under a file label.

This points out, the benefit of a CBMS, if compared with a conventional communication medium, especially appears if the handling of complex information structures is supported.

Furthermore, the users also require possibilities of constructing common information bases. That means, several users want to access jointly an 'information base' by means of the same operations that enable the access to information at the local user agent.

Simultaneously, the users ask for possibilities of introducing selective differences in the access and handling authorisations of the individual users. This means to require the support of organisational contexts.

Organisational Contexts

A communication system should also provide support for organisation and handling of communication. In this context, the technical support of the following models is desirable:

- A message is provided with a given transport route.
- A group specifies organisational rules for transmitting and processing messages of a specific type.

A simple example of the first model is the accounting of travel expenses. Such a communication process involves several persons who - in accordance with their roles - process a form in an order predefined by that form.

An example of organisational regulations is found in the provision of advice to users. If a request is sent to the consulting team, it has to be processed by a team member. In this case the CBMS should enable the team to specify themselves "rules of procedure" which are to be observed when replying:

- For example, the request should automatically be sent to that member who can receive the message first and not to any other member.
- Or the request should automatically be delivered to the member being 'on duty' and, in addition, request and reply should be introduced into the common information base of the team.
- Or the request is delivered to the member "on duty", but request and reply are also mailed to all other members for information.

In extension of available mailing lists and conference services those services are required which provide general, communication-specific coordination tools. These tools should allow the users a free design of communication flows and they should also be applicable outside closed organisational units. This also includes the support of specific office procedures. In order to protect users from being 'processed' there must also be features to break these procedures and to define exceptions. The definition of organisational procedures or communication flows must easily to be modified.

Such an organisational support, however, requires much intuitive feeling from the developers since short-sighted concepts might infringe on the privacy of the user (which will hopefully lead to increasing acceptance difficulties), on the one hand, and, on the other, too rigid concepts would only support already realised organisational structures and cement them so that the development of new organisational structures being specifically suitable for CBMS would be excluded a priori. Therefore, one should rather develop concepts for basic functions which are suitable both for free communication without any prestructuring and for the handling of firmly prestructured tasks. We think that just this point offers the most chances for future development and innovation of computer-based message systems.

References

R. Babatz, U. Pankoke-Babatz, H. Santo, G. Theidig, Experimental Use of KOMEX in the GMD , Computer Compacts April 1983, pp.83

St.R. Hiltz, E.B. Kerr, Computer-Mediated Communication Systems -Status and Evaluation-, (Academic Press, New York London, 1982)

A.W. Holt, P.M. Cashman, Designing Systems to Support Cooperative Activity, An Example from Software Maintenance Management, IEEE COMPSAC, 1981

Th. Kreifelts, Coordination Procedures: A model for cooperative office process', Kommunikation in verteilten Systemen-Anwendungen und Betrieb-, GI/NTG Fachtagung, Berlin Jan. 1983, (Informatik Fachberichte, Bd.60, Springer, Berlin 1983)

M. Ohlson, The Impact of Office Automation on the Organisation: Some Implications for Research and Practice, CACM Nov. 1982, pp.838

J. Palme Experience with the use of the COM computerized, Conferencing System, (FOA Rapport (10166E-M6(h)), Dec. 1981)

H.Santo, R. Babatz, M.Bogen, U.Pankoke-Babatz, G.Theidig, KOMEX V 4.1 User Manual, (Arbeitspapiere der GMD No.71, Dec. 1983)

P. Wißkirchen, Th.Kreifelts, G.Richter, G. Wurch, Informationstechnik und Bürosysteme, (B. G. Teubner Stuttgart, 1983)

PART 4:

SERVICES AND COST/BENEFIT ISSUES

Computer-Based Message Services
H.T. Smith (Editor)
Elsevier Science Publishers B.V. (North-Holland)

ENVOYPOST: A HYBRID ELECTRONIC MAIL SERVICE

D.J. Rhynas
Telecom Canada
Ottawa, Canada

J.R. Wood
Canada Post Corporation
Ottawa, Canada

EnvoyPost™ is a hybrid electronic mail service which combines the Envoy 100™ computer based messaging service of Telecom Canada with the physical delivery network of Canada Post Corporation. Subscribers of Envoy 100 compose messages under the guidance of a special script which prompts for appropriate input, including the mailing address. The message is then transmitted to a daisy wheel printer in a post office closest to the recipient, where it is folded and inserted into a distinctive window envelope for delivery by the letter carrier. The paper outlines why there is a need for hybrid messaging systems and discusses a number of design considerations in implementing a service such as EnvoyPost.

INTRODUCTION

We hear much talk these days about electronic mail. Many forms of communication potentially fall under this umbrella name so it is worth briefly reviewing the concept. One might argue that the telegraph of 100 years ago was in fact a form of electronic mail. A more current definition, however, would be that of computer based messaging. Mail of any sort can be regarded as the third party delivery of posted information. The information is typically enclosed in an envelope of some form which contains addressing information that is used by the system to route the envelope to its correct destination. With computer based messaging, the creation, transmission and reception of the message are all handled electronically. Typically the message is delivered to the recipient's 'mailbox' which he may access at his leisure. At this point the message may be annotated, copied, forwarded, filed or discarded. All mail systems (both postal and electronic) have this attribute of asynchronous reception; that is the sender and recipient need not be on-line at the same time, as is the case for example, with the telephone today.

A hybrid electronic mail system retains the electronic creation and transmission components, but instead produces a hard copy of the message; presentation, in other words, is on paper. The message is then physically delivered to the recipient, similar to conventional mail. As will be shown, such a delivery capability greatly extends the reach and power of computer based message systems.

Despite the burgeoning growth of terminal hardware, communicating word processors, personal computers and executive workstations, not everyone has access to a computer based message system. And this is likely to be the case for some time, particularly with the residential market. From the electronic mail subscriber's viewpoint, he in the past has had to make use of multiple systems and services. Several of his frequent contacts may be accessible electronically, but the one who is not requires him to still be reliant on more traditional office support systems (e.g. dictate, type, proofread, resubmit for typographical corrections, photocopy, envelope and stamp, feed into company internal mail, submit to the Post Office and deliver to recipient's internal mail system).

A hybrid system allows the subscriber to create and edit his text on-line for all recipients. The system will then automatically deliver the message to those who can be reached electronically or print a message in a location close to the recipient for physical delivery. One way of rapidly increasing the reach of computer based message systems is to make the postal universe of addressees available via the medium of a hybrid service. The service allows delivery of messages to be made in a shorter time frame than is possible with conventional mail, and to recipients who are not subscribers.

The Post Office is the oldest communications service organization in existence. It provides a universal service, on demand, and can deliver a message to any address in the country. Moreover, through its agreements with postal administrations throughout the world it provides a low cost, world wide communications facility to its customers.

From the Post Office perspective, up to two thirds of the letter mailstream could be handled electronically over the longer term. At the same time, from the telecommunication carrier's perspective, most addresses currently cannot be reached through an electronic device other than a telephone. Thus, it makes good business sense for both parties to evaluate joint electronic mail endeavours.

This paper commences with a brief overview of the Envoy 100™ text messaging service in Canada. It then describes the design and implementation of EnvoyPost™, a joint venture between Telecom Canada and Canada Post Corporation.

ENVOY 100 OVERVIEW

Envoy 100 is a public text messaging service offered by Telecom Canada (formerly the TransCanada Telephone System) and has been commercially available since July of 1981. It is presently a centralized system which connects to Datapac™, the Canadian packet switched network, by multiple X.25 access lines. The service may be accessed domestically or internationally by the packet network or by the public switched telephone or TWX networks. Essentially any subscriber with an ASCII terminal may exchange messages with other users on a store and forward basis. Since the subscription is related to a 'username' rather than a specific terminal, the user's mailbox may be accessed from anywhere in the world.

Envoy 100 provides a number of features to assist the user in creating, editing and sending messages. Received messages may be selectively retrieved, acted upon, or filed for subsequent on-line retrieval. There are a number of user settable profile options so that the environment may be specifically tailored to meet his needs (as examples, there is a French/English language setting, a time zone setting, options for how incoming messages are to be summarized, etc). In addition a user may elect to call into the system to read new messages or alternatively have them autodelivered, where Envoy will automatically initiate a call to some device with autoanswer capability and deliver the stream of new messages; such a device is most commonly a hardcopy printer but can also be a computer. The complete command repertoire of Envoy is quite extensive and is described in detail in reference 1. A number of enhancements to Envoy are currently under development including the capability to interwork with other computer based message systems (ref 2, 3).

EnvoyPost is an extension to Envoy 100 which interworks with the physical delivery system of Canada Post Corporation. The user creates his message under the guidance of a special script which prompts for the appropriate input, including mailing address. The message is then transmitted to a daisy wheel printer in a post office closest to the recipient, where it is folded and inserted in a distinctive window envelope for next day or same day delivery by the letter carrier.

There are approximately 100,000 ASCII terminals installed in Canada today which could grow to 300,000 by 1985. These figures represent a lower bound given the rapidly expanding numbers of personal computers with communication capability. New electronic services, however, traditionally have long lead times towards implementation by users. To test the potential of EnvoyPost, Telecom Canada and Canada Post decided to commence with a market trial. The one year trial was launched in March of 1983 which provided delivery to 20 major cities. The reach will be extended to cover all of Canada with the full commercial service in March 1984. A separate trial arrangement was established between Telecom Canada and the Electronic Mail Corporation of America, a value-added service firm in the United States which provides access to the U.S. post office E-COM™ service. Diagramatically, the network configuration is illustrated in figure 1.

SERVICE REQUIREMENTS

There were a number of functional requirements laid down in specifying the EnvoyPost service.

From the user's perspective, end-to-end delivery time was an important attribute. The basic service was defined to be next day delivery assuming that the message was printed in the receiving post office by 8:00 PM local time. A premium special delivery grade of service was also defined which provides same day delivery with a final cutoff of 6:00 PM local time.

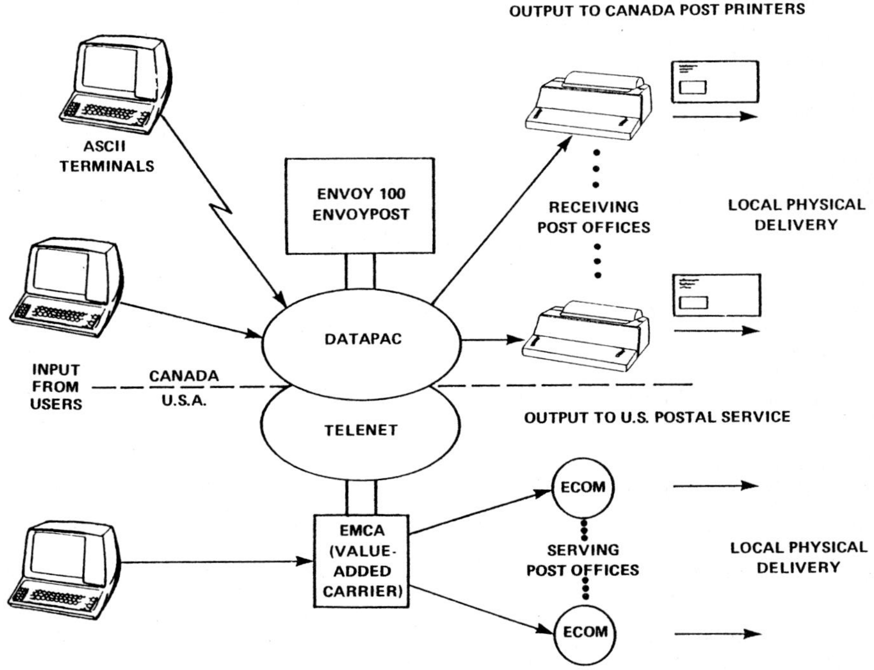

FIGURE 1: ENVOYPOST SERVICE CONFIGURATION

Closely coupled with the delivery time, was the reach of the service. For the market trial, so as not to compromise the next day objective, it was decided to contain the reach to 20 major cities (50% of the population of Canada). To cover all of Canada and maintain the same grade of service, the number of specially equipped post offices will be extended.

Ease of use was deemed to be another important attribute. The basic market requirements were to:

a) Send one letter to one recipient
b) Send one letter to many recipients (postal addresses entered individually)
c) Prompt user in either English or French
d) Have a batch input mechanism for off-line (computer generated) creation of EnvoyPost messages

The user interface was to be prompt driven and 'user friendly' in pointing out any input errors and how they could be corrected. There was to be supporting information on how to use the service, as well as a postal code directory to be kept on-line. In addition, the Envoy subscriber was to have access to all of the conveniences he was accustomed to with the standard electronic mail offering, such as editing capabilities, filing of text, automatically being copied on all messages sent and so on.

Another important attribute was felt to be that of copy quality. Messages were to look like typed business letters rather than the more familiar telegram. They were to be printed on good quality bond paper with standard left and right margins, as well as a bottom margin of at least one inch. Fully formed character printing was to be used, with both upper and lower case characters such that print quality would be of the highest possible clarity and appearance. Customers were to be allowed to input full 80 character lines.

The service had to be attractively priced. The Envoy 100 tariff is usage based at $.30 per 1000 characters in and out of the system, sender pays (that is the sender is billed for the first read of message by a recipient). The EnvoyPost premium was to be handled as a flat rate surcharge on top of the regular usage charges. For the market trial the following prices have been in effect: basic $1.10, special $2.16, U.S. $1.60. As a more concrete example, a one page business letter would cost between $1.50 and $2.50 to send anywhere in North America.

Page layout was important. Envoy would have to format the first page appropriately such that the postal addressing information would line up with the envelope window when the letter was folded. There had to be some provision to handle multipage messages with regard to formatting. In addition, the number of pages in a given message had to be easily foldable to fit in a standard envelope (deemed to be four pages in Canada).

A distinctive envelope was to be used with a readily identifiable logo which would command attention when delivered and would identify, to the recipient, that the electronic mail service was being provided by Canada Post. Indentification of Telecom Canada was to be included in the message header.

Network control was to be possible from a single location, at least during the trial period. The post office printers were to be 'receive only' as local staff were not to be given the facility for inputting messages. It had to be possible to retransmit messages when necessary and to dynamically reconfigure the network to redirect traffic whenever a site was down.

It was decided to have Telecom Canada perform a third party billing function so that the EnvoyPost surcharges would appear on the user's normal Envoy 100 bill. The same billing system was also required to produce revenue statements (division of revenues between the service providers) and various statistical tracking reports e.g., number of messages per week to a given printer location or for a given postal code.

With these needs in mind, Envoy 100 was chosen as the base message switching vehicle; specific solutions to the various requirements are described in the following sections. Potential applications were contract bids, price change notifications, sales bulletins, disseminating stock market information, etc. Because Envoy 100 has a large population of users with personal terminals it was expected that new applications would evolve.

DESIGN CONSIDERATIONS

User Interface

EnvoyPost makes use of a development capability within Envoy 100 known as Envoy Script to support most of the user interface. Envoy Script is essentially a high level programming language which allows the developer to create a line by line prompt sequence and then construct the user's input into a formatted message; it is typically used for specific customer applications such as generating an order form. These attributes enabled the EnvoyPost script to prompt for address information, validate that it would fit within the window (and guide the user if it exceeded the width), and format the postal address in the required page location. Several extensions had to be constructed for the Script language such as the ability to validate a Canadian postal code and a means of verifying that the user's text had not exceeded the page limit. While in text mode the user may make use of the standard Envoy editing commands. The typical user interface prompt sequence for sending a message is illustrated in figure 2.

At the time of sending, the system attempts to match the postal code entered by the user in his mailing address with an entry in a postal code table. It then displays a location message to give the user some assurance that he is indeed sending to the correct part of the country (note again figure 2). If the location is not what the user expected he is prompted again for postal code. If correct, a message posted indication is displayed with a timestamp and a message number which is system unique for that particular message. The user may then go on to do other things.

A similar EnvoyPost batch input script was developed using the same logic, but suppressing all prompts. In this case, all input would be constructed off-line using either a computer or some storage medium such as a diskette or paper tape. After invoking the script the file can then be sent at line speed; all message posted indications or any error messages (e.g., invalid postal code) are logged to an on-line status file which may be queried after the transmission is complete.

A menu driven EnvoyPost information summary and postal code directory were also developed using the Script capability.

Routing and Delivery

The Canadian postal code is a seven character string of the form alpha numeric alpha space numeric alpha numeric; for example K1N 5G1. The first three characters are known as the Forward Sortation Area (FSA) and uniquely identify the receiving post office in Canada. A table was constructed within Envoy which maps each FSA (approximately 4000) with the corresponding printer address. It is possible for multiple FSA's to map onto one printer and as the service grows, the table will continually be updated to support the new printer locations.

As indicated above, at the time of sending, the system performs the postal code lookup to verify that the code is being served. If correct, the message is then placed in an autodelivery queue for the particular printer serving that FSA.

Command? COMPOSE ENVOYPOST

Canada or U.S.A.? CANADA

Name: Mr. B.G. Franklin
Company: MTech Company
Street & #: 85 St. Andrew Street
City: Ottawa
Province: Ontario
Postal Code: K1N 5G1
Delivery Option: BASIC
Text:
(customer enters text of message)

Send? y

Postal Code K1N 5G1 corresponds to METROPOLITAN OTTAWA AREA
Is this the correct destination? y

Msg posted Oct 18, 1983 3:27 PM EDT MSG: YGEU-0730-3872

Same message to another recipient? y

Canada or U.S.A.? U.S.A.

Name: Mr. J. Taller
Company: Morgan Advertising Ltd.
Street & #: 30 Rockefeller Plaza
City: New York
State: NY
Zip Code: 10112

Send? y

Msg posted Oct 18, 1983 3:29 PM EDT MSG: YGEX-0940-2748

Same message to another recipient? n

Another message? n

Command?

FIGURE 2: USER INTERFACE PROMPT SEQUENCE

Within minutes, Envoy sets up a packet network call to the Canada Post printer and the message is printed; the actual time generally depends upon how many messages are queued for that particular printer. If a message has been sent special delivery, it is automatically placed at the head of the queue.

If for any reason the printer cannot be reached or the session is aborted mid-stream, Envoy will automatically go back to the last correctly transmitted message and attempt to recontact the printer. The retry attempts are frequent during the first two hours, at which point a station failure message is automatically sent to the Canada Post network control centre electronic mailbox. After two hours the retry attempts are hourly until the failure condition has been rectified. At any time, the Canada Post administrator may invoke certain Envoy commands which reassign the output queue dynamically so that messages destined for a printer which is not operational may be rerouted to an alternate location. Such an operation is, of course, transparent to the users of the service.

A sample of an actual EnvoyPost message header is included in figure 3. The first part indicates the time of printing. The SEQ # is a concatenation of the date with a sequence number which is incremented for each message sent to that particular printer; in this way the printer operator can easily verify that all messages have been received. The second part of the header indicates when the message was posted by the sender, a system unique message number (which is the same as that seen by the sender in the message posted indication above) and the Envoy user name of the sender. The postal address follows in what is normally considered to be the text of an Envoy message.

In some instances, Canada Post may be unable to deliver a message if, for example, the recipient moved without leaving a forwarding address. The header provides sufficient information for the network control centre to advise the sender electronically via Envoy.

```
            ENVOYPOST MESSAGE   Transmitted by Telecom Canada

PRINTED:      Oct 18, 1983  15:33 EDT
STATION:      *FJP0168
SEQ # :       OCT18.0010

Posted: Tue  Oct 18, 1983   3:27 PM EDT              Msg: YGEU-0730-3872
From:   DJ.RHYNAS/VAS.DESIGN/NTWK.PLNG.DEV/CCTD/CC/BELLCANADA.OPNS
TO:     (PST: K1N 5G1)
Subj:   BASIC DELIVERY


MR. BRIAN G. FRANKLIN                                *CQZ2584
MTECH COMPANY
85 ST. ANDREW STREET
OTTAWA ONTARIO
K1N 5G1
```

FIGURE 3: SAMPLE MESSAGE HEADER

Canada Post Network and Equipment

In establishing a network to meet the service requirements outlined in previous sections of this paper, it was necessary to consider the following:

a) Choice of cities where service would be provided. Cities had to be in Datapac Serving Areas. Service was to be provided in all provinces, to a maximum number of addresses, but without exceeding basic constraints imposed by the limits defined for the trial.

b) Selection of the specific postal facility in each city, and the actual location within that facility. This entailed a consideration of arrangements or processing the mail within the facility and for final delivery to the addressee.

c) Selection of employees with job skills and duties best suited to the operation since this service would not be a full-time job, at least not during the trial period.

d) Ensuring an adequate level of security and confidentiality. Printers had to be in restricted areas.

e) Providing equipment capable of operating reliably in the postal environment, as no special facilities were to be built.

f) Ensuring that adequate maintenance would be available.

The Canada Post network presently consists of twenty-five Envoy 100 autodelivery stations in twenty cities. The electronic mailbox associated with each one of these stations receives all electronic mail bearing the postal codes assigned to the station. Terminals are receive only (RO).

Each autodelivery station is equipped with a high-quality daisy-wheel printer connected to the Datapac network via a dedicated Datapac 3101 Access for ASCII terminal support. Datapac network facilities are leased from Telecom Canada at a regular tariff. Printers are installed in secure areas in main post offices or in major mail processing plants.

The printers selected are capable of using either plastic or metalized printwheels. Metalized printwheels are currently used with carbon ribbons. Metalized wheels were selected to minimize the incidence of spoke failure and to provide consistent print quality over a long period of time. Carbon ribbons were selected to provide the highest possible print quality and to minimize the requirements for cleaning the printwheels.

Printers can be fitted with either a forms tractor or with a cut sheet feeder. A bi-directional forms tractor was selected for use as it was found to provide:

a) More positive control over the top of form positioning
b) More positive control over paper position in general
c) Lower incidence of paper jams or feeding failure
d) Lower cost - less capital investment required
e) Easier set up and adjustment

The overall construction of the forms tractor gave the impression that there was less to go wrong in comparison with the cut sheet feeder and that maintenance requirements would therefore be lower. The choice was made somewhat easier by virtue of the fact that fan-fold bond paper was available with clean-edge perforations. The clean-edge perforation provides pages with edges that approximate the appearance of a cut sheet.

The requirement to allow users a full 80 character line and still provide standard left and right hand margins led to a decision to use 12 pitch printing. Elite 12 was the font style selected. Ten pitch printing would not have allowed the use of 80 character lines with adequate left and right hand margins.

Initially, it was decided that complete control over page and message format would be vested in the Envoy 100 computer with the exception of the left hand margin setting and the top of form position. Envoy was to insert all carriage returns and line feeds, and was also to control pagination, address positioning and right-hand margins. It has been necessary to make some changes in this strategy and they are discussed in the section which deals with Operational Experience during the trial period.

Although daisy wheel printers provide the print quality that was required for this service they are inherently slow devices. At 300 baud the printer easily keeps up with the data transmission. However, data transmission rates of 1200 baud and higher may be implemented in the future. To accommodate this, printers have been equipped with a buffer memory with a capacity of approximately 2600 characters, and three flow control protocols are available. X-On/X-Off is currently in use.

The flow control protocol is also used to interrupt transmission of data under any of the following conditions:

a) Cover open
b) Paper out
c) End of ribbon
d) Printer in check condition
e) Pause switch depressed.

If the error condition is corrected within a predefined time interval, data transmission and printing resume at the point where they ceased, as the printer sends the X-ON control character when RESET is depressed. If the condition is not corrected, the message remains in the autodelivery queue for the station involved, Envoy then invokes the retry routine as described in the previous section.

Printers are equipped with battery protected non-volatile CMOS RAM for retention of an answerback message and several operating parameters. These parameters have to be downline loaded to the printer from the network control centre in Ottawa as no facilities have been provided at the sites for programming. The parameters control a number of printer functions including top-of-form, left hand margin, right hand margin, bottom margin, page size, and carriage home position.

The basic Envoy 100 philosophy is based on the idea that each autodelivery station operator does his own housekeeping, i.e., sets up retransmissions, requests statistical data using the Envoy 100 command structure, etc. Canada Post's Operations personnel required, however, that these functions be handled from a single control centre. Furthermore, provision had to be made to allow mail to be routed to an alternate station whenever an autodelivery station was out of service. Provision also had to be made for downline loading of operating parameters to individual printers. Envoy offered the capability needed to allow Canada Post's network control centre to sign on as any one of the autodelivery stations, set up a retransmission and have the message printed at the autodelivery station. Downline loading routines were made a part of the network control centre software, provided by Canada Post.

Basic network control is performed with a microcomputer programmed to emulate an asynchronous ASCII terminal. A slave printer is available to print out statistical data if necessary.

No discussion of design considerations would be complete without some mention of maintenance philosophy. Electronic mail services must achieve speedy and reliable delivery if they are to be viable. The operator at Canada Post's network control centre is responsible for initiating action to clear faults, and for deciding when and where to reroute mail to maintain delivery schedules. Each fault must be analyzed and an initial decision made as to its probable source, i.e., Datapac, Envoy 100, or the printer. The appropriate maintenance organization must then be notified and service requested.

Canada Post Corporation intends to enter into agreements with other providers of computer-based messaging services as well as with private companies that operate their own internal systems which will permit users of such services and systems to send electronic mail to Canada Post for delivery. The fundamental objective is to provide a universal service which will give the reach provided by Canada Post's delivery network to all those who wish to make use of it. Access to Canada Post's printers is presently possible via the Datapac network. Other networks will be connected when the demand makes it necessary and viable.

U.S. Service

The United States post office offers an electronic mail service known as E-COM (Electronic Computer Originated Mail). It allows large volume mailers to transmit their messages in a specified format to specially equipped serving post offices where they are printed and delivered as part of the first class mail stream. The delivery interval is two days within the continental United States, although typically is is next day delivery throughout most of the major metropolitan centres.

To access this distribution system, Telecom Canada has made an arrangement with EMCA (Electronic Mail Corporation of America), a value-added service firm in New York. When an Envoy 100 subscriber indicates that his message is destined for the States, the script prompts for state and zip code. All U.S. messages are 'loosely' formatted and then autodelivered via Datapac/Telenet to EMCA's computer. Here they are reformatted to comply with the E-COM requirements, bundled with messages from other non-Envoy subscribers and then routed based on zip code to the appropriate U.S. serving post office. EMCA offers this service to its own subscribers and looks after all of the logistic details in interworking with E-COM such as minimum volume of 200 messages per transmission to each serving post office, protocol and format specifications, and monies paid in advance.

In the reverse direction, EMCA's subscribers may send messages to the EnvoyPost system. These messages are appropriately formatted and automatically submitted to Envoy 100 by a batch input script, after which they form part of the normal EnvoyPost stream.

OPERATIONAL EXPERIENCE

Overall, the grade of service and coverage objectives have been well achieved. Customer feedback is very positive and there are a number of innovative applications. One company, described elsewhere at this conference provides comparative annuity quotations to insurance agents; since annuity prices fluctuate daily, EnvoyPost is used to dissemitate information to the company's client base in a very timely manner (ref 4).

With any service introduction there are start up wrinkles and EnvoyPost was no different. This section highlights some observations made to date, primarily from the perspective of Canada Post.

One of the basic tenets of Envoy 100 - indeed of any computer based messaging system - is that input comes from terminals operated by a cross-section of users, many of whom are not skilled in typing or in the operation of terminals. Carriage returns are omitted, text is typed entirely in lower case, cursor controls are used in lieu of the space bar as well as to edit text, etc. Unless the software in the host computer can compensate for these situations the printer will respond to them, resulting in an unsatisfactory document for delivery. The recipient of such a letter has no way of knowing that the problem lies with the sender - he blames the Post Office.

An early problem was encountered with users omitting carriage returns or using 132 column terminals. At the printer, this situation resulted in a partial loss of text. It also interfered with pagination control as line counting was initially based on number of carriage returns. Printing past the right hand edge of the paper has since been eliminated by implementing right hand margin control in the printer. Pagination control has been deleted from the Envoy 100 software and is now achieved by implementing bottom margin control in the printer.

Another problem occurs when the use of cursor controls results in the transmission of escape codes to the printer. The escape codes vary from terminal to terminal but are interpreted by the printer in accordance with its programming. Reverse line feeds cause overprinting; form feeds are sometimes generated, wasting paper; automatic underlining may be activated, margin controls may even be erased. Canada Post is currently investigating the feasibility of making access to the escape code sequences and functions controlled by them more difficult.

Datapac 3101 (compatible with CCITT Recommendations X.3, X.28, X.29) does not use an end-to-end protocol per se. In a recent case, a customer complained of non-delivery of mail. No record of it having been printed could be found, yet the message queue showed it as having been transmitted. It had been transmitted, but a defective EIA cable in the Datapac central office had interrupted the circuit to the printer. Answerback routines at the beginning and end of each message transmission are now being tested to minimize the probability of another occurrence of this nature.

Some difficulties have been experienced in ensuring that postal staff maintain the top-of-form position correctly. There has been a tendency to remove messages from the printer by manually rotating the platen instead of using the form feed push button, and this practice introduces error in the line count which in turn causes top-of-form to be lost. When this occurs, the settings are down-line loaded to the printer and the affected traffic is retransmitted.

Having shared with you the start-up difficulties, it should be pointed out that there have been no insurmountable problems and the service is now operating smoothly.

PLANNED ENHANCEMENTS

Several enhancements are currently under development at the time of writing and will be commercially available for the full service in March of 1984.

Envoy 100 will support a form letter capability which allows a user to set up a distribution list of postal addresses. Each entry in the list may also contain variable text information so it will be possible for the system to automatically send out large numbers of 'personalized' letters in a very convenient manner; e.g., 'Dear Mr. Smith of Ottawa, your account is overdrawn by .....'. The text of the message will also be automatically reformatted depending upon the number and length of the variable text fields.

Another feature to be offered by Canada Post will be that of Signature Service, which for an additional premium will allow the sender to get back a delivery acknowledgement signed by the recipient.

CONCLUSION

The EnvoyPost market trial was successfully launched in March of 1983 and has generated more press coverage than any other service introduction in the history of Telecom Canada. Indeed the response from the market place has been very favourable such that nation-wide coverage will commence in mid-1984. Canada Post, in marrying its service with Envoy 100 has brought the benefits of electronic mail to the public at large.

ACKNOWLEDGEMENT

We gratefully acknowledge the contributions of our colleagues at both Telecom Canada and Canada Post Corporation who were involved in the planning and implementation of EnvoyPost.

REFERENCES

[1] Envoy 100 Reference Manual, Telecom Canada, 1983.

[2] D.J. Rhynas, I. Kerr, 'The Interconnection of Public Electronic Mail Systems', Proceedings of the International Conference on Computer Communications, 1982.

[3] David D. Redell, James E. White, 'Interconnecting Public Electronic Mail Systems', Computer, IEEE Computer Society, September 1983.

[4] C.M. Sandford, 'Making the Right Choice: Public Versus Private Messaging Systems, Proceedings of the IFIP Conference on Computer-Based Message Services, May 1984.

Computer-Based Message Services
H.T. Smith (Editor)
Elsevier Science Publishers B.V. (North-Holland)

MAKING THE RIGHT CHOICE: PUBLIC VS PRIVATE MESSAGING SYSTEMS

Celia M. Sandford
Business Development Department
Telecom Canada
Ottawa, Canada

Today, many organizations are turning to electronic messaging systems to help them improve information flow and decrease costs. One option to be considered when selecting the means of implementing electronic messaging is to use a public service as opposed to purchasing a private electronic mail system. The evaluation criteria that should be used when making this choice are presented using Telecom Canada's public messaging service, Envoy 100, as the example. Two case studies of existing Envoy 100 customers are presented highlighting the benefits of public electronic mail services.

INTRODUCTION

Information flow is a critical issue for most businesses. This information may be in the form of orders, invoices or the agenda for the next customer or committee meeting. Distribution of this information in an accurate, efficient and economical manner is a key-factor that can determine the success or failure of a business or corporation. A missed opportunity can have a significant effect on the company's profitability. Increased general awareness of this problem and the need to stay competitive is forcing many businesses to investigate alternatives to the conventional information transfer mechanisms of telephone, letter, telex or courier. One of the aids in this area that could be applied to most businesses is a computer based electronic messaging system.

After a brief description of the benefits of electronic messaging and the two main messaging application types, this paper analyses the differences between public messaging services and private systems. This analysis covers four areas: reliability/availabiliy, reach, cost, and supplier stability.

BENEFITS OF MESSAGING

Electronic messaging offers that many advantages in improving the information flow process. Statistics prove that many hours of a manager's time are wasted playing telephone tag. This is described as the process of originating and receiving telephone messages when the person you call is not available or you are not available when called.

Messaging systems do not require the originator and recipient to be available at the same time. Although the recipient may not be available while travelling, attending meetings or working flexible hours, messages can still be received and stored in his mailbox. The messages are held by the system and when convenient, the recipient accesses the electronic messaging system to read and answer his outstanding mail. This feature has a significant benefit for businesses with international applications as it increases the 'window' when people in different countries or people working different hours can communicate.

Another less obvious benefit is that the electronic transfer of information decreases preparation and delivery costs compared to traditional means such as Telex, letter or courier. Efficiency is also increased in that the person sending the message is the originator in most cases. The letter or memo does not have to be typed, proof read, then corrected by clerical staff prior to sending. The person who wants to send the information creates it and sends it. This decrease in preparation and delivery time, leaves the messaging user with the extra time available to ensure more accurate thoughtful responses and also increases productivity by providing the necessary information more quickly.

Messaging systems can also save time in the transfer of orders, invoices and other business forms from one company to another. Today many companies have computerized in-house order entry or inventory control systems. Currently paper copies are used to communicate between distributors, suppliers and others. Electronic messaging allows these forms to be transferred electronically reducing the potential errors in converting to paper copies and reducing the information transfer time. This results in improved inventory control and cash flow which allow increases in profitability.

APPLICATIONS

There are two main types of messaging applications:

- personal
- administrative

Personal

In Personal Messaging, users send short informal messages to other people. These messages are in the form of memos, meeting agendas, minutes or brief questions and answers. The recipient and originator are usually individuals not groups. These users usually have direct access to an input device or terminal. Frequently the terminal is on their desk or in their office and used solely by them. Sometimes it is nearby and shared by two or three other people. The conversion to an electronic mail system for personal messaging causes users to quickly depend on the service, expect fast system response times and want a friendly simple user interface. Access to people or groups outside their own organization may be essential to many users as the community of interest grows.

Administrative

In Administrative Messaging the messages are longer, more formal in nature and may take the form of orders, or invoices which are sent to and from groups or departments, not individuals. Accuracy of information transfer and the ability to track and log messages to ensure completeness and reliability are prime considerations. For some applications, the messages are transferred to groups or departments within the same organization. Other applications require that customers external to the organization, input orders directly. External access to the electronic messaging system is a requirement in this case.

These two primary messaging capabilities can then be utilized in various ways. For example, Personal Messaging can be used to co-ordinate a project, in one large company building, or around the world. The number of project team members can be two or two hundred. Administrative Messaging can be used by people within one company located in one building but with multiple departments creating or transferring orders.

TYPES OF SYSTEMS

The corporate messaging needs and the characteristics of the specific applications should be understood prior to choosing the most appropriate messaging system. There is a variety of messaging systems available with various features and capabilities but they can be classified in two ways: PUBLIC or PRIVATE.

Private Systems

A private system is a software package purchased to run on an existing company computer or a complete hardware and software package. It can also be a network of personal computers. The private system, usually located on the customer's premises, is used solely by one organization. All operating, maintenance and support costs are the responsibility of the organization. Examples of this type of system are DECMAIL, INTERCOMM and INFOMAIL. They run on computer hardware manufactured by Digital Equipment, IBM or PRIME.

Public Service

A public service is owned and operated by the service supplier. Customers contract with the service supplier to use a portion of the service's capabilities, and are billed only for the portion they use. The user's responsibility is limited to provisioning terminals or access devices. Envoy 100, an electronic messaging service offered nationally by Telecom Canada, is a typical example of a public service.

Envoy 100, offered in Canada since 1981, is supported on Datapac, the Canadian X.25 packet switching network. The Envoy 100 service is based on Tandem Non-Stop hardware using the Guardian operating system and application software purchased from GTE-Telenet. The software was significantly modified by Telecom Canada to serve the Canadian messaging market. One of its uniquely Canadian features is a user controllable bilingual French-English interface. A user while interacting with Envoy 100 can change his language of operation from French to English. This feature is extremely important in Canada where, although there are two official languages, the majority of the population does not speak both English and French.

Access to Envoy 100 is via standard ASCII asynchronous devices connected to the public switched telephone network (PSTN), the TWX network or devices directly connected via dedicated connection to Datapac. Bulk, non-interactive transfer of messages is also supported using bisynchronous 3780 access.

Introduced in June of 1981, the service is now used by over 500 organizations and 10,000 users. The growth rate of the user base is considerable with over 400 new users added to the service each month. The applications cover personal and administrative messaging, with some users implementing a mixture of both types.

SELECTION CONSIDERATIONS

While the basic functions of message creation, editing and sending are available in all messaging systems, both public and private, there are four aspects of the system under consideration which should be addressed with respect to the application before deciding on the most appropriate system to satisfy the Corporate need.

These aspects are:

- reliability/availability
- reach
- cost
- supplier stability

Reliability/Availability

Availability is key in many messaging applications. The best messaging software is useless if the users can't get time sensitive information from their mailboxes when required or if they loose faith in the system's integrity and start a parallel paper system. If messaging is to be successfully implemented, users must be able to access the service easily and efficiently at their convenience. A busy signal trying to reach your mailbox is as frustrating as a busy signal on the telephone when trying to obtain verbal information from your peers and subordinates.

Private messaging systems, implemented on existing computer hardware operated by the data processing departments in the organization, run concurrently with other programs on the host computer. The usage characteristics for time sharing on management information systems are different than the characteristics and response times needed for electronic messaging. Computer users can adapt or have adapted to limited availability of in-house computer systems and occasional down time is not unexpected. Call blocking during busy periods which prevents system access or slow response times are not unusual circumstances on an in-house computer service. A service availability of 95.00% is acceptable for most in-house computer operations.

The availability demanded for public messaging services is 99.50% or higher. Users slowly become disenchanted with electronic messaging and its benefits do not materialise if it is not as easy to access as the telephone. Public messaging services operate 365 days a year with limited down time for well defined maintenance schedules. Some public services use technically sophisticated hardware and software designed for high reliability messaging applications. To meet these needs Envoy 100 uses Tandem Computers with their Non Stop operating capability. Most hardware failures do not cause a complete failure of the service service; instead, duplicate hardware components take control and operation continues with degraded performance until the component is replaced or repaired.

Personal Messaging users access the system at the same time of day as they use the telephone (mid morning and after lunch). They expect fast response times and easy access. They also access the service after hours and on weekends; therefore, limited, short maintenance windows are a major operating criteria. Adminstrative applications also demand high availability. Delay in creating and sending an order or invoice could result in the company losing an important sale or contract. Reliability is also an important factor to the administrative user. Lost messages due to on-line storage problems could have a significant effect on the company's creditability with its customers.

The messaging system chosen must have adequate communications facilities and processing power to handle the expected loading. The hardware must be provisioned so that potential data loss is minimized.

Reach

Reach is the term used to describe the number of people with whom you can communicate. As in most forms of communications, the value of the service increases with the number of potential recipients who can receive your information. This encompasses various potential access and delivery mechanisms for electronic mail systems.

A private system usually supports the existing access protocols used by the data processing applications that use the computer. Due to the cost involved in implementing new protocols, expansion in this area is often limited.

Only one organization or department uses the system so that the number of potential message recipients is limited. Access to external communications services or networks are also constrained.

Public messaging services support various access device protocols and networks. Envoy 100 supports 3270 access and 3780 access as well as ASCII access from the TWX, PSTN (Public Switched Telephone Network) and Datapac network in Canada and via international packet switching links around the world.

While a private system is used by just one organization, a public service allows users to message between companies or subscribers. This means your suppliers can message you and you won't have to give them access to your private system or carry the cost of their messaging use. Conversely, you can message your customers without changing systems. Many of the dominant national suppliers already have such significant user bases that many company's business associates or competitors are probably represented to some degree in the existing user base. Many applications also make use of bulletin board facilities for distributing information to other subscribers. Public services, of course, have a greater variety of these sources of information.

Some public messaging services also have links to postal and courier companies. Envoy 100's service is called EnvoyPost. This service allows an Envoy 100 user to create and send a message including the Canadian postal address and postal codes. This message is physically printed at a Canada Post Corporation office and delivered the same or the next business day by Canada Post delivery personnel. Another option of the service directs the properly addressed message to the United States ECOM (Electronic Computer Originated Mail) system for physical delivery anywhere in the U.S. These EnvoyPost recipients do not have to be Envoy 100 subscribers. The costs of services such as these are significantly less expensive than traditional forms of communication. An EnvoyPost message of one thousand characters costs about $2.00 to send anywhere in Canada compared to the cost to prepare and send a business letter in Canada of about $6.00. These costs include paper and delivery costs.

The ability to automatically deliver messages to auto answer devices in other countries is also beneficial. Envoy 100 can deliver messages to any U.S. TWX and ASCII PSTN device and is planning an International TELEX connection this year. This facility allows users to address most common messaging devices in the world using one existing terminal.

These examples of input and output features lead to the need for another way to expand your reach. Although your potential messaging application may seem to need limited reach now and you may have specific access devices or terminals in mind, future evolution should be considered. Messaging systems in the 1980's are at the same evolutionary stage as the telephone before 1920. At that time there were many local pockets of telephone users joined together by a local telephone service. In the future, messaging services will evolve like the telephone system to form global networks and standards are being developed to facilitate this interconnection. The current CCITT plennary session will formalize the message protocol sections of the standard in 1984. By 1988 standards concerning other areas of message system interworking should be fixed. These standards will define mandatory and optional features and capabilities of messaging services. Any private systems purchased should be adaptible to this interconnection so that its users are not isolated. This 'public door' concept is mandatory for all services both public and private.

Other public services are also being developed that will support public directories of messaging users, systems and special services. In the future these public directories will allow users to find data and people and easily transfer data and personal messages around the world.

Cost

Hardware, Software and Rates

The cost to implement a private messaging system includes initial fixed costs and on-going operating costs. The initial costs of purchasing an appropriate software package must be considered together with the cost of purchasing the computing and telecommunications hardware to support it. Electronic mail packages are available for some computers for as little as $5,000. More sophisticated hardware and software packages which will support 150-500 users are available for about $200,000. The cost of operating and maintaining these systems must be included in public/private cost comparisons. These costs include hardware and software maintenance, the cost to house the computer in an appropriate environment, Computer Operations staff and customer support personnel. These are all behind the scenes costs. The cost of operating, supporting and maintaining a public service falls to the service provider and is shared by all users and reflected it in the service rates.

Public messaging services charge only for what you use. Their rate plans are usually established based on a reasonably low entry fee. The usage sensitive portion of the rate scheme is either time or volume based. In the case of Envoy 100 the entry fee is a $25-$50 initial service charge, then just $5 per month for Individual User accreditation or $20 per month for a corporate account, with $3 for each user accredited in the corporation. Each time the service is used a $0.30/kilocharacter (1000 character) charge is applied for creating and sending messages to another user's mailbox or for autodelivery to the Datapac network. This usage sensitive charge includes Canadian network access charges via Datapac.

Additional incremental charges are only applied for premium services such as EnvoyPost, or U.S. and Canadian TWX, and DDD delivery. Storage charges are 1/2 cent per thousand characters per day. Messages are kept free of charge on the system for five days after they have been received. These flexible rate plans allow companies to start small to try out the concept and expand as they identify new applications. Volume discounts are usually available for high volume users.

Modelled on the philosophy of the telephone and postal service, Envoy 100 also offers a 'sender pays' concept. The person sending the message pays for the recipient to receive the first copy. This is advantageous for either intercompany or interdivision messaging applications. The charges are allocated to the originator's department or organization and electronic 'junk mail' is discouraged.

Wherever possible, to reduce implementation costs, existing access devices should be used. These could be data processing terminals using 3270 protocol, TWX or Telex machines, personal computers or word processors and standard terminals using asynchronous ASCII access. Supporting access from various networks using many protocols, both synchronous and asynchronous, with high availability is expensive. Forecasting methods must also be implemented to ensure appropriate hardware and communications facilities are implemented as applications grow. Changes in protocol standards or network interfaces must be made to ensure access to the network. As applications grow and develop, new networks or protocols must be supported.

Public services are responsible for providing communications facilities to their services with high reliability. As customer demand is perceived, new protocols are supported. Network interface changes are handled automatically.

Training

Visible to the user is documentation, training and customer support. Most public services provide customer training from many locations. Users of a private system must be trained and supported internally. The costs of training and supporting users can be significant particularly for the first few users. Once a significant user base is established in your company, user synergy exists and users tend to support themselves and in many cases train themselves. User training and support in the early implementation stages is very important for successfull application implementation in your organization. The 'perfect' public or private system can be chosen, yet the project fail, if the application is not correctly implemented and sufficient user support provided. Training and customer documentation is sometimes free or available for a modest cost on Public Services.

Enhancements

Public messaging services continually evolve as customer needs change and as technology advances. To accommodate this evolution in a timely fashion, the Envoy 100 service has an on-going enhancement program. Since its inception in 1981 six major new features have been added as well as numerous minor improvements.

These include:

- the ability to deliver messages to auto answer terminals in Canada
- a bilingual user interface
- support of all Canadian time zones
- EnvoyPost
- interconnection to the U.S. ECOM Service
- 3780 access support
- ability to deliver messages to U.S. TWX and Public Switched Telephone Network devices

Continual feedback from customers and on-going market research provide a continuous stream of customer driven new features.

The flexible rate plans and low start up costs of public services are attractive to small groups of users. The larger initial capital expense costs of a private system are justified for larger numbers of users. The breakeven point varies depending on initial private system costs, number of users supported and traffic. Some small organizations with 150-450 users could obtain a private messaging system for $170,000-360,000 in fixed costs, exclusive of on-going operating and support costs. These on-going private system operations costs could be minimized if a support system and support personnel are in place for other applications.

Supplier Stability

Since electronic mail should, if properly introduced, become as indispensible to your organization as the telephone, or the copier; you must ensure the integrity of the vendor. Although inexpensive packages can be found, at discount prices, only reputable vendors with significant visible investment in the product should be considered. If you need minor support or major expansion, a reputable vendor should be able to supply it.

THE PUBLIC MESSAGING CHOICE

Two Canadian companies who have made the choice to implement their messaging applications on Telecom Canada's public messaging service, Envoy 100, are Domglas, owned by Consolidated Bathurst and CompQuote. These company's applications and the benefits of using a public messaging service illustrate the preceding points.

Domglas

Domglas manufactures glass container ware such as liquor and food bottles for industrial customers on a contract basis. With six production plants, four sales offices and warehouses throughout Canada and the U.S., extensive communication is required to keep operations under control and running smoothly despite the great distances separating locations. Domglas uses the Envoy 100 service to replace telephone calls and letters for co-ordination of export distribution and production and glass mould scheduling. Envoy 100's most valuable features from Domglas' perspective, are the multiple distribution capability by which messages can be sent to all offices involved in one transaction; rapid access to written confirmation of an order to release; and the fact that communication is always successful. The recipient doesn't have to be physically available to receive the message. To Domglas, this means U.S. and Canadian locations can quickly receive messages concerning contracts or orders; thus, orders can be filled and container ware released quickly, frequently within two hours. This function used to take significantly longer using their previous means of communication which was telephone conversations confirmed in writing. Envoy 100 gives Domglas better control over scheduling and ordering of mould equipment for all Domglas plants. They can send copies of messages to people across the country where before they would mail typed or photocopied letters. Unexpected production schedule changes are discussed using Envoy 100 rather than expensive long distance telephone calls. Use of Envoy 100 has meant bottom-line savings via improved information flow for Domglas by allowing them to process orders and release inventory quickly.

CompQuote

CompQuote is a Montreal-based company which provides comparative annuity quotations to insurance agents. The annuities market is a fast-changing environment with approximately 50 life insurance companies providing annuity plans to Canadians. Once individuals who invested in Registered Retirement Savings Plans reach age 60, they can buy an annuity policy which provides monthly income up to age 90 or for the rest of their lives. The company from which an individual chooses to buy an annuity can make a significant difference since rates and comparative ranking changes on a daily basis.

A $25,000 annuity may yield a monthly income of $330 from one company and only $297 from another. This ranking could be reversed the following day. Now, using a public messaging service, Envoy 100, CompQuote provides a same-day comparative quotation service, evaluating 40 life insurance and trust company's current annuity rates and providing ranked comparisons for the top 10 companies plus a listing of all the companies surveyed. The client data, provided by his insurance agent, is fed by CompQuote into a computer system that produces a one-paged personalized comparative quotation in seconds.

This quotation is then immediately sent to the agent via Envoy 100. CompQuote pays for the agent's use of Envoy 100 and the agents only provide their own terminal and modem. If agents do not have a terminal they can receive their quotations via EnvoyPost, the delivery function using CanadaPost delivery personnel. Before using the Envoy 100 public messaging service, CompQuote provided next-day delivery of quotations using expensive telecommunications and overnight messenger services. These communications services cut into CompQuote profits and quotes were not as timely as the agents wanted them to be. Quotations were occasionally read over the telephone but it was feared that mistakes could be made. That was not acceptable.

Use of Envoy 100, a public messaging service with the EnvoyPost feature, has decreased costs four to six times and due to increased speed and efficiency, encouraged agents to increase their use of the CompQuote service. CompQuote chose a public messaging service due to the ability to access other delivery mechanisms such as EnvoyPost, the national availability of the service and its low cost.

SUMMARY

When selecting an electronic messaging system for an organization, the decision should take into account four factors: reliability/availability, cost, reach and supplier stability. The relative importance of each of these factors should be influenced by the application as it is initially perceived. However, don't assume that one electronic messaging application will be sufficient for all time. Once messaging is successfully introduced in an organization and its use matures, other applications will evolve. The most innovative feature set today can be obsolete next year. Don't be misled by basing your decision on the service with the most features, unless these features expand your reach. A calendar is an interesting "attention getter", but if most of your applications are information transfer oriented, the ability to deliver that information anywhere in the world is more important.

Large, centrally located applications with set fixed access protocols and networks might be best implemented on a privately run internal messaging service using special hardware and software. Geographically, dispersed applications that need access from many devices and many networks could best be suited to a public messaging service. Trials or pilot tests can be easily implemented at low cost on public services, but thorough analysis of each application, and it's potential growth should be completed before final long term system selection is made. If a private system is chosen ensure, it has or will have a 'public door'.

The benefits of electronic messaging are many. Effective, efficient, economical communication of information can be a crucial factor in the success of most businesses. Public or private messaging services provide an excellent means of combating the information flow challenge. The selection of the most appropriate service type should be made after thorough analysis of the applications to be supported.

ACKNOWLEDGEMENT

I gratefully acknowledge the contributions of my colleagues at Telecom Canada who assisted in the preparation of this paper.

PART 5:

REGULATORY AND SECURITY CONSIDERATIONS

Computer-Based Message Services
H.T. Smith (Editor)
Elsevier Science Publishers B.V. (North-Holland)

THE INTERCONNECTION OF MESSAGE HANDLING SYSTEMS IN THE LIGHT OF CURRENT CCITT RECOMMENDATIONS

Peter T Kirstein

Department of Computer Science
University College London
London, UK.

The paper analyses recent regulatory practices on the interconnection of public and private networks, with specific emphasis on Message Handling Services. It analyses the emerging CCITT recommendations, and shows how they conflict with some current practices.

1. INTRODUCTION

The attitude of many Governments and telecommunications authorities to the provision of communication services is changing rapidly. Not only are more countries permitting independent provision of basic telecommunications transmission, but the whole area of "Telematic Services" is becoming wide open. Only three years ago many European authorities were believing that Teletex [1] would be the answer to all message services, and that much of this would remain in public hands. Now British Telecom, for example, is offering no less than three commercial electronic message services in addition to Telex and Teletex. Now there is a working group of the Consultative Committee on International Telephones and Telecommunications (CCITT) producing its agreed X400 ff recommendations on Message Handling Systems [2], which included the interconnection of private and public message handling services.

This paper tries to clarify the current picture on the interconnection of public and private computer and data networks, with particular emphasis on the provision of Message Handling Services.

The picture has two aspects - the National and the International. The national schemes depend only on National policies, and these vary widely in the different countries. The international ones are more similar, in that most countries try to follow CCITT recommendations. Of course with the current rapid changes in the CCITT environment, and the widely differing levels of message services in different countries, a uniform stance does not exist. The paper is based on the official policies. In fact these are changing fast. I describe later how several networks are contrary to the policy, but look like being allowed.

In Section 2, I outline my definitions of Terminals and Networks for regulatory purposes, and in Section 3 some of the historical regulations on the interconnection of private and administration facilities. In Section 4, I consider message switching in more detail, and in Section 5 the interconnection aspects of the CCITT X400 recommendations. In Section 6 some current message services are analysed in the light of CCITT recommendations, and some conclusions presented in Section 7.

2. TERMINALS AND NETWORKS

From the viewpoint of the PTTs, there are two important classes of customer objects; terminals and networks. A terminal is a device attached to the Data Communication Equipment (DCE) - usually supplied by the PTT. A terminal, in this parlance, can be a single VDU, a computer, a collection of computers, or a Local Area Computer Network. It must, however, be local to one site with a need for wide area communication. We will adopt the same definition of "terminal" in this paper. A Private Network is any collection of terminals connected by leased (non-switched), wide area, communication channels. Thus Fig 1 shows a number of sites Si connected by leased communication channels C.

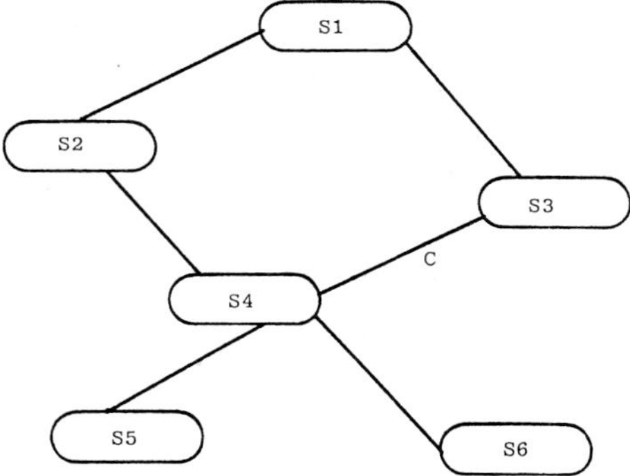

Figure 1 Schematic of sites connected as a private network

This represents a Private Network. In most countries the sites Si must belong to one organisational entity for it to be classed as a Private Network PN. It may then provide various Value Added Services such as switching, multiplexing, message switching etc. If these functions are provided by the PTTs, then we will call it an Administration Network AN.

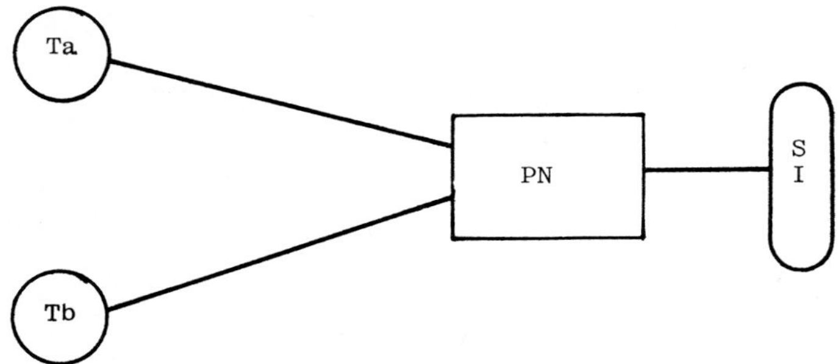

Figure 2 Terminals connected directly to private networks

A Private Network PN offers services to other organisations. Thus the terminals Ta and Tb may be attached, either directly (as in Fig 2) or via an Administration Network, as in Fig 3.

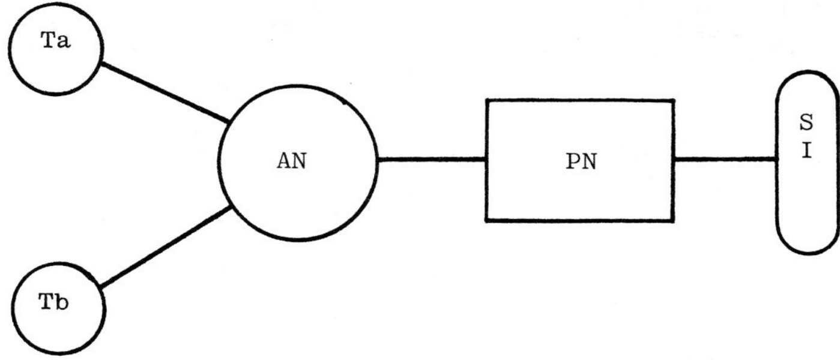

Figure 3 Terminals connected to private network via administration network

As long as the Private Network PN is merely providing computing services for a terminal eg. Ta, there is no problem. If, however, PN is passing data deliberately between Ta and Tb, it may be considered to be acting as a Value Added Carrier (VAC). In this case P may require a special authority or license. In the degenerate case that PN is merely a computer on a single site, it may still require special authority to store and forward data between Ta and Tb. This regulation is the case of the PTT monopoly on message switching, which is at the heart of the considerations of Computer Based Message Services.

3. INTERCONNECTED PRIVATE AND PUBLIC NETWORKS

In most countries, if a single organisation has different sites Si, in one or more countries, it is possible to lease communications channels at fixed cost connecting those sites. This is illustrated in Fig 1. In some countries even here the PTT is sometimes trying to charge a traffic dependent tariff for C. In general, the collection of sites of Fig 1 can be regarded as a Private Network PN, but such a private network can be regarded only as referring to one organisation and one country.

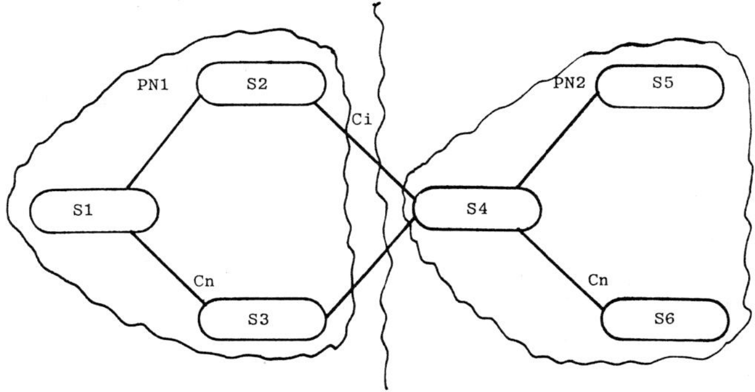

Figure 4 Schematic of two connected Networks in different countries

If the Private Network extends across two countries, as for example in Fig 4, it must usually be regarded as two private networks PN1 and PN2. The traffic which can pass across the national communication channels Cn are purely national affairs. However, the traffic, tariffs and regulations across the international channels, Ci are usually subject to the Committee Consultatif International de Telephones et Telecommunications (CCITT) and/or, in Europe, the Conseil European de Postes et Telecommunications (CEPT).

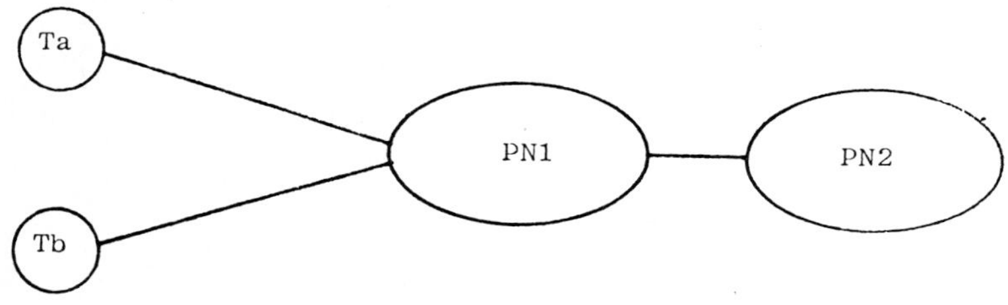

Figure 5 Two connected private networks

Thus in most countries PN1 and PN2, as shown in Fig 5, can be connected directly only if they belong to the same organisation - nationally or internationally. If PN1 and PN2 belong to different organisations, they may be permitted to connect only via a Public Administration Network (AN) as shown in Fig 6.

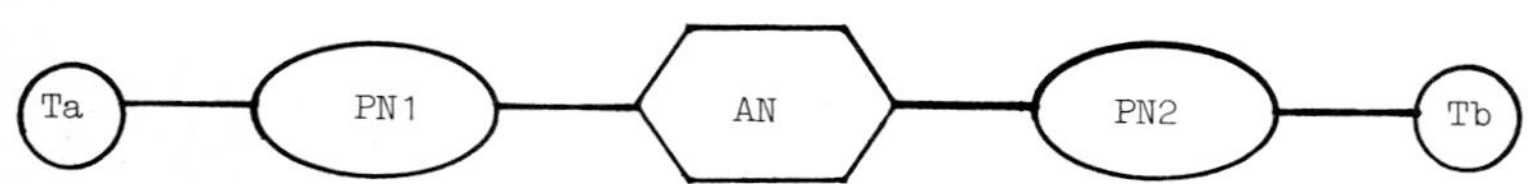

Figure 6 Connection of two private networks via an Administrative one

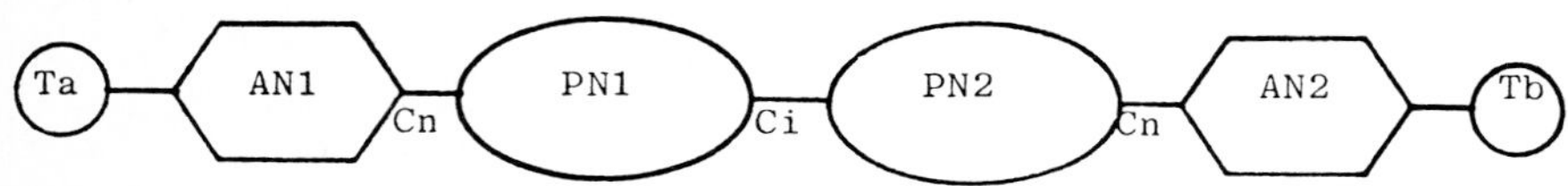

Figure 7 International connection of two private networks and access via two Administration ones

Most Service Bureau organisations provide access to their customers who belong to different organisations. In most countries the leased channel of Fig 2 will be permissible, even if a terminal Ta belongs to a different organisation from PN1. Some countries insist the access must be via an Administration network, as in Fig 3; often the service provider wants the access of Fig 3 in any case, to give a cheaper catchment area for lower activity terminals.

If PN1 and PN2 belong to the same organisation, it is usually permissible for a Terminal Ta, belonging to a different organisation, to access PN2 via PN1 (and possibly a national administration network) as shown in Fig 7. After all both administrations get revenue from the international channel Ci. However, access from Ta to Tb will either be prohibited, or will require, in some countries, that PN be licensed to provide Value Added Services. Sometimes such carriers will even be permitted to let Ta access Tb in Fig 7. However if we have the situation of Fig 8, with three country connection and T5 belonging to a different organisation, PN2 is usually not permitted to act as a relay between PN1 and PN3; only if there is a direct channel C13, so that the topology of Fig 8 degenerates to Fig 7, is Ta permitted to access Tb. In most countries, even if there is no channel C13, a terminal Ta can access resources on PN3.

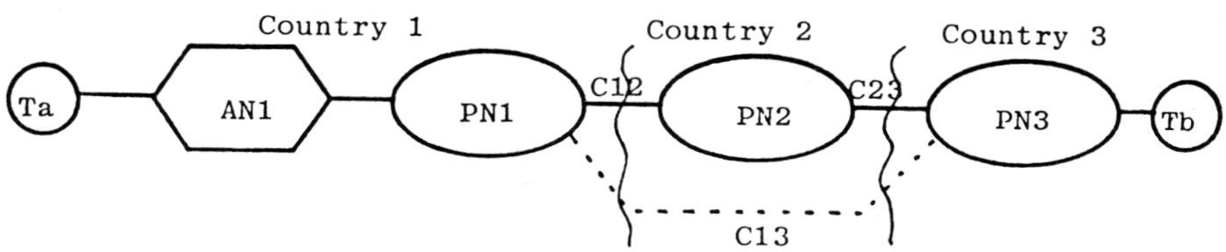

Figure 8 Three country connectivity

4. MESSAGE SWITCHING

If PN represents either a private network or even a single computing entity or Host, in Figs 2 or 3, the rules on passing data from Ta to Tb via PN1 are complex. In the UK, they have been that it is necessary for PN1 to process the data substantially; British Telecom had the monopoly on simple message switching it Ta and Tb belonged to a different organisation from PN1. More recently, in the UK it became permissible for PN1 to do such message switching - but technically it needed to obtain a license from British Telecom and now the Department of Trade and Industry. In the US and Canada, such activity has long been permitted. This led to the ridiculous situation in which one could have two private networks PN1 and PN2 as in Fig 5 in two countries (eg one in Europe and one in the US). Two terminals in the UK were permitted to access PN2 via PN1. PN2 was permitted to provide message switching in its host country. But the message switching of PN2 between Ta and Tb was not permitted.

In many countries the limitations on message switching have now relaxed; in any case they were almost unenforceable. Nor was their meaning clearly defined. For instance, if we take the simple example of Fig 3, and PN1 contains a Computer Based Message System (CBMS), it may be argued that address list expansion, to multiple mail boxes, was "substantial processing".

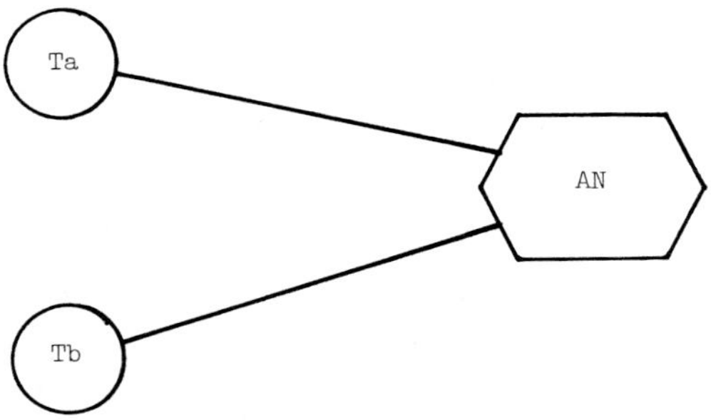

Figure 9 Direct Terminal Interaction via an Administration Network

Many PTTs are trying to push Teletex, which is topologically the simple situation of terminals T3 and T4 communicating directly as in Fig 9. However almost all PTTs realise that Teletex does not have the full functionality of a CBMS, and are trying to decide their role in the provision of CBMS. There is, therefore, a study group on this matter in CCITT, who have proposed a detailed set of draft recommendations [2]. These are discussed in the next section.

5. THE CCITT MESSAGE HANDLING SYSTEM RECOMMENDATIONS

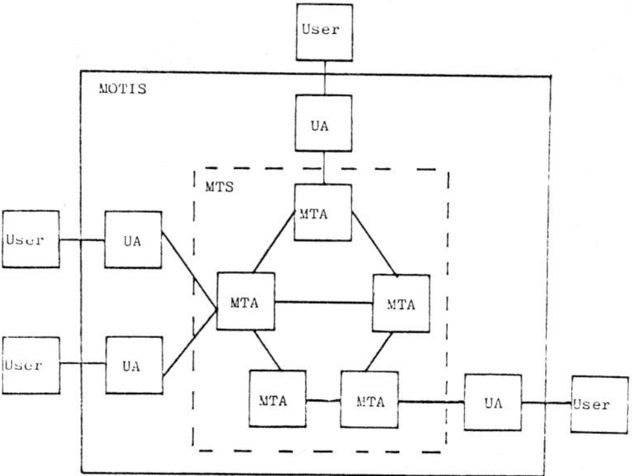

Figure 10 Functional view of the ISO Text Preparation and Interchange model

The CCITT recommendations on Message Handling Systems (MHS) [2] cover a wide range of subjects: service elements, message transfer protocols, service facilities available to users, presentation representation, type conversion, Teletex access, reliable transfer and Open system interconnection. This section only concerns the regulatory considerations. The MHS model has the structure shown in Fig 10. Here UA is the User Agent, which has two functions: it provides the user facilities, allows reception and transmission of message to the Message Transfer Agent (MTA). The UAs and MTAs can either be private or Administration supplied. One or more hosts, together with a collection of users, become a Management Domain (MD). The Management Domains are either Administration Management Domains (ADMD) or private ones (PRMD). The features supported for PRMDs are still under review. However, the rules for them follow very closely those for administration and private networks of Sections 2 and 3.

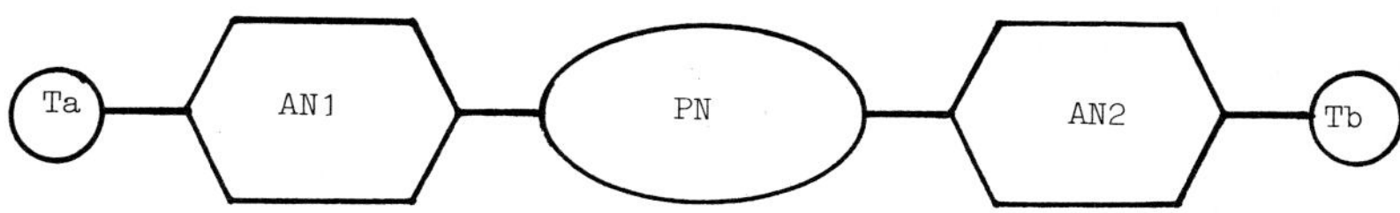

Figure 11 A private network connected to two Administration ones

Thus just as a Private Network PN of Section 2 was limited to one country, so is a PRMD. Just as two PNs must normally connect via an AN, just as in Fig 6, and not directly as in Fig 5, so must PRMDs connect. A PRMD may be connected to two ADMDs, as is PN to AN1 and AN2 in Fig 11; however, traffic from one AN1 may not be relayed through a PN to an AN2. No mention is made of direct connection of two PRMDs. It is not clear whether this is merely an omission, or whether such connection will be prohibited.

There is one hole in the present draft of the recommendations. Apparently the situation of Fig 5, where two PRMDs in different countries, belonging to the same organisation, may be connected together directly is not envisaged. It will be interesting to see if this possibility is permitted in later drafts.

6. VALUE ADDED SERVICES AND SOME CURRENT PRACTICES

The present CCITT recommendations encouraged some value added services relevant to CBMS, and are vague on others. They specifically mention directory services - but are not clear what type of directory services will or can be provided by whom. In particular, it is not clear whether PTTs will provide directory services for private MHSs, where private parties will be permitted to provide directory services for PTT MHSs, and who may do which classes of address list expansion. A similar confusion exists on which types of users will be permitted entries in Public Teletex directories.

In general the recommendations envisage private User Agents (UAs) attached to public MTSs - but it will probably be country dependant whether commercial UAs can pass third party traffic through ADMDs. This will probably be allowed in many countries; more questionably will be the facility to provide third party UA services directly to a private MHS; this may well fall foul of the provisions of Fig 4.

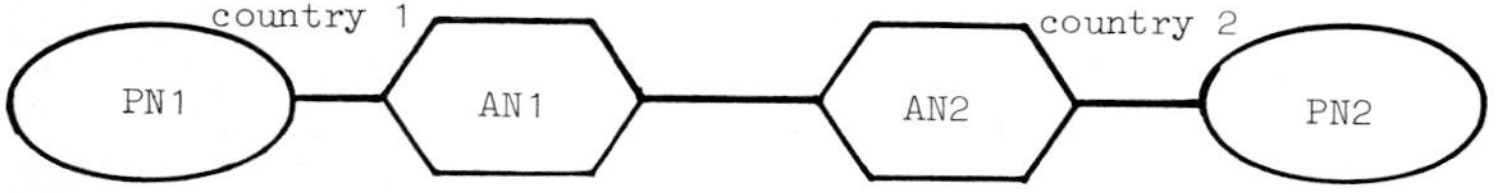

Figure 12 Connection of two private domains in different countries

Some popular current MHSs clearly contravene the current regulations; some are less clear. For example in USENET, [3] individual machines are contacted via the Public Telephone Network, even internationally, and relay further message traffic. Because public services are used, this may well be considered legal. However since an international USENET is really a private MHS, this probably would not be considered as fitting into the picture of Fig 12, and would be disallowed if any international lines were leased. Undoubtedly BITNET [4] should not be permitted internationally. Here you clearly have the situation of Fig 8 (without a C13), and thus have direct connection of private international networks via leased lines, direct connection of private MHSs via leased lines (even international), and international message relaying via local lines between third countries and different ownership of Hosts. This is clearly contravening the recommendations. It looks as if it will be permitted. Presumably this will be an exception because it is a non-commercial service; in any case some countries are asking for volume-based tariffs on the leased lines - i.e. they are not regarding them as normal leased lines.

Certain other commercial systems, in which the message traffic is incidental to other applications - eg financial management - are permitted. These often have a specific, and restricted, charter. Thus SWIFT can provide message services for banks - but not for their customers. Special approved Value Added Services are bridging the gap between the banks and their customers.

7. CONCLUSIONS

The scene on the public and institutional acceptability of Message Handling Services has changed dramatically in the last few years. Where they were publically available only in the US and Canada three years ago, from private bureaus, they are now flourishing. British Telecom in the UK is offering at least three separate systems. Their importance is forcing all parties to consider the problems of interconnection of the systems. One aspect of interconnection is the agreement on standards; here CCITT is leading the way for Administration MDSs, and may persuade the private MDs to follow suit. Another aspect is the regulatory ones; here the current attempt to impede direct connections of private MDs may force them to adopt the CCITT standards - at least to connect to the administration's MDs.

Whether the current recommendations stick is another question. They are complex to implement, and one can expect only a limited subset in the early years. Often this subset may be inadequate to support facilities that private MHSs require. We may expect that if the administration MDs cannot support the necessary facilities (eg encryption, multi-media, delivery confirmation), then the administrations may well have to allow direct interconnection of private systems.

A key problem which must be resolved urgently, to ensure reasonable ability for really widespread use of mail services, both nationally and internationally, is the nature, extent, and source of directory services. Without them, even the current MHSs are having difficulty in extending their services beyond very small communities. This is an area where we must hope public and private Value Added Services will be allowed to coexist - and standards for the coexistence become established.

REFERENCES

1. CCITT: Teletex Service, F.200, ITU, Geneva, 1980.

2. CCITT 5/VII: Recommendations X.401 Message Handling Systems: Basic Service Elements and Optional User Facilities, (and the other seven related CCITT X.400 ff recommendations), ITU, Geneva, November 1983.

3. Nowitz, DA, Lesk, ME: A Dial-up Network of UNIX systems, UNIX Programmer's Manual, 7th edition, Bell Labs, August 1978.

4. BITNET: Because its there, IBM, Perspectives on Computing, Vol 3, No 1, March 1983.

Computer-Based Message Services
H.T. Smith (Editor)
Elsevier Science Publishers B.V. (North-Holland)

CONTRACTS MADE BY ELECTRONIC MAIL: LEGAL ISSUES, TECHNOLOGY AND SERVICES

Julian Newman

City of London Polytechnic
Old Castle Street, London, E1 7NT, United Kingdom

Sharon Harvey

Bedford College of Higher Education
Cauldwell Street, Bedford, MK42 9AH, United Kingdom

Contract law has evolved to fit a concept of "commercial reality". To allow for negotiations at a distance, rules have been defined for postal and instantaneous communication. Technical change now tends to muddy distinctions which were clear at the time the rules were made. This paper explores the issues that may arise from the increasing use of Electronic Message Systems in negotiating contracts.

INTRODUCTION

Developments in communications technology and the liberalisation of public telecommunications policy are hastening the time when business organizations will regularly interact through new electronic media. Just as contracts have been made by conventional postal communication for well over a century, and by Telex for the past 30 years, so Computer Based Message Systems will come to be involved in commercial contractual relationships. Some office system vendors, indeed, already claim that the application of automated techniques can give a company a significant advantage in handling technical contract negotiations.

People do not devote much thought to the law of contract until something goes wrong. A contract may be made in speech as well as in writing, or by combination of the two; many contracts are made with the minimum of formality, and the parties are scarcely aware of the precise time and place at which a contract comes into existence. But questions of time and place can have legal consequences, and may be particularly hard to ascertain where an Electronic Message System (EMS) is the medium for remote communication.

Since neither the legislature nor the courts have yet addressed the matter, it is not possible to give an authoritative account of the law on contracts by EMS, but we believe it is essential to explore the issues that may arise out of the application of this new technology to business communications. The courts are often conservative in adapting to technical or social change, partly because it would be difficult for people to go about their daily business if the law did not take account of pre-established practices and normal standards of reasonable behaviour.

It behoves users and providers of EMS to attend to the legal dimension; hopefully the ensuing discussion will be helpful to users, service-providers and their legal advisers. The approach is based on the law of England and Wales; but the issues are important irrespective of the legal system.

Modern contract law developed in the nineteenth century in response to the expansion of domestic and international trade. Because of the dominance of laissez-faire economic philosophy, the legislature was reluctant to intervene.

Rules were allowed to develop by custom and practice, supplemented judges' decisions resulting from disputes, in adjudicating which the courts have always had regard to considerations of "commercial reality".

THE POSTAL RULES

Before a contract can be said to exist, "There must be some external manifestation of assent, some word spoken or act done by the offeree or his agent, which the law can regard as the communication of the acceptance to the offeror"(1). The offeror may, expressly or by implication, prescribe the mode of acceptance.

One problem that can arise when parties make contracts by communicating over some distance is that the relevant circumstances may change before a reply to the offer is received: the offeror might then wish to withdraw or modify his offer before receiving a reply. What is the legal position if his letter revoking the original offer should cross in the post with the other party's acceptance? This uncertainty is avoided by the doctrine that the contract is made when the letter of acceptance is put into the post-box. If a contract is accepted by telegram, this is treated in the same way as letter-post; but in English law negotiation by Telex is regarded as "instantaneous communication", and thus as comparable to speaking by telephone, despite its being in written form.

The rule that the contract is made when the acceptance is posted is an exception to the general contract rule, that an acceptance must be received by the offeror to be effective. This exception only applies in restricted circumstances. Either it must be clear that the offeror has expressly or by implication prescribed that the post is an acceptable mode of communication. Alternatively, if no mode of acceptance has been specified by the offeror, the nature of the contract and the circumstances in which it was made must be such that postal acceptance was appropriate.

Relevant circumstances will be taken into account in deciding whether a particular communication mode has been specified. These might include a past course of dealings, implying a willingness to be bound by an acceptance made by the same mode in future as was regularly used in the past. But also the mode of communication used in making the particular offer may carry an implication about the mode that should be used for its acceptance. Thus an offer sent by telegram would have been taken as evidence of a request for a speedy reply. If no mode is specified by the offeror then the form of communication to be used for the reply depends on the nature of the offer and the circumstances in which it was made.

The problem of postal acceptance of contracts was first considered by the courts in 1818 (2). The judge considered three possibilities: either the contract was accepted when the letter was put into the post, or when it was delivered to the offeror's address, or when it was brought to the actual attention of the offeror. If the contract were not made when the acceptance was put in the post, there would be no reason why the offeree should be bound in contract unless he knew that his acceptance had been received. So he could request confirmation of acceptance. This could lead to an infinite regress, and inevitable delay in commercial transactions.

Since the offeror can specify the mode of acceptance, he could exclude the post and thereby eliminate the risk that, unknown to the offeree, the letter might not arrive. Since it is for his own benefit that the offeror opts to deal by letter post, it is considered that he thereby waives the normal rule that the contract is not made until he actually receives the acceptance. The acceptance is treated as constructively communicated to him when it is posted, although not in fact communicated to him until he receives it.

During the nineteenth century, judges reinforced the standing of the postal rules by reference to commonsense and the needs of business. In Harris's Case (3), Mellish LJ referred to "mischievous consequences which would follow in commerce" if no such rule were adopted, while Lord Cottenham stated (4) in Dunlop v Higgins that "commonsense tells us that transactions cannot go on without such a rule".

However, the applicability of the postal rules is circumscribed by the restriction that they must not be allowed to result in absurdity and inconvenience, and in Holwell Securities Ltd v Hughes (5) Lawton LJ develops this further: "In my judgement the factors of inconvenience and absurdity are part of a wider principle, namely, that the rule does not apply if, having regard to the circumstances, including the subject matter under consideration, the negotiating parties cannot have intended that there should be a binding agreement until the party accepting an offer ..... had in fact communicated the acceptance to the other."

In 1955, in Entores Ltd v Miles Far East Corporation (6), Denning LJ refused to extend the postal rules to Telex, on the grounds that it is a form of instantaneous communication, although he noted that "in the United States it appears as if instantaneous communications are treated in the same way as postal communications". In the same case Birkett, LJ stated that Telex communications "do not differ in principle from the cases where the parties negotiating a contract are actually in the presence of each other", and Parker LJ stated "as a general rule, a binding contract is made at the place where the offeror receives notification of the acceptance, <u>that is, where the offeror is"</u> (our emphasis).

In the nearly 30 years since that judgement was delivered, commercial and technological developments have made Telex communication much less "instantaneous" in many circumstances. But as recently as 1982 the House of Lords (7) refused to accept the contention that Entores was wrongly decided, despite the recognition that "since 1955 the use of Telex has been greatly expanded and there are many variants of it", and that "the message may not reach, or be intended to reach, the designated recipient immediately ......" (8). However, in that judgement, Lord Wilberforce also stated that no universal rule could cover all such cases; and the courts have not yet had occasion to address themselves to those categories of electronic communication facility that are completely new.

EMS can offer a great variety of services with many combinations and permutations of technical features, and it is not necessarily obvious how these characteristics should be related to the law developed to deal with existing modes of communication. In broad terms, we may ask: should text message systems be assimilated to conventional mail systems, to courier services or to Telex? should sending a message via a voice mail system be treated differently from telephoning and leaving a message on an answering machine? or is it necessary to invoke more fundamental principles to clarify the implications of completely new modes of communication?

At a more detailed level, we may identify the following families of problems:

1 Problems relating to the concepts of "posting", "delivery" and "receipt" in EMS.

2 Problems of applying the concept of "place of occurrence" to electronic communication events, given the possibility of "remote access" to mail-boxes by both parties.

3 Problems arising from the difficulty of applying the concept of "instantaneous communication" as message handling becomes increasingly sophisticated.

4 Problems relating to ownership and control over the message after it has been "posted".

5 Problems relating to possible consequences of using a non-human "agent" in handling and filtering messages, including the use of "active messages" to generate answering messages.

Our discussion concentrates on the first three areas, although we would not wish to underestimate the potential importance of the others. We shall discuss these problems in relation to a classification of relevant features of EMS.

RELEVANT FEATURES OF ELECTRONIC MESSAGE SYSTEMS

We use the term Electronic Message Systems (EMS) to include the full range of communication systems. Thus Computer Mail Systems (CMS) and Telex, for example, are both types of EMS. We divide CMS into Single-Host Mail Systems (SHMS) and Network Mail Systems (NMS). Where we refer simply to CMS, the reference should be taken to cover both Single-Host and Network variants.

In what follows, we ignore certain types of EMS, such as Communicating Word Processors and Facsimile Transmission which are mainly used for communication within a single organization or group, and are unlikely to be used in contract negotiation.

EMS, and their conventional forerunners, can be classified according to both technical and social features. Many features may be quite incidental for present purposes; the technical features that appear potentially important are Addressing Identity and Delay. The relevant social variables are Ownership, Control and Regulation.

By Delay, we mean the possibility of delayed communication. Non-delayed systems are those without storage capacity, which only support instantaneous communication. Conventional Telex and conventional telephone are non-delayed, and so is direct terminal-to-terminal working on a multi-access computer system. Store-and-forward Telex, telephone answering systems and CMS (whether Text or Voice), are delayed. It should be noted that a delayed EMS may also allow instantaneous working. On the other hand, conventional post has a built-in inevitability of delay, which differentiates it from any of the electronic media.

The fact that instantaneous communication is <u>possible</u> by CMS could be taken as grounds for refusing to extend the postal rules to cover them. In Brinkibon, Lord Brandon said "The cases on acceptance by letter and telegram constitute an exception to the general principle .... The reason for the exception is commercial expediency .... That reason .... applies to cases where there is <u>bound to be</u> a <u>substantial</u> interval between the time when the acceptance is sent and the time when it is received" (9, our emphasis).

Identity Addressed may in broad terms be either a Machine (at a place) or a User (or Group). Where communication is directed to a User Identity, this may either be to an electronic mailbox (delayed communication to a user identity) or directly to the terminal where he is logged in (instantaneous communication to a user identity - a facility unlikely to be used for commercial messages). Many NMS are hybrid, in that messages will be addressed to a user identity within a given host machine; but where a NMS provides an automatic routing directory to switch messages to the correct host computer, then addressing may be simply to a User identity.

Ownership and Control of equipment, files and messages may turn out to be relevant to the interpretation of communication events, and to the obligations of parties to a negotiation. Regulations imposed by public policy upon the providers of communication systems might also have a bearing. It should be noted that postal rules do not apply to courier services. An EMS provided under a VANS licence appears to have the characteristics of a courier service rather than a postal service. Privatisation of the main telecommunications carrier, as is currently proceeding in the UK, tends to give any carrier-operated EMS the prima-facie appearance of a courier service, too. Control of both conventional mail and telecommunications by a PTT which is a government department would tend to have the opposite effect, assimilating carrier-provided EMS to postal not courier services, although in the USA Telex has apparently been brought under postal rules (10) despite telecommunications carrier services being in private hands.

In general, the variables of Delay and Addressing Identity appear the most crucial for the problem-families we have listed above; Ownership and Control could be important in some circumstances, moderated by the technical variables, while Regulation would have at most a minor role to play.

"POSTING", "DELIVERY" AND "RECEIPT" IN CMS

If posting, delivery and receipt are the same event in a CMS, then it becomes a form of instantaneous communication, and the postal rules could not be applied; but if there are in principle two or three separate events, then it is non-instantaneous.

A CMS provides a "mailbox" for each user. There is some inconsistency of terminology, with "mailbox" being used by some authorities to refer to a store of messages, and by others to refer to a program which gives users access to these messages. We shall use the term "mailbox" to refer to a file or directory of incoming messages.

The sender creates a file, possibly temporary, containing the message; then he gives a command to "send" this message to another user. On SHMS, it is then immediately added to the recipient's mailbox. On NMS the message may be queued for some time before being transmitted and may indeed be queued more than once in the course of its transmission.

It seems clear enough that "posting" occurs when the sender gives the command to send his message. However, unlike conventional mail, there may be neither legal barrier nor practical obstacle to the sender deleting his message before the addressee has had a chance to read it. Thus the action of "posting" in a CMS may not commit an offeree to acceptance so irrevocably as posting a letter would do. It is possible to make posting irreversible, but this may have unintended negative consequences, which we discuss below.

"Posting" in CMS is at least a readily identifiable event, but "delivery" and "receipt" are much more elusive. A user can decide when he wants to "collect" the messages in his mailbox. To do so he must be logged in to the host computer, possibly through the PSTN and/or through a public or private computer network. Regular users of CMS are likely to log in for many tasks other than sending and receiving mail, since for higher-grade business users systems that only support the mail function tend to be unsuitable even as a communication device (11).

CMS may offer several options when reading mail, e.g. skimming headings, selection by subject or sender, forwarding, delegation. The range of options offered is by no means uniform, and sender and receiver may handle their mail through different UA programs, offering different facilities.

The concept of delivery is also related to responsibility for ensuring successful communication. Where the postal rules do not apply, the offeree is reponsible for seeing that his acceptance is actually communicated to the offeror. However, the offeror could not rely on this in instantaneous communication if he knew that the offeree had attempted to communicate with him, that the attempt had been unsuccessful and that the offeree was not in a position to know that his attempt to communicate had failed, yet he, the offeror, did not notify the offeree of the failure (see below). Facilities for checking the status of users and of messages may be relevant here.

On most CMS the user will be notified of any mail awaiting him when he logs in, and if he is already logged in when a message "arrives" he will be notified of its "arrival" by a prompt, e.g. "YOU HAVE MAIL". This prompt may be displayed immediately, or it may not appear until there is a suitable break in the flow of work. On a SHMS, when the sender gives the command to send his message it becomes almost instantaneously available to the recipient to read. However, if the recipient is not logged in he will not be aware that an attempt has been made to communicate with him. In this respect, the sender is in a similar position to the user of conventional mail: he trusts to the reliability of the postal service, expecting that his letter will be delivered. However, many CMS will also provide "status" information that will enable him to check whether his message has been read, and/or when the addressee last logged in, etc. Some systems also give a warning if one sends a message to a user who has not been logged in recently.

Does "delivery", then, occur when the message is added to a user's mailbox, or when he is notified of its "arrival", or not until he causes the message itself actually to be displayed for him on the VDU, or to be printed out as "hard copy"? On the first interpretation, posting and delivery are simultaneous in a SHMS, and so communication is in a sense "instantaneous" but the situation differs considerably from that envisaged by Denning LJ in his judgement establishing the non-applicability of the postal rules to Telex (12). Lord Denning discusses the possible effects of technical or human failure leading to the non-receipt of the message. He discusses both line failures (which, he says, the offeror can recognise by the stopping of the teleprinter motor) and failures in the receiving apparatus which can be reported by the user at the receiving end. He goes on: "In all the instances I have taken so far, the man who sends the message of acceptance knows that it has not been received, or he has reason to know it. So he must repeat it. But suppose that he does not know that his message did not get home. He thinks it has. This may happen if the listener on the, telephone does not catch the words of acceptance, but nevertheless does not trouble to ask for them to be repeated: or if the ink on the teleprinter fails at the receiving end, but the clerk does not ask for the message to be repeated: so that the man who sends an acceptance reasonably believes that his message has been received. The offeror in such circumstances is clearly bound, because he will be estopped from saying that he did not receive the message of acceptance. It is his own fault that he did not get it. But <u>if there should be a case where the offeror without any fault on his part does not receive the message of acceptance, yet the sender of it reasonably believes it has got home, when it has not, then I think there is no contract</u>."

In Brinkibon, Lord Fraser of Tullybelton also states that "once a message has been received on the offeror's Telex machine, it is not unreasonable to treat it as delivered to the principal offeror, because it is his responsibility to arrange for prompt handling of messages within his own office." (13) With the office becoming "less of a place, and more of a system" (14), one must consider where the limits of this responsibility might now be seen to lie. Is the mailbox or the VDU the equivalent of the "Telex machine"?

Several combinations of circumstances could be envisaged, peculiar to CMS, in which there could be argument about contract, and about responsibility for successful communication. Features intended to guard against fraud or deceit, or to prevent misunderstanding, might in fact have negative effects. For example, inability to delete a message once sent might seem to provide a level of security, but could actually lead to misunderstanding and uncertainty; status information appear to provide an element of reassurance, but could on occasion mislead; etc. We illustrate these possibilities by reference to three hypothetical scenarios.

a) Smith uses a CMS to communicate an offer to Jones, and later changes his mind. Since this particular CMS does not allow Smith to recall or alter his message once sent, he sends a second message revoking his offer. Jones is "off line" at the time the two messages are sent. He logs in next day and receives Smith's offer to which he immediately replies with a message of acceptance. He then reads the next item of mail, which turns out to be Smith's second message, rescinding the offer. Is there a contract?

Here the relevant rule is that the offeree has to know of the revocation, before it becomes effective. So the revocation was not effective when Jones sent his message of acceptance. But there is uncertainty arising from the problem: when is Smith considered to have received Jones's message of acceptance? If this is when the message is delivered at Smith's mailbox (i.e. instantaneous communication), then the offer was actually accepted (acceptance was communicated) before Jones knew of the revocation: so there is a contract. But if the acceptance is not considered to have been communicated until Smith reads it, then Jones may know of the revocation before his acceptance becomes effective, so he does not know if the contract exists until he has checked the status of the acceptance message, and seen that Smith or his agent had read it before he read Smith's message.

b) Smith has made an offer to Jones, who sees the message on his VDU at a time when both he and Smith are logged in. However, at the very time that Jones is composing his letter of acceptance, Smith is composing a letter rescinding the offer. Both men give the command to send their letters at the very same instant. Is there a contract?

All the complexities of scenario (a) apply here; but in addition it could be held that that there was no true consensus, and therefore no contract, or else that the balance of doubt should be in favour of the offeree since the offeror had implicitly taken on the risk of such an occurrence by using a CMS for contract negotiation. A case of this type might lead to records of system status becoming relevant evidence for the existence of the contract, particularly if fine matters of message timing were in question.

c) Smith offers to sell some goods to Jones, and the latter sends a message of acceptance, both by CMS. Smith reads his mail and finds that Jones's message is unintelligible, owing to data corruption. The effect of Smith reading his mail is, of course, that the system records Jones's message to Smith as having been read. Jones seeks status information from the computer, and seeing that Smith has now read his letter of acceptance judges that the contract is now made; he therefore immediately re-sells the goods to Brown and goes out to celebrate, even while Smith is composing a letter to Jones informing him that his

(Jones's) letter was unintelligible. Before Jones has read Smith's second letter, Smith sells the goods to someone else and sends Jones a third letter cancelling the offer.

In this case, the offeror would appear to bear the risk, since he has allowed the medium to be used. However, in the case of a NMS, Ownership and Control might be relevant. If each party owned his own host computer, there might be scope for Smith to argue that the fault lay with, for example, poor hardware or software maintenance on Jones's host computer. However, poor network maintenance would be at the offeror's risk. Any user who had a program handle and acknowledge messages he had not actually read, thus generating misleading status information, would be liable for the consequences.

THE CONCEPT OF "PLACE"

The "place" where the contract is made becomes important in deciding the proper law of a contract made between parties in different countries, and in deciding whether an action may be brought in the English courts where the defendant is outside the jurisdiction (15).

It is thus possible to envisage the situation where two communicators are in two different jurisdictions, and the computer through which they are communicating is in a third jurisdiction. It is the human beings, not the computer, which are parties to the contract; but the place where the contract is made may depend on which definition of "delivery" prevails. If arrival at the mailbox constitutes delivery, then the acceptance is received by the offeror at a time when he is not physically present. If communication of acceptance is taken to be when the message is actually read, then the place of the contract, and hence the law of the contract, may be uncertain to the offeree, which is unsatisfactory. Vice versa, if communication of acceptance is taken to be when the message arrives at the offeror's mailbox, then in effect the postal rules are being applied to EMS, which would be unsatisfactory in a situation in which the offeree could cancel his acceptance message any time up to the offeror reading it.

"INSTANTANEOUS COMMUNICATION" AND SYSTEM SOPHISTICATION

Computers and microcomputers may be used in EMS which are not true CMS. In particular, a computer may be used either as a Switching Device or as a Message Preparation Device. Use of Telex Switches and Store and Forward exchanges implies that a Telex message can be sent but not delivered instantaneously because of the receiver's machine being busy.

The increasing sophistication of the Telex system makes it less and less resemble direct instantaneous person-to-person communication. There are also plans for Telex to interwork with Teletex, which is not only itself a "super-telex", but will also be used as a transport system for NMS. Thus a message might originate within one type of system, but end up in a different system, throwing further doubt upon the assumptions that communicators might reasonably make. This adds further complexity to the situation described by Lord Wilberforce in Brinkibon: "The sender and recipients may not be the principals to the contemplated contract. They may be servants or agents with limited authority. The message may not reach, or be intended to reach, the designated recipient immediately: messages may be sent out of office hours, or at night, with the intention, or on the assumption, that they will be read at a later time ..... The messages may have been sent and/or received through machines operated by third persons ...."(16). The House of Lords judgement in Brinkibon does not however necessarily imply a rigid or narrow view as may be seen from Lord

Wilberforce's further remarks: "No universal rule can cover all such cases; they must be resolved by reference to the intentions of the parties, by sound business practice and, in some cases, by a judgement where the risks should lie."

SOME DILEMMAS

The courts would probably wish to avoid the following:

a) extension of the scope of the postal rules

b) uncertainty about the place and time of contract

c) going against "commercial reality" or "commercial expediency".

The characteristics of EMS, and the different combinations of circumstances that can arise with the interconnection of different EMS, make the reconciliation of these three objectives akin to squaring the circle. In order to apply the Telex precedents to CMS, the latter must be defined as instantaneous communication, which is only possible if posting and delivery/receipt are taken to be simultaneous. Therefore delivery/receipt must be assumed to take place "at the mailbox"; thus the contract is made where the offeror's mailbox host computer is. But this means that the offeror must be deemed to have waived the normal condition, that a contract is not made until he has actually been made aware of the acceptance. This is, in effect, an extension of the postal rules to a rather broad category of modes of communication, using systems which may allow actions by the offeree that would not be possible or permissible by conventional mail. However, in order to avoid this, contract must be said to be made where the offeror is at the time he in fact reads the acceptance. Thus the offeree will be uncertain as to the time, and perhaps the proper law, of the contract.

Legislation would probably confound an already complex picture. The responsibility must lie with users and providers of EMS, to arrive at an appropriate definition of "commercial reality". The legal rules were developed to deal with situations that had been left undefined by the parties. But it is always open to the offeror to specify the mode of acceptance of the offer, and he can do so in sufficient detail to avoid the ambiguities concerning time and place of receipt that we have identified above. Likewise, the proper law of the contract can be explicitly stated in the contract. Until normal commercial practice has developed a system of mutual understanding of the way in which these issues should be handled, parties to negotiation should spell out explicitly in the contracts the intended answers to these questions. The use of standard documents in preparing messages should ease the task of ensuring that this is done; alternatively, service providers could issue a set of standards which they require every user to accept, unless he gives specific notice to the other party that he intends otherwise.

NOTES AND REFERENCES

(1) Cheshire & Fifoot's Law of Contracts (10th edition, 1981). London: Butterworth.
(2) Adams v Linsell, (1818) 1 B & Ald 681
(3) Harris's case: re Imperial Land Co. of Marseilles (1872) LR7 Ch App 587
(4) Dunlop v Higgins, (1848) 1 HLC 381
(5) Holwell Securities Ltd v Hughes, [1974] 1 All ER 161, [1974] 1 WLR 155
(6) Entores, Ltd v Miles Far East Corpn, [1955] 2QB 327, [1955] 2 All ER 493
(7) Brinkibon Ltd v Stalag Stahl und Stahlwahrenhandelsgesellschaft [1982] 1 All ER 293

(8) Lord Wilberforce in Brinkibon (see note 7)

(9) Lord Brandon in Brinkibon (see note 7)

(10) Denning LJ in Entores (see note 5): ".. in the United States of America it appears as if instantaneous communications are treated in the same way as postal communication."

(11) Newman, J C (1981) "Human factors for CBMS for Management Use", in Uhlig, R (ed) Computer Message Systems. Amsterdam: North Holland.

(12) Denning LJ (loc. cit.)

(13) Lord Fraser of Tullybelton in Brinkibon (see note 7)

(14) Tapscott, D (1982) Office Automation: A User-Driven method. New York, NY: Plenum.

(15) Service of a writ outside the jurisdiction may be allowed, at the court's discretion, under RSC Order 11, if the contract was made within the jurisdiction.

(16) See note 7

(17) loc. cit.

Computer-Based Message Services
H.T. Smith (Editor)
Elsevier Science Publishers B.V. (North-Holland)

DESIGNING SECURE MESSAGE SYSTEMS: THE MILITARY MESSAGE SYSTEMS (MMS) PROJECT

Constance L. Heitmeyer
Carl E. Landwehr

Computer Science and Systems Branch
Information Technology Division
Naval Research Laboratory
Washington, D.C. 20375

The goal of the Military Message Systems (MMS) project is to specify the requirements and design of a family of secure military message systems and to build full-scale prototypes of two family members. This paper describes several techniques that are being used in the MMS project: the application of Parnas' program family principle to both the requirements document and the design specification, the definition of an Intermediate Command Language to describe the user services provided by family members, the formulation of an application-based security model to define the security rules that each message system must enforce, and the construction of quick prototypes to validate requirements and to evaluate different user interface designs. The paper concludes by describing the project's current status.

1. Introduction

In the next two decades, the U.S. Department of Defense will need several new computer-based message systems. These systems will have many features in common, providing many of the same user services and enforcing the same security rules. They will also have important differences, such as different user command languages and implementation on different computers. The goal of the Military Message Systems (MMS) project is to specify the requirements and design of a family of secure message systems and to build full-scale prototypes of two family members. One of the prototypes will be designed for a military environment where little message handling is required (e.g., onboard a submarine). The other prototype will perform all of the functions of the first prototype plus additional functions. The intent of the full-scale prototypes is to demonstrate the viability of our approach to building secure systems and to provide a basis for building production-quality systems.

In this paper, we summarize the functional and security requirements of military message systems and then describe the techniques that we are using in the MMS project: application of the program family principle, definition of an Intermediate Command Language to specify required user services, formulation of an application-based security model, and the construction of rapid prototypes. We conclude by describing the current project status.

2. Requirements of Military Message Systems

In recent years, automation has been applied increasingly to the handling of military messages [4]. The primary purpose of military message systems is to process formal messages, i.e., official messages exchanged by military organizations. Formal messages are transmitted over military networks, such as AUTODIN; their format and use is governed by military standards. Future military message systems may also handle informal messages, i.e., unofficial messages exchanged by individuals. Examples of informal messages are those supported by several current message systems available on the ARPA network (e.g., HERMES [10]).

Functional Requirements. Message system operations may be organized into three categories: operations on incoming messages, operations on outgoing messages, and message storage and retrieval. Operations in the first category permit a user to display and print messages that he has received. Second-category operations support the creation, editing, and transmission of outgoing messages. Message storage and retrieval operations allow users to organize messages into message files and to retrieve messages via single keys (e.g., message id) or combinations of keys (e.g., subject and originator). Typically, military systems that process formal messages provide the same operations as systems that process informal messages plus several additional operations, such as distribution determination, action and information assignment, and release [4].

Security Requirements. Each formal military message is composed of several fields, including To, From, Info, Date-Time Group, Subject, Text, Security, and Precedence. A classification, such as UNCLASSIFIED or SECRET, is assigned to each field and to some subfields, e.g., the paragraphs of the Text field; further, the overall message has a classification that is at leastas high as that of any field or subfield. Thus, the Subject field of a message may be classified at a lower level than the message as a whole, and two paragraphs of the Text field may have different classifications.

In some data processing applications, users process information at a single security level for long periods of time. In contrast, message system users often need to handle data of several classifications during a single computer session. For example, a user may wish to compose an UNCLASSIFIED message based in part on a previously received SECRET message. To accomplish this, he may want to simultaneously display the SECRET message and compose the UNCLASSIFIED message. As a second example, the user may wish to scan newly arrived messages and print only those that are UNCLASSIFIED. To do so, he must display messages with several different classifications and then print a hard copy of only the UNCLASSIFIED ones.

Military message systems are required to enforce certain security rules. For example, they must insure that users cannot view messages for which they are not cleared. Unfortunately, most automated systems cannot be trusted to enforce such rules. The result is that many military message systems operate in "system-high" mode: each user is cleared to the level of the most highly classified information on the system. A consequence of system-high operation is that all data leaving the computer system must be classified at the system-high level until a human reviewer assigns the proper classification.

An objective of our research is to design message systems that are multilevel secure. Unlike systems that operate at system-high, multilevel secure systems do not require all users to be cleared to the level of the highest information processed. Moreover, information leaving such a system can be assigned its actual security level rather than the level of the most highly classified information in the system. Unlike a system that operates at system-high, a multilevel system can preserve the different classifications of information that it processes.

3. Techniques Included in our Approach

Our development approach is based on several techniques each of which is discussed below.

Program family principle. Review of the requirements of future message systems suggests that one system will not suffice for all environments. Several similar systems will be needed that share certain functions and enforce military security. Because they will operate in different environments, these systems will have important differences, e.g., in their user command languages, in the communications networks to which they are connected, and in their user terminals.

The design problem is to exploit the similarities of MMS family members without unduly constraining the individual variations that make such system suitable for its particular environment. A message system aboard a submarine, for example, shares certain features with a message system for command center personnel, but it is unreasonable to insist that submarine personnel and command center personnel use exactly the same system. To deal with this problem, we have adopted the program family principle, which requires developers to consider the entire family before building a single member [12, 13].

We are applying the principle to two products: a requirements document and a design document. The MMS requirements document includes (1) a set of user services, where each family member is associated with some subset, and (2) a security model which applies to all members. Because its goal is to describe the shared features of family members, the requirements document excludes features that differentiate family members. The MMS design document will define a module decomposition suitable for all family members. In the module decomposition, the different features of family members are assigned to separate modules, so that different family members can be produced by replacing modules without changing the overall system structure [11]. For example, two family members that are identical except for their user command languages will differ only in their implementation of the user command language module.

Intermediate Command Language. A central feature of the MMS requirements document is use of an Intermediate Command Language (ICL) to describe the user services required by family members. The ICL is designed so that the user services provided by any single family member can be described by some ICL subset. The user invokes ICL statements to manipulate the message system data items (e.g., messages and message files) that each message system supports. Some ICL statements only cause information to be retrieved, e.g., DISPLAY_MSG, while other ICL statements cause information to be modified, e.g., DESTROY_MF (MF is an abbreviation for MESSAGE FILE).

Each ICL statement is an abstract description of a user command in that it specifies the command's user-visible effects without restricting either the command syntax or the physical characteristics of the user's terminal. As noted above, MMS members may differ in their user interfaces. Thus, a user command to display a message may take different forms in different MMS family members. In one system, the user might type "display message"; in a second, he might type "show message"; in a third, he might select the menu item "Display Message" and in a fourth, he might depress a function key labeled "Display Message". Given that the effect of each of these four user commands is identical, i.e., each causes the user terminal to display the specified message, each is associated with the same ICL statement, specifically, DISPLAY_MSG. With this approach, two family members that provide identical services but differ in their user command languages are described by the same ICL subset. Moreover, given two systems where one system performs only a subset of the operations performed by the second, the ICL subset for the smaller system will be contained in the ICL subset for the larger system.

To illustrate the use of the ICL, we include three figures. Figure 1 lists ICL subsets that describe three family members: M0, the receive-only member, which supports the display and storage into message files of incoming messages; M1, which includes all commands of the receive-only member and additional commands for composing and transmitting outgoing messages; and M2, an extension of M1, which includes user commands for the security officer and for enforcing access control on messages and other user-visible data items. Figure 2 contains specifications for three ICL commands, one associated with the data type 'message' and two with the data type 'message file'. Figure 3 provides a scenario that illustrates the correspondence between a particular user command language and the ICL.

Application-Based Security Model. In recent years, the Bell-LaPadula model [2, 3] has dominated efforts to build secure systems. While its complete formal statement is lengthy and complex, the model may be briefly summarized by the following two axioms:

1) the simple security rule, which states that a subject cannot read information for which it is not cleared ("no read up"), and
2) the *-property, which states that a subject cannot move information from an object with a higher security classification to an object with a lower classification ("no write down").

These axioms are to be enforced by restricting the access rights that subjects, e.g., users and processes, have to objects, e.g., files and devices.

Unfortunately, a system that strictly enforces these axioms is often impractical. In many real systems, users occasionally need to perform operations that, although, they do not violate our intuitive notion of security, do violate one of the axioms, i.e., the *-property. To permit such operations, the Bell-LaPadula model introduces the notion of a trusted subject: a subject trusted not to violate security even though it is permitted to violate the *-property.

For example, a user may need to extract an UNCLASSIFIED paragraph from a CONFIDENTIAL document and use it in an UNCLASSIFIED document. A system that strictly enforces the Bell-LaPadula model would prohibit this operation unless it were performed by a trusted subject. Consequently,

M0	M1	M2		
	CREATE_MSG	CREATE_MSG		
	EDIT_MSG	EDIT_MSG		
	UPDATE_MSG	UPDATE MSG		
DISPLAY_MSG	DISPLAY_MSG	DISPLAY_MSG		
	SEND_MSG	SEND_MSG		
	REPLY_MSG	REPLY_MSG		
	INFO_MSG	INFO_MSG		
		ACTION_MSG		
		READDRESS_MSG		
		DUP_MSG		
		SETPERMIT_MSG		
		DISPLAY_MSGAS		
CREATE_MF	CREATE_MF	CREATE_MF		
DESTROY_MF	DESTROY_MF	DESTROY_MF		
DISPLAY_MF	DISPLAY_MF	DISPLAY_MF		
EXPUNGE_MF	EXPUNGE_MF	EXPUNGE_MF		
DELETE_MC	DELETE_MC	DELETE_MC		
UNDELETE_MC	UNDELETE_MC	UNDELETE_MC		
COPY_MC	COPY_MC	COPY_MC		
MOVE_MC	MOVE_MC	MOVE_MC		
	RECLASSIFY_MF	RECLASSIFY_MF		
		DUP_MF		
		SETPERMIT_MF		
		DISPLAY_MFAS		
DISPLAY_MFD	DISPLAY_MFD	DISPLAY_MFD		
		CREATE_TOBJ	CREATE_USER	CREATE_TERM
		DESTROY_TOBJ	DESTROY_USER	DESTROY_TERM
		EDIT_TOBJ	DISPLAY_USER	MAX_TERMCLAS
		UPDATE_TOBJ	CHG_CLEARANCE	DISPLAY_TERM
		DISPLAY_TOBJ	ADD_AROLE	
		COPY@ENT@_TOBJ	REMOVE_AROLE	
		COPYTOBJ_@ENT@	CHG_PASSWORD	
		RECLASSIFY_TOBJ	ADD_CROLE	
		DUP_TOBJ	REMOVE_CROLE	
		SETPERMIT_TOBJ	LOGIN_USER	
		DISPLAY_TOBJAS	LOGOUT_USER	
		DISPLAY_TOBJD		

Figure 1. ICL Subsets for Three MMS Family Members

Note: In the specifications, "x: y" means that x is of type y and "x: y ref" means that x is a reference for a data item of type y. For each command, input parameters are listed first; any output parameters are listed after input parameters and separated from them by a blank line.

ICL Command for Messages

Name	Parameters	Description
DISPLAY_MSG	msgid: message ref OR dmsgid: draft-message ref msg: message OR dmsg: draft-message c: classification	Displays the value of the message with the given reference. Also displays the message classification c.

ICL Commands for Message Files

Name	Parameters	Description
CREATE_MF	mfname: message-file ref c: classification sw: CCR-switch as: setof (access-triple)	Creates a message file with reference mfname, classification c, CCR-switch sw, and access set as. Inserts an entry for mfname in the user's message file directory.

Name	Parameters	Description
MOVE_MC	cid: citation ref mfname: message-file ref	Inserts the message citation with reference cid at the end of message file mfname. Marks 'deleted' the citation with reference cid.

Figure 2. Specifications for Three ICL Commands

The first column shows each user command, the second column the corresponding ICL command (for simplicity, no ICL parameters are given), and the third column the system response. Responses enclosed in brackets are comments; those that are unbracketed are literal responses. Note that message files contain citations, which in turn contain only part of the information in a message, such as classification, the date received, the originator, and the subject.

User Command	ICL	System Response
displ dir	DISPLAY_MFD	msg file directory: heitmeyer clas: UNCLAS inbox TOP SECRET new-ideas CONFIDENTIAL
displ mf new	DISPLAY_MF	message file: inbox classif: TOPSECRET 5 U 6 Mar mcgovern at ISI Re: new ideas 6 S 6 Mar reagan at ISI My new ideas
displ cur msg	DISPLAY_MSG	[msg attached to citation 5 is displayed]
delete mc 5	DELETE_MC	done [msg citation 5 is now marked deleted]
displ nxt msg	DISPLAY_MSG	[msg attached to citation 6 is displayed]
move mc 6 new-ideas	MOVE_MC	refused: citation classif exceeds file classif
create secret mf reagan	CREATE_MF	SECRET file named 'reagan' has been created
move mc 6 reagan	MOVE_MC	done
displ mf all	DISPLAY_MF	message file: inbox classif: TOPSECRET 1 S 2 Feb landwehr security options 2 U 3 Mar lubbes at ISI Re: security 3 T 4 Mar hart at ISI New ideas 4 U 5 Mar mondale at BBN What new ideas? *5 U 6 Mar mcgovern at ISI Re: New ideas *6 S 6 Mar reagan at ISI My new ideas
delete mc 2	DELETE_MC	done
expunge mf	EXPUNGE_MF	done
displ mf all	DISPLAY_MF	message file: inbox classif: TOPSECRET 1 S 2 Feb landwehr security options 2 T 4 Mar hart at ISI New ideas 3 U 5 Mar mondale at BBN What new ideas?
display dir	DISPLAY_MFD	msg file directory: heitmeyer clas: UNCLAS inbox TOP SECRET new-ideas CONFIDENTIAL reagan SECRET
get mf reagan	none	done [reagan is now current file]
displ mf all	DISPLAY_MF	message file: reagan classif: SECRET 1 S 6 Mar reagan at ISI My new ideas

Figure 3. User Scenario

systems based on the Bell-LaPadula model usually contain mechanisms (e.g., the "trusted processes" in SIGMA [1] and in KSOS [9]) that permit some operations that the *-property prohibits.

To avoid these problems, we take a different approach. We believe that a security model should be derived from a specific application. Thus we have defined a single, integrated security model that each member of the MMS family must enforce. The model is intended to allow users to understand security in the context of message systems, to guide the design of military message systems, and to allow certifiers to evaluate such systems.

An informal version of the MMS security model is stated in English and consists of four parts: definitions, user's view of operation, assumptions, and assertions. The definitions section, whose purpose is to establish an explicit basis for the model, includes terms such as classification, clearance, user, and operation, with definitions that correspond to those in general use. To deal with the special security requirements of message systems, the MMS security model introduces some specialized terms, such as object and container. An *object* is defined to be the smallest unit of data that has an explicit classification marking. A *container* is an entity that has a classification marking and may hold objects or other containers. An object removed from a container retains its security label, so extracting an UNCLASSIFIED paragraph from a CONFIDENTIAL message involves no downgrading.

The user's view of MMS operation summarizes the operation of a secure MMS using the terms presented in the definitions section. The four assumptions are security assertions that can only be enforced by systems users; e.g., "The user enters the correct classification when composing, editing, or reclassifying information." The assertions, shown in Figure 4, are rules that each secure message system must enforce. The relationship between the security model and the ICL is that all the assertions must hold following the completion of an ICL command.

We have also defined a formal model, based on set theory, that corresponds to the informal MMS security model. The formal version serves three purposes: (1) it is an example of how an informal model that captures the security requirements of a particular system can be made formal; (2) being abstract, the formal model can be interpreted by others for different but related applications; and (3) it is a basis for proofs about particular message system specifications and implementations.

Rapid prototyping. An important aspect of the MMS project is validation of the MMS requirements. We need to insure that the requirements document is a correct, complete statement of what is required. One way to evaluate the document is to ask user representatives to review both the ICL specifications and the (formal) specification of the MMS model. Unfortunately, users usually find such specifications difficult to understand and thus difficult to evaluate.

As a result, we have chosen instead to use rapid prototypes to validate the requirements [5]. We have identified several ICL subsets. Our plan is to build rapid prototypes that perform the user services specified by these subsets and that enforce the rules defined by the MMS security model. Once the rapid prototypes are implemented and provide sufficient functionality, we will present them to user representatives for evaluation.

Authorization	1.	A user can only invoke an operation on an entity if the user's userID or current role appears in the entity's access set along with that operation and with an index value corresponding to the operand position in which the entity is referred to in the requested operation.
Classification hierarchy	2.	The classification of any container is always at least as high as the maximum of the classifications of the entities it contains.
Changes to objects	3.	Information removed from an object inherits the classification of that object. Information inserted into an object must not have a classification higher than the classification of that object.
Viewing	4.	A user can only view (on some output medium) an entity with a classification less than or equal to the user's clearance and the classification of the output medium. (This assertion applies to entities referred to either directly or indirectly).
Access to CCR entities	5.	A user can have access to an indirectly referenced entity within a container marked "Container Clearance Required" only if the user's clearance is greater than or equal to the classification of that container.
Translating indirect references	6.	A user can obtain the ID for an entity that he has referred to indirectly only if he is authorized to view that entity via that reference.
Labeling requirement	7.	Any entity viewed by a user must be labeled with its classification.
Setting clearances, role sets, device levels	8.	Only a user with the role of System Security Officer can set the clearance and role set recorded for a userID or the classification assigned to a device. A user's current role set can be altered only by that user or by a user with the role of System Security Officer.
Downgrading	9.	No classification marking can be downgraded except by a user with the role of downgrader who has invoked a downgrade operation.
Releasing	10.	No draft message can be released except by a user with the role of releaser. The userID of the releaser must be recorded in the "releaser" field of the draft message.

Figure 4. Assertions of the MMS Security Model

The user feedback that we obtain will then be used to correct and, if necessary, extend both the ICL specifications and the MMS security model.

The rapid prototypes will also be used for other purposes: to assess the suitability of the ICL subsets that specify the user services provided by the full-scale prototypes, to aid in evaluating the design of different user command languages, and to assess the impact of the MMS requirements and the security model on the user interface.

4. Current Status

In September, 1982, an informal version of the MMS security model was published [7]. Based in part on experiments with rapid prototyping and in part on the effort to formalize the security model, this early version has been modified slightly. Statements of both the updated informal version and a new formal version have been completed and are available in [8].

A preliminary description of the Intermediate Command Language for three MMS family members has been completed [6]. Based on experiments with rapid prototypes, some revisions to the ICL are in progress.

Three rapid prototypes have been built: M0, M1, and M2. To date, these prototypes have been used internally to evaluate the ICL specifications and the MMS security model. Shortly, the prototypes will be made available to external users for evaluation.

REFERENCES

[1] S. R. Ames, Jr. and D. R. Oestreicher, "Design of a message system for a multilevel secure environment," in *Proc. 1978 Nat. Comput. Conf.* June 5-8, 1978, pp. 765-771.

[2] D. E. Bell and L. J. LaPadula, "Secure computer system: Unified exposition and Multics interpretation," M74-244, MITRE Corp., Bedford, MA, July 1975.

[3] R. J. Feiertag, K. N. Levitt, and L. Robinson, "Providing multilevel security of a system design," in *Proc. 6th ACM Symp. Operating systems principles, ACM SIGOPS Operating System Rev.*, Vol. 11, No. 5, Nov. 1977, pp. 57-65.

[4] C. L. Heitmeyer and S. H. Wilson, "Military message systems: Current status and future directions," *IEEE Trans. Commun., Vol. COM-28, No. 9, Sept 1980, pp. 1645-1654.*

[5] C. L. Heitmeyer, C. E. Landwehr, and M. R. Cornwell, "The use of quick prototypes in the secure military message systems project," in *ACM SIGSOFT Software Engineering Notes*, Vol. 7, No. 5, Dec 1982, pp. 85-87.

[6] C. L. Heitmeyer, "Intermediate Command Language (ICL) subsets for M0, M1, and M2: Informal specifications," NRL Tech. Memo, Jan. 1984.

[7] C. E. Landwehr and C. Heitmeyer, "Military message systems: Requirements and security model," NRL report, Naval Res. Lab., Wash., DC, Sept. 1982.

[8] C. Landwehr, C. Heitmeyer, and J. McLean, "A security model for military message systems," *ACM Transactions on Computer Systems* (to appear).

[9] E. J. McCauley and P. J. Drongowski, "KSOS: The design of a secure operating system," in *Proc. AFIPS Nat. Comp. Conf.*, June 4-7, pp. 345-353.

[10] C. D. Mooers, "The HERMES guide," BBN report 4995, Bolt, Beranek and Newman, Inc., 10 Moulton St., Cambridge, MA, Aug. 1982.

[11] D. L. Parnas, "On the criteria to be used in decomposing systems into modules," *Commun. Ass. Comput. Mach.*, Vol 15, Dec. 1972.

[12] D. L. Parnas, "On the design and development of program families," *IEEE Trans. Software Eng.*, Vol. SE-2, pp. 1-9, Mar. 1976.

[13] D. L. Parnas, "Designing software for ease of extension and contraction," *IEEE Trans. Software Eng.*, Vol. SE-5, pp. 128-138, Mar. 1979.

PART 6:

CONFERENCE AND MESSAGE SYSTEM INTERCONNECTION

Computer-Based Message Services
H.T. Smith (Editor)
Elsevier Science Publishers B.V. (North-Holland)

INTEGRATION OF ELECTRONIC MAIL AND CONFERENCING SYSTEMS

Steve Kille

Department of Computer Science
University College
London

Two approaches by Electronic Message Handling Systems (MHS) on the distribution of messages to multiple recipients are considered: The use of centrally stored messages on a conferencing system, and the use of distribution lists to deliver messages to individual users. It is shown that these mechanisms are not incompatible, and this is illustrated by work done to integrate systems of these types. Possible developments of future Message Handling Systems are discussed, and it is suggested that this type of integration will be an appropriate mechanism for distributing a message to a range of recipients.

1. INTRODUCTION

Two distinct strands of development in Message Handling Services can be broadly described as messaging systems, and conferencing systems. Both may be considered as having evolved from basic electronic mail systems on single computers. Conferencing systems have emphasised development of the user interface and user communication structuring, whereas messaging systems have emphasised inter-machine distribution aspects. The differences become clear when considering the details of communication between a group of individuals. In messaging systems, messages are sent to destinations explicitly specified by the sender. This is generally used in conjunction with distribution lists, where a specific destination is mapped onto a number of recipients. In a conferencing system, global conference names are specified which map onto a set of recipients. Conference entries are generally stored centrally on a system and structured reading mechanisms are provided. Although these types of system emphasise different aspects of message communication, it is suggested that there is no fundamental distinction. This paper considers the tradeoffs between a variety of such systems and describes developments which will allow the benefits of both styles of working to be achieved.

The first part of the paper takes a pragmatic view of current systems, and describes the nature of conferencing and messaging systems, using three systems in everyday use as examples:

- COM - a centralised conferencing system.
- The Usenet news system - a distributed conferencing system.
- Arpanet style messaging systems

These types of system are also described briefly in terms of the CCITT (IFIP WG 6.5) Message Handling System model [1]. Familiarity with this model is assumed. Work done at University College, London (UCL) to allow interworking between these systems is described. Some problems of integrating a collection of utilities into a coherent system for messaging and conferencing are discussed. They illustrate the tradeoffs which occur, both from the user and system standpoint. This relates particularly to message storage and to the manner in which a user views messages originating on different types of system.

The problem of distributing messages to a large number of users is then considered. Some assumptions as to the nature of the distribution to such sets of users are made, and based on these, an approach to distributing messages is proposed. The protocol requirements of such a service are discussed, and it is suggested that they are satisfied by current Message Handling System standardisation efforts. The problem of naming and addressing of distribution lists / distributed conferences is discussed briefly. It is hoped that this will show the possibility of a more unified approach to message communication.

2. CONFERENCING SYSTEMS

Computer conferencing systems have evolved over a number of years, and should be considered as a distinct form of Message Handling System. The majority of computer conferencing systems are centralised systems, based on one computer and using networks only to provide terminal access to the system. Sebestyen describes in detail the characteristics of such systems, as well as giving references to a good number of systems of this type [2]. This type of system should not be confused with real-time teleconferencing systems.

There is no clear definition of what is required of a system for it to be considered as a computer conferencing system. There are however a number of typical characteristics which are listed below. A message is seen as information to be communicated between users.

(i) Messages are stored in a shared spool area, rather than in an area controlled by an individual user. The philosophy is that messages are a system resource, rather than owned by individuals.

(ii) Communication is structured into conferences, rather than messages to individuals. These conferences would reflect an area being discussed on that conference (e.g. computer networks). Some systems also support messages to individual users, which may be handled in a different manner.

(iii) A user is able to 'subscribe' to a selection of conferences, usually from within the user interface.

(iv) A large number of messages are stored, often in a database, to allow study of earlier conference entries and to provide the functionality discussed below in (v). This aspect requires a significant amount of storage, which tends to lead to such systems existing only on large centralised facilities.

(v) Entries within a conference are structured into sets relating to particular subjects, often simply an entry with comments relating to that entry. More complex possibilities for structuring sets are discussed in [3]. The user interface will generally allow actions to be applied to sets of entries, as well as to individual entries (e.g. skip all entries in the current set).

The COM conferencing system is a good example of a centralised conferencing system [4]. It is of interest at UCL, because many individuals in Europe use COM systems (in particular the University of Stockholm COM), and some of the discussions within these systems are of wider interest. Although some UCL users have made direct use of these facilities, most do not use them because of the effort of connecting to such a remote system. This is owing to the relatively poor performance compared to accessing local systems over a high speed interface, which makes message reading a great deal easier. It is interesting in the context of this paper, because experiments are being performed at Stockholm to communicate with external messaging systems. These include using the JNT Mail Protocol [5], which is also employed at UCL. This functionality has provided the basis for the experiments and structures discussed in section 3.

Perhaps the most widely used distributed conferencing system is the Usenet news system [6]. Conferences within Usenet are termed newsgroups, and this will be used here to denote a Usenet style conference. Whilst this system is crude in many aspects, it is a very useful demonstration of the possibility of interlinking conferencing systems. The following features are salient:

(i) Newsgroups are defined by global hierarchical names (e.g. net.sport.football describes a network wide newsgroup on football).

(ii) There are over 1000 participating sites, and several Megabytes of traffic per week. To handle this, sites must do one of the following:

   (a) Store only a small subset of all the newsgroups.
   (b) Discard entries after a relatively short period of time. This often loses some of the advantages of conferencing systems.
   (c) Allocate a large amount of storage. This cannot be done by many systems.

(iii) Distribution is achieved by passing items on to a set of connected sites. To prevent undue wastage of communication resources, this necessitates a relatively sparse connection of the sites involved. This in turn requires a few 'backbone' sites to handle all newsgroups, and to relay them on to a significant number of other sites. Difficulties associated with this approach are discussed in section 4.

(iv) Although closely related, the newsgroup and user namespaces are separate.

In terms of the CCITT MHS model, a message would be delivered by the Message Transport Service to a User Agent (UA) associated with the conference. The UA would store the message as a conference entry, and provide such functions as determining the set of users allowed to access a given conference. Usenet style distribution to many UAs would be managed at the UA level.

3. MESSAGING SYSTEMS

It is not the purpose of this paper to discuss the detailed nature of messaging systems, which are regarded as a specific type of Message Handling System. This section will focus on those aspects peculiar to such systems which would not usually be provided by conferencing systems. It is suggested later that Message Handling Systems will evolve in a manner which will remove the distinction between the two styles of system. This section therefore focuses on aspects of current messaging systems. All of the systems connected directly or indirectly to UCL, use the text message format specification RFC 822 as the End to End (UA to UA) protocol [7].

Whilst this protocol does not contain some of the features of more recent protocols, there is a great deal of experience with using it to build large systems. The rest of this section lists some of the features of this type of system.

(i) There are a wide variety of systems, operating under many different operating systems. This is possible because there is a full definition of a relatively simple UA to UA protocol (RFC 822).

(ii) Systems may be built on very small computers (e.g personal workstations). This would not be realistic for a conferencing system, in view of storage and processing requirements. However, a personal computer might be used to access a central conferencing facility.

(iii) Messages are delivered to a UA associated with a specific user, as opposed to a UA associated with a conference. This fundamental difference is the basis of all the other features noted.

(iv) Accounting on a per user basis for storage and communication costs is relatively straightforward.

(v) A user may store messages in a manner appropriate to his or her needs. For example, a user might have delivery time processing of messages into a database sorted by keyword search on the message text. This type of functionality would be difficult to provide on a conferencing system where messages are stored centrally.

(vi) The user interface may be chosen to suit the user requirements, and to be closely integrated with the user's environment. In principle, there is no reason why a conferencing interface should not be as flexible, but in practice, the complexity of conferencing storage structures restricts this.

This type of system maps directly onto the CCITT MHS model. A user would be associated with a User Agent (UA). The functionality associated with (v) and (vi) would be provided by the UA.

Distribution lists are usually used in conjunction with messaging systems as a mechanism to distribute a message to multiple recipients. This paper does not attempt to discuss the detailed functionality and problems of distribution lists, which are considered at length by Deutsch [8]. This paper views distribution lists as a value added service, and not as an intrinsic part of the Message Transport Service. This is not the only possible viewpoint, but is one which is gaining increasing favour. Sending to a distribution list is seen as two distinct phases in terms of the CCITT MHS model. First, the message originator sends a message to a UA which performs the list expansion. This UA then sends messages to the final recipient UA, where the message will be processed, most likely by a user. Palme suggests that '...this (use of distribution lists) is not at all the same thing as computer conferencing.' [4]. The next sections suggest that this distinction is only superficial, and that a distribution list mechanism can provide the full functionality needed for distributed computer conferencing.

4. SYSTEM INTERCONNECTION

This section aims to discuss some of the pragmatic work done at UCL to allow users to access conferencing and messaging systems. The interest of this description lies not so much the individual components, but in the overall structuring apparent to the user.

UCL operates MMDF (Multi-channel Memorandum Distribution Facility), a complex RFC 822 based messaging system which provides connectivity with a large number of sites (of order 10000) [9], [10]. This system is used to provide a message relaying service between UK sites and the DARPA Internet [11]. A particular feature of the UCL system is that it contains a number of machines (six at present), which appear to form a homogeneous site from the standpoint of mail addressing. This permits users (about 500 at present) to be moved easily between machines without changing their mail address. This may well be extended to allowing users to receive mail on personal computers. UCL also runs Notesfile, a conferencing system [12]. On many sites, the Notesfile storage and user interface system is used as an integral part of the Usenet news system, whereas at UCL it is used in a purely local manner. Users never send messages directly into the conferencing system, but send them indirectly through the messaging system. This indirection is transparent to the conferencing system user, who is apparently sending a message to a conference. In the UCL namespace, there are entries which are treated as distribution lists. These entries function in two ways: Firstly as pure distribution lists, containing local users (who may be on any machine) and remote users; Secondly, they contain entries which map onto conferences on one or more machine. Each conference will be maintained with deletion and archiving policies appropriate to the subject of the conference: For example, notices of system maintenance are only held for a short while and then deleted, whereas discussions of more substantial interest are held for longer and in some cases archived. In practice, most conferences are held on one machine with a large amount of storage and selected conferences are placed on other machines with relatively short expiry times. This measure of centralisation reduces storage and communication overheads. Users have straightforward access to the conferencing system, and can add their names to distribution lists by use of a simple program. This program either manipulates a list membership file, or sends a message to the list manager, depending on the policy for the list concerned (public or private). Having information available in both forms allows users to choose between the relative merits of conferencing and messaging style interfaces. For lists of marginal interest, the former is likely to be preferred as it allows rapid scanning of sorted entries. For lists of greater interest, the flexibility of a variety of message interfaces may be preferred. A user may choose to use one approach or the other for all of his or her messaging work. Another possible approach is to use messaging interface for all current work, and to utilise the conferencing system purely as an archive mechanism. A unified approach of using one interface to access both conferences and private mailboxes may be optimal in some cases.

The rest of this section discuss how this local functionality is integrated with other global communication facilities. The first example is the handling of large internetwork distribution lists, which are used widely to communicate information. With lists of interest to any UCL users, rather than add users' name to the list, the name of a UCL sublist is added. This then allows local users to easily access the information, either as a distribution list or as a conference without having the difficulty of contacting the list manager. This gives users the possibility of examining lists with minimal effort to see if they are of interest. This mechanism is not applied to external lists which have very limited interest, and cannot be applied to lists with controlled membership, unless the control is distributed in some manner. Few lists of wide interest fall into the latter category.

As well as external distribution lists, access is also given to conferencing systems. The first system considered is the COM system discussed in section 1. This has a mechanism whereby external addresses can be added to conferences, and these will receive a copy of each entry using the JNT Mail Protocol. From the standpoint of the COM conference, this address is regarded as a member of the conference. Conferences can be addressed from the JNT Mail system as <conference@com-site>, and conference names are mapped to this form when they are passed to the JNT Mail Protocol. This allows the COM conferences to be treated in the same manner as external distribution lists. However, from the standpoint of a local user who reads a COM conference as a local conference, no major functional difference is noticed between reading the conference locally and reading the conference on the COM system. One difference is that it is not possible to determine the membership of conferences in a simple manner. It is suggested that although this is a useful function, in general it becomes increasingly difficult to determine as systems become more distributed. Membership of local conferences is still easily accessible. The inverse of this approach is also used, in that COM conferences can become members of external distribution lists.

The handling of the Usenet News system discussed in section 1 is more complex. Due to the structure of the distribution mechanism, duplicate copies of some articles are likely, and there is no messaging mechanism to eliminate these. This function is achieved by injecting incoming articles into a news system. This system does not perform any storage operations, but simply eliminates duplicates and provides the news relay and transmission functionality to other sites. This can be viewed as a component which performs the Usenet protocol functions. Articles are then mapped onto local names which point to local user conferences / distribution lists. The newsgroup name is mapped onto the news system, so that local users can send to the global newsgroup. Unique internal names are chosen to prevent loops from occurring.

5. PROBLEMS FOR FUTURE SYSTEMS

The previous section has shown how, using current messaging and conferencing facilities, distributed conferences can be built using only a messaging system as the basis for communication. The conferencing aspects have been achieved not by special communications protocols, but by structuring within the Message Handling System. This leads to suggestions as to how this approach might be used in future systems.

It is useful to consider the role which distribution lists will play, in a system with connectivity similar to the international telephone system (i.e. having a very large number of potential recipients). The word list will be used, but this may equally well be considered as a distributed conference. Whilst many lists will undoubtedly be very large, those interested in the lists will be a very small percentage of the community, and in some cases users will be widely distributed. This potentially common situation is examined, on the basis that smaller and / or more localised lists are a simpler problem. It is suggested that in most cases where users interested in a list are widely spread, that they will not be spread evenly. For example, a list related to a specialised area of Biochemistry is likely to have membership concentrated in a number of University departments, and specialist firms. In general, a list would be expected to have certain 'pockets' of recipients, together with other isolated recipients.

For a list of this nature, broadcast distribution to all sites which might wish to receive such information would be prohibitively expensive, in view of the relative number of sites which would have to handle items of no local interest. For this reason, it seems likely that lists of this nature will need to have a distribution mechanism of a more structured style: essentially a distribution list mechanism. However, pure list mechanisms lose many of the desirable features of conferencing systems, in particular the ability for users to browse easily through potential areas of interest. This can be overcome by handling the 'leaves' of distribution lists in the manner described: Mapping them onto UAs, which store messages as conference entries and provide a conferencing interface.

The distribution list model discussed in section 3 viewed lists as value added service provided at the UA level. This tree structure can be extended to further levels, either as a multi-level tree or as some more complex structure. An increase in complexity might be justified either to spread the load of providing the list service, or to prevent convoluted relaying. For example, with a list spanning several countries, it might be seen as undesirable to route messages from the UK to France through the USA. The management of such a structure might well be in the hands of an organisation which initially established such a list mechanism. Whilst it is possible that mechanisms to join such lists will be automated, it seems unlikely in view of charging and access control. Thus, a site joining a list by adding an entry which will expand to a local list / conference will be able to provide easy access to this information for users at the site. In this context, a site might be an organisation providing a service for its members, or selling conference facilities. The former is analogous to an organisation subscribing to journals for its workers to study, the latter to a library.

It is worth considering how far proposed messaging standards will go to support this kind of functionality. The major thrust in message standardisation is currently coming from the CCITT [1]. There are other bodies engaged in this area, but all of them are following the work of CCITT to a large extent. It has been suggested that there is a need to build layers on top of the Message Handling System (UA to UA level) to provide a comprehensive service. One important aspect of this higher level of service is message structuring, and office document architectures. This area of active development is not discussed. The consideration of interest here, is whether there is a need for specific conferencing facilities to be built as protocol elements, or if this can be achieved with the proposed MHS protocols. Some proposals such as the GILT protocol [13], have many specific functions for the handling of conferences. It is unfortunate that the potential functionality of such a protocol requires a good deal of detailed access to remote systems for distribution of documents in a reasonably efficient manner. Privacy and security requirements may well prevent such access being allowed. This would imply that distribution structuring must be done with a greater level of human control. One particular feature which should be supported is to have an ID associated with the User Message, and a mechanism to reference this in future messages. Note that this ID should be associated with the document, rather than an individual transmission of a given document. This is provided by the CCITT proposals. This ID is then used by conferencing systems to structure conferences, and in some cases to optimise storage when the same document arrives for two conferences by different paths. Surprisingly, no additional information appears to be needed to provide distributed conferencing facilities using distribution in the manner proposed. It is suggested that additional functionality for controlling conferences (e.g. automatically creating a conference on a remote UA) either in the UA to UA protocol or at a higher level is of limited use, for the reasons given above.

A complex area of some significance, is the handling of Naming and Addressing. Currently, CCITT proposals in this area are somewhat limited. However, IFIP WG 6.5 has made some interesting proposals to be submitted to CCITT which are a substantial improvement [14]. This description is summarised briefly, and it is suggested how the description might be extended to distribution lists. Names are considered as a series of attribute value pairs, which describe a UA in some specific context. The two major contexts of interest are geographical (e.g. like a postal address), and organisational (e.g. country, organisation, and name or job function). It seems undesirable to bind a list name in this manner. It would seem useful to have a context which allowed the list to be described in a global manner. For example in the context of a country, there might be a series of attributes and subattributes describing a discussion list. To allow this type of description, it will be important to have a mechanism (a directory service) to bind this name to the address of a specific UA which will provide the value added list expansion service. The difference between this mechanism, and a flooding style of distribution should be appreciated. However, from the user standpoint, the effect is the same. This mechanism should also be extended to operate within a given context (geographical or organisational), which would provide mechanisms for localised lists, and for naming sublists.

6. CONCLUSIONS

This paper has given a comparison between messaging and conferencing style systems, and discussed the relative merits of each approach in current systems. A pragmatic approach to how such systems have been interconnected is described, and the advantages of this approach explained. It is suggested that in future systems, the distinction between the two approaches will diminish, and conferencing style systems will be used in User Agents without the evolution of standard conferencing protocols. Message distribution can then be achieved without undue waste of the underlying communications resources. This will give the user an integrated view of the message handling namespace, whilst retaining flexibility in the choice of user interface and style of working.

7. REFERENCES

1. CCITT 5/VII, "Recommendations X.400", Message Handling Systems: System Model - Service Elements, November 1983.

2. Sebestyen, I., "Computerised Message Sending and Teleconferencing in an International environment - present and future", Proc. Int. Symp. Computer Message Systems, Ottowa, April 1981.

3. Turoff, M., Hiltz, S.R., "Computer support for group versus individual decisions", IEEE trans. Communications COM-30 no 1, Jan 1982.

4. Palme, J., "Computer Conferencing is More than Electronic Mail", EUTECO, European Teleinformatics Conf. (North Holland), October 1983.

5. Kille, S.E. (editor), "JNT Mail Protocol (revision 1.0)", Joint Network Team, Rutherford Appleton Laboratory, March 1984.

6. Nowitz, D.A., Lesk, M.E., "A Dial-up Network of UNIX systems", UNIX Programmer's Manual, 7th edition, Bell Labs., August 1978.

7. Crocker, D.H., "Standard of the Format of ARPA Internet Text Messages", RFC 822, August 1982.

8. Deutsch, D., "Implementing Distribution Lists in Computer Based Message Systems", IFIP WG 6.5 Conf., Nottingham, May 1984.

9. Crocker, D., Szwkowski, E., Farber, D., "An Internetwork Memo Distribution Capability - MMDF", Proc. 6th. Data Comm Symp, IEEE/ACM, November 1979.

10. Kille, S.E., "The Interconnection of Network Mailsystems", IERE Conf. on Networks and Electronic Office Systems, Reading, September 1983.

11. Cole R.H., et al, "Network Interconnection Facilities at UCL", To be presented at ICCC, Melbourne, September 1984.

12. Essick, R.B., and Kolstad, R., "Notesfile Reference Manual", University of Illinois Technical Report UIUCDCS-R-82-1081, June 1982.

13. Wallerlath, P., "The GILT Abstract Model of a Computer Based Message System", EUTECO, European Teleinformatics Conf. (North Holland), October 1983.

14. IFIP WG 6.5., "A User-friendly Naming Convention for Public Data Networks", IFIP 6.5 working paper, version 2, November 1983.

Computer-Based Message Services
H.T. Smith (Editor)
Elsevier Science Publishers B.V. (North-Holland)

INTERCONNECTION OF THE IBM OFFICE SYSTEM PROFS AND GILT

Guenter Schulze
GMD-Bereich Darmstadt
Rheinstr. 75
D-6100 Darmstadt
Germany F.R.

The IBM office system PROFS is intended to be used as a local CBMS within a distributed message handling system composed of heterogeneous systems. A subset of GILT protocols is chosen for interconnection considering it as a representative of open system protocols. The paper provides a short introduction to PROFS, presents the structure of the interconnection, and describes the architecture of the message systems regarded from the interconnection point of view.

INTRODUCTION

Message systems will be used more and more within organizations and the need for interconnecting them increases, allowing its users to communicate with external users on remote message systems. Because the interconnection shall also apply to available systems of different manufactures, standard communication protocols are needed for interconnection. We have considered a subset of protocols, defined within the GILT project, /7/, as a representative of open system protocols. This subset is expected being very similar to future recommendations or standards in the field of message systems.

Among other systems we use the IBM professional office system PROFS, /1/, as a local CBMS. The primary purpose of adapting PROFS to the subset of GILT protocols has been to enable the inhouse exchange of documents between PROFS and KOMEX, /6/, a conferencing system developed by the GMD and running on a Siemens computer, and, as a member of some research projects, to exchange documents with other project members, e.g. GILT.

The set of selected GILT protocols comprises the network access via X.25, the transport protocol class 0 or S.70, an extended version of CCITT's session protocol S.62, and a subset of the GILT message protocol, /10/,/11/. For X.25 access standard IBM software will be used running in a S/1 computer which acts as a front-end and which interfaces to one virtual machine in the host computer. The implementation of the protocols on top of X.25 is being carried out in cooperation with the IBM scientific center in Heidelberg.

The paper briefly introduces PROFS and the principles of document distribution by PROFS, describes the requirements for interconnection of PROFS to other message systems and the implementation structure within the PROFS environment, and presents an architectural view how the connected message systems are seen from the interconnection standpoint.

THE IBM OFFICE SYSTEM PROFS

The IBM office system PROFS, /1/.../4/, is a VM/370 based application and it is intended to address various textprocessing requirements. It comprises aspects of document creation, filing, storage, retrieval, and distribution. In a later version, calendar scheduling functions were added. Communication to other location is performed by the remote spooling communication system extended by the networking subsystem (RSCS), /5/.

The development of PROFS begun more than 10 years ago by the implementation of a simple mail logging facility. Step by step, more functions were added onto the early prototype predecessor of today's VM/370 operating system. The PROFS system has been improved during some redesign phases and by a joint study with a customer. A more friendly user interface was realized by means of a full screen support in combination with the use of program function keys.

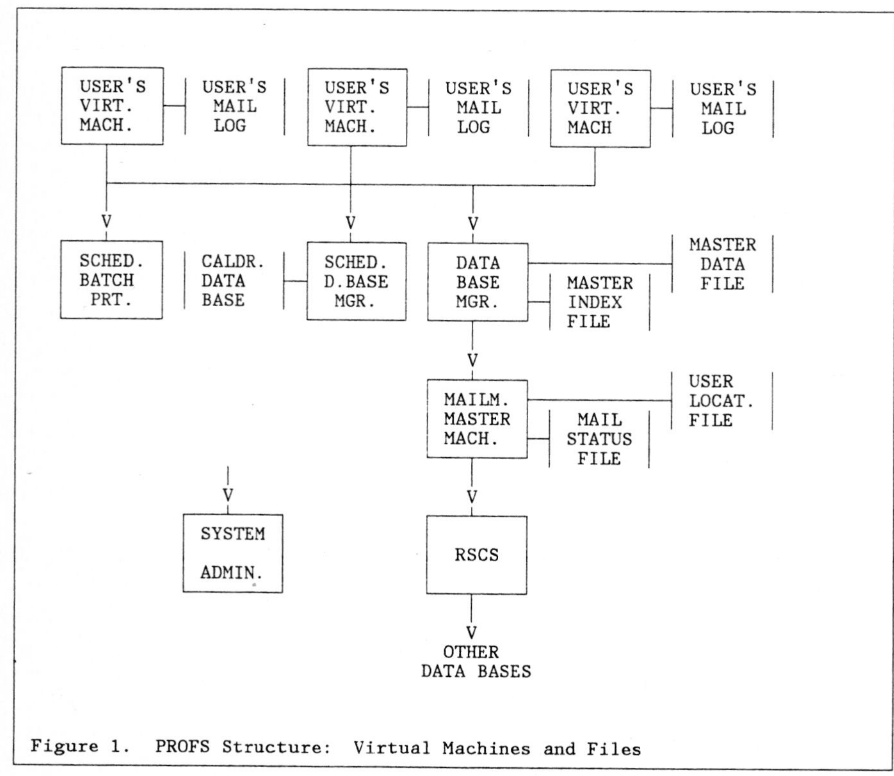

Figure 1. PROFS Structure: Virtual Machines and Files

Today's PROFS consists of the user's virtual machine, the data base manager, the distribution manager, the scheduling facility data base manager, the scheduling facility batch printer, and the system administrator.

Each component resides in an independent virtual machines, and each human user gains access to PROFS via his or her user's virtual machine. Communication to other locations is performed by the remote spooling communication system (RSCS) extended by the networking subsystem. The extension comprises routing and store-and-forward functions.

Functions such as text entry, editing, data manipulation, and management of user's mail log were designed to run in the individual user's virtual machine. The data base manager virtual machine tense to control the common document storage and manage the needed document security, authorization and audit functions. The third component, the distribution manager, delivers and receives electronic documents. The scheduling facility data base manager stores and updates conference room schedules and appointment calendars, and the scheduling facility batch printer prints conference room schedules and appointment calendars. The system administrator is required to install and administer PROFS.

The structure of PROFS with respect to its component virtual machines and associated files is illustrated in Figure 1. All virtual machines except the user's virtual machine and the system administrator virtual machines are running in disconnected mode.

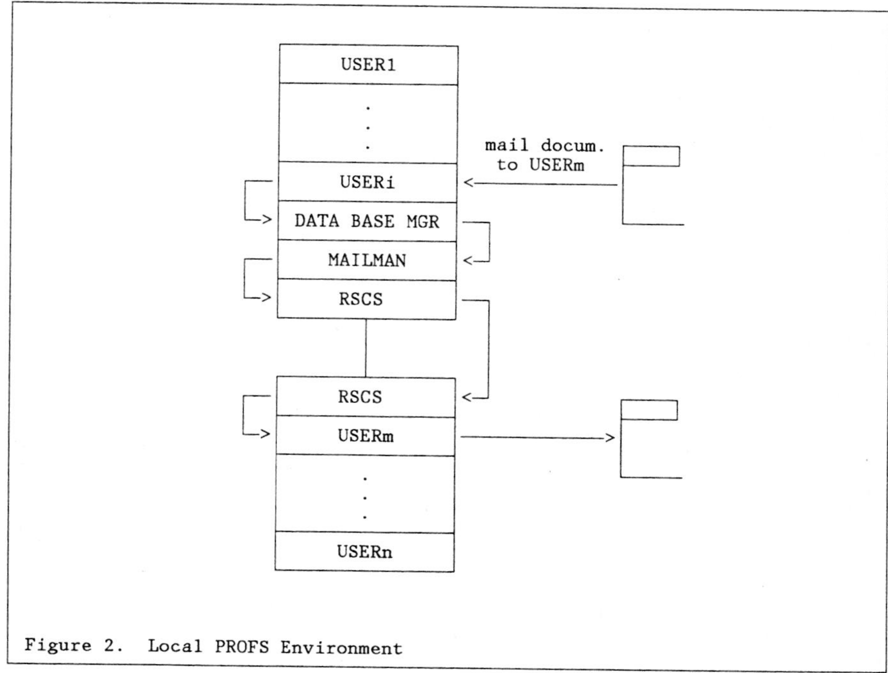

Figure 2. Local PROFS Environment

PROFS DOCUMENT DISTRIBUTION

The transfer facility of RSCS is used as an intersystem file-transfer medium, it acts as a carrier. A comprehensive document distribution facility on top of the RSCS communications layer provides guaranteed delivery with database to database receipt acknowledgement.

The RSCS communications system establishes a network environment which can be used by PROFS in two different ways, either local or remote. In the case of a local environment, the individual user's virtual machines are distributed on different real VM/370 systems but only one central common database is used, see Figure 2. The individual users work with the data entry tools from any one of their real VM/370 systems. Their individual virtual machines communicate with the single central database virtual machine over the local RSCS communication links which are under the control of the central distribution manager (mailman).

If mail is to be sent beyond the local enviroment, the distribution manager communicates with a counterpart distribution manager running at the destination locations as shown in Figure 3. The two distribution managers can exchange electronic documents and update each other's databases.

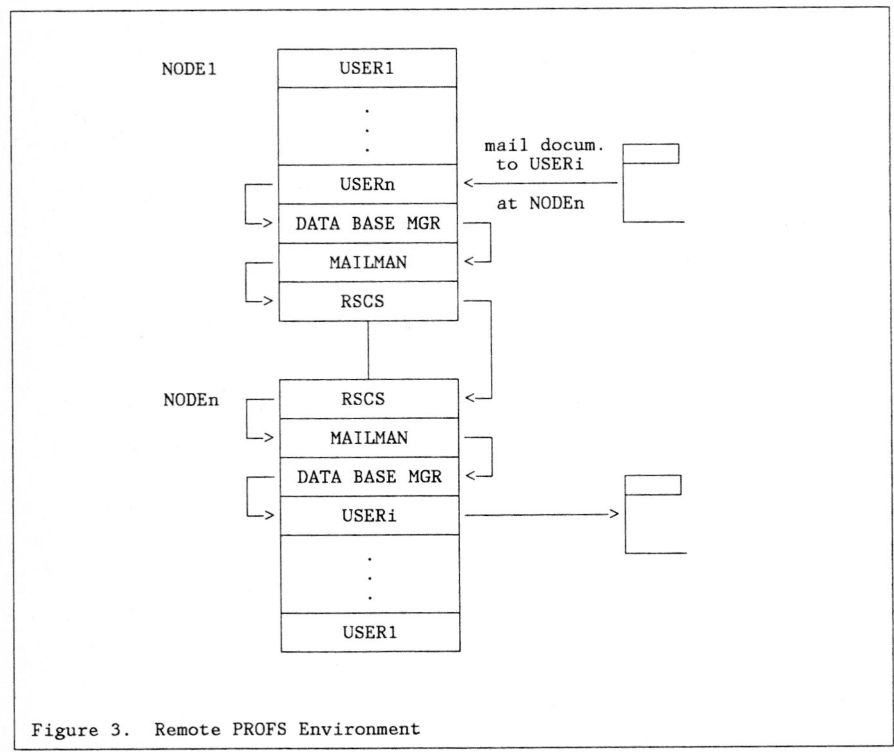

Figure 3. Remote PROFS Environment

REQUIREMENTS FOR INTERCONNECTING PROFS WITH OTHER SYSTEMS

To exchange electronic documents with other non-PROFS systems, the PROFS system should be adapted to a set of open system protocols, rather than adapting the foreign systems to the PROFS/RSCS conventions. We have considered the set of protocols which has been defined within the GILT project as a representative of open system protocols. It is expected that they will be very similar to the ISO and CCITT standards. The set of GILT protocols comprises the transport layer protocol S.70 on top of the network layer and an extended version of S.62 at the session layer. It is further assumed that different already existing and future messaging systems will include 'write document' facilities as a common set of functions. Therefore, the adaptation should concentrate on the implementation of the GILT class 1 message layer protocol. This class contains functions to store an electronic document in a foreign database, but it is not possible to retrieve or read a document from a foreign database. Managing and manipulating conferences and memberships will not be possible either. These functions are contained in the GILT message classes 2 and 3, /10/.

It is intended to start with the Teleletex protocol version, /11/, which contains the message layer protocol elements in a human readable form as a part of the Teletex document. This version also enables users having access to Teletex terminals or Teletex compatible computers to exchange documents with PROFS users.

The GILT subsystem is not intended to replace the RSCS/PROFS subsystem. Both subsystems shall coexist as alternatives and messages will be routed via whichever subsystem the recipient is currently connected to. The local PROFS user need not be involved in the decision of which subsystem to use, he simply adresses the recipients by means of the usual PROFS addressing scheme without any knowledge of the required route.

From the user's point of view, PROFS supports two different ways of addressing. The one commonly used method is the direct addressing scheme. This scheme is based on the assumption that the recipient is known to the system as a PROFS user with its own system-supported personal mailbox. Recipients of this type are addressed by the pair USER-ID/NODE-ID, each 8 bytes in length where NODE-ID addresses the location of the database and USER-ID the user's virtual machine within that location.

The second method is normally used for recipients who do not have PROFS user's virtual machines. In this case, the originating user may address a mailroom facility, instructing PROFS to generate an extra banner page containing the address of the final destination in human readable form. From the message layer protocol's viewpoint, the banner page is a piece of the message content, but it is intended to be interpreted by a human reponsible for distribution of physical mail. Since the structure of the banner page is predefined, this method may also be used to address recipients connected to an open system's environment, if the first addressing method should not be sufficient.

The adaptation should also enable the connection of other types of systems, e.g. the CCITT message handling system MHS as currently defined by a the set of draft recommendations X.MHS0 to X.MHS7, /12/, or it may also include standard IBM RSCS mail.

To realize the proposed adaptation, a new component - the Message

Routing (MSR) virtual machine - is introduced. It is inserted into the communication path between the PROFS mailman and the RSCS virtual machine. It is responsible for switching PROFS or GILT mail to the required target subsystem and must perform message layer protocol conversions if required.

IMPLEMENTATION STRUCTURE

Figure 4 shows a possible configuration of the gateway and the relationship to applications, the RSCS subsystem, and the message transfer service. The message transfer service (MTS) uses the services of the GILT session layer, the transport layer, and the network layer.

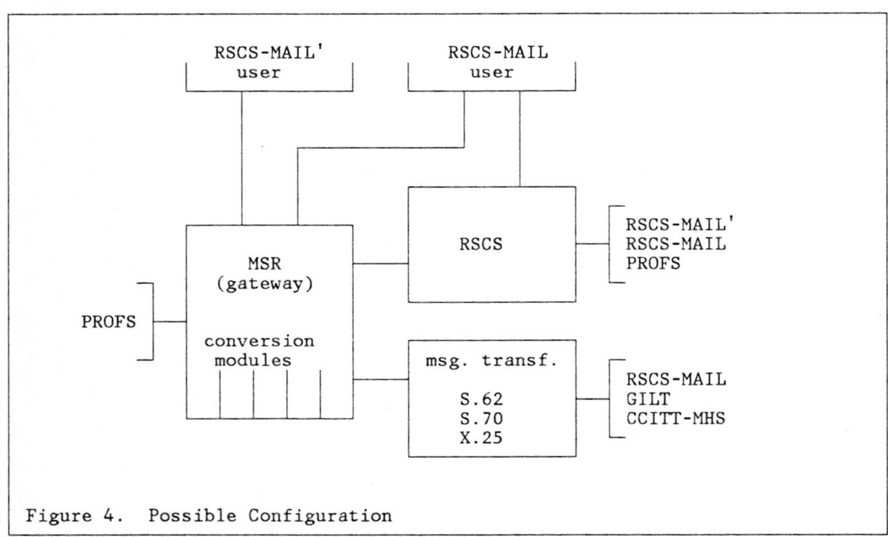

Figure 4. Possible Configuration

The layering structure and their protocols are in conformance to ISO and CCITT open system architecture and their corresponding protocols. The network layer uses X.25, the transport layer S.70, and the session layer a GILT version of S.62.

Figure 5 illustrates the implementation structure. A standard IBM product is used for handling X.25. This package resides in a System/1 which acts as a front end to the host processor. The System/1 communicates with a specific virtual machine via the channel and related channel attachment software package. This virtual machine contains the software handling the transport layer protocol S.70. The S.70 gateway virtual machine communicates with other virtual machines by inter VM communication facilities. A virtual machine of this type, representing a user of the transport service, contains in our case S.62 software and of top of it the message transfer functions. The message transfer service communicates with the message gateway by means of a submit/deliver interface on top of the inter-VM spooling facility.

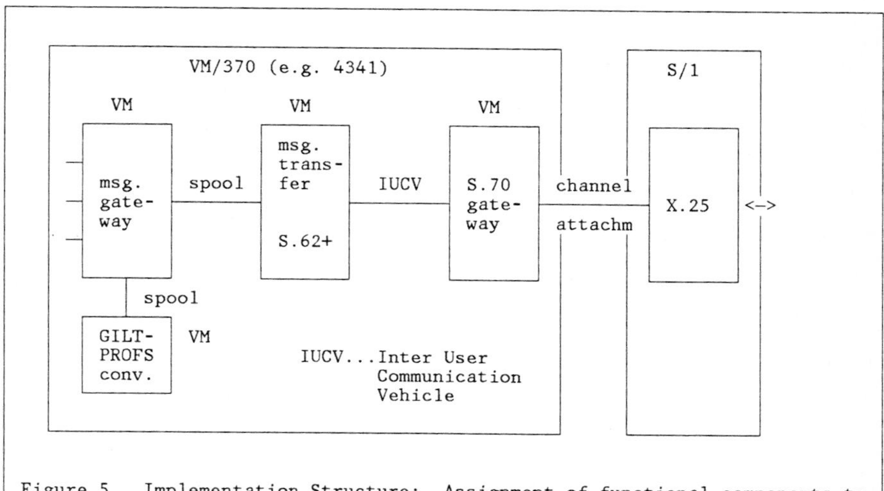

Figure 5. Implementation Structure: Assignment of functional components to system components

The message transfer service uses the session services in order to protect the message from failures which cannot be recovered by transport protocol mechanisms. Such failures may occur if the transport- or endsystem fails and already acknowlegded, but not yet processed, data have been lost. The protection must avoid either duplication or loss of messages. Loss or duplication of messages may occur if synchronisation has been lost, e.g. the receiver of a message may assume the message as a complete one and starts processing, while the sender assumes it is possibly lost and keeps it for further actions. Alternativly, the sender could assume that the message is completly transfered although the receiver couldn't process it due to a failure.

The GILT extensions to S.62 comprise a two way alternate (TWA) data transfer, a two way simultaneous(TWS) data transfer, and a checkpointing initiation from either end. This protocol is similar to the ISO 'Basic Activity Subset' (BAS).

ARCHITECTURE OF THE MESSAGE SYSTEM AS SEEN BY THE GATEWAY

The message gateway will also be able to relay received messages back to other nodes. Therefore this component will be named message routing component (MSR) and it represents the functionallity of an message transfer agent (MTA) in CCITT's model, /12/.

The following description addresses the structure of the message system network as seen from the MSR's viewpoint. The description contains terms which combine the CCITT's and IBM's definitions of message system network architectures, /12/ and /13/.

The MSR sees the external world as a set of subsystems. Each subsystem contains a set of user agents (UAs) belonging to one specific naming management authority. This management authority may be an artificial (or virtual) one; it is the one which is relevant to the MSR for performing the correct translation and routing functions. From the MSR's point of view, the organization of UAs into management authorities may differ from the real organization as seen from the top down to the message system network, due to the fact that messages may be routed through a chain of different gateways.

With relation to a specific instance of a message transfer action, one UA behaves as a source and another as a recipient. A source submits a message to the MSR and a recipient is the target of the message. A set of sources belong to a source management domain (SMD) and a set of recipients to a recipient management domain (RMD). A management domain is a entity which is responsible for the unambiguous naming of the sources or recipients belonging to it.

The MSR receives messages from sources and submits messages to recipients by means of a message transfer service. In order to transfer the message, the MSR must inform the transfer service to which remote access point the message should be transfered. The instance behind this access point is a counterpart of the MSR. It may be a MTA in the CCITT's sense or another MSR. That instance is the representative of the UA with respect to the MSR and it is responsible for further distribution of the message to either the recipient or another MTA. Once the message has been accepted by a receiving MTA, the MSR no longer needs to take care of the message. On the other hand, if the MSR has received and accepted a message it takes full responsibility for further distribution.

The MSR receives messages from a source MTA (SMTA) and submits messages to a recipient MTA (RMTA); it interacts with the message transfer service via a delivery or submission access point, respectively.

The total set of source and recipient MTAs known to the MSR is also normally composed of subsets. Each subset represents a different source or recipient tranfer management domain (STMD or RTMD). A transfer management domain is responsible for the unambiguous naming of MTAs belonging to it.

Within a management domain the corresponding adresses of sources or recipients, or source or recipient MTAs have to be used. However, UAs should also be addressable from outside their management domain. In this case, the addresses used may differ from those defined by their management domain. The use of addresses makes sense only within the context of the corresponding management domain in which they are defined.

Although a UA remains the same it may have different addresses. From the MSR's view, UAs could be unambiguously identified by the concatenation of a management domain name and its associated address. The address represents the related management domain's view (either SMDV or RMDV) of the UA identification. Alternativly, the management domain may be viewed as a definition of the context in which the following address becomes interpretable.

The MSR may identify a source either by

SMD-name/SMDV source address,
or
RMD-name/RMDV source address
for all recipient management domains
accepting that source.

On the other hand, a recipient may be identified by

RMD-name/RMDV recipient address,
or
SMD-name/SMDV recipient address
for all source management domains
allowing addressing of that recipient.

Different representations of addresses for a specific source or recipient gives rise to an identity relation. It defines different address representations for a UA. The management of the identity relation is one of the main tasks of the MSR.

Another important function of the MSR is keeping track of the various routing relationships. This relationships define which MTA or set of MTAs is able to represent a specific recipient and it is used to perform the related message submission and associated MTA addressing functions.

A third relation, named the protocol relation, defines the protocol type of the recipient MTA. The type description comprises the MTA layer protocol type itself and the type of the message body. For example, a PROFS message body consists of document index information and a SCRIPT formatted EBCDIC document and a GILT message has the structure of a Teletex document.

CONCLUSION

The adaptation of already existing message systems to standard communication protocols is becoming increasingly important due to the requirement to enable communication with users of other message systems or with subscribers of public message services. But since the adaptation of the existing systems should not change the user's local interface or affect the remote user's interface, the gateway performing the adaptation must simulate the funtionality which could not be mapped to facilities of the local CBMS.

The major problem detected during the design of the PROFS gateway is the issue of address mapping. A recipient, independent of whether he resides on a PROFS or a non-PROFS system, must be addressed by a system defined user-id and node-id (each being restricted to 8 bytes in length). On the other hand, GILT mailboxes or CCITT user-agents have a considerably more flexible representation, namely O/R-names. Therefore it becomes necessary for the gateway to manage a relatively complex address directory which relates the PROFS view of addresses to the GILT or CCITT view of them and vice versa. Such a directory should be so conceived that it is able to efficiently handle a large community of potential users. We are currently designing the address directory.

Another issue has been the question which of the alternative protocols currently defined should be selected for the starting phase. We have chosen the Teletex based protocol because we expect a relatively large community of potential users having already either Teletex terminals available or Teletex protocols implemented on their computer. Those users may start by a manual interpretation of the message level protocol elements; a stepwise implementation of messaging facilities does not affect the remote users. A subsequent adaptation to the protocols of future public services seem to cause no problems.

REFERENCES

/1/ P.C. Gardener, Jr.,
A system for the automated office environment;
IBM System Journal, Vol. 20, No. 3, 1981

/2/ IBM Professional Office System;
(Programming RPQ PO9O33):
General Information Manual
GH20-2493-0, IBM 1981

/3/ IBM Professional Office System;
Programming RPQ P 09033
User's Guide;
SH20-5503-1; IBM 1983

/4/ IBM Professional Office System:
Programming RPQ P09033
Installation and Administration Guide
SH20-5505-2, IBM 1982

/5/ IBM VM/370
Remote Spooling Communications Subsystem Networking
Allgemeiner Ueberblick
GH12-1379-O, IBM-Deutschland GmbH 1979

/6/ U. Pankoke
Experience with the KOMEX system as an inhouse CBMS
International Working Conference on Computer-Based
Message Services, Nottingham, May 1984

/7/ The GILT Project
General Overview
COST11bis/GILT/010,
University of Duesseldorf, Computing Centre, 1983

/8/ GILT Session Description
COST11bis/GILT/SES/004
University of Duesseldorf, Computing Centre, 1982

/9/ E. Giese
Recommendation for the GILT Session Service Interface
Arbeitspapier Nr. 31
GMD Bereich Darmstadt, Darmstadt, 1983

/10/ GILT: Interconnection of
Computer Based Message and Conference Systems
Green Version
COST11bis/GILT/MES/014
University of Duesseldorf, Computing Centre, 1983

/11/ Teletex GILT Interworking
First Draft
University of Duesseldorf, Computing Centre, May 1983

/12/ Draft Recommendation X.MHS0...X.MHS7
Message Handling Systems
CCITT, June 1983

/13/ Office Information Architectures
Concepts
GC23-0765-0, IBM 1983

Computer-Based Message Services
H.T. Smith (Editor)
Elsevier Science Publishers B.V. (North-Holland)
IFIP, 1984

IMPLEMENTATION OF A DISTRIBUTED CBMS ON A MINIMUM SYSTEM *

Manuel MEDINA, Juan A. ALONSO,
Jordi BALLESTER and Jaime DELGADO

Telecommunication School (E.T.S.E.T.)
Polytechnic University of Catalonia
Apdo. 30.002 - Barcelona-34. SPAIN

This paper describes the implementation of a Computer Based Message System (CBMS) on a multi-microprocessor system. The user of this CBMS can also access other CBMS,s through a public packet switched network, using the ISO standardized protocols. The primitives to communicate CBMS,s and the implementation constraints are discussed.

1.- INTRODUCTION

Three years ago the Telecommunication School Computer Department of the Catalonia Polytechnic University began to work in the field of computer communications. The first step was the implementation of the CCITT X.25 standard |1|. Subsequently, we joined the GILT project, a part of a bigger EEC project called COST 11-bis. The final aim of the GILT project is to interconnect local CBMS,s (Computer Based Message Systems) via public data networks, such as the French TRANSPAC, the German DATEX-P or the new Spanish IBERPAC. Our aim is, not only to implement the CBMS itself and the GILT-proposed communication software needed to achieve interconnection with other remote CBMS,s, but also to do it on a microcomputer system. A lot of effort is required in order to solve the problems caused by the limited memory and processing resources of these systems. In this paper we put forward a minimum CBMS system which is at the same time fully operative and ready for further expansion, when more hardware is added.

2.- MACHINE CONSTRAINTS IMPOSSED BY OUR HARDWARE.

The machine giving physical support to our implementation is a Spanish Z-80 based multimicroprocessor EINA TURBO-800 machine, with up to 7 CPU,s (fig 1) . Each CPU has 64KBytes of dynamic memory, and two serial I/O ports. The operating system used is TURBO-DOS (CP/M compatible), which allows multiprocessing. One of the CPU,s is the master, and it controls the periphéral devices (one floppy disk, one 27 Mb hard disk and the printer) shared by all the slave CPU,s. In our implementation, it also controls the X.25 line, with a throughput of 19.200 bauds. Communication between master and slave CPU,s is accomplished through a programmable synchronous/asynchronous common port. At a first stage only one slave CPU is used.

The programming language used is Pascal/MT+, which allows separate module compilation and linking, even with assembler subroutines.

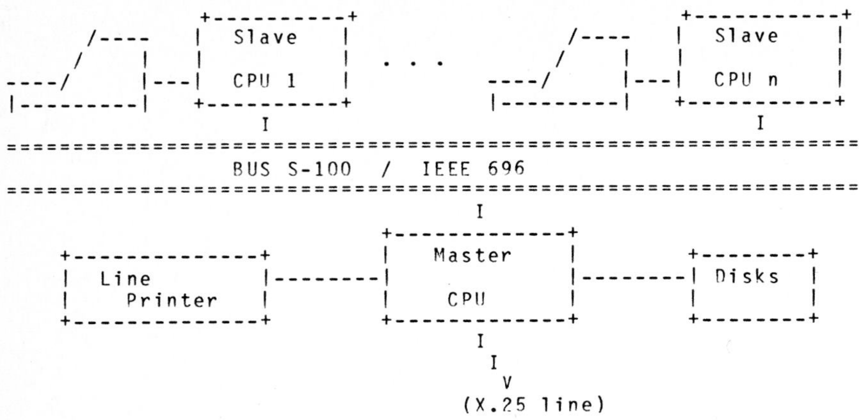

Fig. 1

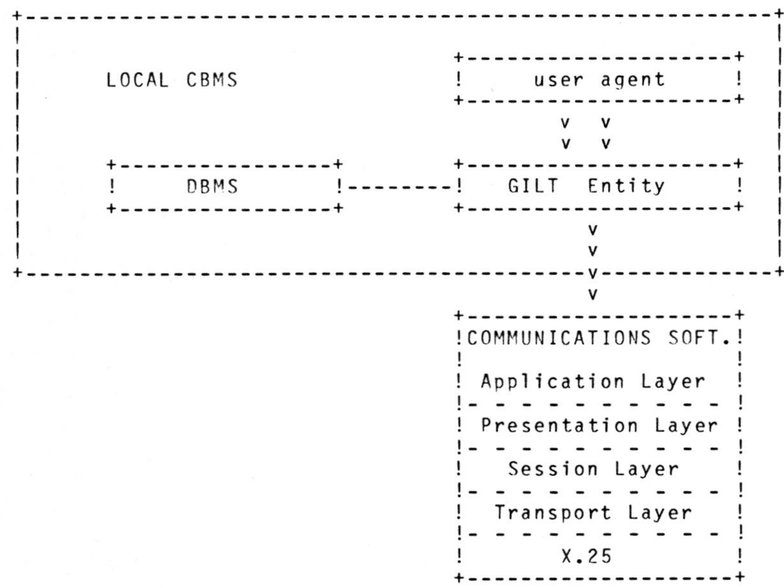

Fig. 2

3.- OVERALL SOFTWARE STRUCTURE.

Figure 2 shows the general structure of the required software. Two main blocs configurate it. First, the CBMS itself, containing in turn a user agent, a database file system and the GILT entity, which manages all the resources offered by the other blocs in order to achieve a successful information handling. Secondly, the communications software based on the ISO architecture for Open Systems Interconnection (OSI) and containing the classical seven protocol layers.

3.1.- The CBMS.

The CBMS is distributed into three separate modules. The GILT entity, responsible for the management of the other modules, the user agent (UA), and the database file system (DBMS).

3.1.1.- **The GILT Entity.**

The GILT entity analyses the requests and responses received from the network and the user agent, verifies their correctness from the protocol point of view, and routes them either to the local DBMS, the user agent or the network. In some cases, one single received request will be split into several requests which will be then sent to other modules, this being the case of a document sent to several mailboxes located at different CBMS,s.

The GILT entity has been implemented according to the abstract model proposed by GILT, (Green Version) |2|. In this model one CBMS is represented by the GILT_store, which is the highest structure level of the whole system (fig 3). This structure contains the list of functions implemented on this CBMS. The CBMS_references associate the logical CBMS_names to the network addresses by which they are accessible.

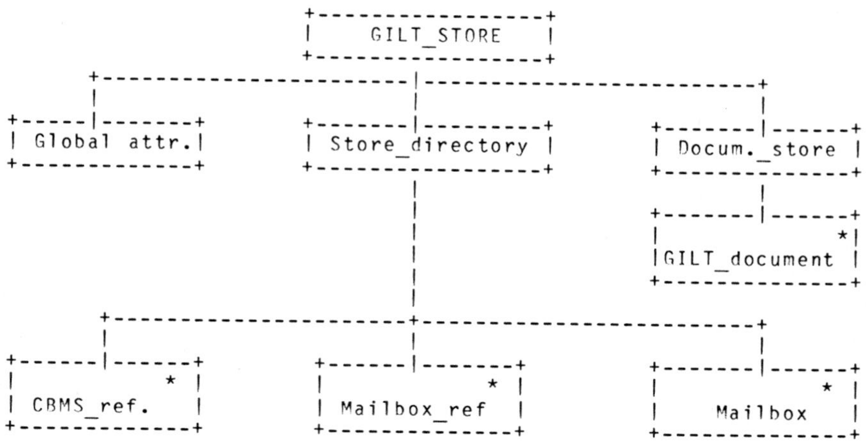

Fig. 3

The mailbox_references (fig. 4) link the known mailbox_names to their CBMS. The mailbox structure represents in the GILT world any entity capable of sending, receiving and storing documents. It has such attributes as access rights and distribution lists, and a set of references to the documents it contains (fig. 4).

Finally, the document store may contain three kinds of documents (fig 5). Document indications, with the information required for identification and retrieval, such as author, creation date, identifier, etc. Short documents, including the document indication and an abstract of it. Complete documents add the document text to the short document.

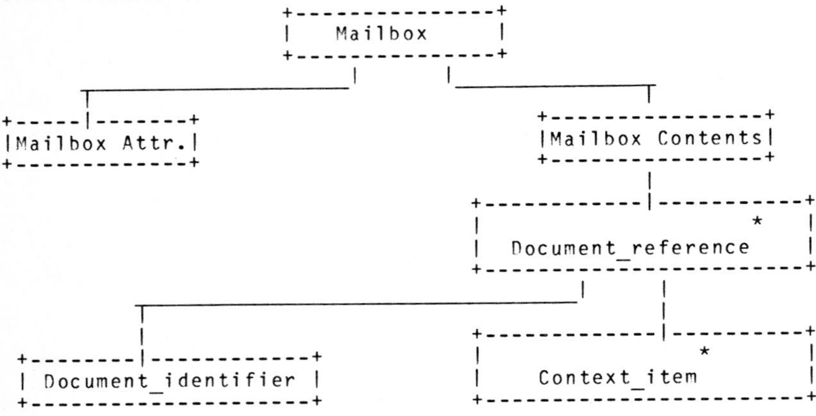

Fig. 4

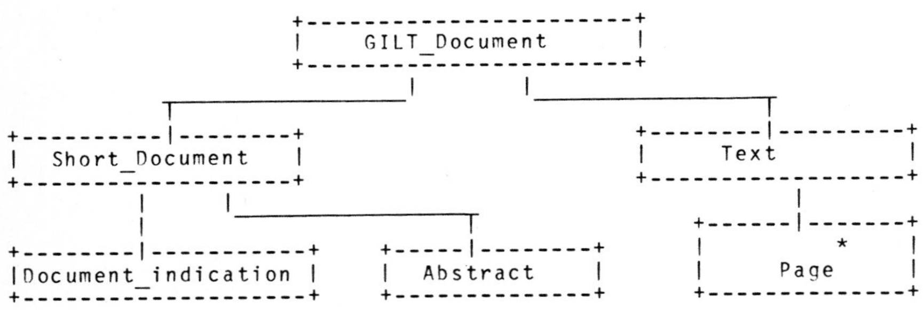

Fig. 5

The GILT CBMS model also defines a set of operations used within the abstract GILT model. These are related to the GILT communication services which provide the means for a CBMS to perform operations on another CBMS. Here is a summary of the operations defined for GILT:

Select_GILT_store: It selects a remote GILT_store.

CBMS_Presentation: It requests the GILT_store capabilities.

CBMS_Authentication: It provides the means for authentication of the remote station.

Deselect_GILT_store: It closes the logical relation existent with a remote GILT_store.

List_CBMS_names: It returns CBMS_names and address information kept by the consulted CBMS.

List_directory, List_mailboxes: These operations return the names of all, some, or one of the mailboxes known to the selected CBMS.

Create_mailbox: It creates a new mailbox.

Delete_mailbox: It deletes an existing mailbox.

Select_mailbox: It finds and selects a mailbox at another CBMS for further operations on it.

Deselect_mailbox: It puts an end to the existent logical connection with a remote mailbox.

Update mailbox attribute operations: They set or update attributes of a mailbox.

Read mailbox attribute operations: They read attribute values of a mailbox.

Write_document: It writes a document into the store of another CBMS and establishes a relation between the document and the selected mailbox.

Read_document: It transfers a document from the remote selected mailbox to the local one.

Send_document: It sends a document to the selected CBMS together with a list of receiver mailboxes, local to that CBMS, to which the document should be linked.

Retrieve_document: It searches and identifies one or more documents in the document store of a CBMS for a requesting mailbox at the selected CBMS.

Get_document: It initiates transmission of document data from documents selected in a previous retrieve_document operation.

In a first stage, only those operations required to do anything meaningful at all, i.e., select_GILT_store, deselect_GILT_store and send_document are to be implemented.

3.1.2.- **The DBMS.**

The DBMS module translates the GILT entity commands into the commands allowed by the local file management system. Since all the information related to the internal structure of the local CBMS (local mailbox attached to it, documents attached to mailboxes, remote known systems identifiers and access points, etc.) is stored in the local database, the GILT entity must access this local database whenever transfer, retrieval or editing operations are involved. A typical example would be the reception of a send_document call from a remote station. The GILT entity should then automatically update the information served by the communication server into the database, and then, retrieve the necessary information from it to create the send_document result. A local user wishing to read the received document should then access his own mailbox in the database.

The functions which are supplied are the same listed for the GILT entity, except those operations that are specific for remote access, such as:

- Send_document.
- Select_, Deselect_ and Identify_GILT_Store.

In order to manage those operations, the DBMS module must be able to handle incompletely specified names and document identification expressions. The mailbox_references (fig. 3), document_identifier (fig. 4) and document_indication (fig. 5), which are part of the GILT_store, act as keys to the access of the stored information. Each terminal bloc of the GILT_Store description given in the figures above mentioned represents a separate file. This permits to have just one copy of a document linked to several mailboxes, which is very useful, considering that, in the GILT concept of conference, some mailboxes are only used for distribution purposes.

3.1.3- The User Agent.

This bloc performs the interfacing task between the human user and the GILT entity. It is intended to make the dialogue process between user and system easier, by displaying the whole list of choices available at any time, and simplifying name specification and identification patterns.

The user has a set of capabilities associated to his/her own mailbox. The main functions provided for normal users, i.e., those without management capabilities, are the same listed for GILT entity, except those used to modify mailbox attributes, which will be only available for the manager user.

3.2.-The Communications Software.

In order to achieve interconnection with other GILT CBMS systems, the GILT group has adopted a series of communication protocol standards which perform the tasks required for a successful transference of information between two computer systems, such as error detection and recovery, resynchronization, network independence, etc.. The communications software has the layered configuration recommended by the ISO in its OSI-RM.

These layers are usually divided into two groups: lower- network-oriented layers and upper-aplication-oriented layers. Lower layers include X.25 layers (up to layer 3, or network layer) and the Transport Layer. The upper layers include the Session layer, used for resynchronization and error recovery purposes, the Presentation layer, which provides basic tools for a communication oriented high level data structure manipulation service, and the Application Layer, with the basic communication services needed to allow cooperation between two CBMS,s.

As far as our implementation is concerned, we have adopted the ECMA Class 0 Transport Protocol |3|, which is the minimum subset of the Transport layer, and gives service to one user. This transport entity will be eventually upgraded to class 2, allowing thus simultaneous multiuser processing. As to the Session Layer we have adopted the S.62 protocol, as proposed in the GILT Standard |4|, which allows compatibility with Teletex terminals. This Session Layer supplies the user with services for creation and management of data units, checkpoints, resynchronization and error recovery. The Presen-tation and Application layers are those defined in the GILT Green Version for CBMS |2|.

4.- OUR IMPLEMENTATION.

4.1.- Multiprocessor Task Allocation.

The prototype of implementation we are doing takes advantage of the multimicroprocessor architecture. One CPU allocates the network-oriented communications entities, i.e., X.25 and layer 4, while the others are responsible for the processing of the application-oriented entities, including layers 5, 6 and 7, the GILT entity, the DBMS and the User Agent (fig 6).

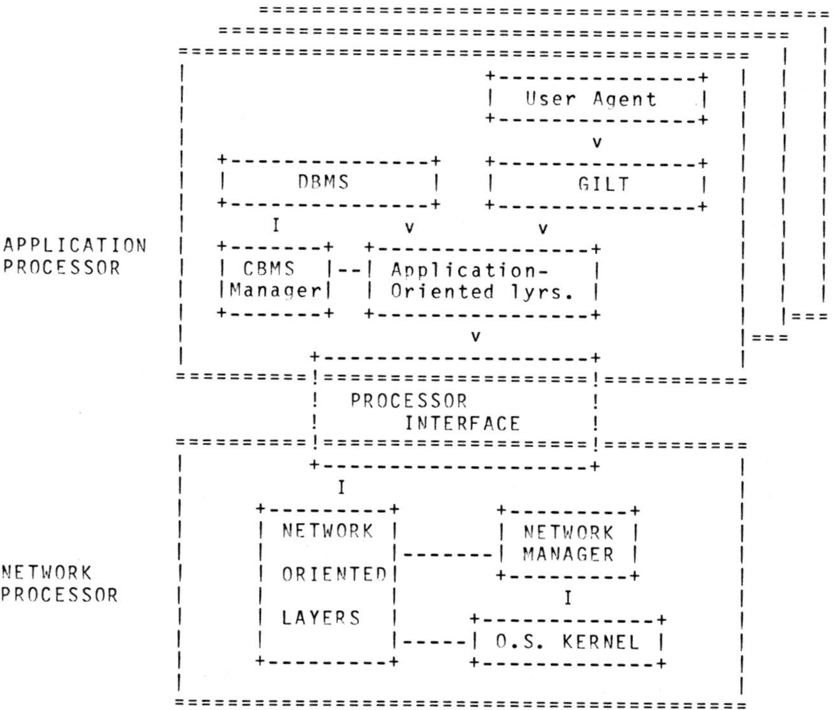

Fig. 6

Two main reasons have led us to make the processor boundary between layers 4 and 5. The first one refers to interlayer communication. This is achieved in two different ways:

Task-to-task : This is used for the lower layers of the communication software. A nucleus of the operating system gives control to the tasks which are ready on a sequential base, while keeps "frozen" those tasks which are waiting for some events to happen or some information to be supplied by other tasks |5|.

Procedure calls : The upper layers use Pascal procedure calls as the means to communicating with each other. This implies that, for instance, when the Presentation and Application layers require the services offered by the Session Layer, they call the session procedure corresponding to this service.

Since the boundary between upper layers and lower layers lies between layers 4 and 5, it seems advisable to place those tasks with the same means of intercommunication within the same CPU environment.

The second reason for this allocation is the possibility of a further expansion of the Transport Protocol service (to ECMA Class 2), with multiuser and network connection multiplexing capabilities, by which several Transport Service users will share the same Transport layer. If the processor boundary is placed between layers 4 and 5, the network processor can be used in a further stage of the project as a sort of front-end communications processor for a set of upper_layers-CBMS processors or even for a more powerful computer system. Figure 6 shows the distribution of tasks per processor.

4.2 - The Network-Processor Task Allocation.

The so called network-processor gives physical support to X.25 and Transport layer processing. It must also manage the operating system nucleus used for communication between tasks. In our implementation, the whole X.25 packet is regarded as being one task (and not three, i.e., one task per layer). The transport protocol entity and the processor interface are the other tasks which the nucleus has to manage. The X.25 packet is clock-interrupt driven, and, therefore, it doesn't work synchronously with the nucleus. It only uses the nucleus task communication primitives to communicate with the transport entity. These consist of semaphores to signal events, and queues to transfer information between tasks.

With this task management configuration, the X.25 packet gets the processor control at periodic intervals of time, processes the information available from the line and/or from the transport entity, and returns the processor control to the O.S. kernel, or to the task that had it when the X.25 interrupt clock signal arrived.

4.3 - The Application Processor Task Allocation.

The application-oriented processor has to manage the upper communication entities, the DBMS, and the GILT entity tasks. Due to lack of memory space, all these tasks cannot reside in dynamic memory simultaneously. This problem must be solved by using overlaying techniques. In this way, only those parts of the software which are really needed for a specific task reside in dynamic memory, while all the rest is stored in disk in form of overlay files. These will be transferred into dynamic memory when they are required for the current new task processing. For example, when the CBMS user is editing a document, all the communication software, i.e., the upper communication entities and the GILT entity communication interface, is not required, and thus, it can be stored in disk until it is needed to send the document. In the same way, when sending the document, the CBMS user agent task will be kept in disk, since it is not needed at all.

4.4 The Manager Blocs.

These parts of the software are used for supervision and control tasks. There are two of such blocs, one being application-oriented and the other network-oriented. They give the system manager the possibility of handling each of the communication entities individually and, at the same time, keeps trace of the successive station states and the information flow occurring in one session.

5 - CONCLUSIONS.

The described implementation of an open CBMS has a very modular structure, which allows an easy implementation on the new multi-microcomputer systems. Many manufacturers offer expansion I/O boards for their computers, with local processing capabilities to handle one or several communication lines, linking the system to data networks or terminals. These boards might allocate the user agent and the communication modules. An intelligent disk controller might allocate the DBMS module and the master CPU would be then responsible for the GILT entity processing.

The use of the same interface between the different modules simplifies the analysis phase of the implementation and at the same time leaves to each module aproximately the same amount of work to do.

The main constraint of the implementation of a distributed mail system on a general purpose microcomputer is the lack of memory space and processing power to run the great amount of software that must be executed. It is almost impossible to implement the seven layers defined by the ISO in its OSI RM and the mail system with only an 8 bit microprocessor available. To have a practical minimum system, there must be a dedicated processor which is responsible for the handling of the lower communications protocols, typically up to Transport layer. From the functional point of view, the minimum system described allows interaction between the local CBMS entity and the network only on an off-line basis, since a single 8 bit microprocessor shows great practical difficulties in supporting simultaneously the mail system user agent and the communications tasks. To enable on-line work with the distributed mail system, it would be necessary either a 16 bit processor with at least 128 Kbytes of dynamic memory to allocate application tasks, or two separate processors, one for communications tasks and another for the user agent.

ACKNOWLEDGEMENTS

The overall module structure of our implementation is the result of the collaboration with the members of the GILT project, with special mention to: R. Speth, P. Wallerath, L. Wosnitza, B. Cappel and H. Zschintzsch from the Duesseldorf University Computer Center.

REFERENCES

|1| X.25. CCITT, yellow book vol. VIII.2, 1981.

|2| "GILT: Interconnection of Computer Based Message and Conference Systems". Green version. Working paper of the GILT-COST.11.BIS project. Univ. Duesseldorf, Computing Center.

|3| Transport Protocol. ECMA - 72. sep. 1982.

|4| S.60. CCITT, yellow book vol VII.2, 1981.

|5| W.A. COLON-CASTRO, D.A. KIRKMAN: "Interfaces between Protocol Layers on a Multiprocessor System". Eighth Data Communications Symposium. ACM SIGCOMM, Computer communicacions review, vol. 13 n.4. oct. 1983.

|6| R. SPETH: "Message Systems and their interconnection". EUTECO oct. 1983. North-Holland publ. T.Kalin Ed.

|7| P. WALLERATH: "The GILT abstract model of a computer based message system". EUTECO oct. 1983. North-Holland publ. T. Kalin Ed.

|8| K.A. BRINGSRUD: "GILT services and protocols for interconnection of open CBMS,s". EUTECO oct. 1983. North-Holland publ. T. Kalin Ed.

|9| R. SPETH et al.: GILT - Open Interconnection of Local Message System in Europe. Submitted to the ICCC. Nov 1984.

---

* The research and developement work reflected on this paper has been possible thanks to a contract, nbr. 4027-79, with the CAICYT, which is a research commission of the Spanish Governement, and another one with the Commission of the European Community into the COST-11bis action.

PART 7:

MESSAGE SERVER IMPLEMENTATIONS

Computer-Based Message Services
H.T. Smith (Editor)
Elsevier Science Publishers B.V. (North-Holland)

MZnet: Mail Service for Personal Micro-Computer Systems

Einar Stefferud, *President, Network Management Associates* and *Visiting Lecturer in Information and Computer Science, University of California at Irvine*

Jerry Sweet, *Department of Information and Computer Science, University of California at Irvine*

Terrance Domae, *School of Engineering, University of California at Los Angeles*

ABSTRACT

Traditional computer mail systems involve a co-resident User Agent (UA) and Mail Transfer System (MTS) on a time-shared host computer which may be connected to other hosts in a network, with new mail posted or delivered directly through co-resident mail-slot programs. To introduce personal micro-computers (PCs) into this environment requires modification of the traditional mail system architecture. To this end, the MZnet project uses a *split-slot* model, placing UA programs on the PCs while leaving MTA programs on a mail relay host which can provide authentication and buffering. The split-slot arrangement might be viewed as a new protocol level which operates somewhere between the currently defined MTS-MTS and UA-UA levels.

Introduction

Mail systems were born and have grown up on large central time sharing systems, often imbedded in large networks of inter-operating computers with a set of distributed processes automatically transferring mail between users. This is certainly the case with the U.S. Department of Defense (DoD) Advanced Research Projects Agency Network (ARPANET) [1] where much of the original computer network mail systems research and development has taken place. Other mail networks such as the Computer Science Network [2] sponsored by the U.S. National Science Foundation, have also used relatively large shared computers lodged in an institutional setting, though they are often connected together with ordinary dial-up telephone links to form a large geographic network. Another U.S. example is USENET [3] which connects thousands of Unix* systems together with informally-supported dial telephone links. Although there have been several attempts, there appear to be no successful mail networks based on small personal computers, such as those that use the CP/M† or MS-DOS‡ operating systems.

The accepted architectural model for computer network mail (first articulated by the IFIP 6.5 Systems Environment Working Group) involves a User Agent (UA) which posts new mail items through a mail slot [4,5,6,7] to a Mail Transfer Agent (MTA) which delivers posted items to designated UA recipients through corresponding delivery slots. When mail is to be delivered to a UA on another host, it is transferred first to another MTA on the recipient user's host, which in turn puts the mail item through its local delivery slot. In this model, a Mail Transfer System (MTS) may be viewed as a collection of MTAs with network connections among them to provide Mail Transfer Services for a large number of users on different host computers.

*UNIX is a Trademark of Bell Laboratories, Inc.

†CP/M is a Trademark of Digital Research, Inc.

‡MS-DOS is a Trademark of Microsoft Corporation.

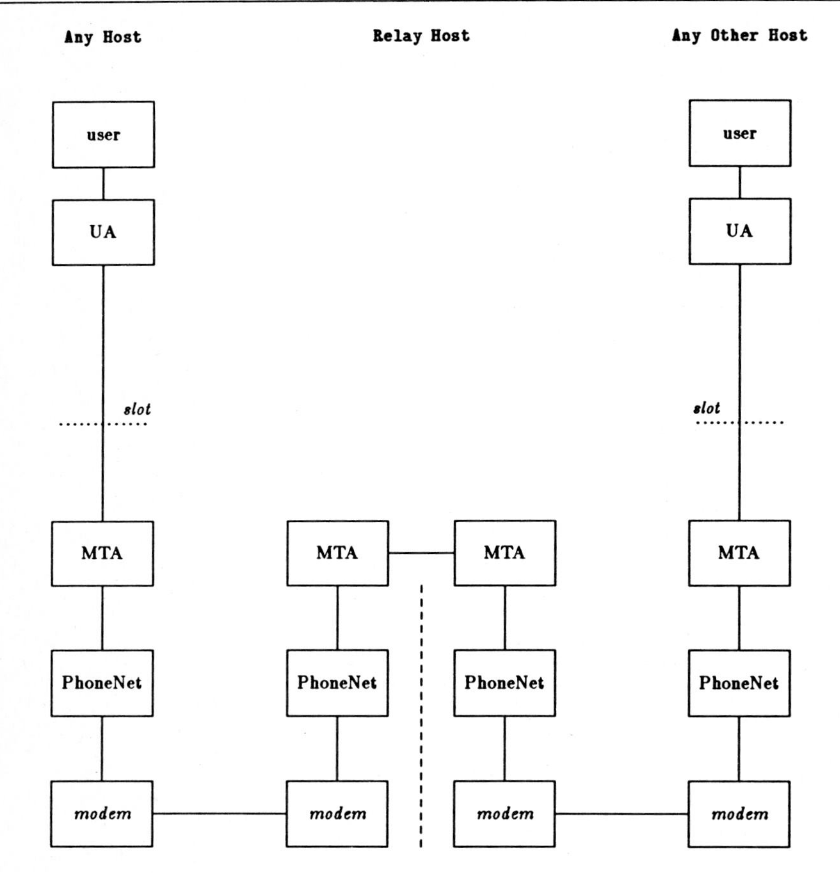

Figure 1. Normal arrangement

Replicating this UA/MTA/MTS model on a personal micro-computer (PC) is not an easy task. Aspects of PCs that make support of this model difficult include limited storage capacities, limited processing capabilities, and the fact that PCs are geared to support a single user rather than several users at once. A PC with limited secondary diskette storage and limited processing capacity (often single-thread) is not well suited to support the full range of automatic interactions between a UA and an MTA, or the necessary interactions between MTAs in an MTS. For example, we do not see any way to certify PC systems for authentication of posted mail. A PC can change its entire character and behavior with insertion of a new program diskette, suggesting that it is the operating system diskettes and their users that must be certified, rather than the computers. Review of certification issues shows that it is not the computer, but its operators and managers that must be certified, and this involves the notions of central management and control. All this is lost in the maze of PCs that we see proliferating on and off our campuses, in and out of our offices and homes.

Thus, we see a need for a new arrangement with the UA separated from its MTA, and using communication protocols to interact with it in ways that resemble MTA-to-MTA interactions. The UA is placed on the PC end, while the more complex tasks performed by the MTA are relegated to the remote host end. The remote MTA must authenticate mail items offered by the PC-based UA, just as it would for a co-located UA, but the task is more difficult because the PC UA is potentially anyone among the public telephone connectable population. This can be handled with password systems, but recognition and identification are not the only services to be provided at the posting slot. Posting also requires some validation of recipient addresses, and validation of the syntax and semantics of certain header fields. Example standards are provided by the U.S. National Bureau of Standards (NBS) and the U.S. DoD ARPANET for the format of mail to be transferred [8,9,10].

The new arrangement described in this paper might be called a *split mail slot* in that the UA side of the slot is split away from the MTA side. Although the UA and MTA may be on opposite ends of a telephone connection, they must still act together as a single processing unit to move mail from one to the other, with all that this may entail. This gives rise to a number of new MTA/UA requirements such as error control for service requests, user intervention to select items for delivery, and user postponement or rejection of delivery without triggering failure notices to senders. These are not serious problems when both MTA and UA are programs running on a single host. For example, with both UA and MTA on the same host, unwanted junk mail is simply deleted at low cost, compared to the cost of deletion after a long delivery transmission time. Better that our PC users be able to discard items without delivery transmission.

OVERVIEW OF THE MZNET ENVIRONMENT

The MZnet project is an undergraduate student effort sponsored within the Information and Computer Science (ICS) Department of the University of California at Irvine (UCI) in Southern California. For the past 2 years, the UCI mail network, known as ZOTnet, has been connected into the Computer Science Network (CSnet) and in 1984, has joined the DoD ARPA Internet with a *Split-Gateway* connection [11] to the University of Southern California Information Sciences Institute (USC-ISI). The MZnet split-slot arrangement may have some similarities to the Split-Slot Internet Gateway at least in name, but the problems and the implementations are quite different.

The UCI ZOTnet environment [13] gives the MZnet project a full-fledged Internet-class mail system as its foundation. The MZnet project objective is to extend this class of mail service to personal computers located in student and faculty residences, offices and laboratories, without waiting for full-blown local area networking to first provide connections. This follows a pattern of making the most of existing facilities to provide a reasonable level of service.

The UCI ZOTnet uses the CSnet-provided MMDF (Multi-channel Memo Distribution Facility) software [12] from the University of Delaware to interconnect two VAX 750 Unix systems with two DEC TOPS-20 systems through a port selector, with dial telephone connection to a CSnet relay [14]. The ZOTnet has since evolved into an ethernet-connected local area network with the aforementioned gateway connection into the DoD Internet. The ZOTnet also connects to USENET with the UUCP protocols, and provides format transformations for mail flowing between protocol domains [15,16]. Adding to the reach of the ZOTnet with MZnet is a natural part of its evolution*.

To this point we have set the context of the MZnet project. The remainder of this paper is devoted to relatively technical discussions of implementation of the PC user agent programs and the split-slot UA/MTA interface.

The MZnet User Agent: CP/MH

CP/MH is a collection of programs designed to work in conjunction with the Micro ZOTnet (MZnet) as an extension of the UCI ZOTnet. CP/MH programs permit a user of a CP/M 2.2-based microcomputer to send and receive ZOTnet mail messages, as well as to manipulate them locally on floppy disks. The CP/MH programs are written in the C programming language and should be portable to similar operating environments, such as MS-DOS, etc.

CP/MH is based on the UCI version of the Rand MH message handling system [17] for the Unix operating system. The major philosophical differences between CP/MH and typical user agents such as MSG [4] and its descendants are those of modularity and of user interface. In CP/MH (as in MH) the user does not invoke a single monolithic program to deal with mail, but rather invokes individual, non-interactive programs with common knowledge of the way messages are stored. Each program has default behavior which can be modified by using Unix-style command line options at time of invocation or through a user profile. Help messages can also be evoked from CP/MH programs.

MESSAGES AND FOLDERS

The format of a CP/MH message adheres more or less to the syntax described in RFC 822 in which a message consists of headers containing information pertaining to the message source and destination, and the message body, separated from the headers by a blank line. An example of such a message might be:

```
Date: 02 Nov 83 23:04:53 PST (Wed)
To: Toto <dog@Univ-Kansas>
From: The Great And Powerful Oz <Oz@Emerald-City>
Subject: What Be Your Excuse?

What's the matter?  I ask you for a simple thing like
"distribute this to Witch@Oz-West," and you can't do it.
You undergrads will do anything to get out of work!

--ozzie
```

Following the MH convention, each message is kept in a separate file. Since a message is simply ASCII text, it can be operated upon by non-CP/MH programs (such as text editors, in particular).

Collections of messages are called *folders*. Under CP/MH, folders are represented by several files: an *info* file, containing maintenance information about the folder, and a set of

*For those who are properly curious about such things, the name "ZOTnet" derives from the cry of the UCI mascot which is the Anteater from the B.C. comic strip, and MZnet is simply a contraction for Micro-ZOTnet.

message files with the same name as the info file, but with unique numeric suffixes (*extensions* in CP/M parlance). An example of this naming scheme might be:

DRAFT	the info file for the **DRAFT** folder
DRAFT.001	message 1 in the folder
DRAFT.002	message 2 in the folder
DRAFT.003	message 3 in the folder

The number of messages that may be stored in a folder is limited primarily by the storage capacity of a floppy disk, but also by the three-digit limit of a CP/M extension.

The info file contains a field named **CURRENT**: specifying the current message number. The current message number signifies the default message operated upon by CP/MH commands using a particular folder. The current message number may be modified by some commands. An example of the contents of the info file **DRAFT** might be

CURRENT: 3

This indicates that the file **DRAFT.003** would be operated upon when default conditions apply (i.e. when no message number is explicitly given to a CP/MH command).

Possible future uses for the info file include named message sequences (a set of messages to which commands may be applied as a whole) and user profile information for application to particular folders (there is presently a single user profile, described shortly).

A floppy diskette may contain more than one folder, but folders do not extend over more than one floppy diskette; therefore two different diskettes may contain folders with the same name.

CP/MH COMMANDS

Commands operating on messages can be divided into several general categories:

Transporting:	sending, receiving
Viewing:	selecting for display, showing header summaries
Creating:	composing, replying, forwarding
Archiving:	categorizing, refiling, deleting, sorting

The architecture of CP/MH permits the simulation of some of these categories using standard CP/M commands when CP/MH, in its present primitive state, does not cover them.

A minimal functionality is presently provided by the following four commands:

COMP	composes mail items: creates a file containing header information taken from a standard or user-specified template. This newly-created file may be edited to fill in the header fields and body.
REPL	replies to mail items: creates a file containing header information appropriate for answering a given mail item. This newly-created file may be edited to change header fields and fill in the body.
SEND	sends mail items: posts selected items through the split-slot from a draft folder.
INC	receives mail items: takes delivery of selected items across the split-slot, incorporating them into a mailbox folder.

These commands, with a few enhancements and modifications appropriate to the CP/M environment, are functionally almost identical to their Unix MH counterparts.

CP/MH commands are invoked like any other CP/M commands such as ED, PIP, or DIR. Command line options are generally preceded by a dash (e.g. **-editor A:ED**), and may be abbreviated. Folder names are preceded by a plus (e.g. **+B:DRAFT**). Messages are identified by numbers or by the special names **first**, **last**, **current**, **next**, and **previous**.

An example of use of a CP/MH command is:

```
comp -edit a:ed -use last +b:draft -log
```

This particular example will edit the last-composed message (the **-use last** option) in the folder **DRAFT** on disk drive **B**: (the **+b:draft** option), using the standard CP/M editor ED on disk drive **A**: (the **-edit a:ed** option), and prompting the user when it is appropriate to change disks (the **-log** option).

All CP/MH commands have a **-help** option which displays all available options for the particular command invoked. Another common option is **-log** which permits the user to change (*relog*) diskettes after invoking a command, for purposes of selecting diskettes with message folders or with editor programs. This is particularly useful on single-drive systems or on systems with diskettes of low storage capacity.

THE PROFILE

If there are options commonly used with a particular CP/MH command, they may be entered in the user profile contained in the file called (naturally enough) **PROFILE**, which must exist on the same diskette on which CP/MH commands reside and from which the commands are invoked. A profile entry consists of a program name followed by a colon and the options to be used with that program, for example:

```
comp:  -editor A:VEDIT +B:outbox -log
repl:  -editor A:VEDIT -log
send:  +B:outbox
inc:  +B:inbox -log
```

Individual profile components are overridden by options given at the time of invocation (e.g. **-noedit** given on the command line will override the **-editor** profile component for a particular command).

The MZnet Split-Slot Mail Transfer System

The MZnet split-slot software implements a peer-to-peer communication protocol between a time-sharing host's MTA and a personal micro-computer (PC) UA. This MZnet protocol extends the UA/MTA/UA model of computer-based message systems (CBMS) to provide a split gateway function between individual PCs and the ZOTnet similar to the UCI ICS split Internet gateway described previously.

THE STRUCTURE OF THE SPLIT-SLOT

The MZnet Split Gateway consists of three distributed processing components:

- A PC running a UA (in MZnet, CP/MH) acting as the mail server.
- A mini/mainframe host running a full MTA (MMDF in MZnet) providing mail relay services.
- A communication protocol (a modified version of MMDF PhoneNet) to connect the two ends of the split-slot.

Although this combination may not be unique, the method by which the MZnet split-slot bonds these parts together uniquely deals with the problems of remote user agents. In addition to overcoming limited storage and processing capacities, remote user agents must deal with

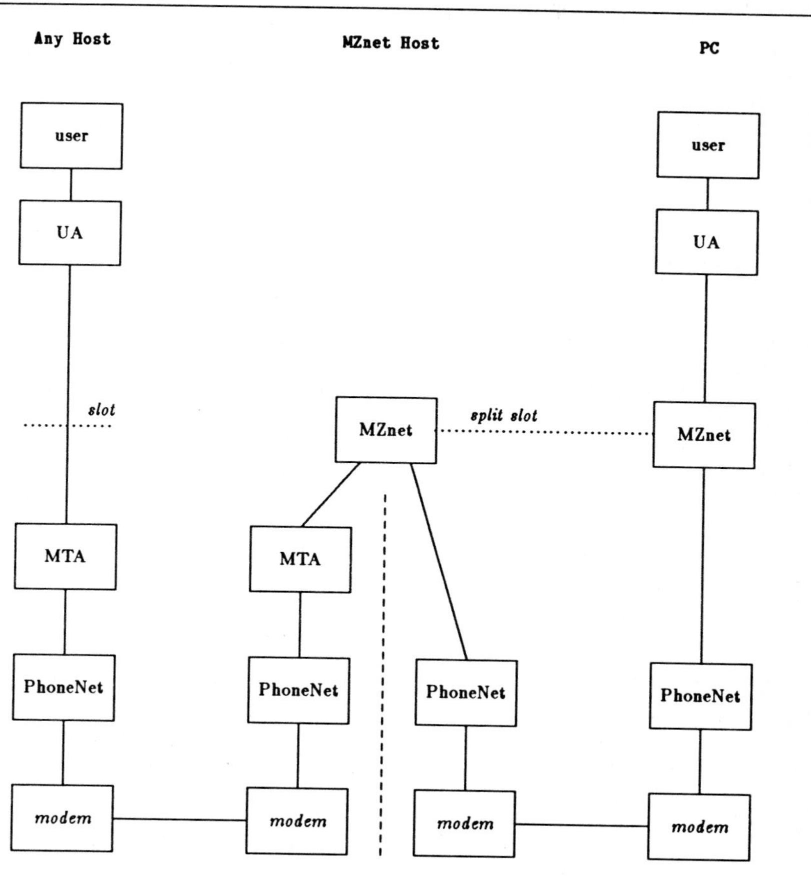

Figure 2. MZnet split-slot arrangement

noisy modem lines, mail software certification, and mail system security problems. The MZnet architecture appears to solve these problems with a clean mail interface for PCs.

THE MZNET MAIL SERVER

The split-slot mail server consists of a set of ***command packet*** programs run from the PC. These programs simply present commands through the PhoneNet communication protocol to the mail relay slave program on the host. Some basic commands are:

PostMail	posts mail drafts to MTA
GetMail	accepts mail from MTA
RemoteScan	displays information about waiting mail
Quit	drops connection between PC and Host

Each command has the form:

Command Request
Data Transmission
Command Termination

For example, the PostMail command is a small program that:

- initiates a command with the Mail Slave by sending the command name (PostMail) encoded within a PhoneNet packet;
- sends a series of PhoneNet packets that contain pieces of the mail item to be posted;
- finally sends a command termination signal to end the transaction without terminating the connection between host and PC.

THE MZNET CHANNEL TO MMDF

The MZnet Channel runs on the MTA host under the University of Delaware's MMDF (Version 1) and is responsible for both delivery of received mail to MZnet users, and posting of MZnet user-originated mail. The MMDF MZnet channel maintains a unique message queue for each registered MZnet user. As new mail items arrive, they are posted to the appropriate queues, where MZnet holds the mail items for pickup by their registered recipients.

To send or receive mail, the MZnet user must attach to the host, log into the public MZnet account, and identify (authenticate) himself. During the MZnet session with the host, the user has access only to that restricted set of functions provided by the MZnet split gateway protocol: he may request delivery of queued mail with GetMail, or post new mail with PostMail. Prior to taking delivery of queued mail, a survey of waiting mail also may be requested with RemoteScan to obtain message size information (among other data) to allow intelligent disposition of mail in the queue.

Hidden within these activities are issues of security and certification. To certify and establish the identity of the user, a second password is requested after logging into the public MZnet account. This certification procedure allows MZnet to certify the source of originated mail. A relatively secure environment is provided by MZnet, as it is the only interface to the host permitted to MZnet users (once beyond the public login procedure), and it offers only the severely restricted set of PhoneNet-encoded commands. Aside from security issues, using a single account to handle all MZnet users reduces demands on system resources.

THE MZNET-PHONENET PROTOCOL

A unique facet of the MZnet system derives from the PhoneNet File Transfer Protocol (FTP). PhoneNet FTP is a simple error-checked packet protocol which transfers ASCII plaintext. PhoneNet encodes any non-plaintext character (or any other character "forbidden" by the idiosyncrasies of the communicating systems) by mapping it onto an "accepted" character set. The accepted character set mapping is determined by a "negotiating" session between the two systems at the start of the PhoneNet session.

MZnet transfers all information (both commands and data) in PhoneNet packets to obtain error control. The MZnet-PhoneNet command FTP tolerates noise with a high degree of success, and in effect, connects both ends of the Split Slot together with a reliable set of virtual wires.

MZNET SESSION EXAMPLE

Here, a typical MZnet session is presented, with the UA commands issued from the PC side of the connection printed in a `typewriter` typeface, and the responses from the host side printed in an *italic* typeface. PhoneNet interactions are indented. The initial connection to the host is accomplished with the `term` program, which provides a simple terminal emulation function. The prompt of the PC for a UA command is "A⟩". Note that passwords are never echoed by the host system.

A⟩ **`term`**
login: **`mznet`**
password:
MZ-Password:
        PhoneNet packet negotiation
Connected.
        exit terminal mode
A⟩ **`send cur`**
        PostMail command
        message text packet transmission
        command terminator
A⟩ **`quit`**
        Quit command
Disconnecting.

Conclusions

The main conclusions of this paper are that small personal computer systems with dial-up phone connections constrain User Agent systems design in ways that require use of a *split-slot* interface between the UA and its supporting Mail Transfer Agent (MTA), and that this interface will best provide the required services if it has error controlled command and data transfer facilities, with interactive behavior.

It is also believed that a good design for the small PC UA is based on a very modular architecture, such as the Rand MH system, which has been used as a pattern for the MZnet UA.

By bringing these concepts together, we expect MZnet to provide reliable UA/MTA service to a distributed set of small personal computers, to match the quality of service that is normally only available from larger mainframe host systems with co-resident UA/MTA pairs.

REFERENCES

[1] SRI-NIC, ARPANET Directory, Network Information Center, SRI International, Menlo Park, California (November 1980).

[2] Comer, D., A Computer Science Research Network CSNET: A History and Status Report, Communications of the ACM, volume 26, number 10 (October 1983) 747-753.

[3] Emerson, S. L., USENET: A Bulletin Board for Unix Users. BYTE, volume 8, number 10 (October 1983) 219-236.

[4] Vittal, J., MSG: A Simple Message System, in: Uhlig (editor), Proceedings of the IFIP TC-6 International Symposium on Computer Message Systems (North-Holland, April 1981).

[5] Deutsch, D., Design of a Message Format Standard, in: Uhlig (editor), Proceedings of the IFIP TC-6 International Symposium on Computer Message Systems (North-Holland, April 1981).

[6] v.Bochmann, G. and Pickens, J. R., A Methodology for the Specification of a Message Transport System, in: Uhlig (editor), Proceedings of the IFIP TC-6 International Symposium on Computer Message Systems (North-Holland, April 1981).

[7] Kerr, I. H., Interconnection of Electronic Mail Systems, in: Uhlig (editor), Proceedings of the IFIP TC-6 International Symposium on Computer Message Systems (North-Holland, April 1981).

[8] Crocker, D., Standard for the Format of ARPA Internet Text Messages (RFC 822) Network Information Center, SRI International, Menlo Park, California (August 1982).

[9] NBS, Message Format for Computer-Based Message Systems, U.S. National Bureau of Standards FIPS Publication 98 (March 1983).

[10] CCITT Study Group VII/5, Draft Recommendation X.MHS1: Message Handling Systems: System Model—Service Elements (version 2), Technical Report, International Telegraph and Telephone Consultative Committee (CCITT) (December 1982).

[11] Rose, M., Low Tech Connections into the ARPA Internet: The RawPacket Split-Gateway, University of California Irvine Techical Report number 216 (February 1984).

[12] Crocker, D., Szurkowski, E., Farber, D. J., An Internet Memo Distribution Facility—MMDF, Proceedings of the Sixth IEEE Data Communications Symposium (November 1979).

[13] Rose, M., The ZOTnet—A Local Area Mailing Network, University of California Irvine Technical Report number 200 (January 1983).

[14] CSNET-CIC, Focus on the University of California, Irvine, CSNET News 2, Bolt, Beranek, and Newman, Cambridge, Massachusetts (October 1983).

[15] Rose, M., Achieving Interoperability Between Two Domains—Connecting the ZOTnet and UUCP Computer Mail Networks, University of California Irvine Technical Report number 201 (January 1983).

[16] Rose, M., Proposed Standard for Message Munging (RFC 886), Network Information Center, SRI International, Menlo Park, California (December 1983).

[17] Borden, B. S., Gaines, R. S., and Shapiro, N.Z., The Rand MH Message Handling System: User's Manual (Rand Corporation, March 1983).

Computer-Based Message Services
H.T. Smith (Editor)
Elsevier Science Publishers B.V. (North-Holland)

A GENERAL PURPOSE MESSAGE GATEWAY ARCHITECTURE

Julian Davies and Reg Quinton

Department of Computer Science
University of Western Ontario
London, Ontario, CANADA N6A 5B7

MLNET is a message-forwarding gateway system which can interface between many different kinds of mail system. We describe the organization of the MLNET processor. It maintains distinct envelope files in its spool areas to accompany the messages. We show how this permits flexibility in interfacing with a great variety of mail systems.

Keywords: Computer based message systems; electronic mail; envelopes; gateways; message transfer services; MLNET

1. INTRODUCTION

MLNET is a system designed to forward mail messages between users on different computer systems. It is designed specifically to permit communication in a non-invasive manner with a diversity of computers. That is to say, MLNET is intended to be operable without forcing a major software effort on each computer connected to the network controller.

The original design for MLNET [1,2] was based on the assumptions that the various computing systems on the network:

(1) have message programs for local use;

(2) probably do not have any support in the operating system for network operations;

(3) may not have any support in the mail program for network functions or "remote users"; and

(4) can be accessed through an interactive asynchronous terminal line, either locally or remotely (perhaps through a network).

A prototype system was coded in Summer 1983, but could not be run regularly because of hardware deficiencies. The hardware situation has improved (as of September 1983) and the software has been reconstructed in Autumn 1983 by the second author.

Our design makes it possible for the gateway processor to poll the various systems in MLNET, logging in as an interactive user, and (if necessary) using the standard mail utility on that system to pick up and deliver messages. This process is governed by scripts which define and control the interactive conversation between the gateway and the target system. The script mechanism models the conversation with the target machine with a kind of finite-state automaton, which is adequate for our purposes. In this design we can easily add new hosts to the network by defining the scripts which control the user dialogues. Figure 1 shows the general network topology.

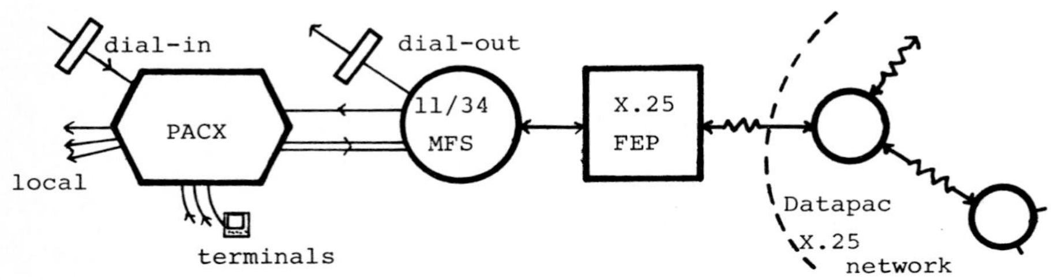

MLNET Network Topology
Figure 1

In the current version of MLNET (revisions are ongoing at the time of writing) the concept of the envelope has been made explicit. In bringing this concept to the foreground, it turns out to be possible to make the gateway much more flexible and capable of connecting to a variety of message systems (not just stand-alone interactive hosts). In particular, it is possible to interface with systems which use a distinct Transfer Layer Protocol, without any major revisions to the existing system. Examples include EAN[3] which conforms with the emerging CCITT P1 and P2 protocols [4-7], and systems using the ARPAnet Simple Mail Transfer protocol [8] or other message transfer protocols.

The "envelope" concept enables messages received through any of these channels to be handled in a uniform manner, and relayed to other systems in the appropriate way, because the Transfer Layer transactions can be converted directly to and from the envelope structure built in this system. The envelope structure we use is simple enough that this kind of interface can be effected with minimum effort.

2. ENVELOPES

The model developed within IFIP WG 6.5 for computer based message systems distinguishes the User Agent layer from the Message Transfer layer (both being sublayers of the Applications Layer in the model for Open Systems Interconnection.) Figure 2 shows this layering. This model has been adopted by ISO and CCITT, with minor modifications [4,9]. In our system, as outlined above, this distinction also proves useful.

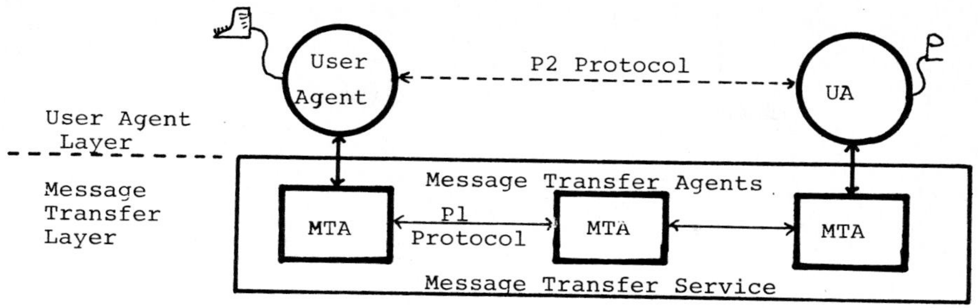

Layered Model for Message Handling
Figure 2

The model also distinguishes between a message and its envelope. The message is an object of the User Agent layer, while the envelope is the property of the message transfer layer, required for addressing and forwarding the message. The message itself is now considered by CCITT to come in two basic forms, shown in Figure 3:

(a) a user message with various header fields, and the message text or a body, possibly structured; or

(b) a notification (typically of delivery or non-delivery) which was presumably not generated within the User Agent layer.

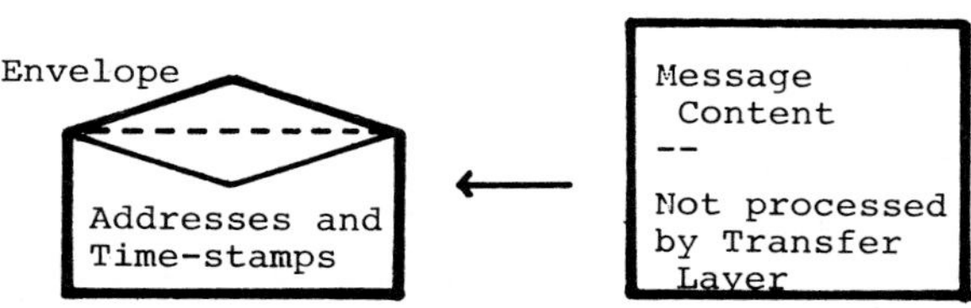

3(a) Message and Envelope

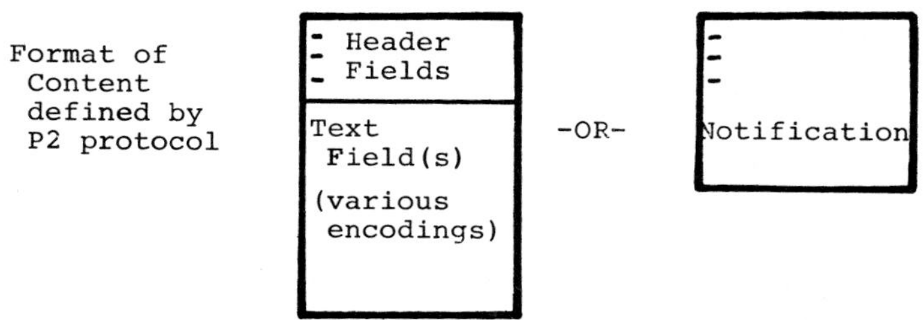

3(b) Types of Message Content

Message Structures
Figure 3

Our system supports both forms of messages, and requires only a minimal structure in user messages. We minimise the structures needed in messages because we wish to interface with a diversity of other message systems.

The envelope is manipulated by message transfer agents. It contains identification of the originator and of recipients for the message, and may collect time-stamps as the message passes through the system. Thus, the transfer agents should not need to examine the message itself (which might have been encrypted) in order to perform their functions.

Semantically, in this model, there is likely to be some redundancy between the information in the envelope and the information in the message header. However, this is comparable to the fact that with ordinary letters, the names and addresses of both sender and receiver often appear on the outside of the envelope and also on the letterhead within. The date of posting may also appear in both places, (though one is put inside by the sender and the other outside by the mail system). Practice in these respects varies somewhat from country to country. At any rate, such duplication of information is harmless, and is an asset when it simplifies the processing.

When we examine existing computer message systems, we find that the distinction between envelope and message is often unclear. In most cases, there is no distinction made between the envelope and the header of the message. This is understandable in single-computer mail systems, where the transfer layer (which needs envelopes) is nonexistent or trivial. However, it can make for some implementation obstacles when trying to integrate such systems into a network, for we have to code specialized procedures to analyse each separate message format.

Another problem, of course, arises over the questions of naming and addressing, which have occupied so much time recently in the Systems Environment subgroups of WG 6.5 [10]

3. THE MLNET GATEWAY

MLNET, as a network of diverse systems, has a gateway processor, also known as the MFS (Message Forwarding System). The MFS makes connections with a number of other systems, mostly (though not necessarily) by polling them--calling them interactively. The MFS regards itself as being at the centre of a star network, though of course the systems sometimes are also connected to other networks and may have direct or alternative connections with each other. The programming effort for MLNET is concentrated on the central node, the gateway, to speed development of the network.

The MFS maintains a set of spool areas, one for each system it contacts. Each spool area may contain several messages. (In the Unix(TM) code, each spool area is a directory, and each message is placed in a file in that directory.) Each MLNET host has its own spool area, and we anticipate also having distinct spool areas for each other network for which MLNET knows of a gateway.

The initial design for MLNET [1] specifies that the MFS has its own mail box for messages on each system it contacts. This mailbox is organized according to the local conventions, and no attempt is made to standardize that aspect. The messages that appear in MLNET's mailbox are assumed to be intended for recipients on other systems.

The MFS will pick up its mail at a system, and determine where to deliver those messages. As stated earlier, MLNET is 'non-invasive', and cannot assume that the local system has provisions for network mail. In particular, the local system need not support any concept of an 'envelope'.

The solution we have adopted to the question of defining envelopes, copes, at least for the interim, by requiring the envelope to appear in the message, in a simple standard format. The envelope for a message, in the simplest case, is one line of text in the message, in the format:

>> <recipient-id> ; <sender-id>

e.g.

>> pdqbach@usndakota; julian davies@uwo-hobbit

Both the <recipient-id> and the <sender-id> are parsed into a user and a host name. A variety of forms is recognised by the MFS for the user identifications. The forms we accept are those used in the Arpanet, Usenet, and other networks we have met. For instance, the above could have been given equivalently as:

>> usndakota!pdqbach ; uwo-hobbit julian davies

where a "!" or a blank may separate a host name from a user name (when no "@" is present). The "!" is a Usenet form, while "@" is an Arpanet separator.

A line in any of these formats is called a routing line. It may be placed within the message automatically by the originating mail program, or it can be typed in manually by the user if necessary. (This makes it possible, if a little cumbersome, to use MLNET even when the local mail program has no special code for it.)

It will be recognized immediately that the routing line is de facto the envelope. That it appears within the message rather than somehow prefacing it is an incidental curiosity. In our system it is permissible to supply several routing lines consecutively, and the whole group supplies the 'envelope' for MLNET. This allows for a single message to be routed to several different persons at (possibly different) hosts.

The user identifications, as described, comprise a host identifier and a user name for that host. This scheme is primitive, but is unavoidable when dealing with systems that do not possess any network-oriented user directories. These identifications should be regarded essentially as user addresses (machine oriented); user names will be accepted in their place when software support is available for a directory service. Although this addressing scheme may appear to be primitive, it has the virtue of making it straightforward to implement gateways to other systems.

As another example, the address "jim@abc-host.CRNET" is parsed as "jim@abc-host" at 'host' (actually network) CRNET. This is then further analyzed to identify a user "jim" on host "abc-host" on the CRNET network.

4. ROUTING IN THE GATEWAY

In our original design for MLNET, the gateway reads messages from a host, and scans them looking for a valid routing line (the envelope). From the routing line, the destination host and userid can be determined. The message (or a copy of it) is then placed in the output spool area for that host. When the message is delivered, the routing line will be reexamined to obtain the userid concerned, and the message can then be posted right to that user.

In the original design, to avoid having to search the whole message again for the routing line, when delivery was made, that line was prepended to the message when it was copied to the requisite spool area. (The current mechanism is described below.)

A couple of other details should be mentioned. The routing line should contain the identity of the originator. This permits a notification to be sent back if the message could not be delivered. The routing line is also permitted to contain flags, as in

>> sclaus@n-pole; rudolph@finland; registered Urgent

The Registered flag causes the MFS to return a notification when (if) the message has been successfully relayed to the destination system. The Urgent flag may expedite forwarding by the MFS. The MFS will also communicate such flags to the receiving system if their functions are supported there. When delivery fails, or if the message is 'registered', a notification can be generated in the gateway which incorporates the responses given by the receiving host.

The Mail program for the DECsystem-10 [11] recognises "external" user addresses, and automatically delivers copies of messages to the MFS's mail box when appropriate, with routing lines generated automatically. It also includes the flags in the routing lines when necessary. This feature makes the DEC-10 mail much more convenient for network mail than would otherwise be the case. Nevertheless, MLNET can be used by systems which have not incorporated those improvements.

5. GATEWAY ENVELOPES

The system described above proved somewhat unsatisfactory, however, and has now been modified. That is to say, just copying the routing line (as supplied in the message) to the start of the copy in the spool area has turned out to be inflexible, especially in dealing with messages containing several routing lines.

The revised implementation keeps the 'envelope' information for the message in a separate file in the spooling area. The mechanism is as follows. When a message is received at the MFS, it is assigned a unique sequence number for internal identification. When the routing line is analysed, the message is put into the spool area, and a separate envelope file is created to go with it.

This envelope file contains various pieces of control information needed by the MFS for control or accounting. The message sequence number, date of reception, size, special flags, originator and the recipient are recorded in the file in a standard structure. Figure 4 shows the format and a sample envelope file.

```
version ; id ; date
sender-spec ; flags
recipient
 blank  another-recipient
  ...
```

4(a) Format of Envelope File

```
A;000062;1983-10-13 16:20:23-4:00
uwo-cs34%reggers;Registered
tom
 dick
 harry
```

4(b) Example Envelope File

The Envelope File Format
Figure 4

This use of a separate file turns out to solve several problems. First, it accommodates messages with multiple routing lines and therefore multiple recipients. It is possible that several of these recipients are actually on the same host, and that one copy of the message can be relayed for all of them. This situation is detected when the system is about to add the message to a spool area. The envelope file for the last message written to that spool area is examined to see whether it has the same sequence number. If it has, the new recipient name is merely added to the envelope file. (The control script will communicate the multiple names to the receiving system in the appropriate manner.)

For reasons of internal organization, when a message is being routed to users on several different hosts (or networks), we build a separate envelope for each destination, which contains the relevant user names for that host (or network).

Another problem solved by the use of envelope files is that the system is no longer tied to a specific format for routing lines, or even to the presence of routing lines as such. It is intended that the envelope file be constructed, gathering the information needed from where it is available. In a user-friendly system it should not be necessary for users to be concerned with providing routing lines or envelopes.

In particular, if the message comes from a Unix or Usenet or Arpanet mailer, it will contain header lines identifying the originator and to whom it is bound. This is also true for some other similar mail programs and networks. Alternatively, if the message comes from EAN or any other CCITT-compatible system, the envelope can be built using data received during the Transfer Level protocol interactions [5]. Similarly with receipt of messages from a SMPT channel [8]. We expect to implement these mechanisms soon.

The separate envelope file will also show its value when the message is to be relayed down a P1- or P3-protocol channel, or an SMTP channel, etc. [8]. The protocol transactions for the relaying can be driven from the envelope file content, whichever protocol is needed. We plan to build software for these functions in the near future.

The envelope file mechanism allows for gradual improvement of the less capable message systems in MLNET. The strategy in the gateway is to build an envelope file from the Transfer Level protocol if such a distinct protocol was used. Otherwise, the message header will be analysed to get the information required. This will be adequate if the originating mailer has some networking capability, and builds headers according to Arpanet RFC-733 for instance [13], or in some other agreed format. These are systems where the envelope information is mixed in with the header fields.

Lastly, if the information for the envelope was not available from either of these sources, the message will be scanned for routing lines, which are analysed as described earlier. If all these fail, the message is undeliverable, and will be discarded. The originator will be notified if he or she can be identified from the message header.

Message Header Transformation

As part of these functions, we are also arranging to reformat messages from certain hosts to assist network users. Some systems put headers on their messages which are text, but not in the common format (RFC-733) used by many other systems. We have installed code which rebuilds the headers of message coming from these systems, using the routing lines if necessary, and constructing an RFC-733 style header. This permits users on other systems to reply to such messages - where the User Agent uses RFC-733 style headers.

To match this, we also have sometimes to convert a header into a non-RFC-733 format, when the message is delivered to a User Agent which expects a different format. Again, the purpose of this, when done, is to enable users to use the existing REPLY or ANSWER command in their user agent, if possible, to reply to messages originating elsewhere in the network.

These tranformations are being made, for instance, (a) to Unix mail, which is "not quite" RFC-733 in its From line, and (b) to messages from VAX/VMS mail (which is an unsophisticated utility).

This transformation of headers will also of course apply to conversions of messages to and from the format defined in X.420 [6].

The trickiest problem encountered with this reformatting of headers, however, also emerged with the envelope construction, and concerns the formats of addresses, and possible specification of routes. Usenet is a primary source of this problem, because of incoherent mail software within that network, and a historical disregard for the distinction between addressing and routing specifications. Other gateways to the Usenet have similar problems. We are attempting, so far as possible, to use domain-oriented addresses in the format name@site.domain in MLNET, for the time being.

6. FUTURE DEVELOPMENTS

We have indicated the likely course of future developments above. The envelope files used within the gateway will increasingly be built using information taken from message headers or from the transfer layer protocol communications.

We expect at some stage to reformat the envelope files to use the same data structure encodings as used in the CCITT envelopes, assuming that this standard will become widespread. In that case, we will be translating routing lines and header lines in messages from other systems. At some stage, perhaps, the messages themselves will be stored internally in a CCITT format; that will be necessary when handling messages containing arbitrary data encodings rather than plain IA5 text.

We plan to extend the mechanisms of this message system gateway to handle messages for conferencing and 'bulletin board' systems.

We expect that network-wide user directory services will become available in future. The MLNET processor will be able to contact the Directory Servers and translate user names on behalf of host systems which cannot handle the DS protocol (perhaps because they lack the network access paths).

7. CONCLUSIONS

We believe we have in MLNET a practical solution to the currently serious problem of a diversity of message systems and networks. Our separation of message text and envelope processing is consistent with the IFIP/CCITT/ISO model for message handling, and provides a uniform structure to handle the enormous variation in message system capabilities. And, in particular, it demonstrates a practical solution to our goal of linking mail programs that were not built to 'know about' the networks. MLNET is now in use at the University of Western Ontario (November 1983) and is linking systems at other places within Canada during 1984 using Datapac connections as well as Usenet telephone links.

The use of message envelope files provides a basis for uniform treatment of messages passing through a message gateway system. Envelope files can be constructed and used within the gateway even though many of the message systems connected to the gateway do not support a mechanism for message envelopes. Where message envelopes are used by the connected systems, protocol translations produce the envelopes needed in each system including the gateway.

References

[1] D J M Davies, Design Plan for MLNET: a computer system for linking Canadian University Computers. CCNG Report E-105, University of Waterloo (May 1982).

[2] D J M Davies, Overview of MLNET. Report No. CS-95, Dept of Computer Science, University of Western Ontario (August 1982).

[3] G W Neufeld, Design of the EAN Messaging System. Proc. CIPS Conference 1983, Ottawa, (May 1983) 144-149.

[4] CCITT; Draft Recommendation X.400: Message Handling Systems: System Model--Service Elements. CCITT, (Geneva, November 1983).

[5] CCITT; Draft Recommendation X.411: Message handling Systems: Message Transfer Layer. CCITT, (Geneva, November 1983).

[6] CCITT; Draft Recommendation X.420: Message Handling Systems: Interpersonal Messaging User Agent Layer. CCITT, (Geneva, November 1983).

[7] CCITT; Draft Recommendation X.410: Message Handling Systems: Remote Operations and Reliable Transfer Service. CCITT, (Geneva, November 1983).

[8] J B Postel, Simple Mail Transfer Protocol. ARPAnet RFC-788. Information Sciences Inst. University of S. California, (November 1981).

[9] D D Redell & J E White; Interconnecting Electronic Mail Systems. Computer, 16, 9, (September 1983) 55-63.

[10] I Cunningham; Message Handling Systems and Protocols. Proc. IEEE, 71, 12 (December 1983) 1425-1430.

[11] IFIP WG6.5; Naming, Addressing and Directory Services for Message Handling Systems. Version 3 (Ed. J E White), IFIP (February 1983).

[12] D J M Davies; Mail User's Manual--Mail Version 4. Report No. CS100, University of Western Ontario (January 1983).

[13] Crocker et al; Standard for the Format of ARPA Network Text Messages. ARPAnet RFC-733, NIC-41952 (November 1977).

PART 8:

TELETEX SYSTEMS

Computer-Based Message Services
H.T. Smith (Editor)
Elsevier Science Publishers B.V. (North-Holland)

A TELETEX BASED MESSAGE HANDLING SERVER

P.A.Carruthers **A.A.Wood**

British Telecommunications,
System Evolution and Standards Dept.
Newcastle System Software Engineering Centre
Newcastle Upon Tyne

The existing CCITT standards for the Teletex service do not cover all aspects of person to person message transfer and a further range of Message Handling System (MHS) standards are emerging to cover this area of communication.

This paper describes the design and implementation of a system supporting full interpersonal message transfer, based on the Teletex service. The system is intended to provide access to the Teletex service for users of a Local Area Network (LAN), but will also allow documents to be routed directly into a user's mail box using MHS action elements. Other action elements are also possible, such as notification of receipt.

The implications of the MHS standards work for such systems is considered, and a number of issues identified.

1. BACKGROUND

In 1981 British Telecom began the process of establishing System Software Engineering Centres (SSEC) in London, Belfast, Ipswich and Newcastle. It was recognised at their inception that good communications were essential for them to inter-relate and function successfully. Each centre was therefore equipped with a Local Area Network (LAN) to provide a flexible software development environment together with Office Automation facilties.

Several projects were initiated by Software Standards and Services Division (SES3) in 1982 to provide specialist servers for the LANs in order to generate a comprehensive private data communications network. One of the most significant of these projects was the provision of a Server allowing access to the new Telematic Service Teletex which would offer interpersonal electronic messaging facilities. This work was undertaken at the Newcastle SSEC and is described in this paper.

2. REQUIREMENTS

The major requirements of the Mail Server were identified at the start of the project as :

2.1 Provision of access via PSTN or PSS to Teletex services (Ref 6) meeting the full requirements of a Teletex installation.

2.2 The capablity of connection to a LAN (either Ethernet or Broadband) giving terminal access concentration.

2.3 To allow access from a wide range of terminal types and give best possible default rendition of the Teletex character set.

2.4 Provision of interpersonal messaging and document delivery (to an individual mailbox) for both internal mail, and external mail between similar servers.

2.5 Provision of security facilities to prevent unauthorised mail access.

2.6 A user friendly interface incorporating editing facilities for document preparation.

2.7 Provision of document filing and retrieval facilities.

2.8 A directory facility for users' names and addresses.

2.9 The ability to accept documents prepared on intelligent terminals or word processors.

The facilities implemented in the current version of the server are explained more fully in Section 4 .

It was obvious from the above requirements that an additional range of application level facilities (particularly a method for communicating, naming, addressing and other document reference information), was required above the Teletex session and presentation levels.

Provision of these facilities grafted onto the Teletex protocols realises a very powerful message/document transfer system capable of communicating directly with the emerging range of telematic terminals.

In defining these messaging and other application facility enhancements account had to be taken of proposed enhancements by CCITT SGVII to the Teletex S series recommendations and work on messaging services by IFIP, CCITT SGVII, ISO, and ECMA (Ref 1, 5, 9 & 10); a longer term aim is the ability of the TMS to communicate with other publicly and privately provided messaging systems.

3. SYSTEM CONCEPTS

Essentially the TMS is a direct messaging system operating from the store of one mail server to the store of a distant mail server or Teletex terminal.

Figure 1 shows the inter-connection of several TMS mail servers and telematic terminals via PSTN or PSS. The dotted box shows proposed future access to a public mail box/store and forward facility supporting Teletex access.

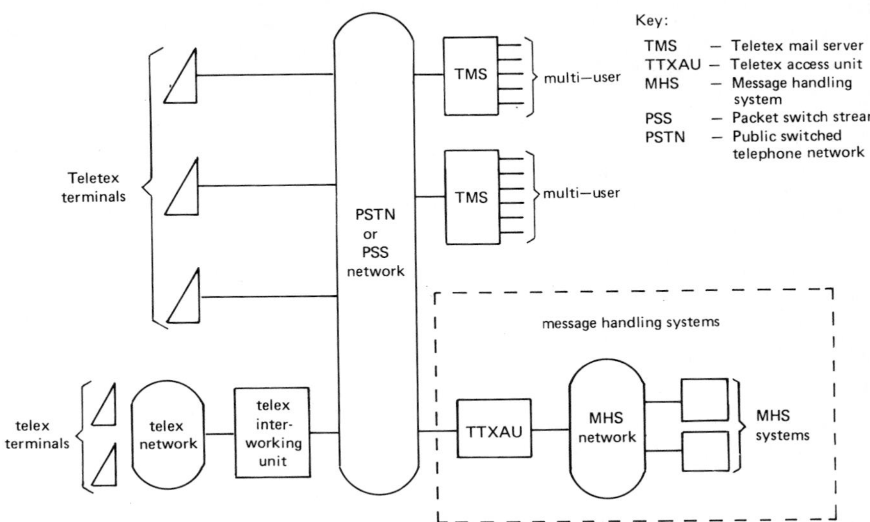

Figure 1 TMS connection to Teletex and other services

Documents and messages are generated by users accessing the local mail server via a wide range of terminal devices used for a variety of other purposes, possibly connected via a LAN or PABX as in Figure 2. Internal mail is stored and distributed by the local server. External mail is either enveloped using a Teletex control document and forwarded to a distant mail server, or alternatively envelope information is included as part of the text document which is forwarded to a Teletex terminal. Incoming mail with envelope information is placed in the appropiate mail box, whereas mail without envelope information, (mail from basic Teletex terminals) is routed to an operator mail box for manual sorting.

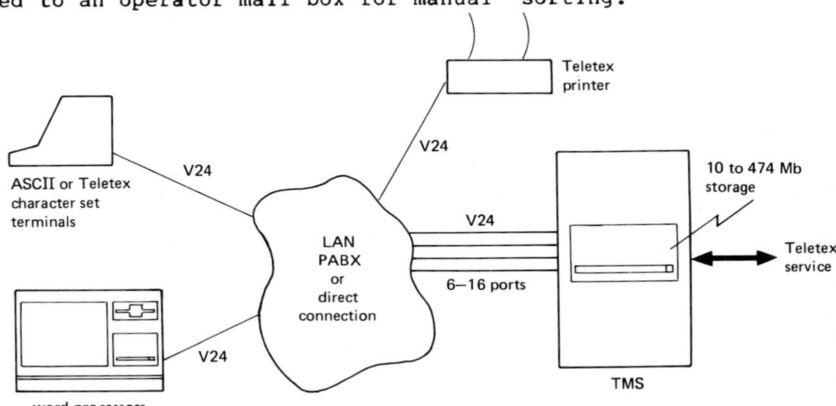

Figure 2 Teletex mail system schematic

4. USER FACILITIES

The TMS system provides the following basic user facilities:

4.1 Document Creation - The system uses a set of directories to allow the creation of documents for sending to known addressees, or unknown addressees at known locations. These directories can be bypassed for sending to unknown locations. The full Teletex character set can be generated from any ASCII terminal using ASCII character sequences.

The text input is monitored for invalid characters, line lengths, or combinations of characters and diacriticals, to prevent the preparation of documents unsuitable for sending via Teletex. A mode is available to provide similar checking on documents to be sent to telex.

4.2 Sending and Receiving Documents - The system maintains queues of documents to be sent, allowing three priority levels. The progress of a document can be monitored by inspection of the terminal log or the status information associated with the document. A printed copy suitable for posting is automatically produced if Teletex transmission is not possible. When the remote location is known to be a compatable TMS system the addressing information is sent as a control document, with the text in a separate Teletex document. The control document carries the names and Terminal ID's of the originator and all addressees on the circulation list in a fixed text format. A TMS system receiving an appropriate control document in association with a normal document will use the addressing information to automatically route that document directly into the addressee's mail box. Any Teletex documents received without an associated control document will be placed in the system operator's mail box for manual sorting and forwarding.

4.3 Document Presentation - On an ASCII terminal, the system will display documents using an approximate rendition using video attributes to indicate, for example, the presence of diacritical marks. The system supports a Teletex printer capable of reproducing the full Teletex character set and control sequences.

4.4 Forwarding and Re-Distributing Documents - The system has been designed to prevent the malicious modification of a document after it has been sent or received, whilst allowing flexible document handling. This is achieved by removing all status information, such as the time and date of delivery, when the document is modified. For example, if the address list for a document is replaced by a new address list, all status information recording the original delivery times will also be removed. Alternativly documents may be annotated and forwarded to a new address list, preserving all of the original addressing and status information.

4.5 Filing and Selection of Documents - The system allows the user to have named files, each containing a number of documents. By default each user will have files named Infile, where incoming documents are stored, and Outfile, where outgoing documents are created. Documents can be copied from one named file into another, allowing documents to be grouped together. Commands are provided for scanning through files for documents matching particular search criteria, eg Sending Date, Subject Text, or an addressee name.

5. HARDWARE

The system is based on the Multibus distributed processing architecture, incorporating the following boards as represented in Figure 3:

a) MC68000 Processor Board - Providing user interface and file management facilities.

b) Intel 8086 Processor Board - Providing transport service and Teletex high level protocols.

c) X25 Board - Providing X25 protocols for the Intel 8086 board.

d) Disk Controller - Supporting up to four disks, each with a capacity of 10M bytes to 474M bytes.

e) Serial Interface Boards - Each supporting 6 or 8 Terminals depending on hardware configuration.

6. SOFTWARE MODULES

Figure 3 also shows the main software modules comprising the system, together with the data paths between the processes. Each facility is allocated to a single process, and data is transfered between processes using a remote procedure call mechanism. The software modules are as follows:

6.1 Transport Service - drives the X25 board, providing call setup and error free transmission.

6.2 Teletex High Level Protocol Process - uses the communications link provided by the transport service to negotiate terminal capabilities, and to transfer and acknowledge Teletex pages. The pages are buffered by this process, a page at a time.

6.3 Transfer Process - drives the Teletex protocol process, supplying pages from documents queued for transmission, and storing received pages.

6.4 File Management Process - manages all files and queues of documents. The process allows documents to be shared between users, but prevents two users from simultaneously modifying the files. Queues of documents are maintained for transmission or printing. This process also maintains central directories of addressee names and locations.

6.5 Print Process - takes documents from the file management process print queues, and performs any convertion of control sequences needed to drive the printer used.

6.6 User Process - provides the user interface, parsing commands and generating the necessary file manager calls. This process also has facilities for supporting ASCII terminals by translating Teletex characters for display as highlighted ASCII, and translating special ASCII character sequences into Teletex characters.

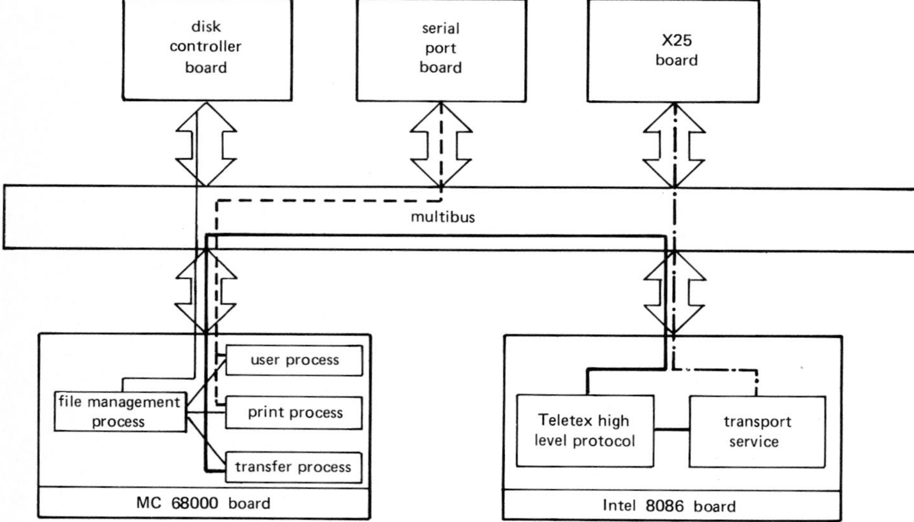

Figure 3 Teletex mail system internal interfaces

7. SOFTWARE MODULE INTERFACES

The interfaces between modules are implemented using a remote procedure call technique, which allows a great deal of flexibility in the design. For example, the command driven user process may be replaced by a menu driven interface without any modification to the other modules; in fact, it is possible to run the system with some users working to a command interface and others with menus.

The remote procedure calls used for accessing the facilities of other processes were each designed to be a repeatable action, allowing further distribution of the software modules into physically distinct hardware connected by Local Area Network technology. It was envisaged at the design stage that a future system could consist of a number of servers on a LAN, as follows:

a) A file server running the file management process software.

b) A print server running the print process software.

c) A Teletex interface unit consisiting of the transfer and Teletex protocol processes.

d) A number of sophisticated user workstations, each running a copy of the user process software.

In the current implementation of the system, these procedure calls use a number of first-in-first-out buffers, or pipes, to transfer information between processes. Data identifying the function required and the parameters for that function call are placed into the pipe to the appropriate process, the process which reads the data executes the function and places the results into the return pipe.

8. FILE STRUCTURES

The file structure in the mail system has been designed to allow efficient sharing of documents between many users. Each user may have a number of named files, each of which may contain pointers to many documents, as shown in Figure 4. A document is identified by the name of the file and the number of the entry in that file. When a document is sent to another user, or copied into another file, the file management process simply creates another pointer in the appropriate file. Additional information is stored in the user's file along with the pointer, such as whether or not the document has been sent or read. This information is used, for example, to prevent the modification of documents which have been received.

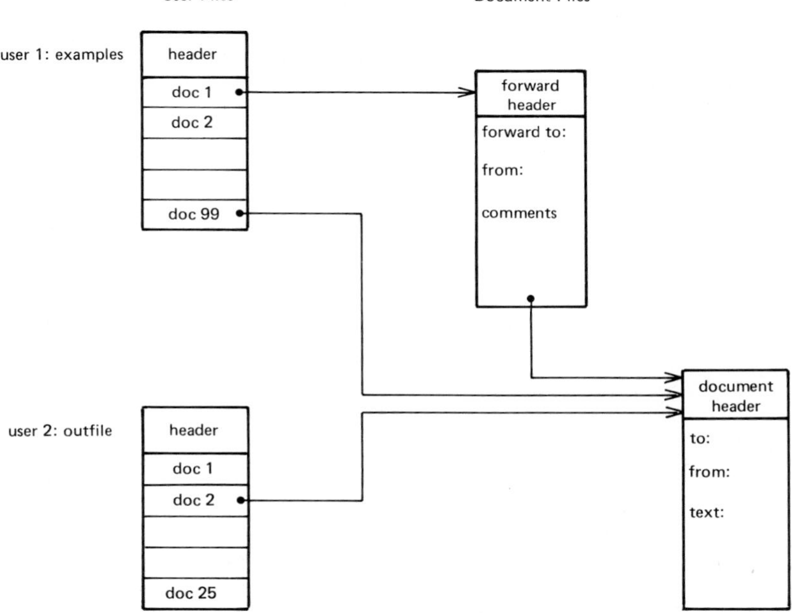

Figure 4 TMS file structure

The documents consist of some header information, such as pointers to various fields in the document, followed by the actual text of the document. The following fields are stored:

* To:
* Copies To:
* From:
* Sent By:
* Subject:
* Text:

The "From" and "Sent By" fields are used to allow the possibility of the document being sent by someone other than the author. The from field is automatically filled with the author's name by the user process when a document is created, to avoid any possibility of fraud. If the sender is not the same as the author, then the "Sent by" field is automatically filled and the author is added to the distribution list, to ensure that he receives a copy of the document.

Forwarded documents are stored in a special type of document file, which only contains the forwarding information and a pointer to the original document, as shown in Figure 4. The file manager automatically chains the forwarded and original document files together when a process reads the document. There is no restriction on the number of times a document may be forwarded. A forwarded document contains the following fields:

* Forwarded To:
* Forwarded Copies To:
* Forwarded From:
* Forwarded By:
* Comments:

9. INTEL 8Ø86 BOARD INTERFACE

The Teletex protocols were implemented in CHILL (Ref 8) to run on an Intel 8Ø86 processor.

Communications between the Intel 8Ø86 and MC68ØØØ is via 128K of dual ported RAM which can be addressed from the MC68ØØØ or the Intel 8Ø86. This memory contains a number of flags for synchronising data transfers between the processors, and a buffer area used for the storage of pages being transfered. A record containing information on the page number, size and starting address in the buffer area is associated with each page and is held with the flags.

When either the Intel 8Ø86 or MC68ØØØ wishes to transfer a document it sets a general flag to request permission to control the buffer area. The other processor will set its own general flag to indicate that it has relinquished control of the shared memory and transfers may begin. The controlling processor may then place a document, a page at a time, into the buffer area and set up the appropriate page record and flag to indicate that the page is ready for transfer. The completion of the transfer is acknowledged using another flag, at which point that page record may be reused. The present system uses three page records, corresponding to the Teletex window size (Ref 7). When all pages of the document have been transferred, the general flag is reset to indicate that the board is in the idle state.

1Ø. MESSAGE HANDLING MODEL PROTOCOLS

The corner-stone of the server is the use of Teletex protocols for document transfer and presentation. The Teletex recommendations however do not address person to person messaging. In terms of the CCITT X2ØØ or ISO layered models Teletex covers up to level 6, the presentation level.

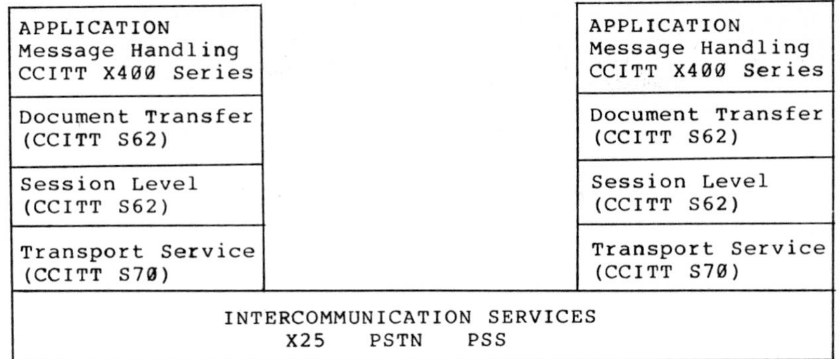

Interpersonal messaging user agent and message transfer facilities reside at level 7. To define the function of the server reference was made to CCITT and IFIP messaging models (Ref 1). One set of draft CCITT recomendations of particular relevance to the server are the X400 series which define all aspects of an interpersonal messaging service. They cover access to messaging systems from a wide variety of devices.

Fig 5 shows the TMS System defined in the terms of the message handling model (Ref 1).

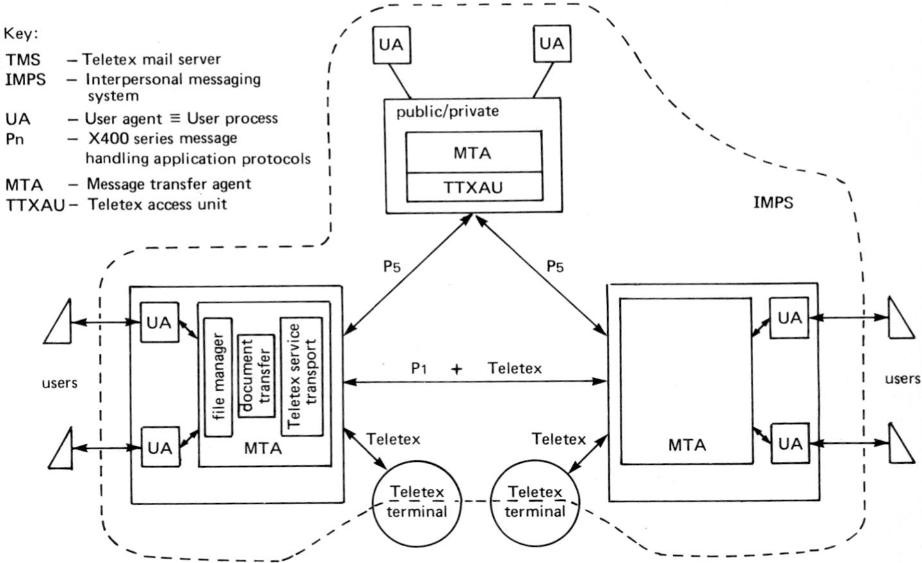

Figure 5 TMS message handling system model

For internal mail operation TMS acts as a single entity. Messages are from one user to another on the same TMS device, via the file management process, which performs all the functions of a Message Transfer Agent (MTA). In this case the Message Transfer Layer (MTL) recommendations do not apply as all messages are local to one device. An internal protocol is used for UA-MTA communication, there is no need for the P3 protocol. The Teletex service is not used.

For external mail operation TMS is part of a global Message Handling System (MHS). Messages are from a user on one TMS device to a user on a different TMS device. This is achieved via the file management and document transfer process in each device. The Teletex service is used to communicate between cooperating mail systems, and Teletex control documents are used to carry the MHS action elements. The CCITT X411 (P1) protocols (Ref 2) were identified as being the most appropriate for communication between TMS systems, but it is recognised that any future MHS Network is unlikely to use Teletex for the lower level session and presentation (document) protocols. It may therefore be necessary to implement CCITT X430 (P5) protocol (Ref 4) to access a Teletex Access Unit (TTXAU) in order to communicate with any future MHS network, regardless of the fact the MHS network will use P1 protocols for MTA to MTA communication.

The current mail server implementation does not fully implement the P1 protocols between TMS systems. Use is made of two basic actions, message sending and receipt notification. The message sending action includes control information (ie number of associated normal documents) message transfer parameters (for example originator and recipient O/R names) and interpersonal messaging parameters. The interpersonal messaging parameters cover aspects such as subject, copy recipients, whether notification of receipt is required, document importance and sensitivity.

A message sending action element is packaged in a Teletex control document (Ref 7) and sent to the distant TMS using Teletex document and session level protocols. This is followed by the sending of an associated normal document or group of normal text documents. Security of delivery and continuity of presentation between TMS systems is ensured by the Teletex service.

Should confirmation of delivery to a distant mail server be required then a notification document will be generated by the distant server. A notification action is initiated by the receiving User Agent to indicate to the sending UA that a message has been read. This facility is optional and an indication is given by the sender in the message delivery action as to whether notification of receipt is required. If one of the alternative recipients is not the operator and the intended recipient is not known then a negative notification could be automaticaly generated.

Communication with other publicly or privately provided message handling systems could be by means of X430 (P5) protocols. This assumes that TTXAU facilties will be provided on the public system.

11. THE FUTURE

It is apparent from much of the above description that neither the S series telematic recommendations nor the X series message handling recommendations fully cover a service of this kind. It seems inevitable that as telematic devices become more complex that it will be desirable to provide delivery on an interpersonal basis and recent work by CCITT Study Group VII on document reference information (Ref 5) shows movement in this direction. However, in the interim the X series recommendations provide the best definition of this application level service. In the longer term it is intended to provide TMS systems with both P5 access protocols for communication with non-Teletex devices and to enhance inter-TMS communication to the P1 protocols.

The current development has resulted in a very powerful electronic mail system which can communicate directly with telematic devices and in addition provides interpersonal messaging facilities. It has the advantage for many users of being located on their own premises giving greater confidence in message security.

The next stage of the development process has begun with the setting up of a system of mail servers sited initially in London and Newcastle. The trial will soon be extended to include systems located in Leeds and Belfast. Operational experience is inevitably leading to various system improvements and should provide a useful input for future standards work.

As the Teletex service becomes operational, interworking with telex and a wide range of Teletex devices will become possible.

12. Acknowledgements

The views expressed here are the authors' personal views and do not represent British Telecom policy statements.

The authors wish to thank the Director of the Systems Evolution and Standards Department of British Telecom for permission to make use of the information contained in this paper.

The assistance and advice of the development team is also gratefully acknowledged.

13. References

[1] X400 Message Handling Systems : System Model - Service Elements. (CCITT Draft Recommendations)

[2] X411 Message Handling Systems : Message Transfer Layer. (CCITT Draft Recommendations)

[3] X420 Message Handling Systems : Interpersonal Messaging User Agent Layer. (CCITT Draft Recommendations)

[4] X430 Message Handling Systems : Access Protocol for Teletex Terminals. (CCITT Draft Recommendations)

[5] Draft Recommendation S.DRI. For Document Reference Information (CCITT Draft Recommendations : SG VIII 24 May - 3 June 1983 TD94.)

[6] F200 Teletex Service (CCITT Yellow Book Recommendations)

[7] S62 Control Procedures for the Teletex Service (CCITT Yellow Book Recommendations)

[8] Z200 CCITT High Level Language (CCITT Yellow Book Recommendations : CHILL)

[9] The Message Orientated Text Interchange System (MOTIS) Model. (International Standards Organisation ISO/TC 97/SC 18/WG4 N59)

[10] Message Interchange Distrubuted Applications Standard MIDA. (European Computer Manufacturers Association July 1983 - Fifth Draft)

Computer-Based Message Services
H.T. Smith (Editor)
Elsevier Science Publishers B.V. (North-Holland)

COMPUTERIZED MESSAGE SENDING AND TELECONFERENCING ON VIDEOTEX THROUGH INTELLIGENT DECODERS, SMART CARDS, AND OPTICAL CARDS

W. Jaburek and I. Sebestyén

Institutes for Information Processing
Technical University Graz
Austrian Computer Society

Computerized message sending is one of the integral services provided on contemporary videotex (VTX) systems. In Austria a computer conferencing system has been designed and implemented using the intelligent videotex decoder MUPID*). The software of the system is based on the standard message sending software of the central VTX host, extended by tele-software modules stored in the VTX central database, in just the same way as normal information frames to provide the computer conferencing features required. After downloading them into an intelligent VTX decoder they augment the standard VTX system to act like a sophisticated teleconferencing system. The paper summarizes the functions of the present teleconferencing system, but also shows vistas for new developments. Special attention is paid to novel peripherals such as the smart card and the optical card, which in principle could be connected to intelligent videotex decoders for message sending and teleconferencing purposes.

1. INTRODUCTION

Interactive videotex - or to use its original name viewdata - is designed as a kind of new computer-supported mass medium with the aim of serving a large user population - both home and professional users. The original idea of videotex is simple and assumes that all households are equipped with a TV set and a telephone. By combining these two pieces of hardware and by adding some electronics to them leads to useful data terminals in households. The additional electronics consist of a decoder for digital-analog decoding of characters into analog signals for the respective optical representation of the codes on the screen of the TV, a modem for modulation and demodulation of digital signals into analog and vice versa for transmission of data over the analog telephone network, and a numerical keypad or alphanumerical keyboard as "input" component of this home data terminal. In such a way inexpensive computer terminals can be placed into homes. These terminals are linked through the public switched telephone network, to a special computer network, the videotex network, to which information and transaction storage and forwarding centers are linked. The transaction storage and forwarding centers are similar in their basic functions to classical time-sharing based computerized message sending and teleconferencing systems. A basic difference between the two lies in the order of magnitude of the number of users supported. While computerized message sending and teleconferencing systems usually support users of about one hundred at the most, videotex based systems are designed for thousands and even more users.

---

*) MUPID was developed by the Institutes for Information Processing (IIG) of the TU Graz and the OCG with the support of the Austrian Federal Ministry for Science and Research and the Austrian PTT.

In the Federal Republic of Germany alone - according to PTT estimates - by 1987 one million videotex subscribers will be linked to the public system, which would be able to fulfill the basic characteristics of a classical computer based messaging and teleconferencing system. To what extent this is already done and how it will be developed further is explained in this paper.

2. MESSAGE SENDING IN STANDARD VIDEOTEX SYSTEMS

Austria's current public videotex system - still based on PRESTEL software - provides two nearly identical ways of message sending: So called response frames and message frames. Both are store and forward messages in principle, i.e. after having been written and sent they are stored in the VTX-central host in the addressee's mailbox and only delivered to a VTX-terminal when the owner of the mailbox tells the VTX-center to do so.

With both message types a special frame with empty fields has first to be retrieved and filled in. Before the message is actually sent it has to be acknowledged by the sender by typing a certain combination of digits.

There are some differences between the two types of messages. The empty response frames are VTX pages created by an information provider. They may only be directed to the information provider's "letter box". Empty message frames on the other hand are created by the VTX-operator, at least in Austria. They may be directed to any VTX subscribers by identifying him by his VTX number (mostly identical or nearly identical with the telephone number).

Retrieval of both types of messages by the recipient is done by simply retrieving the VTX page *930#. All new messages are obtained and read in the order of time received. After the message has been read it may be deleted or archived in a special "letter file" dedicated to each user. The latter files are represented logically by the VTX frame *931# in the Austrian system.

3. MESSAGE SENDING WITH INTELLIGENT VIDEOTEX DECODERS

There are several drawbacks of the standard VTX messaging system used. First of all editing of messages is a rather "processor intensive" task, since the central VTX host has to support a fully fledged editing session for all editing users. In addition the online editing of a message takes several minutes of time resulting in unnecessarily high telecommunication costs. Retrieving messages is done online, too. Paying telecommunication charges for the time needed for reading a message also seems luxurious.

Programmable Intelligent Videotex Decoders (PIDs) like MUPID (cf./MAU82/), may be used to circumvent some limitations of the basic message sending facility of videotex (/MAUR81/, /JAB82/).

By means of special communication teleprograms that could be downloaded from the central VTX system, all message and response frames could be edited in a offline mode, thus without telephone connection to the VTX center. After having finished composing the text, the teleprogram tells the PID to establish the telephone connection to the VTX center and sends the text in a time saving manner.

The retrieval of messages may be supported, too, by appropriate telesoftware. A program would download the whole mail-boxes contents into the local storage of the PID and disconnect the line. Now the recipient may read his mail without being under pressure because of the soaring telecommunication costs.

In addition to these possibilities PIDs, like MUPID also allow the use of a third type of message. As no special characters can be typed into the field of a ordinary VTX message frame (messages may contain only black and white text, whereas with all other VTX frames colours may be used), a special kind of message has been developed, the so called "PID message", which is automatically recognized by PIDs. A PID message is a special short message advising MUPID to retrieve the actual message from a particular VTX frame, which, however, may be a colour graphics page containing vector graphics or even a program to be downloaded into the PID itself.

There are further inconveniences of the present VTX messaging systems. For example the basic VTX message software does not allow the sender to send the same message to more than one recipient without retyping the whole message or at least parts of it. Therefore message sending software has been developed to be used in a PID to send "form" messages to a number of recipients according to a "mailing list" stored in the VTX center.

Another useful piece of software will be encryption and decryption routines for secure transmission of confidential information and for applying digital signatures to electronic documents.

Another software package for the receiver of "VTX mail" would be a program to sort out mail and set priorities for reading.

It can thus be seen that by using PIDs a number of enhanced message sending functions can be realized. That reduces the burden on the VTX central system and provides value-added message services.

4. TELECONFERENCING IN AUSTRIA'S VIDEOTEX SYSTEM

In section 2 and 3 only "one-to-one" or "one-to-many" types of communication via VTX have been discussed. One of the novel possibilities of BTX, however, is "many-to-many" communication called teleconferencing or computer conferencing in the literature. These terms comprise communication based on written text contributed by many authors and distributed via computer and telecommunication systems.

Since early 1983 several versions of such conferencing systems have been publicly tested in Austria's videotex system. The latest called "Btx-FORUM" is described below in some detail.

We faced several problems when implementing our Computer Conferencing (CC) system on VTX. One basic problem, for example, was where to place the messages:

1) In the VTX database?
2) On each participant's local storage?
3) On third party computers connected to the VTX system? (cf figure 1)

Since MUPID in its basic version had no local permanent storage, such as floppy disc, and as up to the beginning of 1984 third party computers were scarcely used in Austria's VTX system, the CC information had to be stored in the VTX central database. This created some problems: in a VTX system only one specific user, the "owner" of the frame, is allowed to update his information frames. Any user having himself identified with another user identification number can read that particular frame if permitted by the owner but cannot alter them. On the other hand two persons using the same identification number of an information provider may update the very same frame at the same time, i.e. the VTX software does not check for double updates.

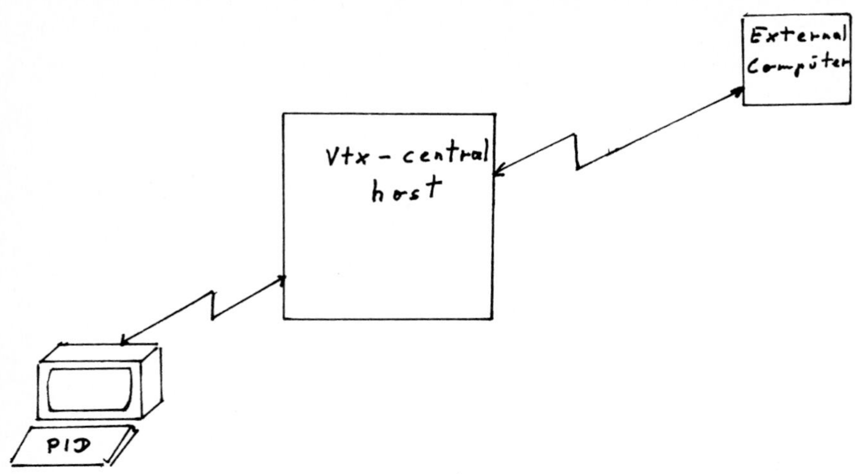

Figure 1
Options for Placing Computer Conferencing Comments in VTX

For this reasong a trick had to be applied when designing the CC system: the comments created by a participant are not directly entered into the VTX database but are first sent to a conference editor by using the above mentioned response frame mechanism. This avoids double update and right of access problems and - assuming that the incoming response frames can be fed into the VTX database by a PID program - no human interaction would be required. Unfortunately no PID is in sole use for this purpose yet. Thus at present conference comments are not entered into the CC system instantaneously, but experience some delay. This is, of course, an inconvenience of our system as it is today.

The picture on the next page provides an overview of the systems's structure and the path of a new comment through the VTX system.

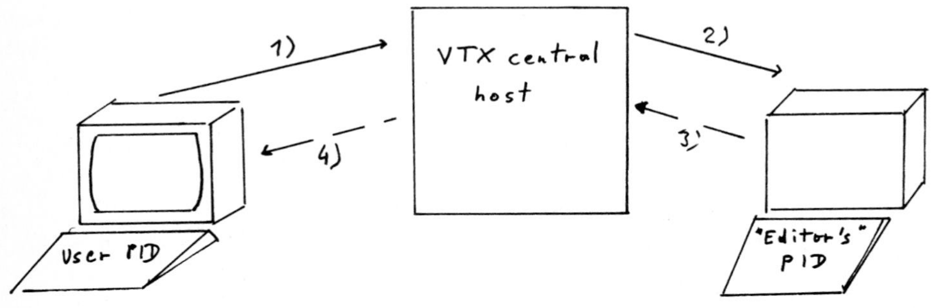

Figure 2
The Structure of the VTX CC System

1) User composes new comment and sends it via VTX message to the editor's PID
2) Editor's PID retrieves new messages and
3) feeds them into the central VTX system's database
4) From there they may be read like "ordinary" VTX frames.

5. SMART CARD - SECURITY AND PRIVACY

As mentioned earlier, this paper considers the potential use of local storage media, especially of smart cards and optical cards for message sending and teleconferencing purposes. For this reason a short overview of both the smart card and the optical card has to be given.

We assume that our new type of videotex system at the terminal side is equipped with intelligent videotex decoders, such as MUPID, augmented with a smart card reader (as used in the French Velizy videotex trial /PI83/, /PI84/ or in some public telephone boxes in France).

The smart card developed in France is a new type of plastic card according to the ISO-Standard 2894 with an internal memory and - most important - internal processing capability. It consists of a microprocessor and microelectronic memory circuits coated with plastics (See figure 3).

Figure 3
A Smart Card

It has a standardized system interface to the card reader, which provides the necessary physical and electrical connections when inserting the card into the reader.

The elements of the smart card and their functions are following:
The microprocessor is the "head" of the card, it controls all memory-accesses, all communication between card memory and the reader, it encrypts and decrypts data and controls the special application programs of the card. It can check, for example, the access right of users or can store data on the card about transactions.

The storage area of the smart card is subdivided into three parts of variable size, depending on the particular application:

i) The Secret memory is only accessable by the microprocessor of the card. External access to it through the card interface is not possible. Since the

secret memory usually contains - depending on the application - the confidential codes of the card holder and/or issuer, and any secret keys for data enciphering, it should not be accessible from outside the card but only through the card's microprocessor.
The smart card is able to check confidential codes such as PIN codes independently by comparing the code entered by the user with the code stored in the card's secret memory. If required, the card holder can himself choose his initial or a new confidential code. In case an incorrect confidential code has been entered several (usually three) times in a series at the same or at different terminals, the card can lock itself into a state preventing all further transactions. Thus the secret memory is the perfect key for identification.

ii) The confidential memory on the other hand is accessable through the external interface for both reading and writing, although only through a confidential user code. Depending on the application this area is usually used to record data about all transactions.

iii) The free access zone is accessable from the external environment freely, without any passwords, or other restrictions. Depending on the application it usually contains information, such as card serial number, card holder's identification, validity period of the card etc.

The smart card offers a very high, practically full, security against any fraud, because of the following characteristics:

i) It is not possible to delete or change data in the transaction area, only new data can be written into it (provided there is space left and access is permitted).

ii) There is no way to change the application program stored in the secrete area.

iii) Access to the confidential memory is only possible through the microprocessor of the card, external access to the secret memory is impossible.

iv) The full content of the smart card thus can not be duplicated, since only the free and the confidential areas are accessible from the external world.

v) The card blocks its operation after a number of predefined unsuccessful attempts when access to the confidential area of the card is made.

The range of applications of the smart card is extremly broad. The card is programmable by the system designer in the most flexible way and its memory can also be flexibly allocated according to usage requirements. The smart card can be used as an easily "transportable" individual data file, containing such data as medical records, personal notebook, identification card, membership cards, lecture book, address book etc. It can also be used as access control for computer systems and as security card for entry into restricted areas. Last but not least the smart card can ideally be used for transactions and telepayment, with and without identification ("anonymity") of its user.

6. OPTICAL CARDS - THE LIBRARY IN YOUR POCKET

The laser recordable optical card is a good example of the new trend towards compact optical memory. The medium is in principle "write once, read only", which makes it perfectly suitable for archiving, identification, recording of transactions and so on. There are a great number of applications in which the above basic characteristics of optical recording are actually more beneficial then an erasable read-write medium. The unit storage costs of this technology are the lowest presently known.

There are basically two types of optical cards.

One, the recordable optical card needs a 'higher' (10 mW) power laser writer for recording information. The card initially is blank. The basis of the card is a polyester film substrate with three layers. On the top is a thick, transparent, plastic coating encapsulation layer, which allows the laser light to pass through unhindered. Under this protective layer is a thin (0.1 micron) layer made of silver grain dispersed in an organic colloidal matrix. This layer reflects about 40% of the light of the reading laser. Data bits are recorded when the writing laser beam melts holes in this reflective layer and also into the third layer, the so-called underlayer. The underlayer consists of the same organic colloid as the reflective layer, but without the silver particles. Its role is to insulate the reflective layer and to increase the laser recording sensitivity. The organic colloidal matrix of the reflective underlayer melts under $200^{o}C$, permitting the use of a semiconductor diode laser. Data bits are encoded as the absence (40% reflectivity) or presence (6% reflectivity) of holes, as determined by the intensity of the reflected light of the reading laser.

In order to ensure that no writing error occurs during the burning process, the so-called DRAW (Direct Read After Write) technique is often used. If the recording is not correct, the whole procedure is repeated on an add-on basis, and the old information is deleted (destroyed). Data on the card may only be added, but not altered (except for DRAW corrections). This capability is utilised for archiving purposes. The nature of the laser burning technology is such that it is unsuitable for mass applications. Thus for recording, i.e. filing of individual text documents it is extremely suitable; however, for making copies in large quantities from the same card it is not.

For this purpose the other type of optical card, the <u>prerecorded optical card</u> (often called optical software card) is much more suitable. The storage capacity of this type of card is identical with the laser burned card. However, because of the complicated replication procedure, costs are higher than those for the first category. But in comparison with other card media its price per bit is still considerably lower by several orders of magnitude. The basic difference between these two types of card is, that on the <u>factory-prerecorded optical card</u> all information is <u>stored at once at production time</u> whereas on the <u>recordable card</u> it is stored <u>continuously at the time of use</u>. The prerecording procedure is similar to that used for analogue videodisc or the digital audio compact disc. It is based on a photolithographic prerecording method, where the recording (replication) of the entire card takes place in one step.

With this technology, mass copying of the same information can be performed extremely cost effectively, the distribution of the card being easy and inexpensive. The data stored is secure as it only can be read, not modified. Making illegal duplicates of the card is costly and impractical. No writing on the medium is possible at the user's side since the reader is only equipped with a low power (1 mW) laser diode identical with those used for the digital audio compact disc system. Because of the high production volumes of such laser diodes, their price is below US $ 50,--.

In principle, a combination of the smart card and the optical card could be imagined. With such an approach a combined reader/writer system would have to be worked out, which would abviously make the peripheral equipment more expensive, perhaps in the range of US $ 1,000. The advantage of such a system would be the built in intelligence of the smart card for identification and/or cryptographical purposes and the inexpensive mass storage capacity of the optical card. Such combined systems do not exist at present.

7. COMPARISON OF CARD MEDIA

Optical cards are different from the smart cards outlined in Chapter 5. The smart card with its embedded microprocessor chip is able to manipulate data and perform intelligent functions in itself, thus being an "active" medium. It also has the

Characteristics	Magnetic stripe card	Smart card (16k)	Optical cards: blank (recordable)	Optical cards: "read only" Type I (prerecorded)	Optical cards: "read only" Type II (prerecorded)
Storage capacity (bits)	1.752	12.000	16.000.000	5.000.000	16.000.000
"Videotex local Storage" capacity (videotex frames - ≈1000 char/frame)	0.2 (not suitable)	1.5 (not suitable)	2.000 (suitable)	625 (suitable)	2.000 (suitable)
"Transaction storage" capacity (Bytes)	219 (not suitable)	1.500 (suitable)	2.000.000 (suitable)	-- (not suitable)	-- (not suitable)
Media costs per card (Volume Pricing)	US $ 0.35	US $ 5	US $ 1.50	US $ 2.50	US $ 5.25
Media costs per bit	¢ 0.02	¢ 0.33	¢ $9.4 \cdot 10^{-6}$	¢ $5 \cdot 10^{-5}$	¢ $3.28 \cdot 10^{-5}$
Media costs per videotex frame	--	--	¢ $7.5 \cdot 10^{-2}$	¢ 0.4	¢ 0.26
Equipment cost (reader/writer) (Volume Pricing)	< US $ 150	< US $ 100	> US $ 600	> US $ 200	> US $ 200

Table 1 Card comparisons

capability to access a certain part of storage (the secret zone) that cannot be reached through the external interface. This is most important for security purposes.

The storage capacity of the smart card is only between 4,000 and 10,000 bits, which only allows storing a limited amount of text. The optical card, however, being the size of a standard credit card, too, has a capacity of 2 Megabytes (!) per side. It is expected that by 1985 /DRB1/ it will be possible to store 10 Megabytes of information per card-side. The present 2 Megabyte storage capacity means that an average of 2,000 (!) videotex frames can be stored on a single card side. (On future cards 10,000 (!) frames. This is one fifth of the present capacity of the Austrian videotex system (!)). Assuming one message to be equal to one videotex frame, 2,000 messages can be archived on one single card side. The future 10 Megabyte version would allow the archival of 10,000 messages per card side. For easier comparison, types and storage capacities of optical and other cards are compared in Table 1.

It can be seen that the magnetic card, which at present is used most frequently for banking purposes, is not really suitable for messaging. Its storage capacity is simply too small for storing messages, transactions or cryptographical programs. The magnetic card is only listed here in order to provide a full picture of the cards available and to underline that it is not suitable for such applications.

The next category, the smart card, is only suitable to a limited degree for message archiving purposes. Its storage capacity is relatively low and its price high. However, it is well suitable for identification and cryptographical application, and whenever local intelligence on the card is needed.

The most suitable card for archiving messages or any other information is the optical card. Its storage capacity is high, the media cost per bit extremely low.

With regard to the equipment cost for reading/writing information onto the card the smart card has considerable advantages over the others, since reading or writing does not require any moving parts.

The magnetic card reader has a built in magnetic read/write head which can be moved either manually or automatically.

The optical card reader is the most sophisticated. It contains moving parts and calls for extremely high precision. Its price is accordingly higher.

At this point it should be said hat all prices given for information should be regarded as approximate prices, variations are possible. Also as time passes, technology improves, and mass production is introduced they will change; usually they get cheaper, but if the technology proves to be more complicated than anticipated (perhaps in the case of the optical card) they might go up.

8. THE ROLE OF INTELLIGENT VTX-DECODERS WITH SMART CARDS - MESSAGE SENDING IN SECURITY

Identification and authentification of a user, especially when fund transfer or message sending is involved, is one of the key problems of videotex systems.

With the use of appropriate identification and authentication techniques and with the introduction of more complex cryptographic methods, however, all requirements of sophisticated electronic message sending can be fulfilled. In this section we describe an intelligent videotex decoder equipped with a smart card reader as an adequate technology.

In principle many types of cryptosystems can be implemented using smart cards, also public-key systems. Public key systems /RIVS78/ have the property that announcing the corresponding encryption keys publicly - let's say through videotex information frames - only allows the encoding of messages but does not give clues for decryption. The decryption keys are only known to the receiver of such messages. They obviously have to be kept secret but have to be remembered, too.

A solution to this problem could be to use smart cards. There the decryption key could be stored either in the secret or in the confidential storage area. Storage in the secret area would ensure that except for the key distributors - e.g. a bank - nobody, not even the user himself, could access the key.

Storage in the confidential area would have the advantage, that the owner of the card could flexibly change its secret key and distribute its public encryption key through videotex.

Public key cryptosystems - as they are known - are also suitable for providing digital signatures. This happens when a user encodes his message with his secret (private) decryption key. In this case decryption of the message - thus testing his authentication - can be done through the user's public key, normally used for encrypting messages to him. It has been proved that such key-pairs in principle exist and can be generated by computers in reasonable time. It can be expected that the first large scale public-key cryptosystem will be in operation in the next few years.

As far as the implementation of such software for videotex is concerned the intelligent videotex decoder and the smart card can share the job. The decoder is better suitable for "number crunching" (thus encrypting and decrypting) and the smart card is better in handling the private (secret) key.

9. THE ROLE OF INTELLIGENT VTX-DECODERS EQUIPPED WITH OPTICAL CARDS, DISTRIBUTED TELECONFERENCING

Classical teleconferencing systems - even the one implemented in the Austrian videotex system-are centralized systems. There is a centralized pool of messages stored and organized on the central videotex database computer. Whenever a user accesses the system, retrieves new or old information messages, types in new contributions, he always deals directly with the system. He uses the central text editor for editing or the database management system for finding a particular keyword in previous messages. There will come a point when the system slows down and it might even collapse. Telecommunication, which is relatively expensive, will always be used while working with the system. Since all functions are centralized, also these tasks are performed through telecommunication and central computers, which could actually be done more economically in a local system.

Using intelligent videotex decoders, many of the central computing functions can be moved into the user's terminal. Editing of text for example can be done locally. The user downloads the textediting telesoftware from the central system and edits his message independently of the central videotex system. Since no telecommunication link is needed during offline editing much of the telecommunication costs can be saved. Only when the message is edited and ready for dispatch is a connection to the central videotex system reestablished.

If, in addition local storage is available, then even the central storage capacity of the teleconferencing system can be reduced and many functions of the system handled locally.

The most used local storage peripheral is obviously magnetic floppy disc, but we want to concentrate on the use of optical cards. It is needless to say that at present such teleconferencing systems are not in use, but they could be soon.

For message sending and teleconferencing purposes the user recordable optical cards could be used. As mentioned earlier up to 16 M bit of information or up to 2.000 messages or conference comments could be stored on one single card. This is more than enough!

The advantage of a system with offline storage for messages is clear. Retrieval of old messages even in full text mode can be made locally, copies of all messages exist at all users, thus there is less danger that data could be lost due to system failure or a similar event. Also, no telecommunication and central computer is needed for such retrieval functions. In combination with gryptographic methods it can be assured that only the owner of the card has access to its messages, i.e. only he is able to decrypt them.

In such message sending system the normal mailbox facility of videotex is used. Messages get written onto an optical card after having been picked up from the mailbox of the user. An appropriate acknowledgement system built into the message sending services of videotex could provide a record of which teleconference participant has seen which comment.

Mass produced prerecorded optical cards could also play a specific role. First, information that is relatively static could be stored and distributed on it, such as a directory of videotex mailbox owners and their addresses, or programcode for the editing, database management, encryption/decryption software.

The storage costs on optical cards are clearly lower than on the central videotex system. At present, costs for a single frame on the Austrian system are between 4 and 9 Shillings (0.25-0.5 US $) per month, the frame cost on the recordable optical card is about 0.75 10^{-3} US $, thus about three orders of magnitude cheaper. For this reason the number of participants in a conference may become particularly big before the cost of all the optical cards becomes as great as or greater than the cost of equivalent storage space in the videotex central database. In this calculation we did not take into account the lower telecommunication needs (and costs) of a distributed optical card based system.

10. CONCLUSIONS

In this paper we have given a review of the state of the art of message sending and teleconferencing in public videotex systems. We have in particular described the ongoing experiments in the Austrian videotex system, the main conclusion being that intelligent videotex decoders are extremely powerful tools for the above applications.

In the second part of the paper we focused on new technologies such as the smart card and the optical card, which could introduce a new generation of videotex based message sending and teleconferencing systems.

Such systems would have the following properties:

a) Through distributed intelligence, only those functions are performed centrally that have to be, otherwise local processing and storage is dominant. This philosophy relieves the central videotex network from unnecessary work. Telecommunication costs of the users are greatly reduced.
b) By using smart cards all problems of identification, security and authentication can easily be solved.
c) The use of optical cards can provide an easy and cheap way for local archiving of messages or conference comments. Massproduced prerecorded optical cards

can be used for distribution and local storage of address lists, and the telesoftware that is needed locally for the intelligent videotex decoder when handling messages or conference comments.

As mentioned, such systems do not exist at present, but we think that they could be built in a relatively short time, and that they would be extremely powerful systems for computerized message sending and teleconferencing.

LITERATURE

/JAB82/ Jaburek, W.:
Videotex - A Communication System,
Report F101 of the Institutes for Information Processing
Graz/Austria 1982,
to appear in Electronic Publishing Review

/MAUP82/ Maurer, H. - Posch, R.:
Der MUPID: Ein Beitrag Österreichs zur Entwicklung von Bildschirmtext,
Report B17 of the Institutes for Information Processing
Graz/Austria 1982

/MAUR81/ Maurer, H. - Rauch, W. - Sebestyên, I.:
Videotex Message Service Systems,
Electronic Publishing Review 1 (1981), 267 - 296

/RIVS78/ Rivest, R.L. - Shamir, A. - Adleman, L.:
A Method for Obtaining Digital Signatures and Public Key Cryptosystems,
Communications of the ACM, Vol. 21 (1978) No. 2, 120 - 126

/DR81/ Drexler, J.:
Optical Data Storage at the Takeoff Point,
Laser Focus, Vol 17 (1981) No 11

/PI83/ Piller, E.:
Die mikroprozessorgesteuerte Speicherkarte CP8,
Microcomputing II,
German Chapter ACM, München 1983, Teubner Verlag, Vol 16

/PI84/ Piller, E.:
Mikroprozessorgesteuerte Speicherkarte im Scheckkarten-Format,
Datenverarbeitung im Europäischen Raum,
ADV Proceedings 1984, forthcoming.